THE INTERNSHIP, PRACTICUM, AND FIELD PLACEMENT HANDBOOK

A GUIDE FOR THE HELPING PROFESSIONS

BRIAN N. BAIRD
Pacific Lutheran University

Prentice Hall
Upper Saddle River, New Jersey 07458

Library of Congress Cataloging-in-Publication Data

Baird, Brian N., (date.)
  The internship, practicum, and field placement handbook : a guide
for the helping professions / Brian N. Baird.
      p.   cm.
  Includes bibliographical references and index.
  ISBN 0-13-475088-8 (paper)
  1. Counselors—Training of.   2. Counseling.   3. Counseling—
Practice.   I. Title.
BF637.C6B26   1996
158'.3—dc20   95-42244
                                                        CIP

Acquisition editor: Heidi Freund
Editorial/production supervision, interior design,
    and electronic page makeup: Mary Araneo
Buyer: Tricia Kenny
Cover designer: Bruce Kenselaar

Printed in the United States of America

10 9 8 7 6 5 4 3

ISBN   0-13-475088-8

PRENTICE-HALL INTERNATIONAL (UK) LIMITED, *London*
PRENTICE-HALL OF AUSTRALIA PTY. LIMITED, *Sydney*
PRENTICE-HALL CANADA INC., *Toronto*
PRENTICE-HALL HISPANOAMERICANA, S.A., *Mexico*
PRENTICE-HALL OF INDIA PRIVATE LIMITED, *New Delhi*
PRENTICE-HALL OF JAPAN, INC., *Tokyo*
SIMON & SCHUSTER ASIA PTE. LTD., *Singapore*
EDITORA PRENTICE-HALL DO BRASIL, LTDA., *Rio de Janeiro*

To Rita Valentine,
who saw me through it all

Contents

PREFACE

Professionals and students in the helping professions consider internships, practicums, and field placements among the most influential experiences of their careers. At the same time, however, students also report that their normal course work typically provides only indirect, and in many cases insufficient, preparation for their first "real world" exposure. This book is designed to bridge the gap between academic coursework and the knowledge, skills, and emotional challenges that are found beyond the classroom.

In writing this book, I sought to draw upon the best information available from psychology, psychiatry, social work, counseling, and other helping professions. Toward that end, I conducted extensive literature reviews of the leading journals and texts in each field. I also consulted with numerous faculty and supervisors in each discipline and in various types of academic institutions and internship settings. Drawing upon personal experience in the role of intern, and having supervised hundreds of students and trainees in beginning and advanced placements, I have tried to write a book that will be valuable at many levels. Whether you are an undergraduate student working for the first time in a field placement or a graduate student completing your final internship, I hope this book will help your work and learning be more effective and more rewarding.

OVERVIEW OF THE CONTENTS

A glance at the table of contents reveals that the book is organized along both chronological and thematic lines. The chapters have been organized sequentially to anticipate the stages interns pass through and the understandings or skills that will be required in those stages. Initial chapters deal with such things as selecting placements and supervisors, meeting staff and clients, and key ethical and legal issues. Middle chapters deal with supervision, working with individuals of diverse cultural and ethnic backgrounds, and self-care. Discussions of termination, finishing the internship, and lessons learned conclude the book. Finally, appendices provide examples of forms useful for establishing learning plans, supervision agreements, ethical guidelines, evaluations, and other procedures.

Because internship training and clinical work involve a constant process of self-exploration and change, the textual material of each chapter is accompanied by self-exploration and experiential learning exercises. I encourage you to use these exercises and be open to the experiences. The more one works in this field the more acutely one realizes the importance of self-examination and understanding.

ACKNOWLEDGMENTS

This book reflects the influence and contributions of many people, and it would not be possible to list everyone to whom I owe a debt of thanks. My many colleagues, friends, and students in recent years, as well as my instructors, supervisors, and mentors during undergraduate, graduate, and post graduate training have all shaped this book and its author. I am grateful for all the positive, and even some of what at the time seemed to be negative, experiences they have given me.

Among the individuals who I want to thank directly, I begin with Andy Carey, who was instrumental in helping formulate the initial plan for this book and provided insightful comments and information throughout its development. Andy's understanding of how students learn and the challenges they face as beginning counselors has been extremely valuable. I have great respect for his skills as a counselor and educator and am fortunate to consider him both a friend and colleague.

I am grateful for the support of Pacific Lutheran University, which granted me the sabbatical leave during which much of the writing of the book was completed. The input and support of my colleagues in the PLU psychology department, especially that of Dana Anderson, Mike Brown, Jerry LeJeune, and Christine Moon, has been and is much appreciated. My secretary, Karen Fleischman, and several student workers also provided great support typing, transcribing my garbled dictation, and helping with countless other details along the way.

The editorial staff of Prentice Hall; Susan Finnemore Brennan in the beginning, Pete Janzow, Heidi Freund, and Mary Araneo have all been most helpful and a pleasure to work with. The reviewers of this book—Phil Abrego, University of Washington; Rickey George, University of Missouri, St. Louis; Robert L. Barret, University of North Carolina, Charlotte; Charles R. Carlson, University of Kentucky; Anthony Di Cesare, Towson State University; James M. Benshoft, University of North Carolina, Greensboro; James Guy, Biola University; Vincent Hevern, LeMoyne College; Steen Halling, Seattle University; and Donald H. Wykoff, Slippery Rock University—provided many fine recommendations for references, content, and other modifications that significantly enhanced the final product. I want to thank each of them for their time, professionalism, and abilities to be direct with criticism and constructive in their suggestions.

Thanks also to some of the many professors and mentors who helped me get into the field and learn some things along the way: Thomas Schenkenberg, Raymond Kesner, Don Strassberg, Dick Hemrick, Randy Linnel, B.J. Fitzgerald, Wilson Walthall, Richard Pasewark, Judith Olson, Max Rardin, Karen Nicholas, Helen Crawford, Leo Sprinkle, Steve Bieber, Geoff Bartol, Lance Harris, Marvin Brown, Mark Seeley, Jarret Kaplan, Vic Ganzer Katherine Mateer, and Tedd Judd. To peers, who shared the challenges and fun: Mike Hawkins, Rick Jensen, Walthall's Warriors, Doreen Daly, Dick Shepherd, Mike Whitley, Warner Karshner, Deborah Frank, and Kirk Strosahl. For friendship and support during dissertation work, Dave Droge and Ray Preiss.

Finally, for their patience and understanding as I spent so many hours on the computer, at the library, and doing everything else it takes to write a book, I owe a huge thanks and more than a few trips skiing to my wife and family.

FOREWORD

Over the years I have had many discussions with colleagues who are charged with the responsibility to train the next generation of psychologists, counselors, and social workers. Although I have often noted the need for a book that deals with the issues encountered in the making of helping professionals, no one has been able to point to a single source or reference that details how one turns well educated students into well functioning professionals. Fortunately, this book answers that call.

My own experiences in graduate school, as well as my experiences serving as an internship supervisor, assure me that nothing is more anxiety-provoking for students than contemplating their internship. For the prospective intern, the tools of the profession have been well established in academic classes, at least at the theoretical level. The internship, however, is different. Now the intern must face the reality of his or her career choice. Does she or he have the ability, the stability, the knowledge, the courage, the humanness, and the skill to become a member of the profession? Will he or she be able to apply these skills to assist others? Is this really the right career path?

Now we have a definitive resource addressing the many issues that interns will face. This book contains almost everything interns, supervisors, and program directors need to know and consider to make the learning experience enjoyable and beneficial to all. There are in-depth discussions of the role of the intern as learner and the realistic, as well as the unrealistic, expectations interns may have. There are comprehensive discussions on finding suitable internship placements, the proper role and goals of the intern as learner, a review of ethical and legal issues, suggestions on how interns may enhance the learning experience through peer group activities, the distinction between supervision and personal therapy, the possible dangers and risks in working with certain patient populations, how to manage time and stress during the experience, and a recognition of the dangers of burnout in the budding professional, to name but a few of the topics covered.

Interns, indeed, even supervisors or program directors, need no longer rely on trial and error to discover successful ways to enhance the learning experience. Here the challenges and obstacles that must be faced and overcome are clearly laid out—both at the macro and micro level. For example, one finds a complete description of how interns conceptualize, develop, and implement peer group learning experiences—an activity that, historically, interns typically had to discover for themselves, often with less than positive outcomes. The chapter on record keeping offers another example of the usefulness of this book. Along with a thorough discussion of the demands of various institutions, issues relating to confidentiality, and recommendations regarding good and bad notes, there are ample examples and exercises to bring lessons about note taking and writing styles rapidly into reality. Many senior clinicians could benefit from this discourse alone. Supervisors and inters will also benefit from the discussion of the similarities and differences between supervision and therapy. Supervision and therapy are not the same, and the proper time and place for each, as well as admonitions to avoid harmful risks of dual role problems, are discussed in a straightforward manner.

To complement such practical information, Dr. Baird also provides a refreshing number of personal experiences designed to help interns realize that everyone makes mistakes, especially those struggling to apply classroom learning to the real world. Throughout the book one finds a great deal of sensitivity to the everyday anxieties, fears, and concerns of interns. Interns will be put at ease with the knowledge that the wide array of feelings they will experience during this learning phase are normal and expected. Interns need not be ashamed or deny their insecurities and fears. These are part of the growth experiences that come with the internship and are to be expected and not avoided.

To his credit, Dr. Baird recognizes that many issues in the field are controversial. Thus, although there are several areas where I hold somewhat different opinions, when discussing these matters Baird states his opinion on the issue

with a well thought out rationale, while acknowledging the viewpoints of others and permitting the reader to follow a different course if desired. In many areas, especially those dealing with ethical and legal matters, the recommendations are stated succinctly and, fortunately, without apology.

No major topic is left untouched by this book. There is an excellent and detailed chapter dealing with the all important but often overlooked issue of diversity in the field. Taboo subjects in graduate programs are openly discussed, including boundary problems between interns and superiors, as well as issues related to the economics of the profession and the guilt many new professionals feel in charging a fee for their services.

I consider this book to be essential reading for students, interns, supervisors, and program directors. All of the topics covered should be mandatory aspects of internship seminars and/or professional issues courses. This book will help to strengthen and upgrade the training experience to the benefit of all.

Bruce E. Bennett, Ph.D.
Executive Director
American Psychological Association Insurance Trust

CHAPTER 1

PREPARATION

I've learned more in this experience than I have in any of my classes. Every student should have the opportunity to do a practicum.

Every day there was something new that I realized I didn't know. If for no other reason than that I'm glad I did an internship.

Comments from student evaluations
of their practicum and internship experiences

THEORY INTO PRACTICE

A friend of mine who was working overseas in the Peace Corps decided it would be fun to teach the children of his village how to play baseball. The children were enthusiastic and eager to learn, so he rounded up some equipment, drew pictures of the playing field, explained the rules of the game, and had everyone practice throwing, catching, and hitting the ball. He even gave them a test that included questions about the number of balls and strikes allowed, how many outs per inning, the distance between bases, and famous players of the past. With the basics mastered, the class improvised a field in a nearby pasture, divided up into two teams, and prepared to play ball.

As the villagers looked on, the excited children took the field. The teacher asked the children if they were ready, and all assured him that they understood what to do. The lead-off batter, a wiry young boy of thirteen, looked nervous but determined. My friend surveyed the field and aligned his players. Then, taking an exaggerated windup, he delivered the first baseball pitch the village had ever witnessed.

To everyone's astonishment, the batter smacked the ball into deep left field. The boy was so shocked by this that he just stood watching as the teacher shouted for him to "Run, Run, Run!" Turning to see how his team fared as fielders, my friend found that all of his players had left their positions and were running as fast as they could around the bases, tagging each one, screaming, laughing, and heading for home plate. The ball, meanwhile, rolled to a stop far out in the field with no one making any effort to chase it.

When the commotion subsided, my friend was the only player left on the field. All of his team, and at last the batter, had raced from the field to home and were thrilled with how many runs they believed they had just scored. "Somewhere," my friend declared to himself, "we've got a gap between theory and practice." With that, he ran for first base and raced around the diamond just as his players had. When he crossed home plate he made baseball history by scoring the tenth run from a single hit. His students loved it and the village still talks about the game today.

Students beginning their first practicum or field placement can identify with my friend's players. Enthusiasm, nervousness, determination, and uncertainty will be familiar feelings. Regardless of all the coursework and study one may have, there is no substitute for real experience. Only by getting out there and trying things can we discover what we do or do not know.

That is why field placements are so valuable. They give you the chance to experience firsthand what you have been studying in your readings and classes. You will quickly discover that reading in a textbook about schizophrenia, alcoholism, child abuse, or other issues is not the same as meeting and interacting with real people who experience the situations or conditions you have studied. So too, reading about, or role playing, therapy and counseling techniques in a classroom is much different than actually participating in therapy sessions.

You will also discover that many of the things you need to know in "the real world," such as ethical and legal issues, how to write case notes, how to deal with supervision, and a host of other topics, probably have not been addressed sufficiently in your academic classes. Even when subjects have been studied in class, as my friend learned from his base running fielders, instructors too often assume that students will be able to transfer what they learn in the classroom directly to the field. Students recognize this error the moment they enter their internship and say to themselves, "Now what do I do?" My goal in writing this book is to help you answer that question.

TERMINOLOGY

FIELD PLACEMENTS, PRACTICUMS, OR INTERNSHIPS?

Before going further, a few words are in order about terminology and the people this book is designed to assist. Rather surprisingly, there is no clear consensus about what certain terms, such as internship, practicum, and field placement, mean. It is generally recognized that all such terms refer to some form of learning beyond the traditional classroom setting. However, in reviewing the literature and speaking with colleagues, one discovers that different disciplines within the helping professions prefer different titles for comparable experiences. Even within the same discipline, programs at different institutions may use different labels for the same sort of experience or may use the same label to describe very different experiences.

In the field of psychology, for example, the term "internship" is used to describe the year-long placement that doctorate level students in clinical psychology must complete before receiving their degree. Field placements of shorter duration, or that entail less responsibility, are often referred to by terms such as practicum, externship, or sometimes as field work. That is generally the case, but it is not always so. Hevern (1994) reported that, of undergraduate psychology pro-

grams responding to his survey, 34.9 percent used the term *internship*, 27.1 percent *practicum*, 13 percent *field experience,* and 8.9 percent *field work* as course titles or descriptors for their undergraduate field studies. Clearly, "internship" is not always reserved for graduate studies, and it is quite common to find courses titled "practicum" or "field experience" at both the undergraduate and graduate levels.

Crossing disciplines, one finds that social work and counseling programs often speak of "field work" or "field placements" rather than internships to describe their applied field training. However, this is by no means universal and those who employ a different nomenclature would undoubtedly be quick to challenge this observation. It must also be recognized that similar terms from graduate programs are likely to be used to describe undergraduate field work. Once again, the meaning of a term can be rather ambiguous.

For the author of a textbook, this poses a problem. This book deals with issues that are common across multiple disciplines and for students at various levels of study and training. Most of the topics will be of interest to students at all levels but some will be of primary concern to those who have never worked in the field before, while others will be most suited for students in graduate studies who have already received extensive academic training and perhaps some prior field work.

To encompass the many related disciplines and readers, the title of this book refers to "Internships, Practicums, and Field Placements." That broad title acknowledges the different approaches to naming and the different levels of students who will read this book, but it is hardly a felicitous phrase for repeated use in the text. Thus, there is a need for a more succinct terminology.

Having reviewed the various options, I find the two best terms to be field placement or practicum. Field placement has the advantage of clearly indicating that the learning is taking place beyond the classroom. Similarly, the word "practicum" directly implies the practical nature of the learning experience. The only problem with these terms is that, although they accurately describe the nature of the learning experience, they do not carry with them a corresponding pronoun for identifying the person doing the learning. How does one refer to the people doing the field experience or practicum? One certainly could say "field experience trainee" or "practicum student," but, again, these are rather tedious for repeated use in text.

This leaves us with the term *internship*. This is admittedly not as descriptive as the alternatives and it tends to be employed more by some disciplines than others, but it does have the noteworthy advantage of an accompanying pronoun, i.e., "intern." Such matters of literary convenience should perhaps not dictate choices of terminology, but given the extant ambiguity of all the available titles and the frequent usage of internship by many programs, I have chosen in most instances to refer to internships and interns throughout this text. The reader should not infer that this terminology refers to a specific level of training or disciplinary focus. Rather, internships and interns should be seen simply as convenient labels referring to any applied field studies beyond the classroom. On occasion, terms other than *internship* will appear throughout the text. This will often happen because other authors who will be quoted use different terminology in their discipline or their personal writing. It may also occur because I have tried to honor such terminology when discussing the work of other authors. Given the present introduction, I trust that readers will recognize and work with whatever terms are being used.

THERAPY, COUNSELING, AND TREATMENT

Just as there is ambiguity about what to call internships, there is also a question about how to refer to what interns do at their internship. In large part this is because interns do many different things. Depending on the nature of the internship, the academic training and experience of the intern, and the individual's interests and skills, interns may be involved in a variety of activities. For most beginning interns the primary focus of the internship will be observation or informal interactions with clients. At more advanced levels, interns will be involved in direct service delivery. Some interns will manage cases, others will participate in assessment, and many will be involved in therapy or counseling.

With so many different activities, no single word can encompass all of what interns might do. Perhaps the easiest solution would be to coin a new verb, the infinitive of which would be "to intern." This could have the circular definition of "that which interns do," and it could apply to any profession or academic discipline in which internships are offered. Rather than resorting to circular neologisms, in this book I will refer in general to "therapy" or "treatment."

As with the decision to use "internship," this choice should not be meant to favor certain types of treatment or certain disciplines. Instead, it is intended to encompass the wide spectrum of activities that are intended to assist clients. This means that "treatment" will include the activities of disciplines and professions that refer to their work as therapy, counseling, or by other related terms. Treatment, as I have used it here, includes physical or other interventions by interns in physical, occupational, or speech therapies. In its broadest sense, treatment could also refer to case management, assessment, play with children at a day-care center, and any other such activities designed to help clients.

What this means, of course, is that in this book I have made a purposeful decision to use a term ambiguously because I wish to avoid semantic debates and because this book is intended to serve the needs of many different interns and programs. This decision may trouble some, but my hope is that the value of the book as a whole will far outweigh whatever differences might arise over initial semantic differences.

SUPERVISORS AND INSTRUCTORS

With the exception of the final internship training for advanced graduate students, in most internship experiences students will be under the guidance of persons in two different roles. To clarify the terminology regarding these individuals, I will use the word "instructors" in reference to faculty from the student's educational institution who monitor the student's progress and interface with those employed by the field placement site itself. Those who directly monitor and direct the student's work at the placement site will be referred to as "supervisors."

In all field work, students should work closely with both their academic instructor and their field supervisor. Although the amount of direct contact students will have with instructors or supervisors will vary from program to program and across placements, throughout this book I will emphasize repeatedly that both instructors and supervisors should be kept closely informed of the intern's activities and should be notified of any concerns or problems that develop.

FINDING AND SELECTING A PLACEMENT

Considering the importance of field experiences, it is surprising how little has been written about how placements are selected and how interns should be matched to specific placement sites. Just as there is no consensus on what to call field learning experiences, i.e. internships, there are also many different models for how such experiences are managed.

Holtzman and Raskin (1989) studied the process of field placement selection across different social work programs and concluded that the procedures used vary widely. At one end of the spectrum are academic programs that leave almost everything up to the student. In such programs students are tasked with locating potential internship sites, contacting staff, arranging for permission to participate, finding a supervisor, and coordinating with an academic instructor. By comparison, other schools exercise control over every element of the internship experience. These schools have identified certain internship sites and supervisors with whom they work every year. Students seeking internships are required to work with one of these placement sites and there are specific learning activities that all students are expected to perform. Sometimes students are allowed to select among the various prearranged internships, but in other programs the choice is made for the student based on the department's assessment of the student's abilities and learning needs.

Just as the process of field placement selection varies, there are also different models for how academic institutions and field placements conduct and coordinate field learning experiences. In some programs, the educational institution continues to have primary control over the student's education in the field. In others, educational responsibility is largely left to the field setting and supervisor. Bogo and Globerman

(1995) provide an informative review of some of the most common models, comparing them in terms of commitment to education, support and resources, degree and effectiveness of collaboration, and communication and reciprocity.

The reason for identifying the different models available is not to argue here that one model is necessarily better or worse than the others. Rather, it is to familiarize you with the range of programs that exist so you can have a sense of where your particular institution stands relative to others. Describing different internship models also helps introduce material that follows in this chapter. If your academic program makes all of the internship arrangements for students, the sections on finding internship sites and supervisors may be of less interest to you than it will be for those who are given relatively little structure in their internship studies. If you find that some of this initial material is not pertinent to your situation, you may wish to skim it and move on to the discussion of internship agreements. On the other hand, if your program provides little structure or support for its interns, the material that follows should be quite helpful.

MEETING WITH YOUR INSTRUCTOR

The first task for interns is to meet with the academic instructor who will work with you during your internship. Some academic programs offer structured classes to go along with internships. Other programs leave internship support or supervision for students and instructors to arrange individually. In either case, initial contact with an instructor is vital for a number of reasons.

The most important reason to work with your instructor from the outset is to ensure that you receive the best possible educational experience from your internship. Instructors can help you select placements or supervisors that are best suited to your needs and they may assist in making contact with placement sites or individual supervisors. If your department has established procedures governing internships, meeting with your instructor from the beginning will ensure that you follow those procedures. Necessary paperwork may be required before you begin an internship and there may be certain requirements for you to receive credit or a grade for your internship.

An additional concern that many interns do not realize is the liability risks that instructors and supervisors face when their students work in the field (Zakutansky & Sirles, 1993). Given this shared liability, the faculty in your department must be involved in all aspects of your internship, from the very beginning until the conclusion.

PEERS AND CAMPUS RESOURCES FOR LOCATING INTERNSHIPS

While instructors will generally be your primary source for internship recommendations, other students who have done internships may also recommend potential internship sites.

Along with identifying placements to pursue, your peers may be able to suggest places to avoid. Such information can be valuable but it is important to keep in mind that another student's experiences will not necessarily match yours. Still, if a student advises that a certain internship amounted to little more than typing data into a computer or watching TV on the midnight shift, you can predict that the learning opportunities at that placement may be limited.

Along with instructors and students as resources, many campuses have offices specifically dedicated to coordinating field learning experiences. These often go by names such as "Cooperative Education" or "Community Learning" programs. Agencies with available internship positions typically send position announcements to these offices, which then post them for students. Even though you may not have heard of a program of this sort on your campus, check around to see if one is available. The program at my institution is outstanding but I am continually surprised at how many students do not take advantage of its services or even know that it exists.

While on the subject of campus resources, one other resource to check is your campus "Career Services" or "Job Placement" center. You may be less likely to find internship openings there but it is a good idea to get to know the career services people and the services they provide. Internships provide an excellent opportunity to begin developing your job application file and honing the interview skills that will be needed when you eventually apply for "real jobs" (Pitts, 1992). Career service offices can help you develop those skills. They can also help you write a vita or resume, and many offices will help you establish a complete job application file including letters of references and other material commonly requested by employers. These offices also receive regular announcements of position openings, so it is a good idea to stop by periodically to see if they have received word of any openings in your area.

COMMUNITY RESOURCES

Interns who look to faculty or campus resources sometimes overlook the many community information sources that can also be resources. If there is a community mental health center in your area you may be able to call and ask if they have lists of local agencies that you might contact. Many communities also have volunteer coordinating programs that are designed to help match programs with volunteers. United Way sometimes supports such programs. Another possible resource would be a telephone crisis line. This may sound surprising at first, but crisis lines make referrals to programs of all kinds. As a result, many crisis lines have books listing different agencies.

Two other sources that all communities have are newspapers and phone books. In the newspaper, classified advertisements sometimes list position openings in agencies that also may offer internships. Try looking in the Employment Offerings or Help Wanted section under the headings of "counselor," "mental health," "therapist," or under your specific discipline's title. These may be listed alphabetically in the general section or you might find them in special sections for "Health Care" positions. The added benefit of finding positions this way is the possibility of locating a paid position for an internship. The disadvantage is that such positions may require more job experience than beginning interns have. Also, in some paid positions it may be more difficult to find suitable supervision. That should not discourage one from calling to discuss a position. Interns often start a position as a student in an unpaid status but are later hired in a paid capacity as openings become available. If you inquire about a position that requires more experience than you presently have, do not be afraid to suggest you work as an unpaid intern in order to gain the requisite experience.

Because advertisements in newspapers will only identify agencies with current position openings, a more reliable source of placements is your phone book. The Yellow Pages listings under "Counseling," "Mental Health," and "Social Service Organizations" will have numbers for many agencies. Some phone books also include special pages listing numbers for community services and agencies. Depending on your area of interest and the requirements of your program, other listings that may be of help include "Schools," "Clergy," "Child Care," and "Hospitals." You may also want to look in the phone book under directory headings for your specific discipline.

National, state, and local professional associations can also be useful resources for finding placements. Most organizations have membership directories that could be used to contact individuals working in settings or areas in which you are interested. Many professions also maintain national catalogues, listing available field training opportunities. These catalogues tend to be directed more toward graduate training, but one can often find opportunities for undergraduates as well.

CHOOSING A PLACEMENT

Finding potential placements is the first step. The next step is to select an internship from among the possibilities. I encourage interns to approach this process thoughtfully because it is important that your first clinical experience be positive. As an intern you may not feel as if you can afford to be too choosy about internships because, after all, you are the one seeking the position. Nevertheless, you will be giving substantial amounts of your own time and resources to the internship so you have a right to consider carefully where you are most likely to get the most benefit.

In an effort to make the process of matching students and placements more efficient and successful, Brownstein (1981) described a process for organizing data on placement opportunities and student characteristics. Building upon

Brownstein's model I have developed information forms for placement sites and for student interns. These forms, which are most useful for placements located near one's academic institution, are provided in Appendices A and B. One form gives interns the opportunity to list their interests, experience, available times, and other information relevant to internship selection. The parallel form presents agency information regarding location, types of clients, treatment approaches, supervision, and available days and times etc.. Comparing information from the intern and agency allows instructors, students, and the agency to make more informed decisions about the suitability of a given placement for a specific intern. Such information may also help reduce the likelihood of placements that do not work out (Holtzman & Raskin, 1989).

Another approach to selecting internship sites was described by Brill, Wolkin, and McKeel (1987) who noted that students seeking predoctoral internships in clinical psychology must choose from several hundred possibilities. To help narrow this field, Brill et al. suggest that prospective interns use a visualization exercise in which ideal short- and long-term training goals and opportunities are imagined. Insights gained from that process are then considered as the intern and instructor review information and materials collected by previous interns. Special emphasis is placed on seeking acceptance to programs that have had positive experiences with other interns from the same university. Applicants are also advised to apply to a limited number of sites rather than dissipating their resources on many different locations. This allows for greater attention to those sites that are chosen and tends to make the quality of applications to those locations higher.

SUPERVISION

Although many interns select placements based on clients served, location, treatment approach, or other considerations, perhaps the most important factor to consider involves the professionals with whom you will work and be supervised. Particularly in more advanced internships, the quality of the internship experience is directly related to the quality of the supervision received. This observation has also been made by Munson (1989), who developed what he called a "Bill of Rights" for supervision. In describing the "rights" of supervisees Munson commented, "Increasingly, I have come to appreciate that supervision is the most important educational experience any clinical practitioner undergoes" (p. 2).

Munson went on to list fifteen things that supervisees have a "right to expect that a supervisor will be." The list included such qualities as being a master teacher, having confidence in knowledge but openness to questioning, the ability to accept criticism without defensiveness, orienting the student to the internship setting, and knowledge of, and adherence to, ethical standards. Not all supervisors will possess all of Munson's desired qualities, but his list can help interns and supervisors identify some of the characteristics that lead to positive supervisory experiences.

For interns who are selecting placements, the basic question to ask about a supervisor is: "Is this someone I think I can work with and who I think would be interested in helping me learn?" In answering this question one must consider the supervisor's personality, qualifications, areas of interest, and her or his willingness and ability to give you sufficient supervision time and instruction. You also should take into account your level of development as a therapist and your personality. Stoltenberg (1981), Heppner and Roehlke (1984), and Friedman and Kaslow (1986) have all described the developmental stages of supervision and suggest that the needs of supervisees change with experience. Other authors, (Kaiser, 1992; Rabinowitz, Heppner & Roehlke, 1986; Gandolfo & Brown, 1987), have emphasized that at all levels of training, supervisees need supervisors who are encouraging and supportive.

Apart from competence and experience, your personality and learning needs should also be considered. You may be naturally suited to a nurturing environment and a supervisor who provides a great deal of direction. Others may benefit more with less direction and greater autonomy. The most important point is to try and find a supervisor who is able and willing to work with you as an individual to best meet your personality and learning needs.

Another area to consider in selecting a supervisor is compatibility of clinical philosophy or approach. Many interns broaden their views and become more confident when they are placed with supervisors from different theoretical orientations than their own, but others have experienced significant conflicts. While placement with a supervisor of different orientation can be very growth producing, if the supervisor or intern are dogmatic and intolerant of differing views, it can leave both feeling frustrated and discouraged. Thus, while you should not limit yourself to working with supervisors who share your therapeutic philosophy, it is important for you to be open to new ideas and to select a supervisor who is willing to consider different approaches.

The best way to get to know potential supervisors is to schedule a meeting or phone interview with them. Remember that in this meeting both of you will be trying to evaluate how well an internship together would work. Supervisors will want to know what your academic training and practical experiences are. They will also be interested in your personality. Can they rely on you? Are you diligent in your work? Will you take suggestions or instructions well? And, will it be in some way worth the supervisor's time to supervise you?

Hersh and Poey (1987) offer a number of useful suggestions to help prospective interns prepare for interviews. In addition to the areas mentioned above, they advise interns to describe why they want to work in the specific internship site and what their goals there will be. Holloway and Roehlke (1987), in a comprehensive review of internships in counseling psychology, discuss selection issues and identify the qualifications considered most important by graduate internship selection committees. They emphasize the importance of prior experience, academic credentials, and letters of recommendation.

For your part, you will be asking some of the same questions your supervisor asks about you (Pitts, 1992). You will be interested in their experience as a professional and their training and experience as a supervisor. You will also want to know if the supervisor will be a good teacher, someone who lets you take some risks and make mistakes in the process of learning but who is also there with guidance and support when you need it. One further question you should ask is how much time the supervisor has to spend with you. More will be said about this in regard to internship agreements, but before you reach the stage of formalizing your arrangement you should know whether or not the supervisor can devote sufficient time to working with you. It would also be a very good idea to read Chapter 5 before finalizing an internship and supervisory arrangement. That chapter deals at length with theories, models, and practical issues relating to supervision.

LEARNING OPPORTUNITIES

Along with identifying a supervisor with whom you would like to do an internship, you should also consider the kinds of learning opportunities that will be available to you. It is especially important to clarify this before starting an internship. The lack of sufficiently interesting or challenging learning opportunities is one of the most common causes of complaints and frustration for interns. It is not infrequent for interns to select what appear to be ideal placements only to discover that all they are allowed to do is code data for research, help with reorganizing files, or "babysit" students while teachers or counselors are out of the room. Clarifying from the outset what opportunities you desire, and what the internship can and will make available to you, can go a long way toward preventing such disappointments. If you know other students who have been at the same internship site you may want to ask what their experiences were.

In your first internship most of the focus will be on learning by observing. This means you should have the opportunity to observe many different elements of the activities at your placement. Ideally, interns should have at least some opportunity to observe everything that goes on, from staff meetings and paperwork to direct treatment and other service delivery. This gives interns the broadest exposure to all elements of the placement. It is important for interns to know both the rewarding and the mundane aspects of the profession.

As their abilities and training allow, interns will gradually go beyond observational learning and begin to accept responsibility for becoming involved in clinical activities.

This must be closely coordinated with the supervisor, but your goal should be to take new challenges in stages, pushing yourself slightly each time but never extending beyond your level of competence. For example, if you have been a participant observer in a group for several months, your supervisor might encourage you to become more involved in facilitating the group. Or, if you have read a number of reports about clients, you might want to try your hand at writing a report. The exact nature and extent of your involvement should evolve as you gain experience in your internship and your supervisor develops more knowledge of, and confidence in, your abilities. Again, the main point is that if you hope to have a certain kind of experience on your internship you should check with potential placements and supervisors to determine if that experience will be available to you.

TREATMENT APPROACHES

Internships provide your best opportunity to experience firsthand what a therapy or technique that appeals to you in theory is like in actual practice. If you have a particular interest in a treatment approach, you may want to seek a placement where you can receive supervision and experience in that approach. As noted in the discussion of supervision, it is a good idea to discuss the matter of theoretical orientation with your potential supervisor and your faculty instructor. Often, within an agency there are people who practice from a number of different orientations. If one person cannot provide you with the training you need they may be able to refer you to another professional who can.

If you already have experience in one intervention approach, I would encourage you to consider seeking training in a completely different approach. This does not mean you must become a "convert" to the other approach. It merely suggests that you be open to different methods and give them a try to see what there is to learn from another perspective. When they actually experience a different approach in practice, interns who may have once been quite critical come to recognize that each method has something useful to offer.

CLIENTS

The next factor to consider in selecting a placement is the type of clients served by the program. Just as it is advisable for interns to be exposed to a variety of treatment approaches, experience with diverse client groups is also desirable. In your first internships, the exact makeup of the client population is less important than the fact that you are out in the real world working with people. Still, there is nothing wrong with seeking a placement based on the types of clients served. If you want to eventually work with a specific client group, it might be ideal to find a placement with a program for that group.

Even if you cannot find a program involving precisely the client group that most interests you, there will likely be many other placements in which you can still receive valuable experiences. For most students, a generalized background of experience is probably more beneficial than premature specialization. You can specialize in your final years of graduate training or after you receive your degree, but in the beginning it is a good idea to be flexible and open to different types of training experiences and different client groups.

In my own training, I specifically sought opportunities to work with clients of virtually all ages and diagnostic groups. By selecting a series of internship and practicum placements I was eventually able to work with clients ranging from small children to elderly adults and with diagnostic groups ranging from college students in a counseling center to patients in a unit for mentally ill offenders. In each placement I learned something new and expanded both my awareness and skills. This diversity of experience also helped me gain a clearer sense of the kinds of therapy and clients that I was most interested in and for which my skills were best suited.

PROGRAMS AND SETTINGS

Theoretical approaches and client types are frequently foremost on interns' minds when they select internships, but you should also consider the different kinds of internship settings available. For example, although the ages of the clients may be similar, an internship in a school setting would likely be much different than an internship in a home for runaway adolescents. Similarly, although many of the clients served, and treatment techniques found, in mental health clinics may be similar to those of inpatient facilities, there will be important differences that are specific to each type of setting. Thus, apart from the clients served and the treatment approaches used, if you only have experience in one kind of setting, a placement in a completely different setting could be very educational for you.

CAREER PLANS

Most interns should avoid premature specialization, but this does not mean you should completely ignore your career plans when you choose an internship. This is particularly important if you hope to seek employment or further education in the field soon after you complete your internship. Interns who are about to enter the job market or go on to further studies often desire placement sites that make them more marketable to potential employers or graduate schools. This is a reasonable strategy because the experience gained in an internship, and the letters of recommendation from internship supervisors, can be very helpful. If you are planning to seek employment, you may want to check the job market to identify the kinds of skills and experience that employers are looking for. Similarly, if graduate studies are a goal, you may want to contact graduate schools and ask what sorts of experiences they look for in applicants.

If your career or academic plans are not yet clear, you may wish to discuss any career or educational questions with your instructor before you choose an internship. By getting a sense of your interests and the options available, you can better select an internship that gives you the experience to help make decisions about future career directions.

PRACTICAL ISSUES: LOCATION AND TIMES

The issues addressed thus far have primarily been concerned with the nature and quality of clinical experience and training you will receive. More mundane, but not to be overlooked, are such practical considerations as where the placement is located and how your available days and times match those of the placement site.

If you can, try to pick placement sites that are readily accessible to you. This will allow you to spend more time at the placement site and less time in transit. In some areas you should also consider safety factors associated with getting to and from a placement. Wherever you find an internship it is a good idea to ask your supervisor and other staff members about any safety issues associated with the location. Sometimes you may find that areas assumed to be "terribly dangerous" are really not such a problem if a few precautions are taken. Do not be embarrassed to express any concerns or to ask your coworkers for their suggestions.

With regard to time, it is important for interns to be on their placement site at regularly scheduled times. Ideally, interns should be at the placement a minimum of two to three hours a day for at least three days per week. Interns who are on site at irregular or infrequent times do not fully integrate into the routine of the placement. Unless interns are present on a regular basis, staff and clients are unlikely to be sufficiently comfortable or confident with them to really involve them in activities. Interns should keep in mind, too, that in so far as the internship serves as preparation for employment, reliably keeping established hours is an important part of demonstrating one's employment readiness.

As you consider your schedule and make arrangements with an internship placement, be as realistic as possible about the times in which you will be available. Many interns do not heed this advice and overextend themselves as a result. This typically happens because interns have a great desire to learn and will try to do whatever their placement sites ask. The motivation to learn is admirable, but if you extend yourself too far you may end up disappointing yourself and the agency.

When you schedule times with your internship do not forget to consider other factors in your life, including family, friends, and other course work. Try to take into account predictable "crunch" times that can be anticipated in your academic or personal schedule. For example, if you know that midterms and finals will demand additional amounts of time for study, or if you will be working on a thesis or dissertation, talk about that with your supervisor and make arrange-

ments well in advance. Similarly, if you are involved in extracurricular activities, take these into consideration as you schedule your internship. If it is evident that academic and other time demands will severely limit the time available for an internship, or if your schedule is so variable that you cannot set aside consistent times for the internship, you might want to consider doing the internship at some other time or perhaps changing other elements of your schedule to better accommodate the internship. It is better to forego an internship than to try to force one into an overcrowded schedule and have a bad experience as a result.

One final note about internship schedules. Although I have emphasized the importance of keeping consistent schedules, the activities of many agencies vary from day to day and at different times of the day. To get a feel for the rhythms of your placement, try to be at the internship at other times in addition to your regularly scheduled times. This can be particularly valuable in institutional placements or other residential settings where clients are present around the clock. In such placements, the activities and atmosphere on evenings or weekends can differ remarkably from the 8-to-5 weekday hours. Interns who can come in during the evening or join staff and clients on weekend outings often will see a much different side of the clients and institution. Those occasions can also provide excellent opportunities to interact with and get to know clients or staff on a more personal level.

COMPETENCE AND SAFETY

The final consideration to mention here is by no means the least important. When you select an internship, you should give careful consideration to your level of ability and training in relation to the tasks you will be expected to perform. An internship should stretch your knowledge and skills but you must not extend beyond your abilities to a point that would be dangerous for yourself or your clients. If the kinds of clients served, or the technical demands of treatment, assessment, or other services are beyond your current abilities, you should recognize this and discuss it with your instructor and supervisor.

This principle not only applies in selecting an internship, it also holds throughout whatever internship you eventually select. If at any time you are asked to do something that exceeds your skill and knowledge and might therefore be hazardous, you should express this to your supervisor or instructor and be sure that you have the necessary support or assistance before proceeding. More will be said about this issue in Chapter 3, which deals with ethical issues.

EXERCISE

If you have not already done so, turn to the internship forms in the Appendix and complete the student form. I suggest that you then give a copy of the form to your instructor and supervisor. Completing the form will help you examine your abilities and needs and the information you provide may enable your supervisor to be more aware of, and hence better able to meet, your educational goals.

INTERNSHIP AGREEMENTS

Once you have found a placement, supervisor, and learning opportunities that suit your needs, the next step is to establish an agreement about what the internship will entail. Two types of agreements should be formalized before you begin an internship. First, there should be a written agreement between your academic institution and the internship site. Next, together with your instructor and supervisor, an agreement should be formulated to describe the nature of your individual internship experience. Establishing such agreements in writing at the outset will help avoid later misunderstandings or confusion about what the internship site and supervisor expect of you and what you expect of them.

INSTITUTIONAL AGREEMENTS
There was a time when internship arrangements were left rather informal. Agencies in the field and academic institutions alike recognized the need to train students, and collaborative arrangements were made relatively easily between instructors and field-work supervisors. In many instances, a simple word-of-mouth agreement on the telephone was sufficient to make the arrangements for an internship. In other cases, a friendly letter was drafted to make things official.

As society and health care have become increasingly litigious, the need for more formal and detailed internship agreements has grown. In the current climate, it would probably be unwise for interns, internship sites, or academic institutions to be involved in internships or similar field learning experiences without a written agreement of some form.

Because no two internship sites or academic programs are identical, there is no single model for such agreements. There are, however, a number of common ingredients that should be addressed (Thibadeau & Christian, 1985). In a study of elements included in social work field-training agreements, Gelman and Wardell (1988) analyzed survey responses from 271 social-work programs, including both graduate and undergraduate programs. In addition to questionnaire responses, the same survey collected actual training agreements from 92 of the responding schools (Gelman, 1990). Based on this information, Gelman identified four types of training agreements. These ranged from what he described as "Friendly," essentially the sort of cordial, nonlegalistic-letter type arrangements described earlier, to a much more technical document dealing primarily with liability avoidance. Gelman labeled this fourth type the "Disclaimer" agreement. Gelman's data

suggested that about half of the agreements he analyzed could be classified in the "Friendly" category, while only a relative handful fit the "Disclaimer" model. The bulk of the remaining agreements were described as "Cooperative/Joint" agreements, which are the kinds of agreements Gelman finds preferable for most programs.

"Cooperative/Joint" agreements typically begin by recognizing the importance, mutual benefits, and shared responsibilities of field learning opportunities for the academic institutions, students, and field placements. This initial recognition is then followed by a description of the agreed-upon expectations for each of the parties involved. The expectations for the field setting include such things as allowing the student to observe or participate in specified activities, providing certain kinds of learning activities, providing supervision by persons with specific qualifications and at specified frequencies, and maintaining contact with the academic institution and instructor. For its part, the academic institution affirms that the student is in good standing and has sufficient preparation to participate in the specified internship activities. The academic institution also agrees to provide a liaison instructor to work with the field setting. The agreement may also clarify the role of the instructor and address the evaluation process to be used. The student's responsibilities as described in such agreements include adhering to the professional code of ethics, attending the internship as scheduled, carrying out any agreed-upon responsibilities, and informing the supervisor and instructor of any problems or concerns. Guidelines for dress and conduct, and, again, a description of evaluation procedures are sometimes also included in the description of the student's responsibilities.

Legal concerns are also addressed in these documents, particularly in regard to liability issues. Two main concerns that are addressed are: 1.) The possibility that the intern might be involved in activities that injure or otherwise harm a client or other person at the internship site, and 2.) The possibility that the intern might be injured or otherwise harmed while at the internship site. Portions of the agreement that deal with these issues specify how responsibilities will be shared in the event of such incidents. This includes clarification of liability insurance.

Many field agencies provide both liability and injury coverage for interns under their existing insurance for volunteers or employees. If this is the case, it is essential for the intern and school to complete any necessary paperwork officially designating the intern as a member of the class of individuals covered by the policy. The fact and extent of such coverage should also be specified in the field learning agreement.

Apart from, or in addition to, any agency liability protection, Gelman found that 60 percent of the schools with "Cooperative/Joint" types of agreements provide liability protection for their students. In addition to this institutional policy, some schools also expect individual students to obtain their own insurance. Other programs leave the matter of insurance for students entirely up to the students. In any case, the field learning agreement should clearly specify who holds what insurance and the extent and limitations of coverage. The same applies to insurance for the field placement supervisor and for the academic internship instructor.

Depending on the nature of the academic program and internship, field learning agreements may include additional information or address other issues, but as a minimum the matters addressed above should be covered. The agreement should then be signed by the academic instructor, field supervisor, and by responsible administrators for the university and field agency. In many instances students sign these documents as well.

Given the concerns about liability and other legal matters, it is advisable for attorneys and risk management officers from both the academic institution and field agency to be involved in drafting and reviewing field learning agreements. At the same time, however, Gelman has expressed concern that if the attorneys who draft or review these documents are unfamiliar with the importance and function of field learning, they may become so detailed or restrictive that field learning will no longer be possible. What is needed is for the academic institution and agency to recognize the need for field learning and then work collaboratively to ensure that the learning experience is safe for clients, students, supervisors, instructors, and others. Well-crafted field learning agreements are an important part of that process, but they cannot substitute for responsible, professional practice on the part of all those involved.

I would like to add one final note in this context. Whether or not your academic program or internship currently operates under the type of formal agreement just described, as an intern it is in your best interest to clarify the issues that such agreements address. If a written agreement exists between your school and agency, be sure to obtain a copy, read it, and understand how it affects your role, responsibilities, and risks. The best person to ask about this is your academic instructor. If a written field agreement does not exist, you may wish to raise your concerns tactfully and ask your instructor for some form of written clarification of at least the issues relating to liability. More will be said about liability and other legal and ethical issues in Chapter 3 of this book. Most interns would be well advised to read that chapter carefully before beginning their internship.

INDIVIDUAL INTERNSHIP AGREEMENTS

A sample individual internship agreement form is provided in Appendix C. As illustrated by that form, internship agreements should record the days and hours you will be expected to work, what your responsibilities will be, and the nature and extent of supervision to be provided. The internship agreement should also provide space to identify what your goals are and how you hope to achieve them during the internship. If, as part of your internship or class, you will be expected to produce some form of product, such as a written paper, journal, research report, etc., this should be included in the agreement. When the agreement has been completed and is acceptable to your supervisor, your instructor, and to you, there should be a space for each of you to sign agreeing to the terms of the agreement. Each person should then keep a copy of this form.

Part of the value of formalizing an agreement in this way is that it encourages people to be clear about their expectations and commitments from the outset. As Costa (1994) and Freeman (1993) point out, providing this structure can help reduce the anxiety that trainees often feel as they start a new internship. By sitting down to write the agreement, the intern, instructor, and supervisor can work out the details of exactly when the intern will be expected at the placement, when supervision will be provided, what sorts of activities the intern can observe and participate in, and how the intern's performance will be evaluated.

EVALUATION

Because each internship offers different experiences and sets different expectations, and because interns differ in their personal goals, it is a good idea to be involved in the evaluation process from the outset. In order to avoid future misunderstandings, the evaluation and grading criteria and process should be agreed upon by interns, instructors, and supervisors before the internship begins. This way everyone can work together to ensure that the evaluation process is productive and contributes to the overall learning experience of the internship.

If your instructor or supervisor has an established format for evaluation, you should review that carefully to be sure you understand it. If your instructor or supervisor does not have a fixed format, you may want to consider the sample evaluation forms provided in Appendices D and E. Whatever evaluation system is used, try to avoid the temptation to focus excessively on the letter grade you will receive. Instead, you should seek and be receptive to feedback that helps improve your clinical knowledge and performance. If you focus more on a grade than upon learning, you may be inclined not to take on new challenges for fear you will not do well and your grade might suffer.

One way to prevent this is to work out an arrangement with your instructor or supervisor that allows and encourages you to recognize your own areas for development and to try new skills. Evaluation that considers improvement in performance along with level of skill is one example of how this can be handled. You can probably identify other options as well. Whatever system you arrive at for evaluation, be sure you understand it and that your instructor and placement supervisor are in agreement with the process and criteria. Evaluations are discussed in more detail in Chapter 5, which deals with supervision issues.

MAKING THE MOST OF YOUR INTERNSHIP

When the steps discussed in this chapter are completed, you should be ready to start your internship. Before moving on to other topics, I want to conclude this chapter by offering some tips for how to make the most of your internship and how to use this book.

ACADEMIA MEETS THE "REAL WORLD"

One thing that all interns discover is that internships require a much different set of skills and knowledge than academic classes. Formal academic classes emphasize knowledge of facts. The focus of most academic exams is on "what" you know, and the "what" that you must know has been explicitly taught in the class. By the time they are in college, most students know this system pretty well. If you pay attention in class, study hard, and memorize the material, you are likely to pass the exam. Contrast this situation with the internship world.

In the internship, the focus is not on "what you know," but "what you can do." Being able to identify the founders of every major therapy technique, or describing in detail five theories of personality, are all fine if you are in a class, but they may be of limited use at your internship. This is not to say such things are unimportant or cannot be very useful, but their use comes not from simply knowing them. At your internship, usefulness of information depends on what you do with it and how you relate it to the situations you encounter. Ronnestad and Skovholt (1993) comment on this, noting:

> . . . the large theory-practice gulf experienced by the student. The student is immediately exposed to extensive new theoretical and empirical information and is then expected to perform adequately in practicum (p. 396).

Students are not alone in recognizing this gap. Raskin (1994) reported that experts in the study of field education in social work offered consensus agreement with a statement that "The lack of fit between classroom courses and field teaching is still evident in field instruction" (p. 82).

The other difference between internships and classroom study is that it is never clear beforehand just what you will have to know. One of the truest statements I know about life in general also applies to internships. The statement is: "Life gives the test first, then the lesson." At an internship, clients do not say to you, "Tomorrow we will deal with how my father abused me for six years then died of a heart attack as he was yelling at me for not cleaning my room. Study hard how to

respond to this issue so you will know what to do when we talk about it." There is no "study guide" to help you prepare. At any given moment you may be called upon to use any knowledge or skills you have and possibly some you do not have. Therefore, your study approach must prepare you with the skills of understanding people and interactions in general. It must also teach you to be flexible, to think on your feet, to expect the unexpected, and to understand that the "grades" are not at all what you are accustomed to.

If you expect the internship to be just like class but taking place in the community, you surely will be surprised, almost certainly will be confused, and you may not do very well. On the other hand, if you appreciate that the experience is related to, yet markedly different from, academic coursework, you are more likely to benefit from and succeed at your internship.

REMEMBER YOU ARE A STUDENT

Internships are not the same as class, but your role at the internship will still primarily be to learn. This is helpful to remember because it frees you from feeling you must already know everything. Friedman and Kaslow (1986) have described how, in the early stage of training, supervisees are "frequently plagued by the self-doubts and ambivalent feelings which reflect both the inchoate nature of their professional identities and the minimal degree of skill they as yet have amassed with which to perform their work" (p. 36). Similar observations have been made by Kaslow and Rice (1987) in their discussion of the developmental phases interns experience during their placements.

One way to reduce the pressure that comes with this phase of training is to be honest about your limited skill or knowledge. If there is something you do not know, you can simply say "I don't know." If you see or hear something you do not understand, you can ask your supervisor or instructor for an explanation. Your goal at an internship is not to impress everyone with how smart or skilled you are. In contrast to trainees who try to disguise what they do for fear of looking foolish or ignorant, I encourage students to be open about how much they need to learn. If you can do this and admit that there are things you do not know but want to learn, your internship will be much more educational.

MAKE THE MOST OF IGNORANCE

For many students, the suggestion to be open about their own ignorance sounds like it will leave them feeling vulnerable. To an extent this is true, but when you think about it some of the most valuable learning and growth take place when we are vulnerable. Moreover, it is a mistake to assume that vulnerability is synonymous with helplessness or incompetence. It is helpful to remind interns that their ignorance can be an advantage. Precisely because they are not expected to know everything, interns can ask questions that others might be afraid to raise. Similarly, because interns are new to settings, they may see things in new ways that people who have worked in a setting for years have never noticed. By acknowledging what you do not yet know, you not only enhance your potential to learn, you also gain a unique kind of permission and influence that is not always accorded to professionals. You should appreciate this opportunity while you still have it. When you obtain your degree and are in the role of professional, it may not be so easy to admit that you do not know everything.

Work Near Your "Learning Edge"

If acknowledging what you do not know is a first step toward learning, being willing to take some risks and extend yourself is a key second step. Internships give you the opportunity to try new skills that you may have only read about before. In order to develop these skills you have to test them and learn from both your successes and your mistakes. A concept that is useful to interns, and that will later be useful in treatment, is the idea of a learning edge. This term refers to the point just beyond one's present level of knowledge or skill. It is not so far ahead that we are in danger of making mistakes that could be calamitous for ourselves or others, but it is beyond our habitual level of functioning and comfort.

In your internship, you will often be right at your learning edge. If you find yourself feeling too comfortable, you should probably talk with your supervisor about extending your activities in some way. If you recognize that there is an area of knowledge or skill that you need to develop, you can expect that it will be a bit uncomfortable but you must also realize that you need to accept this discomfort and push yourself in order to advance. Apart from specific skills you might develop or information you might acquire, becoming familiar and comfortable with your own learning edge is one of the most important lessons you can learn from internships.

Remember That You DO Know Some Things

Along with developing and trying out your skills, the internship should also give you a chance to bring together information learned during your academic program. Although internships are not the same as academic courses, internships can provide valuable opportunities to review what you have studied in your classes. Courses in human development, culture, gender issues, community systems, theories of personality, assessment, abnormal psychology, and other subjects are all relevant to your internship.

I emphasize the importance of integrating your knowledge because it frequently happens that students who have recently studied a subject in class seem to forget what they learned when they begin their internship. Try to avoid that mistake. If you have had a course in human development consider what you learned as you work with people of different

ages. If you have taken a theories of personality class, ask yourself how different theorists might view the people in your clinical setting. If you are working in a community agency, give some thought to ways in which knowledge from a community systems course helps you understand the agency and its clients. Such opportunities will strengthen your understanding of what you learned in class and will give you the chance to compare theory with reality. Again, the emphasis is not just on what you know. It is on what you can do with that knowledge in the context of your internship.

GET HELP WHEN YOU NEED IT

The final suggestion is one that will be offered repeatedly in this text: If you have any problems or questions on your internship, be sure to get assistance. During your internship, it is essential that you recognize when situations or assignments are beyond your ability and you need help to deal with them. You may need help with anything from questions about ethics to how to write a certain kind of case note. It might also happen that you are working with a particularly challenging client, or perhaps you are not getting along well with a staff member or supervisor. Whatever the difficulty, when problems develop, get help and do so early.

People you can use as resources include your faculty instructor, placement supervisor, peers, and other faculty or staff. If none of these persons are available, other professionals outside the setting or university may also be helpful. The main point is to realize that you are not alone and you are not expected to be able to do everything yourself. Again, this is something you must practice not only in your internship. It is a fundamental principle of responsible professional conduct; you will be off to a good start if you follow it in your first placement.

Because it is absolutely essential that interns be willing to seek help and know where to get help if they need it in an emergency, it is a good idea to complete the "Crisis Contact" information form provided in Appendix F. That form lists the names, phone numbers, and other information needed to contact site supervisors, faculty instructors, or other individuals as "backup" if the immediate supervisors or instructors are not available. This may not seem necessary at present, but if a crisis occurs in the middle of the night and you cannot locate your primary supervisor or instructor for help, you will be very glad to have the numbers of other contacts readily available. Having needed just such support when I was an intern, and having provided it to students in my roles as supervisor and instructor, I cannot emphasize this too strongly. Complete the form when you start your internship, keep a copy at work and home, and use it whenever you need help. Any supervisor or faculty worth their salt would much rather be called unnecessarily than to find out later that they were not consulted about something important.

USING THIS BOOK

I have already described how internships are different than ordinary academic classes. With that in mind, it should not be surprising that this book is not a typical textbook.

RESOURCES AND REFERENCES

In writing this book I have tried to present information that will be immediately relevant to your internship. All of the chapters have been designed to address the skills or issues that are most likely to emerge during your internship and that are certain to be part of your eventual work as a professional. I hope you will use the book as a reference source to help prepare yourself for the internship and to answer questions that arise along the way. At the same time, however, I recognize that entire books have been written about the topics of each of the chapters.

Because a text of this length cannot possibly cover everything there is to know in any area, this book is best viewed as a starting point. If you need additional information for your work, or if you are curious about a topic, I hope you will consult the references that are cited within the text. Your instructor, supervisor, and peers can also offer useful suggestions.

READING AS ACTIVE INTERACTION

It is a cliché, but nevertheless true, that you get out of things what you put into them. If you read this book like any other textbook and primarily look to highlight things that might be on a test, you will be wasting your time. This book is not meant to be read that way. As you read you should ask questions, make connections, and consider the implications for your own work. You should seek clarification of things you do not understand and challenge my ideas if you disagree with them. I want you to feel free to write in the margins, highlight key ideas because they interest you, take notes, and discuss your reading with peers and supervisors.

The process should not be just "I wrote the book—now you read it." Rather, it should be "Here are some of my ideas and information, now what do you think?" Whatever your reaction, what matters most is that you have some reaction. That will get things started and learning can proceed from there.

DOING THE EXERCISES

Part of the reason I enjoy working with interns is that I believe strongly in the value of experiential and discovery based learning. In helping interns make the most of their experiences I see the task as both to provide information and stimulate thinking in new ways. In this book, one of the ways I will try to stimulate thinking is by providing exercises relating to the topics of each chapter.

If your goal is simply to "get through" the book, or if you are pressed for time, you may be tempted to skim over an exercise or suggested activity. I hope you will resist that temptation and devote some time to the exercises. It may be that a given exercise is unnecessary for you, but you will not really know unless you test your knowledge. It is one thing to say to yourself that you already know something, but it is another matter to really explore and reflect on an issue in a structured, systematic way. In my experience as an instructor and supervisor, and in my own work as a practicing clinician, I am constantly surprised by how often I think I know something but then discover a completely new insight or understanding that I had not been aware of before.

INTRODUCTION TO JOURNAL WORK

Consistent with the emphasis on active learning and self-reflection, personal journal work can be an exceptionally valuable part of your internship experience. Effective journal use takes time, but journals that are done well provide a unique and valuable form of learning.

Unfortunately, many students and instructors who use journals do not make the most of the process because they are not clear about what should go into a journal or why. To make the most of journal work you should use a journal to: 1.) Record experiences at your internship. 2.) Reflect on your experiences in order to better understand such things as your emotional reactions, thoughts about clients, impressions of treatment, etc. 3.) Make notes about questions, ideas, or discoveries that you wish to discuss or study further. 4.) Complete exercises presented throughout this text.

A RECORD OF EXPERIENCES, REACTIONS, AND THOUGHTS

I recommend to interns that for every day at their internship, they make a journal entry that begins by listing the day, date, and the hours they were at the internship. The entry should then list and briefly describe the major activities you were involved in at the internship that day. A convenient way to do this is to follow a chronological format, noting activities, clients, and staff you worked with, and any other salient information for the day. Remember confidentiality issues as you write in your journal. As will be discussed in greater detail in Chapter 3, it is good practice to use generic terms or single-letter abbreviations, rather than names, to signify clients. An example of a journal entry of this type is offered below:

Thursday, April 21, 199-, 10:00 A.M.–2:00 P.M.
10:00–10:30. Met with Rachel (Supervisor) and followed up on yesterday's group. Agreed that J. and R. had dominated group. B. was distracted by something but we do not know what. We will discuss these observations in tomorrow's group. Also spoke with Rachel about plans

to be at conference next Friday. She approved of my absence. In staff meeting the following Wednesday, I will report back to staff about the conference.

10:30–12:00. Participated in recreation activities with clients under supervision of Robert Jones, Rec Therapist. Played softball at Jefferson park. Close game and clients seemed to enjoy it.

12:00–1:00. Lunch in dining room. Ate with two clients I had not met before. A. and N. Today was A's first day and she was nervous but seemed to be coping. N. has been here three weeks. He is looking forward to visit from his family this weekend.

1:00–2:00. Administered and scored the Beck Depression Inventory for F. Discussed results with supervisor and with F. Wrote brief summary for patient records.

In addition to journal entries describing events of the day, you should also establish a record in which you keep a running total of the number of hours spent in different activities, such as milieu observation, assessment, therapy, case conferences, etc. If you conduct intake interviews, write case reports, or perform psychological assessments, a count of these should be maintained including specific information about which tests were given, interpreted, and/or scored by you.

Recording your experiences in the internship serves several purposes. As documentation of your activities, your journal can help your supervisor or instructor keep apprised of what you are doing. Your journal record also will be useful later on when you seek employment and are asked to indicate your experience in various clinical activities. The record in which you document numbers of interviews, therapy sessions, and assessments, etc., will be especially useful for this purpose. Such information is often requested for graduate-level internships and, in many states, it is required as part of the professional licensing process.

Along with serving as records of what you have done, the process of keeping regular journal entries helps to establish a habit of record keeping. Accurate and current records are essential to responsible clinical practice, but record keeping is often neglected (Kagle, 1993). By getting into the practice of keeping records each day, you are less likely to develop poor record-keeping practices later on. In order for this function to be served and for your journal records to be accurate, you must avoid the rather common intern strategy of neglecting the journal until the end of the term and then trying to fill it in by memory. If you have an extraordinary memory or are skilled at making things up, that approach might satisfy an instructor's requirements but it fails to meet the spirit of the activity and ultimately deprives you of the benefits to be gained from a journal. To avoid this practice, as part of the time allot-

ted for your internship you should include a few minutes at the end of each working day for writing in your journal. This way you will have the information fresh in your mind and will not have to scramble for time later on.

REFLECTION AND EXPLORATION

The record-keeping function of journals is important in itself, but their real value emerges when interns go beyond record keeping and use journals as a place for deeper reflection on their experiences. By using journals as opportunities to explore and process their experiences, interns can gain a deeper understanding of clients, the internship setting, the clinical process, and, most importantly, themselves. When used in this manner, journaling becomes a form of "self-supervision" and can markedly enhance the benefits of the journal and the internship.

To illustrate this approach to journal work, suppose an intern noticed that a client who usually was quite talkative seemed extremely quiet. That observation might lead the intern to think and write about what might be associated with the change in the client's behavior. The intern might consider recent events at the internship or in the client's life. The general mood of the placement could also be taken into account, as could topics and stages of therapy, anticipated events on the unit, and a host of other pertinent factors. It is not necessary for the intern to arrive at "the right" explanation in the journal. What really matters is that the intern is involved in the process of observing things carefully and trying to understand them.

Of course it is not possible for interns to engage in detailed exploration of every event that happens every day at the internship. This means you will have to be selective about what you choose to write about in your journal. One approach is to focus on two or three main ideas or concerns and write about these in detail. An intern might attend to the progress of a specific client, changes in the setting, supervision experiences, or other topics of interest.

Whatever external events your journal addresses, for maximum benefit it is essential to include internal observations in your journal. Interns should use journals to reflect on their emotional reactions, thoughts, and behaviors. The goal of this reflection should not be to "evaluate" or reach conclusions about whether you did things well or poorly. Rather, the goal is to reflect on what you experienced or did in order to increase self-awareness and understanding. A journal entry from one of my students illustrates this process well:

> One of the students at the school really blew up at me today. T. has kind of been a favorite for me and we usually get along great. Today he was causing all kinds of trouble so I asked him what was up. He totally lost it. He called me all kinds of names and acted like he wanted to hit me. I was blown away. I didn't understand what caused him to act like that and I was really hurt by what he said. I felt like maybe it was my fault that he was so upset and that I should have been able to do

something to help calm him down. It was especially hard because some of the other kids saw it all and so did a couple of the staff. The staff were nice afterwards but still I felt like I'd screwed up. I'm supposed to be here to help these kids and sometimes it seems like there's nothing I can do to really reach them. Sometimes I wonder if I need everyone to like me too much.

This process of self-reflection can go a long way toward helping interns work through, and learn from, their experiences. It also provides a useful basis for discussions with instructors or supervisors. The key to making the process worthwhile is to be as open and honest as you can about what you thought, felt, or did and what your impressions are after you have time to reflect.

NOTING QUESTIONS, IDEAS, AND DISCOVERIES

Because ideas that arise during the course of an internship might be forgotten before you have a chance to discuss them, you can also use your journal to record any questions, exciting insights, or discoveries you want to remember. Questions about treatment approaches, agency procedures, or specific client diagnoses or behaviors would be examples of the kinds of things an intern might want to note in a journal and later address with a supervisor. Discoveries could include particular themes that appear to be crucial for certain clients, newly acquired skills to emphasize in the future, or perhaps some ideas for possible research. Ideas for research can be particularly helpful if you are looking for thesis or dissertation topics.

EXERCISES FROM THE TEXT

The final journal function pertains to the exercises you will encounter throughout this book. I have already addressed the importance of these exercises as vehicles for learning. Journals are an excellent place to write about and keep your responses to the exercises. By keeping your work in the journal you will be able to refer to it later in class discussions or supervision sessions. In the future, when you have been practicing for a few years, you can look back in your journal and remember where you started.

REFERENCES

Bogo, M., & Globerman, J. (1995). Creating effective university-field partnerships: An analysis of two inter-organization models for field education. *Journal of Teaching in Social Work, 11*, 177–192.

Brill, R., Wolkin, J., & McKeel, N. (1987). Strategies for selecting and securing the predoctoral clinical internship of choice. In R. H. Dana & W. T. May (Eds.), *Internship training in professional psychology* (pp. 220–226). Washington, DC: Hemisphere Publishing Corporation.

Brownstein, C. (1981). Practicum issues: A placement planning model. *Journal of Education for Social Work, 17*(3), 25–28.

Costa, L. (1994). Reducing anxiety in live supervision. *Counselor Education and Supervision, 34*, 30–40.

Freeman, S. C. (1993). Structure in counseling supervision. *The Clinical Supervisor, 11*, 245–252.

Friedman, D., & Kaslow, N. J. (1986). The development of professional identity in psychotherapists: Six stages in the supervision process. In F. W. Kaslow (Ed.), *Supervision and training: Models, dilemmas and challenges.* New York: Haworth Press.

Gandolfo, R. L., & Brown, R. (1987). Psychology intern ratings of actual and ideal supervision of psychotherapy. *The Journal of Training and Practice in Professional Psychology, 1*, 15-28.

Gelman, S. R. (1990). The crafting of fieldwork training agreements. *Journal of Social Work Education, 26*, 65-75.

Gelman, S. R., & Wardell, P. J. (1988). Who's responsible? The field liability dilemma. *Journal of Social Work Education, 24*, 70-78.

Heppner, P. P., & Roehlke, H. J. (1984). Differences among supervisees at different levels of training: Implications for a developmental model of supervision. *Journal of Counseling Psychology, 31*, 76-90.

Hersh, J. B., & Poey, K. (1987). A proposed interviewing guide for intern applicants. In R. H. Dana & W. T. May (Eds.), *Internship training in professional psychology* (pp. 217-220). Washington, DC: Hemisphere Publishing Corporation.

Hevern, V. W. (1994). *Faculty supervision of undergraduate field experience coursework.* Paper presented at the annual meeting of the American Psychological Association, Los Angeles, CA.

Holloway, E. L., & Roehlke, H. J. (1987). Internship: The applied training of a counseling psychologist. *The Counseling Psychologist, 15*, 205–206.

Holtzman, R. F., & Raskin, M. S. (1989). Why placements fail: Study results. *The Clinical Supervisor, 6*, 123–136.

Kagle, J. D. (1993). Record keeping: Directions for the 1990s. *Social Work, 38*, 190–196.

Kaiser, T. L. (1992). The supervisory relationship: An identification of the primary relationship and an application of two theories of ethical relationships. *Journal of Marital and Family Therapy, 18*, 283–296.

Kaslow, N. J., & Rice, D. G. (1987). Developmental stresses of psychology internship training: What training staff can do to help. In R. H. Dana & W. T. May (Eds.), *Internship training in professional psychology* (pp. 443–453). Washington, DC: Hemisphere Publishing Corporation.

Munson, C. E. (1989) Editorial. *The Clinical Supervisor, 7*(1) 1–4.

Pitts, J. H. (1992). Organizing a practicum and internship program in counselor education. *Counselor Education and Supervision, 31*, 196–207.

Rabinowitz, F. E., Heppner P. P., & Roehlke H. J. (1986). Descriptive study of process and outcome variables of supervision over time. *Journal of Counseling Psychology, 33*, 292–300.

Raskin, M. S. (1994). The Delphi study in field instruction revisited: Expert consensus on issues and research priorities. *Journal of Social Work Education, 30*, 75–89.

Ronnestad, M. H., & Skovholt, T. M. (1993). Supervision of beginning and advanced graduate students of counseling and psychotherapy. *Journal of Counseling and Development, 71,* 396–405.

Stoltenberg, C. (1981). Approaching supervision from a developmental perspective: The counselor complexity model. *Journal of Counseling Psychology, 28,* 59–65.

Thibadeau, S. F., & Christian, W. P. (1985). Developing an effective practicum program at the human service agency. *The Behavior Therapist, 8,* 31–34.

Zakutansky, T. J., & Sirles, E. A. (1993). Ethical and legal issues in field education: Shared responsibility and risk. *Journal of Social Work Education, 29,* 338–347.

CHAPTER 2

GETTING STARTED

One of the great things about aphorisms is that for every famous saying there is an equal and opposite saying. Two sayings, mutually contradictory of course, relate particularly well to internships. The first is, "You never get a second chance to make a first impression." The counterpoint advice is, "Don't judge a book by its cover." As you begin your internship, keep in mind the importance of the first impressions you make upon others. Remember also not to judge an internship setting or the people there based solely on your first impressions.

This chapter addresses common questions and concerns that arise in the first few days of an internship. It also discusses the role of the intern, some of the opportunities you can expect, and the limitations inherent in internships. Typical areas of concern for interns include such things as how to identify oneself, working with other staff, meeting clients, charging fees for service, managing paperwork, and coping with other tasks that are part of professional life but will probably be new to most interns.

FIRST IMPRESSIONS

When you begin an internship, first impressions will go both ways. On the one hand, you will be introduced to the staff, clients, and the internship facility and you will begin to form your own impressions of them. At the same time, the staff

and clients with whom you work will begin to form impressions of you. Because first impressions can leave lasting effects, you should think about what kind of first impression you want to give others.

It would be foolish for anyone to tell interns exactly what they should wear or precisely how they should act their first days on the job. Fortunately, "power ties" are not an expected part of the helping professional's wardrobe. Nevertheless, interns would be well advised to consider the nature of their internship setting, the kinds of activities they will be involved in, and what the institutional norms are for attire and conduct. Most people have had the awkward experience of arriving at an event for which they were either dressed more formally or informally than everyone else. One way to avoid this experience at internships is to ask your supervisor beforehand what the norms for clothing are and what activities will be happening on the first day.

The value of this simple advice was demonstrated by the experience of an intern who, keen on making the best first impression he could, arrived at his internship the first day dressed in a suit and tie. The intern could not have looked finer, but it happened that his first day was "games" day at the internship site. Everyone else on staff was wearing shorts or jeans because, among other things, the games day activities included softball, egg tossing, and a tug-of-war through a mud pit. Dressed as he was, the intern did not participate in any of the events. What could have been a wonderful way to get to know people resulted in a rather uncomfortable experience of feeling out of place.

Experiences in the opposite direction have also befallen interns. One student who went to his first internship dressed in his usual campus attire of shorts, a tee shirt, and sandals, was summarily sent away by his supervisor and told to come back the next day more suitably dressed as a professional. Needless to say, this was not the best way to begin a relationship.

As these examples demonstrate, the key to starting off on the right foot is to get a sense of what the expectations are at the internship and to try to match those. This does not, as some students feel, mean you are selling yourself out or losing your individuality. It simply means you recognize that, in a way, you are a guest at the internship and it is a sign of respect to dress and conduct yourself in a way that respects the customs and needs of the internship. Just as therapists or counselors must understand the needs of clients and adapt their interventions accordingly, interns should consider the institutional needs of their placement site.

While interns should consider the first impressions they will make on others, many people at the internship will not be as concerned about the first impressions they make on the interns. This is only to be expected. As mentioned earlier, the experience and perspectives of staff are substantially different than those of interns.

A year ago one of our promising young interns returned from the first day at her internship site terribly distraught and convinced that the next three months were sure to be awful. When she had gone to visit her supervisor he was at first too busy to meet with her. When finally they did meet late in the day, he asked a lot of questions about her approach to treatment, her experience, and what she was doing there. During their conversation he corrected some of the things she said, he used "rough" language, and he never asked about who she was as a person. As she described it, the supervisor seemed to be more of a prosecuting attorney than a future mentor. Almost in tears, she said to her instructor, "I'm sure there's no way we'll ever get along. I'm sure he hates me already and I just can't work with someone like that."

In some cases this conclusion might have been correct, but the instructor knew the supervisor and was aware that his style was often perceived to be gruff. The instructor also knew that the supervisor was extremely dedicated to his clients and to the interns he trained. The gruffness was in part his natural style, in part because he was overworked, and in part his way of getting past the surface talk to see how interns performed in response to stress. The supervisor had worked with many different interns and had come to believe that, given the clients and the nature of the work at that internship site, interns had to be able to cope with confrontation.

In response to requests from the intern, the instructor called the supervisor who reported that, contrary to the intern's first impressions, he was quite impressed by her and thought she would work out just fine. The next day he apologized for any misunderstandings, complimented the intern on how she had responded, then set to work providing the intern with the best training and supervision received by any student that semester. Not all supervisory relationships work out as well as this one did, but it demonstrated the importance of not making decisions based solely on first impressions.

ENTHUSIASM MEETS EXPERIENCE

Supervisors and staff who work with interns consistently say that the greatest thing interns bring to placements is a sense of enthusiasm and optimism. Fresh from their studies and eager to try out their knowledge and skills, some interns practically radiate energy. Other interns, perhaps less sure of themselves, may radiate insecurity. All interns have in common the fact that they bring something new to the institution. This is one of the reasons institutions and supervisors agree to accept interns. For the most part, they appreciate the new perspectives interns can bring and they value the opportunity to be part of training future professionals.

While the presence of interns is valued by many professionals, interns should also be aware that their own perspective and experience differs markedly from the experience of the staff and clients who are already at a placement. Caught up as they are in their own feelings and in all there is to do and learn, interns often do not pause to think about this difference.

For the intern, each placement is a new and potentially exciting experience. Throughout their time in the placement, interns will be on the steep upward slope of the learning curve and every day can bring new discoveries and opportunities. By comparison, many of the staff at placement sites will have worked there for years. Their perspective will differ markedly from the intern's because they already know the people, system, and clients with whom they work. They may also have seen many interns come and go. As a result, although the internship experience is unique to the intern, having interns at the site is not so unique to the staff and they may not share in the intern's sense of novelty or enthusiasm.

This does not mean the staff are any less invested than interns in the treatment of clients. It simply means their perspective will differ from that of the interns. One long-time staff member explained it to an intern by comparing the experience to "falling in love versus marriage. The initial sense of wonder is fantastic but it can't be maintained forever. That doesn't mean the love is gone, it just means it has taken a different form that might not be so easy to see from the outside."

That same staff member went on to point out another factor that differs for staff and interns. For interns, the experience is known to be limited in time. At the completion of the internship the intern will go back to school, move on to another internship, or do something else, but seldom will the intern stay on at the site. Staff, on the other hand, were there before the interns came and will be there after the interns leave. This is part of the reason interns sometimes feel as though some staff members do not reach out to form the kinds of close contacts that interns might desire. The staff may have become accustomed to interns coming and going; it is not realistic to expect them to form repeated close contacts that will almost certainly be temporary. Of course, many interns do form valuable and lasting relationships with supervisors and others at internships, but it is helpful for interns to understand the situation so they will not be disappointed if such relationships do not develop.

EXERCISE

Take a moment to think about the role of intern as viewed from several different perspectives. For example, how do each of the following view interns: Supervisors? Other professional staff? Staff with less formal education? Administrators? Clients? The interns themselves? As you think about these perspectives, ask what positive ideas might each group hold about interns and what negative ideas might they have. Giving some thought to this beforehand will better prepare you for the different relationships and reactions you will encounter during your internship.

THE ROLE OF THE INTERN

The role of intern occupies a gray area somewhere between student and professional. As an intern, you will still have many things to learn but you may also be counted on to possess certain knowledge and skills. Depending on your experience and training you may be given gradually increasing responsibilities, but your position will probably not be equal to that of full staff. This ambiguity is compounded by the fact that others at the internship, including staff and clients, may also be unclear about what interns are and what the purpose of the internship is.

Your role as intern may be further complicated by precedents set by previous interns. Many placement sites have had a number of interns over the years and the interns who preceded you will have created certain expectations, positive or negative, to which you are likely to be compared. If the previous intern was terrific, you are more likely to be welcomed to the placement but there may be high standards to match. If the former intern did not do well at the internship there may be a negative attitude toward interns that could carry over to you. These possibilities are mentioned not because you can really do anything about what preceded you, but because it might help you to understand that the ways in which people relate to you will often be influenced by other experiences that have nothing to do with you as an individual.

Two simple principles can help interns deal with role ambiguity and any precedents that other interns may have set. Those principles are: 1.) Be honest with yourself and with others, and; 2.) Do your best. This may sound simplistic, but many interns have reported that remembering these basic principles helped them keep it together when things became confusing at placements.

Being honest with yourself means you accept that your role is ambiguous not only for you but for others as well. It also means that you are open about your relative strengths and limitations. If you have no experience doing something, let people know and be open to learning. If you have some experience or knowledge, do not be afraid to share it. If situations arise in which you need clarification about your role or the expectations others have, do not try to read people's minds. Ask for clarification and be willing to share your own thoughts and feelings about the matter.

Doing your best means that you do not have to be the world's greatest therapist, social worker, or counselor and it is not your sole responsibility to save all of the clients or do everything anyone asks of you. As an intern you should set high standards for yourself but do not set or try to meet unrealistic expectations. You are at your internship to learn, not to prove you already know. If people around you seem much more experienced than you, do not be intimidated. They probably do have more experience and that gives you the opportunity to learn. Enjoy that opportunity and make the most of it.

THE ROLE OF THE PROFESSIONAL

Because interns are in the process of exploring their profession, it is important to consider how the role of professional differs from that of student. Perhaps the most important difference between professionals and students is that professionals are expected to meet certain standards of conduct that are not expected of students.

Earlier, I described the student who was sent home from an internship because he was not dressed suitably. In addition to dress there are standards for the kind of language that is acceptable, the way one relates to others on the job, and the quality of work one produces. Professional and student standards are also different in regard to more mundane but nevertheless important details such as coming to work on time, keeping appointments, etc. Students typically have a great deal of freedom in each of these areas but the professional must be prompt, reliable, and act in ways that maintain an image of respectability.

To some students, everything that was just described may sound too controlling or pretentious and they may want nothing to do with it. As one intern, who was very bright and had excellent clinical skills, said, "Hey, I am who I am and they can take it or leave it. I'm not going to look or act like somebody I'm not." In spite of his otherwise strong clinical skills, this young man had difficulty understanding the position of his internship.

At his university, this student had not needed to worry a great deal about image. If he came to class late he missed material, but that was his responsibility and he was able to manage it. Similarly, his appearance did not matter to his professors. If he performed well on tests and assignments he earned the grades and that was it. This was all as it should be while the student was at the university. But the student's internship placement did not have the same luxuries the student enjoyed.

The ability of placements to reach clients and, sometimes, to receive financial support, depends a great deal on the image they convey to the community. Some programs in certain settings can, like students on campus, "get away with" unusual appearances or approaches. But most treatment settings do not have that freedom. Many programs maintain a precarious balance of funding and are dependent on the image they convey to funding sources and the community. This dependence is complicated by the fact that, due to the nature of human services, many programs have images that are suspect from the beginning. If treatment staff begin to look or act in ways that are too discrepant from the expectations of people responsible for funding, programs may well lose their financial support and, hence, their ability to serve clients. This may seem unfair, and appearance may not have anything to do with the quality of service provided, but to the outside world trying to judge a program, appearance is often all they have to go on. Perhaps it is not "right," but interns must understand that reality and appreciate the constraints within which their placements operate.

Apart from the public image of a program, administrators and supervisors must also be sensitive to the impressions that clients will have of treatment staff. Many clients are willing to work with a therapist almost regardless of his or her appearance, as long as the therapist is believed to be competent. But there are also clients, equally in need of treatment, who simply will not work with someone who does not, at least to some degree, match their expectations for professionals. While no one can or should be all things to all clients, part of becoming a professional is learning to adapt one's own conduct, within certain limits, to meet the needs of the client.

For most students this will not be a problem, but if you find it difficult to balance your personal identity with your professional role, you might want to select another internship that more closely matches your style. I also encourage you to understand that meeting standards does not mean abandoning your individuality. If all professionals were clones they would not be able to meet the needs of diverse clients. There is room and need for individuality among therapists, but it is also your responsibility to find ways to remain an individual while still serving your internship and clients.

When I work with students who choose to dress or act differently than the norm I almost never tell them they must change in order to work as interns. That is not my role and, frankly, I enjoy the diversity. In fact, at various times in my life I have certainly not met "the norm" myself and I would have resented greatly having someone tell me how I had to dress or act. What I do tell interns is that they owe it to themselves and to their placement and clients to think seriously about the effects of their appearance and actions. Interns must also realize that there may be certain placements, supervisors, or clients who will have narrower limits of tolerance than the intern might be comfortable with. Some interns may not be able to work within those limits so they will have to either make adjustments or forego that particular training opportunity in favor of something else. Again, part of becoming a professional is finding ways to balance your individuality with your professional role. There are countless ways to do this and the internship is a perfect time to experiment and discover what does or does not work.

MEETING CLIENTS

When they first begin placements one of the most common concerns of interns is how they will be received by clients.

EXERCISE

Before reading further, write down some of your hopes and concerns about meeting clients. Talk about these with your peers and, if possible, with students who have recently completed internship experiences. Also schedule some time to discuss these issues with your supervisor and instructor. They will undoubtedly be familiar with these issues already, but it can be very useful for you to express any concerns openly.

In most cases, anxieties of interns about meeting clients are often quite different from realities. In spite of the common fears of interns, most clients readily accept interns and relate to them as they do to other staff members. Clients generally understand the need to train future professionals. Some are even solicitous, wanting to help ensure that the interns have a good experience. Other clients may be overly accepting of interns, and some will be extremely trusting of the intern's skills. Friedman and Kaslow (1986) contrasted the supervisee's anxieties with the patient's trust by noting that patient reactions "attest to the fact that at least one member of the trainee-patient dyad believes that the former is actually a therapist" (p. 34).

This does not mean all clients will welcome all interns. There will be clients who reject working with interns and want to work with a "real therapist." Clients who resist working with the intern can be very intimidating and remarkably able to make interns feel unwelcome or incompetent.

As interns prepare for their first interactions with clients, they should understand that whether clients are extremely trusting, instantly hostile, or react in some other way, the intern's task is to understand these reactions in the clinical context. This means that interns should not necessarily be overly flattered by clients who are immediately trusting, nor should they be deeply hurt or intimidated by clients who are initially distant or hostile. Instead, the intern should try to understand the client's reaction from the client's perspective and be aware that each interaction is part of the overall clinical process. It also helps to remind interns once again that they should beware of first impressions, both positive and negative, because first impressions can often be misleading.

Along with concerns about how clients will respond to them, interns also ask questions about how they should introduce themselves to clients. As recommended earlier, the best practice is to be honest. When asked, interns should say they are interns, tell their field of study and, if it is relevant, explain a bit about why they are at the internship. For example, "Hi, I'm Alyson Jones. I'm an intern in counseling and I'll be working here for the next three months." That is usually sufficient. If more information is requested, such as what experience you have, you should also be honest about that. If you have experience working with a certain treatment approach or setting it is fine to say so. If you have no such experience, you might say, "I haven't had any experience working in a setting of this kind. That's why I'm here. I'll be working closely with my supervisor and hopefully I can learn some things."

With regard to supervision, Zakutansky and Sirles (1993) assert that whenever interns will be working directly with clients the intern's field supervisor should make it a point to meet directly with the clients at the start of treatment. In addition to ensuring that clients are aware that the intern is being supervised, meeting with the supervisor allows clients to know that there is someone they can speak with if they have concerns about their treatment. These issues are discussed further in Chapter 3 in the context of the ethical obligation to provide "informed consent." Before working directly with clients, all interns should read that chapter carefully and be well versed in their ethical obligations.

AGE AND EXPERIENCE ISSUES WITH CLIENTS

The age and experience of interns are two issues that sometimes arise when interns meet clients. These are particularly likely with undergraduate students, many of whom will be in their early twenties or perhaps even in their late teens. For interns in this group, their age is seldom a problem if they are working with young children or early teens. It may, however, become an issue if clients are close in age or if clients are older than the intern. Clients in late adolescence or older adults sometimes ask questions like, "So how can somebody your age have anything to tell me?"

In response to such questions interns should first try to understand what the question might mean to the client. Does it mean, for example, that the client is sincerely interested in the treatment program and wants to know he or she can rely on the intern for help? Or, does it mean that the client is interested in taking a position of power over the intern because that is how the client relates to most people? What else might a question of this type mean to clients?

How one understands the meaning of the client's question should help in forming a response. As a general guideline, interns need not be defensive about age, experience, or, for that matter, any other issues on which they might be challenged by clients. Instead, the intern might wish to acknowledge the importance of the question. Then, without being defensive, the intern may explore any specific concerns or issues with the client. This displays genuine concern for the client's needs and shows that the intern is honest. An example of one way this might occur in practice is offered below.

A male client has been court ordered to seek counseling because he has abused his wife and children. The dialogue below takes place when the client meets a new intern who will be working with the client's primary therapist. The intern will also be observing interactions between the client and his family members.

Client (rather gruffly): So you're an intern from the college, huh? How old are you?

Intern: I'm twenty-one. And you?

Client: Forty-two. Old enough to be your father. (Pauses for a moment looking over the intern. Then, with some hostility asks) What the hell are you supposed to tell me that I don't already know?

Intern (calmly but assertively): I'm not sure I'm here to "tell" you anything. I'm mainly here to observe and learn. But it sounds like you're wondering about my age and whether or not I know what I'm doing.

Client: That's exactly what I'm thinking. I don't need any know-it-all kid telling me how to raise my family. I've got enough of those already.

Intern: I don't think it's my job to tell you how to raise your family. I might be able listen to how things are going and maybe help you folks get things back together.

Client: Yeah. We'll see.

In this example, the client appears to want to diminish the intern's credibility. This reaction may be based on legitimate concerns about the intern's qualifications or it may be an attempt to shift the focus from the client's reason for being in treatment to questions about why the intern is there. The intern's response is thoroughly professional. She does not attempt to elicit the client's approval on the spot, nor does she become defensive, counterattack, or apologize. Instead, she stays right with the client and with the interaction process. She acknowledges the presence and legitimacy of the client's concerns and offers to do what she can to be of help. That is all that can reasonably be expected.

An interaction such as this would probably not be very pleasant for the intern or the client, but not all clinical work is pleasant. It may also happen that in spite of the intern's best efforts a client will continue to be hostile and challenging. This can make things even more unpleasant, but it provides important clinical information that can help the intern understand the client. The intern should keep in mind that, on the one hand, it is perfectly legitimate for clients to have questions about the intern's age and experience. At the same time, however, the real issue of importance is the issue the client brings, not the intern's age. By remaining professional and receiving what the client is saying without becoming defensive, the intern can help keep the focus where it needs to be.

TIME LIMITS

The example just presented demonstrated how clients can resist working with interns. This happens on occasion, but the reverse situation often poses a more vexing problem. Although some clients may not want to work with interns, it also happens that clients will form very close connections with interns. One reason for this may be that many clients are in great need and interns are usually approachable, interested, and eager to work with them. While relationships between interns and clients can be highly beneficial to both, they also raise unique clinical issues that must be carefully considered in selecting clients to work with interns and in developing treatment approaches.

One of the real strengths of interns is that their enthusiasm and openness often makes it possible to form contacts with clients who may have been given up on by others. Indeed, some experienced supervisors make a habit of assigning the most "hopeless" cases to interns because they have learned that, where others may have failed, the enthusiasm and effort of an intern can sometimes break through.

At the same time, however, interns know from the first day that their time at a placement will be limited and that termination may be inevitable within just a few months after the internship begins. Under such circumstances, is it therapeutic, or even fair, to encourage interns and clients to build relationships when it is known that their contact will end in a very short time?

There is no easy answer to this question but it must be addressed. The first thing that must be done is for interns to be very clear about the time limits of their placements. Interns must be clear about this with staff, clients, and, most importantly, with themselves. This means that when they begin working with individual clients, in groups, on projects, or whatever else they may participate in, interns must inform those involved of the time constraints. This is part of the previously mentioned informed consent process.

Interns must also remember their own time constraints;

they should avoid creating unrealistic fantasies about what can be accomplished or should be attempted within the time available. It is not honest, for example, to tell clients the intern will always be there for them if the intern knows that in another two months he or she will be gone. Similarly, taking on a project that will require a year to complete is unwise if the internship only lasts six months. It may be difficult to limit a relationship with a client or decline involvement in a project that is interesting, but it is better to be realistic than to create false hopes that will inevitably lead to disappointment.

When interns hear this advice they sometimes wonder if they should avoid working with any clients or projects at all. That would be going too far. Rather than avoiding all involvement or contact, the wise response is to be selective about one's involvement. This is the second element of working within limited time. Not all cases or projects will require extended time periods. Many clients can be helped within a few weeks or months and many projects can also be completed in a short time. One of the intern's responsibilities is to select cases and activities wisely. Supervisors should also play a role in this and should be aware of time constraints when they assign interns to clients or duties. If an intern is assigned a case or project for which time limitations will pose a problem, the intern should discuss this with the supervisor.

A third element to working within time constraints is to consider the approaches used. It is not necessary to limit involvement to short-term cases or activities as long as the treatment selected takes the time factor into account and includes provisions for continuing the treatment or other work after the intern leaves. Time constraints can also be dealt with by working with clients in the presence of another professional who will continue the case when the intern leaves. Arrangements of this type often involve interns seeing clients jointly with their supervisor. The supervisor can then maintain the case after the internship concludes. A comparable situation also holds when the intern is involved in treatment groups. Because the group provides the continuity for clients, there is a less dramatic change when an intern leaves.

However the matter of time limits is addressed, interns are well advised to consider termination issues even before they accept a case. By thinking about termination as part of selecting cases and choosing intervention techniques, many potential difficulties of termination can be prevented from the outset (Penn, 1990). More will be said about concluding treatment in Chapter 12, but, for the reasons described here interns should keep time limits in mind at all stages of their internship and work with clients.

FEES FOR SERVICE

Most interns who are just starting out will not have to deal with charging for their individual services, but the agencies where you work will very likely have at least some fees. As you gain in experience and training you may begin to see clients on a fee-for-service basis yourself. Whether or not this is part of your internship, for many interns the question of charging for helping people is an awkward issue.

There are several reasons why interns find it difficult to charge for services. One reason is simply that it is a new experience. Most interns will have worked for pay before, but the work was probably at a different type of job that did not require the intern to directly collect a fee. If a previous job did require that you collect fees, the service provided probably seemed more tangible than therapy or other social services. For example, tutoring, teaching, waiting tables, sales, construction, and other jobs may all require that one ask customers for payment, but in each of these situations it seems relatively clear what the payment is for. In the case of human service professions it is not always as clear what the service is or how much it is worth.

A second, and more vexing, factor that makes it difficult to charge fees is that charging for service feels like it conflicts with the altruistic motives that brought many interns to the helping professions. If a person goes into a profession out of a desire to help people, but then charges those people money, the conflict between altruism and the profit motive is likely to create dissonance. Resolving this dissonance is not easy because one runs the risk of compromising the altruism or simply rationalizing away one's sense of guilt. I must confess that I am not always comfortable with the matter of charging for what I do, but I will explain in a moment how I deal with the issue. Before I do, however, a third issue must be addressed that is inextricably connected to the question of fees for service. This issue revolves around the question "Does treatment work at all, regardless of who practices it?" This is particularly relevant to interns who are training in psychotherapy or counseling. Friedman and Kaslow (1986) consider this a perfectly understandable question for interns and they note that:

> It is highly unusual for a trainee to enter the field with a firmly entrenched belief in the efficacy of psychotherapy. It is therefore very much the task of supervisors and teachers to nurture the growth of the trainee's faith in the power of the healing process. (p. 37)

In my own work, I deal with the issue of charging for service in several ways. To begin with, it may help to recognize that what human service professionals are really billing for is our time. We are not necessarily promising to "cure" clients or solve their problems. We are, however, agreeing to spend time with clients and do the best we can to help them in some way. Psychologists, counselors, and social workers are not the only professionals who bill for services in this way. Attorneys, physicians, and many others bill in similar ways. The common element to these professions is that billing is based on the professional's time. Attorneys do not always win their cases and doctors do not always cure

their patients. Professional services are offered to and paid for by clients because the knowledge and training the professionals have received are believed to be valuable by the client. The central principle is that the professional's time is of value. Thus, when you charge clients, what you are really charging for is your time and the skills and knowledge you apply during that time.

In addition to time spent directly with clients, Callahan (1994) reminds clinicians that direct contact with a client is not the only time the therapist or counselor will spend on that case. Taking notes, correspondence, scoring and writing test reports, etc., all take time and must be considered when professionals determine their fees and how much they actually receive for their services.

One of the reasons professional services are valued is that the professional has dedicated a great deal of time and money to receiving education and training. The training alone does not guarantee that a person is competent, but it is hoped that certain skills and knowledge have been acquired during training and will be of use as the professional works with clients. Because admission to professional training is selective and is usually followed by further screening for licensing, it is also assumed that professionals possess a degree of intelligence and knowledge that will be of use in their work. Finally, possession of a professional degree and license also implies that the individual is bound to act within certain established ethical constraints designed to protect the client.

This brings us to the issue of whether or not interns are sufficiently skilled to justify charging for services. By their nature, internships involve a trainee working in a clinical setting under the guidance and instruction of a supervisor. This means that the intern is not working independently. Interns work closely with supervisors who help them review cases and who review the interns' treatment with clients. Thus, when clients are billed for services provided by interns, they are not being charged solely for the intern's time. The bill must also include the time of the supervisor and the resources of their internship site. What is more, although interns may not yet be ready for independent practice, this does not mean their time is without value. Many interns, particularly those completing graduate degrees, are in fact quite skilled and, in conjunction with the aid of their supervisor and the support and resources of their internship site, it is thoroughly appropriate that they bill and be compensated for their services.

Two other topics merit brief mention here in regard to fees. First, although interns are unlikely to deal with the matter directly themselves, the process of collecting fees when clients fail to pay can raise delicate and ambiguous ethical issues (Goodman, 1994). Although interns may not deal with this process personally, they should be aware of the process and any related informed consent issues. For example, in some agencies unpaid client bills will be given to a collection agency. That possibility should be shared with clients at the outset of treatment. Interns should ask their supervisor about this issue before starting treatment and must be sure clients are aware of billing and collection issues.

It should also be mentioned in this context that the issue of collections agencies and clinical fees is controversial and may be associated with increased risks of liability suits for confidentiality breeches. In light of this concern, some experts in legal issues have advised against the practice, arguing that the fees that might be obtained through such means are probably not sufficient to justify the risks (Eric Harris, personal communication, February 3, 1995).

A second issue of interest has to do with how different client types may relate to fees in different ways. Rabkin (1994) offers a brief discussion of how clients with diagnoses such as Dependent Personality, Obsessive Compulsive Personality, etc., may react in unique ways to fees and how this reaction can become part of the therapeutically useful material therapists address in treatment. Interns who encounter difficulties in dealing with fee issues with certain clients may find Rabkin's ideas particularly useful.

IS TREATMENT EFFECTIVE?

Still, two big questions about charging fees remain. Is treatment really helpful and worth paying for? and, How does one reconcile altruistic motives with billing for services?

The answer to whether or not therapy and counseling are really helpful is a qualified but confident yes. Although a number of methodological issues complicate research in this area, numerous reviews (Crits-Christoph, 1992; Jacobson & Addis, 1993; Kazdin, 1991; Lambert, Weber & Sykes, 1993; Lipsey & Wilson, 1993; Lee, Picard & Blain, 1994; Shadish, et al., 1993; Whiston & Sexton, 1993) have concluded that for most clients, including adults, children, couples, and families, psychotherapy has positive effects and produces results superior to what would be expected if the client had not been in therapy or had received placebo treatment. Strupp and Binder (1992) note that "Improvements from psychotherapy are surprisingly durable. . ." (p 123). Strupp and Binder go on to acknowledge that relapse will affect a percentage of patients, but this should not necessarily be considered a treatment failure ". . . it is now considered entirely reasonable for patients to seek further therapy when stresses and associated problems recur" (ibid.).

That is the good news. Now for some qualification and a few words of caution. Although research suggests that, overall, therapy has positive effects as compared to control and placebo groups, it has been difficult, with the exception of certain behavioral treatments for specific anxiety disorders, to demonstrate that different therapy approaches produce markedly different outcomes (Luborsky, Singer & Luborsky, 1975). There has also been substantial discussion about how one defines and measures outcomes and how they should be compared across studies (Ankuta & Abeles, 1993; Speer, 1992).

Some years ago, Paul (1967) pointed out that one should not simply ask if therapy in general is effective. Instead, one should ask,

> What treatment, by whom, is most effective for this individual with that specific problem, and under which set of circumstances? (p. 111)

The goal of answering those questions is certainly appealing, but as Beutler (1991) has explained, the number of variables involved and the research techniques and designs that have been used thus far have made it impossible to identify the optimal combination of patient characteristics and psychotherapy approaches. As a result, to date about all that can be stated with confidence regarding therapy differences is what Whiston and Sexton (1993) concluded:

> On the whole, the research indicates that no one theory is any more effective than any other. Similarly, adherence to any one theory or approach does not guarantee successful outcome. (p. 48)

Given the previously mentioned evidence that "therapy" broadly defined is generally effective, the lack of conclusive evidence that one therapy approach is necessarily superior to another need not be disheartening. It does, however, suggest that the heated arguments that sometimes arise between therapists of different "schools" are in most cases based on philosophical differences rather than empirical evidence.

Of greater concern than arguments over theoretical superiority is evidence that between 6 percent (Orlinsky & Howard, 1980) and 11 percent (Shapiro & Shapiro, 1982) may get worse rather than better in therapy. Strupp (1989) identified some of the factors, notably "communications that are experienced by patients as pejorative" (p. 717) that may contribute to negative outcomes. Strupp argues that therapists need to be more attentive to such factors in their practice and in training of students. This means we must be mindful of the fact that we have the potential to do harm as well as good and that the "effectiveness" of our interventions will not always be in positive directions.

ALTRUISM VERSUS MONEY

The question of altruism versus monetary incentive remains. To some extent the issue may be out of your hands at your internship. If the placement site has a policy on fees for service you may simply have to work with that as long as you are at the placement. That structures your response to a large extent for the moment but it does not really "solve" the question for you individually.

A second consideration regarding charging for treatment is that charging fees may enhance the effectiveness of therapy. Conolley and Bonner (1991) presented videotaped counseling simulations to undergraduate students and then asked the students to rate the counselor. All students observed the same videotape, but before assigning their ratings the students were given descriptions of the counselor's background, including her credentials and her fee structure. Results showed that compared to students who were told the counselor charged $25 per hour, students who were told the counselor charged $80 rated the counselor significantly higher in "credibility, attractiveness, expertness and overall counseling behavior" (p. 357). Interestingly, students who were told the counselor used a sliding fee scale, that is, from $25 to $80, depending on the client's income, gave ratings that on average were between the $25 and $80 groups but did not differ significantly from either the high-fee or low-fee group. The authors noted that the use of students rather than "real clients" as raters, and the use of a video simulation of counseling may limit generalizability of the findings. Nevertheless, to the extent that these findings suggest that fees may be related to perceptions of counselors, it may also be that fees will have an impact on therapy effectiveness.

Somewhat different findings were reported by Wong (1994), who asked students and university staff to rate credibility of therapists described as charging either $70, $90, or $115. Given these rates, no significant differences were found for credibility ratings by either students or staff. Wong concluded from this that as long as fees are in the range similar to usual professional fees, cost differences may not substantially affect credibility ratings. For a review of other research on this topic, see Herron and Sitkowski (1986) and Waehler, Hardin and Rogers (1994).

Apart from the question of therapeutic effectiveness there is also a matter of pride involved for many clients who sincerely need help but do not want to accept "charity." For these clients it is important to respect both their need and their pride and allow them to pay for services to the best of their ability.

Of course the arguments offered above could simply be justifications for charging fees when one's real incentive is not so much therapeutic effectiveness but lining one's own pockets. Ultimately, individuals must make their own judgments about their motives and the relationship between those motives, fees, and therapy. While I would not presume to tell interns what they "should" do, it might be helpful at this point to share my personal perspectives on this issue.

I did not enter this field because I wanted to "get rich." If that was my goal I could have pursued any number of other occupations. My primary motive was the desire to help people and society in the best way I could. In selecting a profession, I tried to identify one in which I could contribute to society and to others while at the same time putting food on the table for myself and my family. In other words, I set out to find a way to reconcile altruistic motives with the legitimate need to earn an income. For me, it was not altruism *versus* income, it was altruism *and* income. The helping professions seemed to fit that aim well. I have found that many of the same motives that lead me to this field are shared by my students and interns. Similar motives have been described by Berger (1995), who noted that very few of the senior therapists he interviewed even mentioned financial rewards as a factor sustaining their commitment and enthusiasm for the profession.

As noted earlier, when fees are charged for therapy, what we are really charging for is our time and the years of training and study that went into developing our skills. Many agencies and professionals work on a sliding scale in which clients are charged according to their ability to pay. Consistent with personal values and the code of ethics of our professions, a portion of clinical services are also provided free as a direct service to the community. The key point is that whether I am charging full fee, reduced fees, or I am providing services gratis, I believe my time and skills are valuable and merit fair compensation. As long as I am doing my best and my fees are reasonable, I feel I am balancing altruistic motives with financial needs.

INOCULATION: WHAT *NOT* TO LEARN

To conclude this chapter, let us change directions and, instead of describing things you should learn on your internship, discuss some things you should not learn.

Throughout this book you will be encouraged to be open to learning. But that does not mean you must uncritically model everything you observe or accept everything you are told as truth. This point is raised now because interns sometimes begin to model behaviors that are not necessarily worthy of emulating. Modeling and listening are wonderful ways to learn, but it behooves you to be aware and thoughtful about the behaviors you observe or the information you receive.

Let me demonstrate the point through an example. In some placement sites staff members constantly express negative attitudes toward clients. They may display this through a hostile tone of voice, derogatory statements, meanspirited "jokes," or in other overt or subtle ways. Interns who observe this attitude may not feel comfortable with it at first, but if the atmosphere of a setting and the behavior of the staff set an example of negativity it is easy for the intern to adopt similar attitudes and behaviors, often without even realizing what is happening. I have observed interns who began with positive, idealistic feelings begin to shift toward negativity and hostility within just a few weeks at a placement. When I point this out, the interns are often surprised and somewhat ashamed of themselves, but most are glad to have the feedback and to understand what they have modeled and why.

As another example of how interns can adopt behaviors that are countertherapeutic, in many placement sites it is common for staff to use what might be called "stock" words or phrases when speaking to or about clients. One example, which is admittedly a pet peeve of mine, is the word "inappropriate." In my opinion, this is probably the most overused word in all the helping professions. For instance, in response to a client's statement or action a staff member might say "Tim, that is inappropriate." Or, a therapist might write a note that says "Tim acted very inappropriately in group today." I recently attended a conference in which a speaker used the words appropriate or inappropriate more than twenty times in five minutes of a presentation. Interns observe this usage and quickly incorporate it into their own vocabulary. Unfortunately, more often than not, the word "inappropriate" is used in ways that are countertherapeutic, i.e., that block rather than enhance intern and client understanding and growth. As a result, interns who model the use of the word "inappropriate" are learning a behavior that will inhibit rather than enhance their therapeutic development.

When I introduce this example into discussions with interns (and sometimes supervisors) who are already working in the field, many protest that they and the rest of the staff use the word inappropriate all the time and they do not hear anything wrong with it. Others argue that it is just a word and I am making too much out of it. In response to this, I offer two observations. First, the fact that interns have so quickly adopted and, perhaps more importantly, accepted the terminology is evidence of just what I have been saying about how people model unconsciously and why it is important to be careful with what one models. Second, in regard to the word "inappropriate" per se, I find it useful to ask interns what they mean when they say "inappropriate." Most interns initially have great difficulty defining their meaning without resorting to a tautology of using the term to define itself. When they do begin to work toward a definition it becomes apparent that the meaning of "inappropriate" depends on the situation. It is also evident that, in general, the word is used very broadly to express generic staff displeasure or disapproval of a client's behavior.

In place of "inappropriate" I suggest that professionals and clients would benefit by abandoning such a broad term and confronting more specifically the real issues that are involved in a given situation. For example, suppose a client said to a staff member he thought the staff member was ugly. Instead of saying "Tim, that is inappropriate," the staff member might be more specific and respond by saying, "That hurts my feelings when you say that," or "You sound angry today. Shall we talk about what is going on?" The first response, "That's inappropriate," does not tell the client what is inappropriate, why it is inappropriate, or what "inappropriate" means. By comparison, the alternatives give specific information about the effects of the statement or about possible motives behind the statement. "That's inappropriate" might "shut the client up" but it is much less likely to promote a genuinely therapeutic interaction. Formulating an alternative

response might require more effort and insight from the staff, but compared to a meaningless reflex response it is much more likely to be therapeutic.

Misuse of the term "inappropriate" is but one example of how interns model behaviors without thinking about the purpose of the behaviors or why they are modeling them. Other terms or phrases that are used excessively and imprecisely include "manipulative," "denial," "acting out," "resistant," "doing it to get attention," and certain diagnostic categories that come in or out of vogue. If you are attentive, you will no doubt encounter others along the way.

This is not to say that the words described above should never be used or that their mere utterance will be damaging to clients. It must be stressed, however, that words are among the primary tools of treatment and it is vital that interns learn to use them thoughtfully. By raising the subject here, my goal is to inoculate interns against uncritical acceptance of words, behaviors, or attitudes that would inhibit their development. The thing that is most crucial to avoid is not some specific word or action; it is the tendency of all of us to imitate behavior, accept information, or adopt attitudes without thinking for ourselves about what we are doing. Beginning with your internship and throughout your career, you should think about everything you do and observe. You should ask questions and seek explanations. If done politely, this can be a valuable learning experience not only for you but also for staff, many of whom may not have thought carefully about the issues themselves.

Thus, as you begin your internship, strive to avoid preconceptions and be open to learning but, at the same time, think carefully about what you are observing and learning. In the end, the ability to think critically and wisely is the most important thing you can gain from any internship experience.

REFERENCES

Ankuta, G. Y., & Abeles, N. (1993). Client satisfaction, clinical significance, and meaningful change in psychotherapy. *Professional Psychology: Research and Practice, 24*, 70–74.

Berger, M. (1995). Sustaining the professional self: Conversations with senior psychotherapists. In M. B. Sussman (Ed.) *A perilous calling: The hazards of psychotherapy practice.* (pp. 302–321). New York: John Wiley and Sons.

Beutler, L. E. (1991). Have all won and must all have prizes? Revisiting Luborsky et al.'s verdict. *Journal of Consulting and Clinical Psychology, 59*, 226–232.

Callahan, T. R. (1994). Being paid for what you do. *The Independent Practitioner* (Bulletin of the Division of Independent Practice, Division 42 of the American Psychological Association), *14(1)*, 25–26.

Conolley, J. C., & Bonner, M. (1991). The effects of counselor fee and title on perceptions of counselor behavior. *Journal of Counseling and Development, 69*, 356–358.

Crits-Christoph, P. (1992). The efficacy of brief dynamic-psychotherapy: A meta-analysis. *American Journal of Psychiatry, 149,* 151–158.

Friedman, D., & Kaslow, N. J. (1986). The development of professional identity in psychotherapists: Six stages in the supervision process. In F. W. Kaslow (Ed.), *Supervision and training: Models, dilemmas and challenges.* New York: Haworth Press.

Goodman, K. J. (1994). When patients don't pay: Practical aspects of fee collection. *The Independent Practitioner* (Bulletin of the Division of Independent Practice, Division 42 of the American Psychological Association), *14(1),* 24–25.

Herron, W. G., & Sitkowski, S. (1986). Effect of fees on psychotherapy: What is the evidence? *Professional Psychology: Research and Practice, 17,* 347–351.

Hill, C. E., & Corbett, M. M. (1993). A perspective on the history of process and outcome research in counseling psychology. *Journal of Counseling Psychology, 40,* 3–24.

Jacobson, N. S., & Addis, M. E. (1993). Research on couples and couple therapy: What do we know? Where are we going? *Journal of Consulting and Clinical Psychology, 61,* 85–93.

Kazdin, A. E. (1991). Effectiveness of psychotherapy with children and adolescents. *Journal of Consulting and Clinical Psychology, 59,* 785–798.

Lambert, M. J., Weber, F. D., & Sykes, J. D. (1993). *Psychotherapy versus placebo therapies: A review of the meta-analytic literature.* Poster session presented at the Annual Meeting of the Western Psychological Association, Phoenix, AZ.

Lee, C. M., Picard, M., & Blain, M. D. (1994). A methodological and substantive review of intervention outcome studies for families undergoing divorce. *Journal of Family Psychology, 8,* 3–15.

Lipsey, M. W., & Wilson, D. B. (1993). The efficacy of psychological, educational, and behavioral treatment: Confirmation from meta-analysis. *American Psychologist, 48,* 1181–1209.

Luborsky, L., Singer, B., & Luborsky, L. (1975). Comparative studies of psychotherapy: Is it true that "everyone has won and all must have prizes"? *Archives of General Psychiatry, 32,* 995–1008.

Orlinsky, D. E., & Howard, K. I. (1980). Gender and psychotherapeutic outcome. In A. M. Brodsky & R. Hare-Mustin (Eds.), *Handbook of psychotherapy and behavior change,* (pp. 3–34). New York: Guilford Press.

Paul, G. (1967). Strategy in outcome research in psychotherapy. *Journal of Counseling Psychology, 29,* 268–282.

Penn. L. S. (1990). When the therapist must leave: Forced termination of psychodynamic therapy. *Professional Psychology: Research and Practice, 21,* 379–384.

Rabkin, L. Y. (1994). On some character styles and fees in psychotherapy. *The Independent Practitioner* (Bulletin of the Division of Independent Practice, Division 42 of the American Psychological Association), *14(1),* 26–28.

Shadish, W. R., Montgomery, L. M., Wilson, P., Wilson, M. R., Bright, I., & Okwumabua, T. (1993). Effects of family and marital psychotherapies: A meta-analysis. *Journal of Consulting and Clinical Psychology, 61,* 992–1002.

Shapiro, D. A., & Shapiro, D. (1982). Meta-analysis of comparative therapy outcome studies: A replication and refinement. *Psychological Bulletin, 92,* 581–604.

Speer, D. C. (1992). Clinically significant change: Jacobson and Truax (1991) Revisited. *Journal of Consulting and Clinical Psychology, 60,* 402–408.

Strupp, H. H. (1989). Psychotherapy: Can the practitioner learn from the researcher? *American Psychologist, 44,* 717–724.

Strupp, H. H., & Binder, J. L. (1992). Current developments in psychotherapy. *The Independent Practitioner* (Bulletin of the Division of Independent Practice, Division 42 of the American Psychological Association), *12(3),* 119–124.

Waehler, C. A., Hardin, S. I., & Rogers, J. R. (1994). College students' perceptions of the relationship between fee and counseling. *Journal of Counseling and Development, 73,* 88–93.

Whiston, S. C., & Sexton, T. L. (1993). An overview of psychotherapy outcome research: Implications for practice. *Professional Psychology: Research and Practice, 24,* 43–52.

Wong, J. L. (1994). Lay theories of psychotherapy and perceptions of therapists: A replication and extension of Furnham and Wardley. *Journal of Clinical Psychology, 50,* 624–632.

Zakutansky, T. J., & Sirles, E. A. (1993). Ethical and legal issues in field education: Shared responsibility and risk. *Journal of Social Work Education, 29,* 338–347.

CHAPTER 3

ETHICAL AND LEGAL ISSUES

The first rule of medicine is Do No Harm. The same rule applies to internships. One of the ways the helping professions have sought to ensure quality treatment and reduce the potential for harm to clients is through the establishment of formal ethics codes or standards. The states have also worked to protect the well-being of consumers by enacting regulations and laws governing the licensing and practice of various professions. This chapter discusses key ethical and legal issues relating to clinical practice and internships.

ETHICAL GUIDELINES OF THE HELPING PROFESSIONS

Membership in professional organizations carries with it a commitment on the part of each member to adhere to the ethical guidelines of the organization. Ethics codes are not handed down as final "truths from above." They are arrived at through extended discussion and review among the organization's members. As conditions change, ethics codes are updated. Indeed, even before a code has been officially published, debate may have begun on how the code may need to be modified and improved (Keith-Spiegel, 1994). During the time an ethics code is in effect, members are expected to abide by that code. In some states, licensing and practice laws incorporate the professional ethics codes into law.

Not all ethical standards are identical for all professions, but most professional ethics codes share certain basic principles (Kitchener, 1984). Ethical guidelines for several of the leading professional organizations can be found in the references listed below. Again, be aware that ethical standards evolve over time and in some instances undergo substantial revisions. Thus, it may happen that more recent versions of certain codes will become available. In general, these can be obtained from the sources listed below.

American Association for Counseling and Development (Now American Counseling Association) (1988). "Ethical Standards of the American Association for Counseling and Development (3rd Revision), AACD Governing Council, March 1988," *Journal of Counseling and Development*, 67, September, 4–8. (See also below for most recent revision.)

American Counseling Association (1995) *American Counseling Association Code of Ethics and Standards of Practice*. Alexandria, VA: Author.

American Association for Marriage and Family Therapy (1990). *Code of ethical principles for marriage and family therapists*. Washington, DC: Author.

American College Personnel Association (1989). *Statement of ethical principles and standards*. Alexandria, VA: Author.

American Psychological Association (1992). Ethical principles of psychologists and code of conduct. *American Psychologist, 46,* 1597–1611.

American School Counselor Association (1984) *Ethical standards for school counselors.* Alexandria, VA: Author.

Association for Specialists in Group Work (1990). Ethical guidelines for group counselors: ASGW 1989 Revision. *The Journal for Specialists in Group Work, 15,* 119–126.

National Association of Social Workers (1993). *NASW Code of Ethics.* Silver Spring, MD: Author.

SPECIFIC ETHICAL GUIDELINES

In addition to general ethical guidelines, some organizations, such as the American Psychological Association (APA), have developed more specific guidelines that apply to clinical practitioners. The APA's "Ethical Principles of Psychologists, General Guidelines for Providers of Psychological Services" (APA Board of Professional Affairs, 1987) is an example of such practitioner guidelines. The APA has also published "Guidelines for Providers of Psychological Services to Ethnic, Linguistic and Culturally Diverse Populations" (APA Office of Ethnic Minority Affairs, 1993). Similar standards have been proposed for counselors (Ibrahim & Arredondo, 1986).

ENFORCEMENT OF ETHICAL STANDARDS

Interns and professionals should be aware that ethical guidelines are established by professional organizations to govern the conduct of their members. Organizations have established procedures for investigating ethics complaints and disciplining members who are found to have violated ethical standards (Ethics Committee of the APA, 1992; AACD Ethics Committee, 1991). Within the governing organizations, consequences of ethical violations can range from warnings and required educational efforts to dismissal from the organization.

Because ethical guidelines are established by organizations to govern member conduct, they do not formally apply to practitioners who are not members of the organizations. Thus, a psychologist who is not a member of the American Psychological Association cannot be sanctioned by the organization for violating its ethics codes. The same is true for members of other professions and organizations. That does not mean there will be no consequences for unethical conduct. Students, in particular, should know that violations of ethical standards for their profession can be considered grounds for academic discipline and possibly dismissal from a training program. For an informative review of this issue see Cobb (1994).

ETHICS AND LAW

Ethics are not the same as laws, but ethical principles of leading professional organizations are often incorporated into the licensing and practice laws of individual states. To the extent that state licensing laws incorporate or parallel professional ethical standards, practitioners who violate those laws face possible loss of license as well as possible criminal prosecution for certain violations (Swenson, 1993). Civil actions for monetary damages may also result from unethical actions (Bennett, Bryant, VandenBos & Greenwood, 1990). One should also be aware that laws vary from state to state and are continually evolving as new cases arise. Therefore, you must make it a regular practice to update yourself on current laws within your state and on current practices regarding confidentiality and other ethical constraints. For detailed discussion of legal issues relating to clinical work, see Swenson's "Psychology and Law for the Helping Professions" (Swenson, 1993); "Professional Liability and Risk Management" (Bennett et al., 1990); "Ethics, Legalities, and Professional Practice Issues in Marriage and Family Therapy (Vesper & Brock, 1990); and "The Psychologist's Legal Handbook" (Stromberg et al., 1988).

ETHICAL AGREEMENT FORMS FOR INTERNS

In an effort to ensure that interns will be informed about and adhere to ethical standards, I require each intern I supervise to read and sign the Ethical Guidelines form presented in Appendix G. I then keep this form in my class records for future information purposes. As you will see, the form covers some of the essential guidelines that all professionals must know and follow. It also provides space for the intern, the field supervisor, and the instructor to sign indicating that this material has been addressed, along with any local or placement-specific ethical concerns.

ONGOING ETHICS STUDY AND TRAINING

Reading and signing the ethics form should not be considered the last word on ethics. Rather, it is a fundamental starting point from which further discussion and ongoing evaluation should proceed. A highly recommended source is an article by Zakutansky and Sirles (1993), which identifies six intern and supervisor relationships and reviews ethical and legal issues relevant to each. The relationships are "(1) student-client; (2) student-field instructor; (3) field instructor-client; (4) field instructor-field liaison (representing the social work program's field staff); (5) student field liaison; and (6) field liaison-client (p. 338)." If you eventually start treating clients, it may be useful to review an article by DePauw (1986). In this article, she offers a "timeline" perspective in which she reviews major ethical issues in sequence as they pertain to phases of counseling.

In addition to such readings, you should maintain a discussion of ethics with your instructor, supervisor, and peers and should plan to participate in periodic continuing education in ethics. As Welfel and Lipsitz (1984) observed in a review of research on ethical training, mere knowledge of ethical codes does not guarantee ethical behavior. In the same journal issue, dedicated specifically to ethical decision making, Kitchener (1984) pointed out that no ethical code can be written to handle all situations that might arise. What is more, in certain instances, adhering to one element of an ethical code may conflict with a different portion of the same code.

Kitchener distinguishes between ethical principles and codes of ethics, noting that codes of ethics derive from underlying ethical principles. Included among the principles shared by virtually all helping professions are: respect for autonomy, avoiding harm, and promoting good, truthfulness, and justice. Kitchener asserts that when ethical dilemmas or conflicts are faced, awareness of these principles provides the basis for decisions to be reached through a process of critical thought and evaluation.

The material that follows in this chapter discusses key ethical principles in some detail, but it is important to recognize that ethics cannot be boiled down to a simple "cookbook" of dos and don'ts. Ethical conduct requires a continuous process of self-monitoring, reflection, and careful thought. Throughout your training as an intern and your work as a professional it is incumbent upon you to know and understand not only the letter of the ethical codes, but their spirit, rationale, and practical implications.

COMPETENCE

The first and most important principle of most ethics codes is to operate within one's level of competence. Consistent with the principle of "Do No Harm," knowing our limits means that no matter how much we may want to help others, we must recognize the extent and limitations of our abilities and seek assistance or supervision when we need it.

The importance of knowing one's abilities and limits should make intuitive sense, but, in the desire to help, it is easy to imagine that we are more capable than we actually are. Unfortunately, this lesson is often learned "the hard way" as we start something with the best of intentions only to wind up in a mess when the situation exceeds our abilities. A personal experience in a nonclinical setting may help to demonstrate both how easy it is to overestimate abilities and the possible consequences of making that mistake.

As a break from clinical work and teaching, I sometimes go whitewater kayaking. In kayaking, especially when one is learning, there are frequent occasions when one must exit the boat and swim for safety. There are also times when other boaters are swimming and need to be rescued. In these situations the power and speed of rivers can be overwhelming and one quickly learns that rivers are no place for the unprepared.

In river rescue situations the first priority, even before that of trying to help a victim, is to not endanger yourself. As one river rescue expert explained it, "If you go jumping into a river to help someone and you don't know what you're doing, the odds of you effecting a rescue are very, very small. Instead, the odds are high that you will become a second victim and you may actually cause the victim and yourself to drown. Bravado and heroic intentions do not impress the river."

I observed this firsthand when an inexperienced kayaker tried to help a swimming boater by getting the swimmer to the apparent safety of a fallen tree that lay on the water surface. What neither the kayaker nor the swimmer realized was that trees in rivers, although they look safe, are actually among the most deadly hazards. The river pushes against the tree with incredible force and even a relatively gentle current can easily entrap kayakers or swimmers. In this case, that is exactly what happened. When they reached the downed tree, the kayaker's boat overturned, trapping the would-be rescuer and the victim underwater, where they were unable to extricate themselves. Both people would almost certainly have drowned had it not been for a more experienced boater who saw what was happening and managed to free them. If not for the skill of the more trained boater, the swimmer and the rescuer would have died.

The purpose of this analogy is not to scare you away from your field placement (or from kayaking). Rather, it is to encourage you to be well aware of your limitations and not get in over your head. Just as beginners cannot fully appreciate the skill required to run expert rivers or rescue swimmers, casual observers of clinical work often believe it consists of little more than listening to other people talk. This idea, that anyone can do human service work without any training, is not only wrong, it is dangerous. Beginning trainees who try to provide treatment, assessment, or other services on their own without supervision are surely going beyond their limits. They might get lucky and do some good, but they might also get unlucky and do a great deal of harm to their clients and themselves.

Good intentions are no substitute for competence. One of the purposes of ethics is to remind us that we are not always the best judges of our own abilities and conduct. Simply because you want to believe you can help someone does not mean you are justified in proceeding. In all of your clinical work, make it a practice to ask yourself as objectively and honestly as possible if you have any real training or experience in the skills required to work with a given individual or situation. Then, go a step further and ask yourself how you would be able to provide objective evidence of your competence if required to do so by an ethics review board or a court of law.

This first principle is so important that if students learn nothing else in their internship they must at least learn how much they do not know. The fact is that no matter how much you study, there will never be a time when your knowledge is not vastly exceeded by your ignorance. From your first internship experience to the end of your career, you must continually strive to recognize when you need help and never be afraid or embarrassed to seek it. Until you have at least several years of experience, supervision should be an essential part of all your work and training. Further, throughout your career, you should always seek supervision when you work with particularly difficult cases or if your own performance may be adversely affected by personal issues.

You should also recognize that at no point in your career will you know everything you need to know. There is always room to learn more and in most states some form of continuing education credit is required for licensing. In my own practice, I read multiple professional journals, attend far more than the required numbers of hours of continuing education each year, and regularly consult with other professionals about challenging cases. Even with these measures, there are still many times when I recognize that I am not adequately trained to deal with certain clients or issues. In such cases one should not hesitate to seek supervision or to refer to other professionals with greater skills in the needed areas.

One final note about competence. Students sometimes believe that because they are students or interns they will not be held accountable for their actions as they would if they were professionals. This is not necessarily the case. Particularly when students are at more advanced levels of training and are given primary responsibility for a client's care, the students must recognize that they". . . are acting in a professional role, and with this status comes the responsibility to uphold the same legal, professional, and ethical standards. . ." (Zakutansky & Sirles, 1993, p. 339). Students should also be aware that if they act unethically or if their actions harm a client, they will not be the only ones held responsible. Their supervisors and instructors may also be held accountable. Thus, in considering your actions recognize that part of accepting the role of intern means accepting the responsibility that goes with it.

INFORMED CONSENT

The ethical principle of informed consent means that clients have a right to be informed about the treatment, assessment, or other services they will receive before they agree to participate in or receive those services. When applied in practice, this principle dictates that, in order to ensure informed consent, clients must be given certain information in a manner and language that they can understand. At a minimum, clients should be informed about each of the following subjects (Harris, 1995).

1. They should be made aware of the qualifications of the person providing treatment. This includes the degrees, clinical experience, specialized training, licenses, etc., the person has received.
2. In the case of interns, clients should know that the treatment provider is an intern and will be supervised. The intern's educational and training background should also be explained.
3. Clients should be given the name and qualifications of the intern's supervisor and should have an opportunity to meet with that supervisor if they wish. Clients should also know how they can contact the supervisor if they have any questions or concerns in the future.
4. Clients should know the nature of supervision, including the frequency of supervision and the activities it will entail, e.g., reviewing case notes, listening to tapes of sessions, etc.
5. Clients should be informed about the nature of the treatment or assessment to be provided. This includes a brief description of the approach to treatment or the purpose of an assessment and the instruments that will be used.
6. The frequency and duration of treatment sessions, as well as a reasonable estimate of the typical number of sessions involved to treat a given concern, should be explained.
7. The client's responsibilities for participating in treatment must be made clear. For example, the client should be expected to attend scheduled appointments, notify the therapist in advance if appointments must be canceled or changed, follow through with any assignments, etc.
8. Fees must be explained. Issues include the costs per session or per assessment and whether or not there are charges for missed sessions. How and when are payments to be made and the procedures that will be followed if payment is not made have to be explained. This discussion should also cover how insurance provider contacts will be managed and how this impacts confidentiality.
9. If a client's insurance policy limits the number of sessions the insurance company will pay for, an agreement must be reached about how to proceed if more sessions are needed and the client is unable to pay without the assistance of the insurance (Appelbaum, 1993).
10. Confidentiality must be spelled out. The nature and limitations of confidentiality, including a specific discussion of any limitations to confidentiality of what is said in treatment, as well as what is contained in the client's records, should be communicated.
11. An opportunity for questions to be answered should be provided before beginning treatment or at any time during treatment.

While informing patients of the issues described above, it is also a good idea to document that the information has been provided and understood. A sample form that addresses informed consent issues is presented in Appendix H. This form covers each of the critical topics and provides a place for clients to sign indicating that they have read, understand,

and have asked any questions about the treatment they will be receiving.

Documentation of informed consent serves several functions. By scrupulously documenting that patients have been informed, therapists ensure that they are adhering to this ethical principle and are providing what is considered to be a key element of care. If questions arise later about treatment, fees, confidentiality, or other matters, documenting that the client was informed about such things can be extraordinarily helpful. This is especially important if legal issues, such as malpractice proceedings, arise. You should also be aware that in many states, such documentation is required by state ethical guidelines and or laws. Thus, developing the habit of completing informed consent forms is a wise, and in some cases legally mandated, practice for interns and professionals alike.

CONFIDENTIALITY

Insofar as openness and honesty are essential ingredients of treatment, confidentiality is considered a necessary condition for effective therapy (Swenson, 1993). Along with competence and informed consent, many helping professionals consider confidentiality to be their primary ethical responsibility (Crowe et al., 1985).

The essence of confidentiality is the principle that clients have the right to determine who will have access to information about them and their treatment. In clinical settings, clients need to feel that the information they share will stay with the professional and not be released without their permission. Without this assurance, clients are less likely to explore and express their thoughts and feelings freely. This, in turn, is likely to inhibit the client's willingness to share certain information and may distort the treatment process (Nowell & Spruill, 1993). At the same time, however, clients also must be aware of limits to confidentiality so they can make informed choices.

Survey research suggests that clients and the general public share the belief that confidentiality is important (Claibornet al., 1994). On the other hand, Rubanowitz (1987) has reported that many of those surveyed believe there are instances, for example if crimes have been or are likely to be committed, in which the therapist should inform the necessary authorities even though it means violating the client's confidentiality.

In spite of, or perhaps because of, its importance, confidentiality is the issue most frequently identified as a source of ethical dilemmas for clinicians and educators (Pope & Vetter, 1992; Hayman & Covert, 1986; Stadler & Paul, 1986). Considering the high value placed on confidentiality, and the frequency of ethical dilemmas it poses, interns must fully understand the principle of confidentiality, know how to avoid violating confidentiality through carelessness, and appreciate the consequences of such violations. Interns also need to know that confidentiality is not fully guaranteed by their role or the clinical setting in which they work. There are exceptions in which you may, sometimes must, divulge information about clients. You need to know what such situations are, how to deal with them, and how to inform clients of these limitations to confidentiality.

The discussion that follows addresses general issues of confidentiality that apply to most settings. While the guidelines that are offered should be helpful, be aware that certain therapy approaches pose unique problems and some settings may follow very specific approaches to protect confidentiality. Placements serving minors, persons who are HIV positive, drug and alcohol treatment programs, and other settings may all have special precautions and procedures. Group therapy and family therapy also pose certain unique ethical and legal issues with regard to confidentiality (Paradise & Kirby, 1990; Vesper & Brock, 1990). In all settings, at the beginning of the field experience, the intern should ask specifically about confidentiality policy. If at any time questions arise pertaining to confidentiality, you should consult your supervisor and/or instructor.

RELEASE OF INFORMATION

In order to protect confidentiality, certain standards and guidelines must be followed scrupulously. First, no one other than the client should be given any information—written, verbal, or otherwise—about the client without explicit written and signed permission from the client. In most settings, standard "Release of Information" forms are used. These typically provide space to identify the person(s) who will receive the information, the purpose for the release, the specific information to be released, the form in which the information will be communicated, the date of the release, the time period for which the release is to be valid, the name of the person authorized to release the information, the name of the client, and the signature of the client and the primary therapist or other professional (Bennett et al., 1990).

In practice, this requirement for written permission means that if someone calls or comes into an office claiming to have the client's permission to see their records or discuss their case, one must not share records, discuss the case, or even acknowledge that the person is a client unless there is written permission authorizing such disclosure to the individual requesting the information. This may feel like a nuisance but it is necessary.

If problems arise you can cope with insistent or demanding people by saying something like, "I'm sorry, but I cannot share any information unless I have a signed release of information form. I'm sure you understand how important confidentiality is, and I'll be glad to provide you with whatever information I can as soon as a signed release of information is available." Note that this statement does not acknowledge that the individual in question is a client. It merely says a release is necessary for any information to be shared. If the person requesting the information does not accept this explanation or is insistent that they be given information, you can refer them to a supervisor. Under no circumstances should you let urgency, pressure, or inconvenience lead to laxity or carelessness about obtaining written releases.

SAFEGUARDING RECORDS

In order to ensure the confidentiality of records, all case notes, records, and other written or recorded information about the client should be kept in locked file cabinets. You should not leave notes, files, or other material with client names out in the open where others might see them inadvertently. As a further precaution, the words "Confidential Records" can be printed or stamped on all records. If case notes are kept on computers, access to the files should be restricted in some way and the computer screen with notes should not be left on for others to see should the clinician be absent.

If interns keep class notebooks or journals, these should be carefully maintained so they are not lost or misplaced. As an added precaution, interns should mark clearly on the outside of their notebooks that the material is confidential and should be returned unopened to the owner. I have all of our interns who keep journals write in bold letters on the front: "Confidential Personal Journal—If Found, Please Return to (Intern's Name and Address)." In your writing for journals or classes, the identity of clients should be disguised via pseudonyms or false initials such as Mr. X or Ms. B. Avoid the use of real initials or first names only as these can easily be connected to the actual individual.

SHARING INFORMATION WITH COLLEAGUES

Guidelines for sharing information with outside sources are relatively clear and, with the few exceptions to be discussed later, the rule can be summarized succinctly as "Not without written permission from the client." Questions about sharing information with colleagues within an internship placement are not as easily answered. As each setting and situation are different, it may be helpful to offer a general framework you can use to help make your decisions. This framework revolves around the "W" question words, who, why, what, where, when, and how. Before sharing information about a client with anyone you should ask yourself:

First: Who is this person? Has the client given permission for them to have the information? What is their role or authority within the clinical setting? What professional training do they have? What is their relationship to the client,? What do you think of their clinical skills, ethical knowledge, etc.? Also ask yourself if the other person knows about and respects the principle of confidentiality.

Second: Why do they want the information? Are they involved in the client's treatment in some way? Are they just curious? Are they seeking information to help them understand the client, or are they likely to use it in some counterproductive way.

Third: What information is being requested? Is the person asking for data such as address, phone, etc., or are they asking for clinical information about the nature of the client's concerns or background? Are they asking for general impressions from tests or interviews or do they want specific scores or answers to specific questions? Remember that merely because someone is asking for a certain type of information does not mean you should provide the information requested. Depending on the circumstances, you may choose to offer summaries or general impressions rather than specific test results or interview responses. You may also choose to offer no information at all if there is a probability that it will not be used responsibly and professionally.

Fourth: Where are you? Is the setting private, or are you in a public place where others could easily overhear your discussion? Are the office doors closed? Could people in the waiting room hear you? Are other clients nearby?

Fifth: When should you discuss the information? Is now the best time to share information? Will you have adequate time to discuss and explain things or will you be rushed and not do an adequate job? Would it be better to schedule a specific time and place rather than sharing things in passing?

Sixth: How will you share the information? Is it best to discuss information directly one on one or can you accomplish the task over the phone? Should you formalize the exchange of information in writing, either by providing the information itself in written form or by keeping notes of the conversation? What are the relative pros and cons of direct verbal versus written exchange?

If you ask these questions immediately and automatically each time you consider sharing information about a client, the chances of carelessness will be significantly reduced. Still, mistakes can happen. To demonstrate this, consider the following examples of how confidentiality was inadvertently violated by trained clinicians who were not thinking or acting with sufficient care.

INADVERTENT CONFIDENTIALITY VIOLATIONS

A psychologist with twenty-five years experience was invited to a large introductory psychology class to discuss clinical issues. In the course of his talk he described a case study in which he mentioned that the patient was a fifty-year-old man, divorced, with two daughters. At this point, confidentiality was still protected. However, the speaker went on to name the town the client lived in, then said that the client owned a local Ford dealership, was a past president of Rotary, and had been struggling with a serious drinking problem for several years. The psychologist never actually divulged the client's name but in the midsize community where this occurred it was easy enough for several people in the class to know who the client was.

As a second example, over lunch in a local restaurant, an intern and his social work supervisor were discussing a family the intern was seeing. At the end of the lunch they arose to find that the same family had been sitting one booth away. Thinking about the discussion later, the intern realized he had said some rather critical things about certain family members and he was extremely troubled about how to deal with this in the next session.

EFFECTS OF CONFIDENTIALITY VIOLATIONS

To appreciate the significance of breaks in confidentiality, imagine yourself as the client in the situations just described. How would you react to hearing your personal case discussed before a class in such a way that people would know your identity? What would be your reaction to the next therapy session if you had heard your therapist discuss your case over lunch? Would you even go to therapy or would you simply terminate with no explanation?

Also ask how you might feel as a current or potential therapy client if you heard a therapist discussing some other client. Even for those other than the clients themselves, merely knowing that therapists speak in such ways about clients could cause people to avoid the therapy process entirely.

The clinical implications of confidentiality violations should be sufficient to promote caution, but there are also liability issues to consider. Many states have laws protecting confidentiality of clients. Violations of such laws are subject to criminal prosecution. In addition to the possibility of criminal prosecution, if a client is harmed in some way by a therapist's breech of confidentiality the client may well sue for damages (Conte & Karasu, 1990; Schwartz, 1989; Swenson, 1993). Because confidentiality is such a fundamental condition of therapy, a judge or jury would not be likely to look positively on an intern's or professional's carelessness in such matters.

EXCEPTIONS TO CONFIDENTIALITY

The matter of confidentiality is complicated by the fact that there are certain occasions in which information about clients may or must be shared with others (Schwartz, 1989). This is further complicated by legal uncertainties and differences in interpretation and statutes for different states. In the space available here, only a brief review of this topic can be provided, but the information that follows should be sufficient to help you appreciate both the importance and complexities

of this issue. Again, you are strongly encouraged to study this matter in more detail in the references cited at the beginning and end of the chapter and in consultation with your supervisor and instructors. You should also familiarize yourself with state laws regarding this issue.

Without attempting to provide specific guidance for each situation, five instances will be identified in which absolute confidentiality may not hold and information may need to be revealed. The main message in this discussion is to inform interns that under no circumstances should one give a client the often heard but erroneous assurance that "nothing you say or do will be shared with anyone else without your permission." That simply is not always true and clients have a right to know the exceptions.

Swenson speaks of therapists giving clients a "psychological Miranda warning" about limits to confidentiality (Swenson, 1993, p.70). This reference to the Miranda ruling means that therapists should tell clients beforehand how information from clinical interactions might be used in court. This allows clients to use their own discretion about what they will or will not discuss in therapy.

Findings of Miller and Thelen (1986) support this principle, showing that most subjects want to be informed of confidentiality limits beforehand. In spite of this finding and the clearly stated ethical principle, Nicolai and Scott (1994) report that of the respondents to their survey regarding informed consent procedures and child abuse reporting, almost 20 percent of respondents "indicated that they sometimes, rarely, or never provide this information to clients and more than 5 percent misleadingly tell clients that everything disclosed in therapy is confidential" (p. 159). Nicolai and Scott express their concern about this finding, stating:

> Without explicit presentation of information regarding confidentiality limits, the novice client may well assume that all disclosures, regardless of content, will be kept confidential. Moreover, clinicians who tell clients that everything they say will be held in confidence are clearly putting clients, as well as themselves, at risk. (p. 158)

Briefly, the five main exceptions to confidentiality occur in: 1.) Cases of abuse. 2.) Cases in which clients are considered dangerous to themselves. 3.) Cases in which a client intends to harm others. 4.) Certain legal proceedings in which the case notes and other records can be subpoenaed. 5.) Requests by insurance providers for case notes to assess the necessity for and benefits of services.

PRIVILEGED COMMUNICATION

Before discussing the exceptions to confidentiality, it will be helpful to introduce and explain the concept of privileged communications. Privilege is a legal term referring to the rights of individuals to withhold information requested by a court. Such privileges are established by law and pertain to professions and relationships such as the relationship between attorney and client, physician and patient, communications with members of the clergy, and, in most states, communications between clients and officially recognized mental health practitioners including psychologists, social workers, counselors, and others recognized by the states.

As Swenson (1993) explains the rationale for such protections, "These are relationships in which the legislatures consider the benefits of confidentiality more important than a court's need for evidence" (p. 135).

It is important to understand that the legal right of privilege resides with the client, also referred to as the "holder" of the privilege. This means that it is the client's prerogative, not the therapist's, to decide to waive privilege and allow information to be disclosed. Except in certain circumstances to be discussed in a moment, the therapist's obligation is to protect the client's privilege whenever it is applicable. Therapists must understand that if they refuse to release information, they are doing so on behalf of the client's privilege, not because the therapist holds the privilege. Similarly, therapists must realize that, apart from situations explicitly allowing or requiring confidentiality to be broken, the therapist cannot unilaterally waive a client's privilege for them. Unless the client has voluntarily waived privileges or the courts have specifically ordered otherwise, the therapist has a duty to assert the client's privilege and not release information.

Although the principle of privileged information protects client confidentiality in most cases, certain legal exceptions apply. Just as courts have ruled that clients have privilege to not disclose information shared with therapists, the courts have also determined that in certain circumstances therapists must release information, whether or not the client would concur. Swenson explains that under normal circumstances, "a therapist is not liable for violating a client's privacy rights if the therapist discloses information covered by an exception or because a law mandates disclosure" (p. 135). Examples of such conditions are described below.

As a preface to the discussion that follows, it should be emphasized again that this material is intended to help you understand the issues that you should consider in dealing with confidential material. Laws vary from state to state and change with time. Therefore, this should not be taken as legal advice. You are responsible to understand and abide by the laws of your state and the practices of your agency. If you have any questions or specific concerns arise, consult with your instructor, supervisor, state organization, professional insurance provider, or attorney.

ABUSE

In most states, specific laws require those in the helping and teaching professions to report instances of known or suspected abuse of children (Kalichman, 1993; Swenson, 1993). This principle, which primarily applies to instances of child abuse, but which may also apply to abuse of disabled or elderly adults, is designed to protect vulnerable individuals from harm. Under abuse reporting laws, if a child tells a therapist that he or she is being physically or sexually abused, or if the child has bruises or other injuries that suggest abuse, or if the therapist has other clear grounds to believe physical, sexual, or emotional abuse are occurring, the therapist is obligated to notify agencies that will intervene to investigate the matter and protect the child. These agencies are generally referred to as Child Protective Services, Children's Services Division, or, more commonly in practice, by acronyms such as CPS, CSD, etc.

In most states that require professionals to report abuse, the laws also protect those who report from civil liability, providing the reports are filed in good faith and without malice. Failure to report abuse may result in criminal penalties or in civil actions (Howing & Wodarski, 1992). A brief but informative and thought-provoking history and analysis of the effects of mandatory reporting laws is provided by Hutchinson (1993). For a discussion of some of the complications and ambiguities in legal protections that such reporting laws may entail see Alexander (1993).

Howing and Wodarski (1992) have provided an informative review of both the legal and clinical issues associated with child abuse and neglect. They note that, given the incidence of child abuse, it is highly likely that professionals will come in contact with cases of suspected abuse. They also emphasize, as does Swenson (1993), that laws vary among the states and there are many instances in which ambiguity in the law or uncertainty within a specific case make the task of knowing when to report complex.

Abuse situations are further complicated by concerns about how clients or families will react if a therapist files a report with a protective services agency. In this context, Howing and Wodarski reiterate the advice to inform clients in advance of limitations to confidentiality. They also suggest that treatment is not always harmed and can sometimes be enhanced if a therapist discusses such concerns and responsibilities with clients and incorporates the abuse reporting, investigation, and response into the overall context of treatment.

In your own work as an intern you should speak with your supervisor and instructor to be sure you are informed about the abuse reporting laws in your state. You should also know the procedures to follow if you have reason to believe a client is being abused or is abusing someone else. Such procedures must always include: notification of confidentiality limits at the outset of therapy, careful documentation of information, and consultation with supervisors and instructors. The charge of abuse is very serious and professionals must not be hasty in reporting cases. On the other hand, if there are sound reasons to believe that abuse is occurring, the professional or intern may be responsible to report the abuse and they must know what their legal responsibility is. In all such situations, interns must inform and consult with their placement supervisor and faculty instructor whenever such questions arise.

Dangerousness to Self

When clients are considered to be at risk of harming themselves therapists are obligated to take measures to prevent such harm. If clients recognize the danger and are willing to go along with protective measures for their own benefit, confidentiality is not usually a problem. The therapist simply has the client complete required release of information forms, then proceeds to take the necessary measures to ensure the client's well being. This may require voluntary hospitalization or other protective measures to care for the client.

Matters are more complicated when the therapist has reason to believe the client is at serious risk of self-harm but the client is not willing to comply with treatment recommendations. In these situations the therapist may have to take steps to seek involuntary commitment to a hospital unit or pursue some other treatment option to ensure the client's safety.

Procedures for obtaining involuntary treatment vary, but a common scenario is for the therapist to contact specifically designated mental health specialists who then evaluate the client and determine the need for commitment or other treatment. In general, as long as the therapist is acting in good faith and using sound professional judgment, pursuing such measures is protected by law, even though it means releasing information about the client to certain agencies or officials without the client's permission. Again, however, this is a general rule and one should check carefully about the procedures to be followed in each case and location. One should also be sure to carefully document the information on which decisions were made and the steps taken in response. Further guidelines for dealing with suicidal patients are offered by Jobes and Berman (1993) and Sommers-Flanagan and Sommers-Flanagan (1995).

Intent to Harm Others ("Tarasoff" Situations)

A second situation in which clinicians may be required to divulge information relating to dangerousness arises when a client makes explicit threats or statements of intent to harm another person. This situation is now commonly know in the professions as a Tarasoff case, based on an incident in which a client told a therapist he wanted to harm a specific individual. The therapist believed the client was serious and took steps to pursue involuntary commitment, but the therapist did not manage to directly warn the intended victim. Several months later, the client, who had since dropped out of therapy, killed the young woman he had earlier threatened to harm. The therapist was then sued for damages for not having warned the victim. Reviews of the Tarasoff case have been provided by Fulero (1988) and Slovenko (1988), both of whom discuss in detail the initial case and subsequent implications. Special Tarasoff-related considerations and implications for HIV patients are reviewed by Stanard and Hazler (1995).

The Tarasoff case, from which the principle known as "the duty to warn" evolved, has since gone through a series of appeals and the definition of the duty to warn has itself continued to evolve. More will be said about the problems of assessing dangerousness in a later chapter. The key point to be remembered here is that if you have good reason to believe someone seriously intends to harm another person, you may be required to take every reasonable step necessary to warn the intended victim and responsible authorities such as the police. This will sometimes mean that information is divulged about a client without the client's permission. That obligation places therapists in a difficult bind, particularly if, as Leong, Eth and Silva (1992) have reported, the records of therapists who warn of potentially dangerous clients may later be used in criminal prosecution of the client.

Strategies for dealing with potentially dangerous clients have been described by Monahan (1993). Critical steps recommended by Monahan include: training and knowledge of risk assessment, examination of the client's past and current clinical record, direct inquiries of the patient, and estimation of the risk and development of a responsible plan. It is beyond the scope of this chapter to go into more detail on this topic, but, again, if you encounter situations you are unsure of you should immediately seek assistance from supervisors and instructors, from your professional organization, and, if necessary, from legal counsel. Also, you should be careful to document fully the steps you take and the information on which you base your decisions. This will help ensure that you follow sound clinical practice. If something unfortunate happens in spite of your best efforts, accurate documentation and sound consultation can help reduce your personal risks of liability.

Legal Proceedings and Court Orders

A fourth situation in which you may be forced to reveal information about a client is if you are ordered to do so by the court. This may come about through a variety of processes but one of the more common reasons involves civil suits for damages (Schwartz, 1989). If, for example, a therapist is seeing a client who sues someone else claiming the other person's actions caused psychological harm to the client, the attorney for the defendant may have the right to subpoena the plaintiff's psychological and medical records. If, in cases such as these, your records are requested by someone other than the client, it is advisable to do everything you can to not release information unless you are granted a release of information from the client. Attorneys usually advise plaintiffs that their records may be requested in such proceedings and the possible review of clinical information will be taken into consideration in the decision to pursue a lawsuit. Nevertheless, there may be instances in which a client will not sign a release of information to share information with the opposition's attorney. In that event the treatment professional may be ordered to comply with court orders to release the information.

Whether or not the client has signed such a release, if a court order requires it, the records must be released. Be sure, however, that before you release any records without the client's permission, you have in fact been ordered to do so by a court. Merely receiving a letter from an attorney indicating that your records have been requested does not constitute a court order and you are not, therefore, required to comply. You should also know that a subpoena to appear before a court is not the same as a court order demanding records. If you receive a subpoena to appear without a specific order to produce your records, you should preserve the client's privilege and not release records unless specifically ordered to do so, in writing, by the court. It should also go without saying that in any of these situations you should consult with your attorney and, again, with your instructor and supervisor.

In light of the possibility for release of information through court order, three pieces of advice emerge. First, clients should be informed of this possibility at the start of therapy. This reduces the risk of later suit if the clinician made some inaccurate comment such as "there is no way anyone can have access to your records without your permission." Second, clinicians might want to be selective in what they put in their case notes. This matter is discussed in more detail in Chapter 8. Third, again, before releasing any information without a client's permission, consult with an attorney to be sure that the court order or other request has legal authority and cannot be refused.

INSURANCE COMPANY INQUIRIES

Unfortunately, as health care reform and other efforts to curtail costs have increased, there has been a corresponding increase in the intrusiveness of some insurers demanding to see copies of therapy case notes for patients they have insured. Technically speaking, requests by insurance companies for treatment information do not typically constitute exceptions to confidentiality because clients have often (but not always) consented, either in the process of registering for treatment or when signing up for an insurance policy, to have their medical records available to the insurer for review. Even though they have signed such agreements, many clients are not fully aware of the implications. When it comes to psychotherapy notes, clients are apt to be especially sensitive about releasing notes to third parties.

In response to the possibility that insurers will request records and case notes, practitioners can take several steps to help preserve the confidentiality of clients' personal information. First, as noted earlier, therapists should inform clients from the outset of any potential limitations to confidential-

ity. In relation to insurers, clients may choose to sign a release authorizing the therapist to send copies of case notes, or, clients may prefer to simply pay for the treatment entirely on their own in order to prevent the intrusion.

Regrettably, there have been increasing reports of clients who choose not to seek needed treatment because they so resent or are embarrassed by the intrusive questions of insurers. As insurers seek to "prescreen" clients before authorizing therapy, this may become an even more serious problem. For a suicidal patient, victim of sexual abuse, or anyone facing serious distress to have to discuss this with an anonymous insurance representative before meeting with a qualified therapist of their choosing is, in my judgment, extraordinarily countertherapeutic and potentially dangerous. Professional organizations are working to prevent or contain such intrusions and I encourage professionals and interns to support those efforts.

Along with advising clients of the prospect of case reviews, therapists can also screen what goes into notes and what kinds of notes they take. In place of "process" notes, which are used by therapists to record critical personal information and therapist's observations of the client's dynamics, many therapists who anticipate third-party record reviews are tending toward records that exclude much of the personal information and focus instead on identifying specific problem areas, treatment goals, and the interventions related directly to these (Kagle, 1993). Therapists are also reporting that they keep both process and problem-oriented types of notes, sharing the latter with insurers if requested and keeping the notes containing more personal information confidential.

Another approach used by many therapists is simply to limit what they put in their case notes. For example, if a client were to discuss marital infidelity, the therapist might record something like, "we spoke again today about relationship issues." This will help the therapist recall what was discussed but does not contain information specific enough to be embarrassing. As long as the therapist is able to recall what the abbreviated notes mean, this is not a problem. However, if the patient is not seen for several years in therapy the therapist may not recall the case and such notes would not offer very much help. Further, if the case is transferred to another therapist, or if someone turns to the notes while providing crisis coverage, the new therapist may not be aware of some of the most important underlying issues. In these cases, the practice of keeping two sets of notes might be preferable, providing that the therapists who might provide backup coverage are aware that second notes exist and how to obtain them.

Because I am personally opposed to sharing case notes with insurers, in my practice I prefer to avoid sending any type of case notes. Instead, with the client's permission, I send separate letters briefly summarizing the nature of our treatment, the number of sessions provided, the progress to date, and the prognosis. In most cases, insurers appreciate the need for confidentiality and this has proven sufficient. If the insurer requests additional information I then discuss this with the client to be sure he or she knows that the case notes may be shared. If the client expresses concern, I may write a second letter indicating that the client and I are concerned about sharing direct case notes because they contain sensitive material. I then offer still more detailed summaries of the major focus and methods of treatment. Finally, and only as a last resort, if the client has consented and it is absolutely necessary in order to receive reimbursement, I will reluctantly share copies of notes with the insurer. Again, however, this is something I oppose where possible and always consider as I think about the content of what goes into my notes. For an extended review of ethical and legal issues relating to managed care and insurance, see Appelbaum (1993).

CONFIDENTIALITY WITH MINORS

This discussion of confidentiality concludes with a topic that is frequently raised by interns but, unfortunately, has no simple answers. This question deals with confidentiality issues in the treatment of minors. In working with minors, the principle of confidentiality becomes more complicated because the client's right to confidentiality must be balanced with the rights and responsibilities of parents to be informed about their children's well-being and treatment. This problem can be particularly acute in school settings, where, in addition to balancing confidentiality of students and rights of parents, counselors must also work within legal guidelines and district or school policies (Huey, 1986).

Unfortunately, ethical guidelines of the different disciplines provide relatively little clear direction regarding confidentiality and work with minors. The lack of specificity in the ethical guidelines is understandable when one realizes that, as we have seen elsewhere in the area of professional ethics, laws and precedent vary across states and are continually evolving. For example, Swenson reports that the "age of majority," i.e., the age at which "a minor legally changes to the status of an adult" is 18 in some states, 19 in others, and 21 in others (Swenson, 1993). This diversity of state laws makes specific recommendations hazardous. Nevertheless, there is merit in considering several general guidelines to working with minors.

Gustafson and McNamara (1987) reviewed both legal and developmental considerations relating to confidentiality with minors. With regard to developmental factors, they note that in empirical studies (Belter & Grisso, 1984), 15-year-olds performed as well as 21-year-olds in assessment of their understanding of client's rights. Other studies (Kaser-Boyd, Adelman & Taylor, 1985) have shown that therapy risks and benefits can be identified by minors, including minors with learning and behavioral problems. In general, it appears that children after the age of about twelve years old have a better understanding of confidentiality and related issues than do younger children. This is consistent with the conclusions of the American Psychiatric Association's Task Force on Confidentiality of Children's and Adolescent's Clinical Records. That task force recommended that the age of consent to release confidential information be set at 12 years or over (American Psychiatric Association, 1979).

This recommendation is useful, but it must be applied with caution because some states have laws that grant parents or guardians access to medical and educational records until the child is 18 years old. Given the apparent contradiction between ethical principles and state laws, Gustafson and McNamara recommend that therapists working with minors or families should establish a written professional service agreement that explicitly states the conditions of confidentiality within which therapy will be provided. This should be reviewed with each person involved, then signed and made part of the client's permanent record. By reviewing conditions and signing an agreement beforehand, the possibility of later misunderstanding or conflict is reduced. This process also gives clients and therapists the right to decide if they will participate in therapy under the established conditions.

I concur with the recommendation of professional service contracts, but I would add that such contracts should be established for all clients, not just minors, and these contracts should reflect local laws. As noted at the outset of this discussion, all clients should be informed from the beginning of therapy what the extent and limitations of confidentiality will be. Further, it is emphasized again that interns must discuss confidentiality and other treatment issues carefully with their supervisors before initiating treatment with minors. I am familiar with instances in which trainees got themselves and their agencies into potentially serious trouble by treating minors and offering advice contrary to the wishes and legal rights of parents. The trainees were well intentioned but misguided and their efforts wound up creating more problems than they attempted to solve. By consulting carefully with supervisors those problems could have been avoided.

DUAL RELATIONSHIPS

The therapeutic relationship is unique. To protect the integrity of therapy, professional ethics prohibit the formation of "dual relationships." Dual relationships encompass a wide spectrum of interactions, but the underlying principle is that the therapist must avoid becoming involved in relationships or roles that could compromise the therapeutic process for the client (Kagle & Giebelhausen, 1994; Boryrs & Pope, 1989; Kitchener, 1988). Dual relationships can include such things as serving as a counselor for a student who lives in the same dormitory as you, agreeing to treat a coworker, or seeing your landlord's family member in exchange for rent reduction. In more malignant and destructive forms, dual relationships can take the form of romantic or sexual contacts between therapist and client.

The danger of dual relationships lies in the possibility that therapists will in some way, consciously or unconsciously, let one aspect of their non-professional relationship with clients interfere with their treatment relationship. Kagle and Giebelhausen (1994) explain that:

> Dual relationships involve boundary violations. They cross the line between the therapeutic relationship and a second relationship, undermining the distinctive nature of the therapeutic relationship, blurring the roles of practitioner and client, and permitting the abuse of power. (p. 217)

The concept and examples of boundary violations have also been addressed by Gutheil and Gabbard (1993), who delineate some of the most common areas in which boundaries may get crossed in therapy. These include issues relating to the roles of therapist and patients, the timing of therapy sessions, location of interactions, payment, attire, gifts, language, therapist self-disclosure, and physical contact.

In addition to considering the effects of boundary violations on the patient's treatment, Gutheil and Gabbard emphasize that what appear to be minor initial deviations from standard practice may lead to more consequential violations. They also point out that in relation to legal actions, particularly those concerning physical intimacy between clients and therapists, evidence of certain nonsexual boundary violations may be interpreted as evidence that sexual violations also took place. As they phrase the matter,

> To summarize the foregoing more concisely, albeit metaphorically, smoke usually leads to fire; one can, however, find smoke where there is no fire, and yet fact finders may assume that where there's smoke, there's fire. (p. 189)

It is important to understand that the interference generated by dual relationships can come from the client, the therapist, or both, but it is always the therapist's responsibility to deal responsibly and ethically with the situation. If, for example, a therapist were to accept a neighbor as a client, such small matters as the neighbor's anger about the therapist's barking dog could easily block the more important issues that should be addressed in therapy. Similarly, if interns are involved with an on-campus clinic as part of their training, they should probably not accept as clients other students with whom they are likely to share classes. The danger would be that things said in therapy could impact classroom interactions or that classroom discussions could influence therapy. The best way to avoid such conflicting roles is not to accept as clients persons with whom one already has another relationship.

Essential to the strictures against dual relationships is the realization that, as therapists and humans, we are not the best judges of when our own actions might be swayed by conflicting roles. This means the decision of whether or not to become involved in a dual relationship is not really left to the individual to decide. It is simply prohibited. Although this might on occasion be unnecessary and may even be counter to the perceived needs of certain clients, in the vast majority of cases, scrupulous avoidance of dual relationships will be in the best interests of therapist and client alike. Again, the safest route is always to avoid any form of dual relationship.

SEXUAL RELATIONSHIPS WITH CLIENTS

The most destructive and legally consequential forms of dual relationships are those involving romantic or sexual contacts with clients. As noted earlier, the prohibition against dual relationships is designed to take certain options away from therapists. In the case of sexual relationships, this is particularly important and valid. The ethical codes of every major professional organization in the helping professions specifically proscribe sexual relationships with clients (Kagle & Giebelhausen, 1994). Failure to heed this principle has lead many otherwise fine clinicians into deep trouble and caused lasting and serious harm to people they initially set out to help.

Lest any therapist believe that having sex with clients is somehow beneficial to the client, or that clients and therapists are just like any two other adults and can freely engage in whatever form of relationship that develops, the research and clinical evidence is clearly to the contrary. Although some (Williams, 1992) have raised questions about the difficulties of conducting empirical studies of this subject, those studies that have been done, e.g., Bouhoutsos et al. (1983) have concluded that among those sampled in their research, the vast majority of cases involving therapist-patient sex produced negative consequences for the patient. At the very least, when sexual contacts develop, the therapy process is almost certain to be diverted from its original and legitimate goal and becomes obscured or lost entirely in the sexual relationship.

Survey data are further supported by the clinical experience of therapists who have treated patients whose former therapists engaged in sexual overtures or contact. Many clients of therapist who have formed sexual relationships with them find it extremely difficult ever again to trust a supposed "helping" professional. Lasting feelings include mistrust, guilt, humiliation, and anger. Pope and Bouhoutsos (1986), whose book, *Sexual Intimacy between Therapists and Patients*, should be required reading for all human service professionals, describe clients as suffering from what they identify as the Therapist-Patient Sex Syndrome. Along with the feelings of mistrust and guilt, many of the symptoms of this syndrome are similar to those of Post-Traumatic Stress Disorder. Pope and Bouhoutsos also note that there is an increased risk of suicide among clients who have been sexually abused by their therapist. This means that therapists who engage in such relationships with their clients are putting the clients at risk not only of psychological damage, but also of death.

If the damage to clients is not sufficient to promote

responsible behavior on the part of clinicians, legal and professional sanctions provide added weight (Pope, 1993). It bears repeating that every professional organization explicitly forbids sexual contact with clients. Violation of this rule leads to almost certain sanction or dismissal from the professional organization. It can also lead to loss of license.

An additional and increasingly consequential result of sexual misconduct is that subsequent applications for malpractice insurance are likely to be denied. Further, because managed care companies and other health insurance companies are becoming increasingly selective about the providers whose services they endorse, professionals who have been sanctioned for sexual misconduct are unlikely to be approved for third-party reimbursement. Together, these consequences may effectively terminate one's professional career. For interns and students in the helping professions, sexual misconduct will almost surely lead to dismissal from training, thereby ending ones career before it has begun (Cobb, 1994).

In addition to ethical standards and sanctions by professional organizations, many states also have laws against such contact (Appelbaum, 1990; Strasburger, Jorgenson & Randles, 1991). This makes therapist-patient sex not only an ethical but also a criminal matter. The reason for such laws is that practitioners who are not members of professional organizations cannot be sanctioned by such organizations. Therefore, states have acted to make all practitioners responsible for ethical conduct, regardless of their membership status. Appelbaum (1990) reviewed existing laws and concluded that, "In almost all circumstances, the crime is considered a felony, and both prison sentences and fines may be imposed."

Along with criminal laws, in all states the possibility of civil suits for damages exists (Jorgenson, Randles & Strasburger, 1991) and the protection against such suits is often very limited. An added effect of therapist-patient sexual contact can be found in the fact that professional liability insurance premiums for therapists and counselors have increased markedly, largely due to claims against professionals for sexual contact. To contain these costs, insurers are beginning to limit the amount of damages the insurance company will pay for such claims. In many policies, the liability insurance company agrees to defend such cases but will not pay for any damages. Thus, the costs of any damages would come directly from the therapist's financial or material assets. This policy is designed to place more of the burden on the clinician who violated the ethics to begin with. Some have argued, however, that this may instead be limiting the damages victims can collect (Pope, 1990).

The final point to be made here has to do with the statute of limitations for sexual misconduct by therapists. Unlike crimes such as theft or burglary, for which one cannot be prosecuted beyond a fixed period of time, in the case of sexual abuse some states do not "start the clock" on the statute of limitations until the victim becomes aware of the damage.

This might be several years or longer after the actual events took place. It is also worth mentioning that, in regard to disciplinary actions by licensing boards and professional organizations, there may be no statute of limitations. There have been cases in which clients filed complaints with review boards for actions alleged to have occurred more than a decade earlier (E. Harris, Feb. 3, 1995, personal communication).

The situation as it is described above and as it exists in law and professional standards must be clearly understood: helping professionals who have sexual relationships with clients are likely to be expelled from the profession, lose their license, be excluded from further practice, stand to lose large sums of money, may face the possibility of a prison sentence, and could be the target of complaints for an indefinite time after the misconduct occurs.

Maintaining Professional Boundaries and Dealing with Feelings of Attraction

It should be clear from the discussion thus far that therapist-client sex is almost certain to have lasting and severe negative effects on the client and the therapist. The consequences may also be devastating to others in the therapist's life, including family, friends, and professional colleagues, not to mention to the profession itself.

These facts highlight the strictures against and consequences of therapist-patient sex, but there is also a need to consider how sexual contact between therapist and patients can be prevented and how interns can be trained to deal with sexual issues in therapy more effectively.

In an effort to educate patients about this subject, the American Psychological Association's Committee on Women in Psychology (1989) published a brochure to inform patients about the ethical and clinical implications of therapist-patient sex. This brochure identifies the kinds of behaviors that would be considered unethical in a therapy relationship. It then proceeds to inform clients of their options for dealing with the therapist in question and for filing formal complaints and legal actions. The brochure emphasizes that most therapists are responsible individuals who adhere to ethical standards, but for the well-being of clients and the profession it is important for clients to know what constitutes unethical behavior and how to deal with it.

Thorn, Shealy, and Briggs (1993) have demonstrated that brochures of this type are received favorably by clients and therapists and that the brochures enhance client awareness of the issues and ethical standards. Although prepared by psychologists under the auspices of the American Psychological Association, the principles outlined in the brochure apply to all of the helping professions and would usefully be shared with clients regardless of the discipline or training of the therapist. Other approaches to educating clients about ethics and their rights, and the availability of victim advocacy and self-help groups have been described by Hotelling (1988).

Along with efforts to increase awareness among clients, in recent years increasing attention has been given to addressing the issue as part of academic and internship training (Rodolfa et al., 1990; Vasquez, 1988). Rodolfa et al. (1994) found that of 389 survey respondents identified as working in university counseling centers, only 12 percent stated that they had never been attracted to any client. Pope, Keith-Spiegel, and Tabachnick (1986) have reported survey results indicating that 95 percent of male and 76 percent of female therapists surveyed reported having been sexually attracted to clients at least on occasion. Sixty-three percent expressed feeling guilty, anxious, or confused by their attraction.

In spite of the frequency of therapist attraction and the feelings that are evoked as a consequence, a later survey by Pope and Tabachnick (1993), which also addressed feelings of fear and anger toward clients, revealed that half of those surveyed said they had received either poor or no training in how to deal with the issue of sexual attraction. On more positive notes, the same survey indicated that 25 percent of the sample considered their training to have been good to excellent. Another encouraging finding comes from Pope et al.'s 1986 results, which indicated that 57 percent of the psychologists sought supervision or consultation when they were attracted to clients.

Pope et al. (1986) emphasize several points that are particularly relevant to interns. Because it is evidently common for therapists to experience attraction to clients, it is essential that this matter be addressed openly in training programs. In this process, there is a need to recognize the fundamental distinction between experiencing feelings of attraction and acting on those feelings. Students need to feel that it is safe to discuss feelings of attraction without fear that their instructors or supervisors will condemn, ridicule, or intrusively question them. In helping students understand and explore issues of attraction, instructors and supervisors must model the kind of professionalism that they expect students to develop and exhibit as therapists.

When dealing with feelings of attraction in therapy it can be particularly useful to watch for subtle signs that therapeutic boundaries are being crossed. In the discussion of boundary violations alluded to earlier in this chapter, Gutheil and Gabbard (1993) note that role boundaries are fundamental to issues relating to boundary violations. They propose a key question to help therapists understand and evaluate this issue. In evaluating their behavior in relation to boundaries, therapists should ask themselves "Is this what a therapist does?" (p. 190)

Gutheil and Gabbard (1993), along with Simon (1989) and Gabbard (1989), point out that in most instances a common sequence of events leads to physical intimacy with patients. This sequence typically begins with apparently innocuous actions, then progresses to problematic levels. Referring to what they call the "slippery slope" scenario, Gutheil and Gabbard describe a:

> . . . transition from a last-name to first-name basis; then personal conversation intruding on the clinical work; then some body contact (e.g., pats on the shoulder, massages, progressing to hugs); then trips outside the office; then sessions during lunch, sometimes with alcoholic beverages; then dinner; then movies or other social events; and finally sexual intercourse. (p. 188)

Recognizing this sequence can provide an early warning system to interns and therapists. If you find yourself dressing differently because a certain client will be seen that day; scheduling appointments later, or allowing sessions to run longer for some clients; if you are revealing more about your personal life than is typical; if you think about a client more than is normal for you when you are away from your office, if you are suggesting or accepting opportunities to meet outside of therapy; or if other behaviors are beyond your usual conduct, you should recognize that something unusual is happening and it should be explored in supervision.

This issue is so important to the well-being of clients, therapists, and the integrity of our professions, that it is incumbent on interns and professionals to deal with it responsibly and ethically. If during your internship, or at any time in your career, you find yourself crossing therapeutic boundaries, feeling sexually attracted to a client, or if a client is attracted to you, seek supervision. You will not be the first or the last person to find yourself in this situation, but it is essential that you deal with it professionally. An excellent additional resource on this subject is Pope, Sonne, and Holroyd's *Sexual Feelings in Psychotherapy* (1993).

NONSEXUAL DUAL RELATIONSHIPS

Because sexual relationships between therapists and clients can be so damaging, they have received the bulk of attention in discussions about the ethics of dual relationships. Less destructive, but still problematic, are dual relationships that do not involve sexual or romantic contact. Examples of such relationships were alluded to earlier, as in the case of accepting as clients neighbors, fellow students, or coworkers.

In most instances these situations can be dealt with by simply referring the individuals to other professionals. There are, however, conditions under which referral may not be practical. Barnett and Yutrzenka (1994), Sobel (1992), and Hargrove (1986) have all pointed out that in certain rural settings there may be limited numbers of practitioners available. In these circumstances, it is very likely that practitioners will sooner or later be asked to treat clients with whom they have some relationship apart from therapy. In rural settings it is also likely that practitioners who may not have known a client prior to beginning treatment will later encounter that client in some other role after treatment has begun. For example, a therapist might discover that a former or present client is a member of a service or social organization or is the coach of the opposing little league or youth soccer team.

In a survey of ethical dilemmas encountered by psychologists, Pope and Vetter (1992) found that circumstances such as those just described are by no means infrequent in rural settings. Based on their findings, Pope and Vetter recommended that future ethical codes take geographical concerns into account and should more clearly distinguish between situations in which dual relationships may or may not be therapeutically acceptable.

The most important issue for practitioners is keeping the well-being and best interests of the client foremost. The difficult challenge is to know when and how different roles or relationships might conflict with the treatment process. No ethical code can successfully identify every possible contingency or specify exactly what professionals must do in all circumstances. Therefore, in ambiguous conditions the professional must use discretion and judgment. However, as noted earlier, our own judgment can sometimes betray us.

To guard against this, Barnett and Yutrzenka (1994) offer useful advice to professionals who, for reasons of geography or other factors, may treat persons with whom they have other relationships. Among other things, Barnett and Yutrzenka recommend that professionals directly acknowledge the fact of their different relationships and seek to "compartmentalize roles, not relationships." In other words, professionals in rural communities must have their own identity and relate amicably to other community members, clients and nonclients alike. Compartmentalizing roles means that therapy issues should not be raised with clients outside the context of the therapy interaction, but issues that happen outside therapy which might impact the treatment process may need to be dealt with directly in therapy. This possibility should be addressed with clients at the beginning of treatment.

Being extremely cognizant of confidentiality is also particularly important in small communities, as is scrupulous documentation of your actions and the rationale behind them. Other precautions recommended by Barnett and Yutrzenka include trying to know yourself as well as you can but also consulting with other professionals who can help recognize any signs that you might deny or minimize potentially problematic issues. If no other professionals are available in your local community, you may want to establish regular phone contact or consultation with other professionals in your region who are sensitive to these issues and would be honest and supportive with you. Finally, even though local referral options may be limited in some settings, Barnett and Yutrzenka advise that professionals should make contact with any other possible resources in the community or area and should be willing to refer whenever a dual relationship conflict does or might occur.

RELATIONSHIPS BETWEEN EDUCATORS, SUPERVISORS, AND TRAINEES

As a final point in the discussion of dual relationships, it should be noted that the ethical guidelines identified in this section also apply to relationships between supervisors, instructors, and students (Miller & Larrabee, 1995; Bowman, Hatley & Bowman, 1995; Larrabee & Miller, 1993; Harrar, VandeCreek & Knapp, 1990). Much as sexual contact between therapists and clients breaks down the therapy process, sexual relationships between supervisors and interns are likely to interfere with the supervision process (Jacobs, 1991). Recognizing this fact, the APA formally stated in the 1992 code of ethics that:

> 1.19 (b) Psychologists do not engage in sexual relationships with students or supervisees in training over whom the psychologist has evaluative or direct authority, because such relationships are so likely to impair judgment or be exploitative. (APA, 1992)

In addition to impairing the direct supervisory relationship, the potential for sexual relationships between supervisor and trainee can also make open discussion about therapist-client attraction particularly difficult. At the conclusion of their 1986 article, Pope et al. stressed that in discussing issues of attraction, students must be safe from educators who might use such issues as openings to establish intimate relationships with the students themselves.

It is regrettable that this matter must be addressed, but the data suggest that sexual contacts between therapists and clients and between instructors and students is not uncommon. Pope, Levenson, and Schover (1979) reported that 16.5 percent of women respondents and 3 percent of male respondents reported that during their graduate training they had sexual contact with psychology educators. Among educators, 8 percent of women and 19 percent of men reported having engaged in sexual relations with their supervisees. This survey also suggested that those who are involved in such interactions as students may be more likely to violate the comparable ethical standard as professionals. Comparable, though slightly lower, percentages have been reported by Thoreson et al. (1993) and by Miller and Larrabee (1995).

Results similar to those of Pope et al. were found by Robinson and Reid (1985) who found that 13 percent of women respondents indicated that they had experienced sexual contact with their educators during their graduate education. This research also indicated that 48 percent of the respondents had experienced some form of sexual harassment as graduate students. Consistent with studies suggesting that therapist-patient sex is harmful to clients, 95 percent of those who had experienced sexual contact or harassment felt it was detrimental. In reviewing these and other studies of sexual contact or harassment, Bartell and Rubin (1990) noted that many respondents did not feel sexual contact with instructors was coercive at the time it occurred. In retrospect, however, the majority see some degree of coercion and consider it to be an ethical problem (Glaser & Thorpe, 1986). A similar change in attitude over time was reported by Miller and Larrabee's respondents (1995).

With regard to the issue of sexual harassment, the APA Ethical Code contains language defining and proscribing sexual harassment. Principle 1.11 states:

> (a) Psychologists do not engage in sexual harassment. Sexual harassment is sexual solicitation, physical advances, or verbal or nonverbal conduct that is sexual in nature, that occurs in connection with the psychologist's activities or roles as a psychologist, and that either: (1) is unwelcome, is offensive, or creates a hostile workplace environment, and the psychologist knows or is told this; or (2) is sufficiently severe or intense to be abusive to a reasonable person in the context. Sexual harassment can consist of a single intense or severe act or multiple persistent or pervasive acts. (APA, 1992)

Proscriptions against multiple relationships and harassment are also contained in the AACD Ethical Standards, (Sections A. 9 and B.14 respectively) (AACD, 1988) and in the Code of Ethics of the NASW.

It is evident that the problems of educator-student sexual contact and harassment are real and ongoing. It is also evident that such harassment is contrary to the ethical standards of the professions. If you are placed in an uncomfortable position due to the unwanted comments or actions of an instructor, supervisor, coworker, or peer, you should know that you have the right to file a grievance and demand that the behavior be stopped. I suggest that students who are harassed file formal complaints both with their academic institution and with any professional organizations or licensing bodies with which the harasser might be affiliated. For harassment to stop, everyone in the helping professions must understand the problem, adhere to the principles themselves, seek supervision when necessary, and report violations whenever they occur. Then, the consequences of violations must be certain, meaningful, and effective.

LIABILITY AND INSURANCE

The final topics to be addressed in this chapter are professional liability and liability insurance. Although interns are less likely than practicing professionals to be the target of malpractice lawsuits, interns are by no means immune from such suits. For this reason, Pitts (1992) has urged counseling programs to require liability insurance for all practicum and internship students. In addition to providing financial protection, Pitts points out that obtaining such insurance acquaints students with "this reality of professional life." (p. 207)

Because many students will not be familiar with the nature of liability claims and the purpose of liability insurance, a brief review may be helpful. For more extensive dis-

cussion, see an article by Conte and Karasu (1990) or books by Bennett et al. (1990) and Swenson (1993).

ELEMENTS OF MALPRACTICE

Bennett et al. (1990) introduce their discussion of malpractice by explaining that:

> When a practitioner undertakes to treat, diagnose, assess, or in any way advise or provide psychological services to a client, that practitioner is obliged to exercise a certain standard of care and service delivery. For the practitioner to be found negligent, it must be shown that he or she did not exercise the standard and, by failing to do so, injured the client (the plaintiff in the suit). (p. 34)

Malpractice suits are special cases within the broader category of "negligence." By virtue of their professional status and their relationship with clients, those in the helping professions have a responsibility to provide care that meets the standards of their profession. If a professional is sued for malpractice, plaintiffs must successfully prove each of four "critical elements." These are: 1.) The existence of a professional relationship between therapist and client. 2.) The existence of a standard of care and the failure of the practitioner to meet that standard in the care of the client. 3.) That the client suffered some form of harm or injury. 4.) That the client's harm or injury was caused by the practitioner's failure to meet the standard of care. (Conte & Karasu, 1990; Bennett et al., 1990)

The best way to deal with lawsuits is to prevent them from happening by practicing within the standards of care of one's profession. Bennett et al. (1990) have provided useful "Focus Lists" to help practitioners review their procedures and ensure they are up to standards. The length of such lists prohibits their inclusion here, but I encourage interns and supervisors to consult the original source, review the lists, and refer back to them periodically to ensure that standards are being maintained.

With regard to specific issues that are often associated with liability claims, the ethical and legal proscriptions against dual relationships and sexual conduct have already been discussed. The importance of informed consent and confidentiality have also been addressed. If clinicians follow these guidelines they will reduce the potential basis for the most common successful suits. Two other areas that are often of concern over liability are suicidal patients and Tarasoff-type situations. Extended review of these issues is beyond the present scope of this chapter. For useful suggestions regarding the clinical treatment of suicidal patients and ways of reducing associated liability, see Sommers-Flanagan and Sommers-Flanagan (1995) and Jobes and Berman (1993). For principles to follow in regard to Tarasoff-type situations, see Monahan (1993). In cases involving patients with HIV, see Stanard and Hazlen (1995).

LIABILITY INSURANCE

Conte and Karasu (1990) point out that lawsuits against psychotherapists are relatively rare and that proving all four elements of malpractice suits is not easy. As a result, only about 20 percent of cases result in judgments against the psychotherapist and the "average cost of claims is under $22,000" (Bennett et al., 1990, p. 31).

These figures notwithstanding, Bennett et al. emphasize that practitioners should have insurance for several reasons. Even if one's practice is perfectly within standards, there is no guarantee that a lawsuit will not be filed or that one would emerge unscathed from such a suit. A practitioner who is successfully sued could be required to pay damages as high or higher than hundreds of thousands of dollars. Furthermore, regardless of the outcome of a lawsuit, the process of defending against the suit can be financially and emotionally expensive. An added benefit of such insurance is that some providers, such as the American Psychological Association's Insurance Trust, have begun to provide toll-free legal consultation with psychologist/attorneys. The goal of this service is to prevent problems from developing or to catch them as early as possible.

The costs of liability insurance for psychologists, counselors, social workers, and others remains low relative to certain medical professions. Nevertheless, the frequency and size of claims has increased (Conte & Karasu, 1990) as has the cost of insurance. Fortunately, liability insurance is available to interns for much lower rates than for fully licensed professionals. Interns can obtain more information about such insurance by contacting their national organizations or by contacting the insurance providers themselves.

When you look into liability insurance, you will discover that two types of policies are offered. These are called "claims-based" and "occurrence-based." (For more detailed information consult Bennett et al. (1990) or your professional organization's insurance provider.) Understanding the differences in policies is important because the type of policy you choose will influence how much you pay and how you are covered.

Briefly, claims-based insurance provides coverage for acts that occur during the time you are insured as long as you hold the policy, but the coverage stops when you no longer carry the policy. This means that if you let a policy expire or choose to retire and no longer carry the policy, your insurer would no longer provide coverage even if you are sued for something that occurred when you did practice and did have the policy. In other words, when you discontinue the policy, your protection is also discontinued, regardless of when the event for which you are being sued occurred. On the other hand, as long as you hold a claims-based policy, you will be covered for any events that happened while you were insured under that policy, providing that you are still insured under the policy.

The advantage of claims-based policies is that they are usually less expensive than occurrence based policies during the first years they are held. The cost increases with each subsequent year because the insurer is then providing protection for the year in which the policy is now held, as well as for events that may have occurred in previous years. If you wish to discontinue a claims-based policy, you must realize that doing so discontinues your protection against suits even if the suit concerns something that happened when you were insured. You can, however, purchase special coverage called a "tail" or "rider," which will insure you for a period of time following termination of your regular policy. Some policies also carry a clause that if one has held claims-based insurance for a number of years and then retires from practice, the "tail" coverage is applied free of charge.

The other type of policy, "occurrence-based," provides protection for events that occurred during the time you held the policy, regardless of whether or not you are still carrying the insurance at the time you are sued. This type of policy is typically more expensive to begin with, but once you purchase an occurrence policy you are covered essentially forever for the period in which you held the insurance. If someone sues you for an event that happened five years earlier, as long as you held an occurrence-based policy at that time, you will be covered, even though you may not hold the policy at the time you are actually sued.

As you evaluate different types of liability insurance policies, be sure to examine matters other than simply price and the surface differences between claims- or occurrence-based policies. Among the other factors that should be considered are: What types of activities, situations, or expenses are not covered under the policy? Does the coverage include defense costs along with damages in the payment limits or are these figured separately? What is the financial security and history of the company providing the insurance (if your insurance provider goes bankrupt you effectively become uninsured)?

This discussion has been intended to provide an introductory overview and should not be taken as constituting legal or financial advice. As with all insurance, it is essential to read the conditions of the terms carefully and to compare policies offered by different providers. This is particularly important in the case of malpractice insurance for interns. Such coverage may not apply to all internship placements or all activities of interns. You may also find that your internship site carries its own insurance for interns and it may not be necessary for you to purchase your own. However, before deciding that you do not need coverage of your own, it is advisable to have written assurance that you are covered under the agency policy and that such coverage includes both defense and damage costs. Be sure that you understand the nature and limitations of any coverage your internship provides or you purchase for yourself, and consider these factors carefully in light of your own activities as a student, intern, or as an employee.

SUMMARY

Ethical guidelines exist to protect the well-being of clients, practitioners, and the profession. As a trainee, it is incumbent upon you to be well versed in the principles established by your profession and within your work settings. This chapter has reviewed key ethical issues that are most relevant to interns, but as has been repeated throughout the chapter, you are strongly advised to review the ethical standards of your profession and to discuss these with your peers, instructors, and supervisors. Finally, as noted throughout this chapter, ethical and legal standards evolve and change over time. Therefore, the review offered here is part of a process that you should continue throughout your training.

REFERENCES

Alexander, R., Jr. (1993). The legal liability of social workers after DeShaney. *Social Work*, *38*, 64–68.

Allen, V. B., Sampson, J. P., Jr., & Herlihy, B. (1988). Details of the 1988 AACD Ethical Standards. *Journal of Counseling and Development*, *67*, 157–158.

American Association for Counseling and Development (1988). "Ethical Standards of the American Association for Counseling and Development (3rd Revision), AACD Governing Council, March 1988." *Journal of Counseling and Development*, *67*, 4–8.

American Association for Counseling and Development Ethics Committee (1991). Report of the AACD Ethics Committee: 1989–1991. *Journal of Counseling and Development*, *70*, 278–280.

American Association for Marriage and Family Therapy (1990). *Code of ethical principles for marriage and family therapists.* Washington, DC: Author.

American Counseling Association (1995). American Counseling Association Code of Ethics and Standards of Practice. Alexandria, VA: Author.

American Psychiatric Association, (1979). Task force on confidentiality in children's and adolescent's records. *American Journal of Psychiatry*, *136*, 138–144.

American Psychological Association (1992). Ethical principles of psychologists and code of conduct. *American Psychologist*, *46*, 1597–1611.

———. (1990). Ethical principles of psychologists. *American Psychologist*, *45*, 390–395

American Psychological Association, Board of Professional Affairs (1987). General guidelines for providers of psychological services. *American Psychologist*, *42*, 712–723.

American Psychological Association Office of Ethnic Minority Affairs (1993). Guidelines for providers of psychological services to ethnic, linguistic and culturally diverse populations. *American Psychologist*, *48*, 45–48.

Appelbaum, P. S. (1993). Legal liability and managed care. *American Psychologist*, *48*, 251–257.

Appelbaum, P. S. (1990). Statutes regulating patient-therapist sex. *Hospital and Community Psychiatry*, *41*, 15–16.

Association for Specialists in Group Work (1990). Ethical guidelines for group counselors: ASGW 1989 Revision. *The Journal for Specialists in Group Work*, *15*, 119–126.

Barnett, J. E., & Yutrzenka, B. A. (1994). Nonsexual dual relationships in professional practice, with special applications to rural and military communities. *The Independent Practitioner: Bulletin of the Division of Independent Practice, American Psychological Association*, *14* (5), 243–248.

Bartell, P. A., & Rubin, L. J. (1990). Dangerous liaisons: Sexual intimacies in supervision. *Professional Psychology: Research and Practice*, *21*, 442–450.

Belter, R. W., & Grisso, T. (1984). Children's recognition of rights violations in counseling. *Professional Psychology: Research and Practice*, *15*, 899–910.

Bennett, B. E., Bryant, B. K., VandenBos, G. R., & Greenwood, A. (1990). *Professional Liability and Risk Management.* Washington DC: American Psychological Association.

Boryrs, D. S., & Pope, K. S. (1989). Dual relationships between therapist and client: A national study of psychologists, psychiatrists and social workers. *Professional Psychology: Research and Practice*, *20*, 283–293.

Bouhoutsos, J., Holroyd, J., Lerman, H., Forer, B. R., & Greenberg, M. (1983). Sexual intimacy between psychotherapists and patients. *Professional Psychology*, *14*, 185–196.

Bowman, V. E., Hatley, L. D., & Bowman, R. L. (1995). Faculty-student relationships: The dual role controversy. *Counselor Education and Supervision*, *34*, 232–242.

Claiborn, C. D., Berberoglu, L. S., Nerison, R. M., & Somberg, D. R. (1994). The client's perspective: Ethical judgments and perceptions of therapist practices. *Professional Psychology: Research and Practice*, *25*, 268–274.

Cobb, N. H. (1994). Court-recommended guidelines for managing unethical students and working with university lawyers. *Journal of Social Work Education*, *30*, 18–31.

Committee on Women in Psychology—American Psychological Association (1989). If sex enters into the psychotherapy relationship. *Professional Psychology: Research and Practice*, *20*, 112–115.

Conte, H. R., & Karasu, T. B. (1990). Malpractice in psychotherapy: An overview. *American Journal of Psychotherapy*, *44*, 232–246.

Crowe, M., Grogan, J., Jacobs, R., Lindsey, C., & Mark, M. (1985). Delineation of the roles of clinical psychology. *Professional Psychology: Research and Practice*, *16*, 124–137.

DePauw, M. E. (1986). Avoiding ethical violations: A timeline perspective for individual counseling. *Journal of Counseling and Development*, *64*, 303–305.

Ethics Committee of the American Psychological Association (1992). Rules and procedures: October 1, 1992. *American Psychologist*, *47*, 1612–1628.

Ethics Update (1988, December). *APA Monitor*, *19*, 36.

Fulero, S. M. (1988). Tarasoff: 10 years later. *Professional Psychology, Research and Practice*, *19*, 184–190.

Gabbard, G. O. (Ed.) (1989). *Sexual exploitation in professional relationships.* Washington, DC: American Psychiatric Press.

Glaser, R. D., & Thorpe, J. S. (1986). Unethical intimacy: A survey of sexual contact and advances between psychology educators and female graduate students. *American Psychologist, 41*, 43–51.

Gustafson, K. E., & McNamara, J. R. (1987). Confidentiality with minor clients: Issues and guidelines for therapists. *Professional Psychology: Research and Practice, 18*, 503–508.

Gutheil, T. G., & Gabbard, G. O. (1993). The concept of boundaries in clinical practice: Theoretical and risk management dimensions. *American Journal of Psychiatry, 150*, 188–196.

Hargrove, D. S. (1986). Ethical issues in rural mental health practice. *Professional Psychology: Research and Practice, 17*, 20–23.

Harrar, W. R., VandeCreek, L., & Knapp, S. (1990). Ethical and legal aspects of clinical supervision. *Professional Psychology: Research and Practice, 21*, 37–41.

Harris, E. A. (1995). The importance of risk management in a managed care environment. In M. B. Sussman (Ed.) *A perilous calling: The hazards of psychotherapy practice.* (pp. 247–258). New York: John Wiley and Sons.

Hayman, P. M., & Covert, J. A. (1986). Ethical dilemmas in college counseling centers. Special Issue: Professional Ethics. *Journal of Counseling and Development, 64*, 318–321.

Hotelling, K. (1988). Ethical, legal, and administrative options to address sexual relationships between counselor and client. *Journal of Counseling and Development, 67*, 233–237.

Howing, P. T., & Wodarski, J. S. (1992). Legal requisites for social workers in child abuse and neglect situations. *Social Work, 37*, 330–335.

Huey, W. C. (1986). Ethical concerns in school counseling. *Journal of Counseling and Development, 64*, 321–322.

Hutchinson, E. D. (1993) Mandatory reporting laws: Child protective case finding gone awry. *Social Work, 38*, 56–63.

Ibrahim, F. A., & Arredondo, P. M. (1986) Ethical standards for cross-cultural counseling: Counselor preparation, practice, assessment, and research. *Journal of Counseling and Development, 64*, 349–352.

Jacobs., C. (1991). Violations of the supervisory relationship: An ethical and educational blind spot. *Social Work, 36*, 130–135.

Jobes, D. A., & Berman, A. L. (1993). Suicide and malpractice liability: Assessing and revising policies, procedures, and practice in outpatient settings. *Professional Psychology: Research and Practice, 24*, 91–99.

Jorgenson, L., Randles, R., & Strasburger, L. (1991). The furor over psychotherapist-patient sexual contact: New solutions to an old problem. *William and Mary Law Review, 32*, 643–729.

Kagle, J. D. (1993). Record keeping: Directions for the 1990s. *Social Work, 38*, 190–196.

Kagle, J. D., & Giebelhausen, P. N. (1994). Dual relationships and professional boundaries. *Social Work, 39*, 213–220.

Kalichman, S. C. (1993). *Mandated reporting of suspected child abuse: Ethics, law, and policy.* Washington DC: American Psychological Association.

Kaser-Boyd, N., Adelman, H., & Taylor, L., (1985). Minors' ability to identify risks and benefits of therapy. *Professional Psychology: Research and Practice, 16*, 411–417.

Keith-Spiegel, P. (1994). The 1992 Ethics Code: Boon or bane. *Professional Psychology: Research and Practice, 25*, 315–317.

Kitchener, K. S. (1984). Intuition, critical evaluation and ethical principles: The foundation for ethical decisions in counseling psychology. *The Counseling Psychologist, 12*,(3), 43–56.

Kitchener, K. S. (1988). Dual relationships: What makes them so problematic? *Journal of Counseling and Development, 67*, 217–221.

Larrabee, M. J., & Miller, G. M. (1993). An examination of sexual intimacy in supervision. *The Clinical Supervisor, 11*, 103–126.

Leong, G. B., Eth, S., & Silva, J. A. (1992) The psychotherapist as witness for the prosecution: The criminalization of Tarasoff. *American Journal of Psychiatry, 149*, 1011–1015.

Miller, D. J., & Thelen, M. H. (1986). Knowledge and beliefs about confidentiality in psychotherapy. *Professional Psychology: Research and Practice, 17*, 15–19.

Miller, G. M., & Larrabee, M. J. (1995). Sexual intimacy in counselor education and supervision: A national survey. *Counselor Education and Supervision, 34*, 332–343.

Monahan. J. (1993). Limiting therapist exposure to Tarasoff liability: Guidelines for risk containment. *American Psychologist, 48*, 242–250.

National Association of Social Workers (1990). *Code of ethics.* Silver Spring, MD: Author.

Nicolai, K. M., & Scott, N. A. (1994). Provision of confidentiality information and its relation to child abuse reporting. *Professional Psychology: Research and Practice, 25*, 154–160.

Nowell, D., & Spruill, J. (1993). If it's not absolutely confidential, will information be disclosed? *Professional Psychology: Research and Practice, 24*, 367–369.

Paradise, L. V., & Kirby, P. C. (1990). Some perspectives on the legal liability of group counseling in private practice. *The Journal for Specialists in Group Work, 2*, 114–118.

Pitts, J. H. (1992). Organizing a practicum and internship program in counselor education. *Counselor Education and Supervision, 31*, 196–207.

Pope, K. S. (1990) Therapist-patient sex as sex abuse: Six scientific, professional and practical dilemmas in addressing victimization and rehabilitation. *Professional Psychology: Research and Practice, 21*, 227–239.

———. (1993). Licensing disciplinary actions for psychologists who have been sexually involved with a client: Some information about offenders. *Professional Psychology: Research and Practice, 24*, 374–377.

Pope, K. S., & Bouhoutsos, J. C. (1986). *Sexual intimacy between therapists and patients.* New York: Praeger.

Pope, K. S., Keith-Spiegel, P., & Tabachnic, B. G. (1986). Sexual attraction to clients: The human therapist and the (sometimes) inhuman training system. *American Psychologist, 41*, 147–158.

Pope, K. S., Levenson, H., and Schover, L. (1979). Sexual intimacy in psychology training: Results and implications of a national survey. *American Psychologist, 34*, 682–689.

Pope, K. S., Sonne, J. L., & Holroyd, J. (1993). *Sexual feelings in psychotherapy.* Washington, DC: American Psychological Association.

Pope, K. S., & Tabachnick, B. G. (1993). Therapists' anger, hate, fear, and sexual feelings: National survey of therapist responses, client characteristics, critical events, formal complaints, and training. *Professional Psychology: Research and Practice, 24,* 142–152.

Pope, K. S., & Vetter, V. V. (1992). Ethical dilemmas encountered by members of the American Psychological Association: A national survey. *American Psychologist, 47,* 397–411.

Robinson, W. L., & Reid, P. T. (1985). Sexual intimacies in psychology revisited. *Professional Psychology: Research and Practice, 16,* 512–520.

Rodolfa, E., Hall, T., Holms, V., Davena, A., Komatz, D., Antunez, M., & Hall, A. (1994). The management of sexual feelings in therapy. *Professional Psychology: Research and Practice, 25,* 168–172.

Rodolfa, E. R., Kitzrow, M., Vohra, S., & Wilson, B. (1990). Training interns to respond to sexual dilemmas. *Professional Psychology: Research and Practice, 21,* 313–315.

Rubanowitz, D. E. (1987). Public attitudes toward psychotherapist-client confidentiality. *Professional Psychology: Research and Practice, 18,* 613–618.

Schwartz, G. (1989). Confidentiality revisited. *Social Work, 34,* 223–226.

Simon, R. I. (1989). Sexual exploitation of patients: How it begins before it happens. *Psychiatry Annals, 19,* 104–122.

Slovenko, R. (1988). The therapist's duty to warn or protect third persons. *The Journal of Psychiatry and Law, Spring,* 139–192.

Sobel, S. B. (1992). Small town practice of psychotherapy: Ethical and personal dilemmas. *Psychotherapy and Private Practice, 10,* 61–69.

Sommers-Flanagan, J., & Sommers-Flanagan, R. (1995). Intake interviewing with suicidal patients: A systematic approach. *Professional Psychology: Research and Practice, 26,* 41–47.

Stadler, H., & Paul R. D. (1986). Counselor educators' preparation in ethics. *Journal of Counseling and Development, 64,* 328–330.

Stanard, R., & Hazler, R. (1995). Legal and ethical implications of HIV and duty to warn for counselors: Does Tarasoff apply? *Journal of Counseling and Development, 73,* 397–400.

Strasburger, L. H., Jorgenson, L., & Randles, R. (1991). Criminalization of psychotherapist-patient sex. *American Journal of Psychiatry, 148,* 859–863.

Stromberg, C. D., Haggarty, D. J., Leibenluft, R. F., McMillian, M. H., Mishkin, B., Rubin, B. L., & Trilling, H. R. (1988). *The psychologist's legal handbook.* Council for the National Register of Health Service Providers in Psychology.

Swenson, L. C. (1993). *Psychology and law for the helping professions.* Pacific Grove, CA: Brooks /Cole.

Thoreson, R. W., Shaughnessy, P., Heppner, P. P., & Cook, S. W. (1993). Sexual contact during and after the professional relationship: Attitudes and practices of male counselors. *Journal of Counseling and Development, 71,* 429–434.

Thorn, B. E., Shealy, R. C., & Briggs, S. C. (1993). Sexual misconduct in psychotherapy: Reactions to a consumer-oriented brochure. *Professional Psychology: Research and Practice, 24,* 75–82.

Vasquez, M.J.T (1988). Counselor-client sexual contact: Implications for ethics training. *Journal of Counseling and Development, 67,* 238–241.

Vesper, J. H., & Brock, G. W. (1990). *Ethics, legalities, and professional practice issues in marriage and family therapy.* Boston: Allyn and Bacon.

Welfel, E. R., & Lipsitz, N. E. (1984). The ethical behavior of professional psychologists: A critical analysis of the research. *The Counseling Psychologist, 12,*(3), 31–42.

Williams, M. H. (1992). Exploitation and inference: Mapping the damage from therapist-patient sexual involvement. *American Psychologist, 47,* 412–421.

Zakutansky, T. J., & Sirles, E. A. (1993). Ethical and legal issues in field education: Shared responsibility and risk. *Journal of Social Work Education, 29,* 338–347.

CHAPTER 4

Internship Classes and Peer Groups

Internships can be tremendous learning opportunities, but they can also feel pretty lonely if you are not connected to others who are having similar experiences. If an internship class or peer group is part of your program, you have the chance to learn from the experiences of your peers as well as from your own internship. Classes and peer groups provide a place for you to try out skills during the normal course of discussion and through activities such as role plays. Internship classes and groups also give peers a chance to share in the excitement of discoveries and successes or offer a much needed emotional support when the internship experience feels too uncomfortable or confusing (Hayes, 1990).

This chapter describes some of the common activities and necessary ingredients for successful internship classes and peer groups. Reading the chapter will give you a better idea of how internship classes and peer groups function, ways to give and receive feedback, models for peer group supervision, and other topics. If you are part of an established class or group for interns, your instructor may address many of the topics that are discussed in this chapter. If classes or groups are not established at your internship, you may want to consider organizing peer study groups on your own. To help you do this, we begin with a few suggestions for how to form peer study or supervision groups with other interns.

FORMING INTERNSHIP PEER GROUPS

Before describing internship groups, a distinction should be made between peer study or support groups and the friendly gatherings that take place apart from work or school. For example, interns might get together informally as a group to go canoeing or bicycling after work or classes. Others might see films together every weekend or perhaps someone might organize monthly potlucks. Some of the best parties I ever had in graduate school were with fellow interns or graduate students. These get-togethers are very important, but such gatherings are different from peer learning groups. If you want to focus on peer learning and support you will need a structure and setting that are conducive to that work.

In some settings there are many interns from the same discipline and perhaps even from the same school. In these settings it is usually simple to form peer groups. You just talk with your peers, see if they are interested in getting together, and find a convenient time and place to meet. Because I believe peer groups are extremely important, I encourage interns to ask their supervisors to allow time and a location where interns can meet during the regular working hours as part of their training. Most internships are happy to support such requests.

If you are at an internship site where there are few or no other interns, or where there are no other interns from your discipline, the process of forming a peer group may be more difficult. Under such circumstances you may need to expand your horizons and speak with students from other disciplines or who are doing internships at other placements. Although this requires more effort, there are advantages to meeting with interns from other disciplines or settings. Students from other disciplines will bring perspectives and information that you may not have been exposed to in your own training. Similarly, interns working in other placements may have experience working with completely different clients or treatment approaches than are found at your placement. Interacting with one another can expand everyone's awareness and bring valuable insights that might not come from a more homogeneous peer group.

MODELS OF PEER GROUP LEARNING

A number of different models have been proposed for peer group learning and peer supervision. Benshoff (1993) has developed an approach to peer supervision that combines goal setting, journal article discussion, reviews of taped therapy sessions, case presentations, and evaluation and termination discussion. In studies of the effectiveness of this approach, Benshoff found that the vast majority of students rated the experience of peer supervision positively and felt that they had gained useful input and information from the process. Subjects reported that the peer supervision felt more relaxed than more traditional supervision and they appreciated the feeling of being free from grading or other evaluation by supervisors.

In a somewhat similar model described by Borders (1991), individual interns or counselors take turns receiving assistance from their peer group. In this approach, the peer learning process begins with the interns seeking assistance by specifying questions they would like addressed and the kinds of feedback they are seeking. This is followed by presentation of a taped therapy session or a description of a case. As they listen to the case, peers in the group take different roles or focus on different aspects of the interaction. For example, one person might focus on the nonverbal behavior of the therapist or client. Another might listen for the sequence of the content addressed. Group members might also be invited to view the session from different roles. These roles might include the client, therapist, or significant people in the client's life. Another approach to the case would be for different members to listen from different theoretical perspectives. Some members might approach the case from a behavioral perspective, others from a psychodynamic model, and still others from a cognitive framework.

Borders points out that the focus, roles, or theoretical perspectives assigned to or chosen for group members provide instructional experiences for the group as well as for the person receiving the supervision. Interns who need to develop greater nonverbal awareness can be assigned to focus on this

element of the interaction, while those who are learning about a certain theoretical model can apply that model as they view the case. Borders also notes that because the role of observer relieves the stress experienced as a therapist, trainees are often able to notice things or display skills as observers that they have not yet manifested when they are in the therapy role themselves.

When the tape or description of the case concludes, peers give feedback based on the initial question posed and the roles or perspective each individual assumed while the case was presented. As peers give feedback, the supervisor or another group member monitor the feedback to note any patterns that emerge and to observe the process of the group. The individual receiving the feedback can ask questions of the observers and is invited to reflect on how the feedback has or has not helped address the questions that were raised at the outset of the session.

Many of the elements described by Benshoff and Borders are also found in a model developed by Wilbur et al. (1991). Their Structured Group Supervision (SGS) model includes five phases: "The Request-for-Assistance Statement," "The Questioning Period and Identification of Focus," "The Feedback Statements," a "Pause Period," "The Supervisee Response," and finally an "Optional Discussion Period." Wilbur et al. note that during the request for assistance the supervisee may seek assistance with technical skills, personal growth, or integrating aspects of the therapy process. During the questioning period, group members use a "round-robin" technique, taking turns, with each member asking one question of the supervisee. Depending on the nature and focus of the initial request for assistance, the group members ask questions that tend to focus on what Wilbur et al. describe as "skill-development and task-process," "personal growth and psycho-process," or "socio-process." These different foci are also referred to as "extra-, intra-, or interpersonal," respectively.

Following the questioning, group members offer feedback relating to the initial request for assistance. The supervisee can take notes during this feedback but is asked to remain silent and not respond to the feedback. Wilbur et al. point out that this reduces the common "Yes but. . ." or "I have tried that already" types of responses that supervisees often give to feedback. Group members are encouraged to offer feedback in the form of statements such as "If this were my client. . .," or, "If I were in your situation. . . ."

Perhaps the most unique feature of the SGS model is the "pause period" that follows the feedback statements. It was noted above that during the feedback the supervisee can take notes but is not allowed to respond verbally. Following the feedback, there is a period of ten-to-fifteen minutes during which the supervisee is invited to think about the feedback but is not allowed to discuss the case further with group members. Group members may take a brief break to have coffee or interact with one another, but the supervisee's task is to reflect on the feedback.

In my experience, the concept of structuring a time for reflection is particularly valuable. The overriding U.S. and Canadian cultures, and academia in particular, place a premium on quick responses and give relatively little value to thoughtful reflection. Yet instantaneous responses make it difficult for recipients of feedback to fully explore what they have heard or how they are reacting to the feedback. Quick responses also tend to go hand in hand with defensiveness rather than open receiving of feedback. By structuring time for thought, supervisees are encouraged to give deeper attention and consideration to the feedback they have received. This is likely to lead to more effective learning and it models the importance of careful thought and time in the therapy process.

When sufficient time has elapsed for a period of reflection, the group gets back together and the supervisee responds to the feedback he or she has received. This may include sharing of new insights, identification of what feedback seemed particularly helpful and why, or any other comments the supervisee wants to make. If time allows, the supervisee's response can be followed by an open discussion period.

ELEMENTS OF SUCCESSFUL CLASSES AND GROUPS

For classes or peer groups to be most effective, they need to include many of the same elements that are essential to effective therapy or counseling. Trust, support, openness, honest feedback, safety, and willingness to explore and experiment are all ingredients of successful groups. Peer support is also vital and is often cited by our interns as the single most important element of internship classes.

Internship classes are enhanced when students and instructors remember to intentionally address and promote a positive, supportive atmosphere within the group. One of the ways to do this is by talking about the topic directly within the class. Interns are asked to share how they think the class is going, how they feel about working together, and to express any desires or concerns they might have for the class. As you work with your internship class or peer group, you may find it helpful to ask yourself and your group some of these same questions. The exercise below is designed to assist in that process.

EXERCISE

As a beginning toward developing a caring class or peer group, each intern may wish to explore several questions:

1. Am I willing to take some risks myself, ask for help, and be open about my questions, areas of competence, and feelings of inadequacy?
2. Am I willing and able to empathize with and support my peers as they deal with difficulties in their internship and in the class?
3. Am I willing and able to empathize with and support my peers as they deal with success and accomplishments in their internship and in the class?
4. As I imagine it and as I demonstrate it in my behavior, what is my goal in this class? Am I seeking to learn and help others learn, or am I: a) Just trying to get the grade, b) Trying to improve my status by showing what a good clinician I am? What is my real goal in this class?
5. Do I realize that it often seems easier to understand what is happening from the outside looking in? This means we must be gentle with ourselves when someone else points out something we had overlooked. We must also be gentle with our peers if we recognize something in their work that they had been overlooking.
6. When I have something to ask or say to another student do I act on this or am I passive and quiet? If I do act, is it in a way that conveys respect and empathy? If I do not speak up, is it because of my own characteristics or because I determined in this instance that my input or questions were not necessary at this time?

OFFERING FEEDBACK TO PEERS

As part of an internship class or study group, you will be involved in a give and take of ideas, observations, and suggestions. For this process to be most effective, it is helpful to keep in mind certain guidelines for giving and receiving feedback. Kadushin (1985), in his book on supervision, offered nine guidelines for supervisors to use in giving feedback to supervisees. These guidelines addressed the importance of offering feedback soon after an action; giving specific rather than vague feedback; focusing on concrete, objective behaviors; keeping feedback descriptive rather than judgmental; focusing on behaviors of the person receiving the feedback rather than their personal qualities; and offering feedback in the form of tentative statements instead of authoritative conclusions or directions. Kadushin also stressed the importance of positive feedback and of considering feedback as part of an idea-sharing, rather than advice-giving process. Finally, Kadushin reminds us that feedback must be selective and not overwhelm the recipient by the amount or the nature of the feedback offered. Similar recommendations have been offered by Woit and Brownlee (1995) in their description of "reflecting teams" as a clinical tool and as a classroom learning activity.

Whenever one offers feedback about a case, and particularly for students offering suggestions for peers, it is important to remember that the role of outside observer is much easier than the role of therapist. Observations that might seem "obvious" to an outsider might be difficult to recognize or accept when one is directly involved in the complex role of treatment provider (Borders, 1991). Thus, peers should not let themselves become overly confident or feel superior to one another if it happens that one person recognizes something about a case that others did not.

While remembering that it is often easier to be in the role of observer, peers should also not forget that whatever impressions they might draw from a case description or tape, there will always be many things that they do not know about the history of the case or the interaction between the therapist and client. This suggests another reason to avoid becoming overly confident as an observer. It is entirely possible that overconfidence is based not on an accurate impression but on misunderstanding the case.

Consistent with the principles of the two previous paragraphs and with Kadushin's suggestions, it is a good idea for interns to offer feedback to one another with a degree of "intentional tentativeness" rather than as conclusive statements. Instead of making statements phrased as "This client is clearly manipulating you!" or, "At that point you should have asked him to. . . ," peers might try, "As I watched the tape I got a feeling the client was trying to get your approval or permission. Did you have that feeling too or is something else happening?," or, "I wonder what might have happened if you had asked the client to. . . ."

Phrasing feedback in this way respects the difference between observer and therapist and does not imply that the observer has "all the answers." This practice is not only useful in peer feedback. It is also a valuable technique in therapy. Just as observers of therapy can mistakenly think they have the answers for their peers, therapists can sometimes think they have the answers for their clients. Tentative phrasing can help reduce resistance and encourage clients to explore possibilities.

THE IMPORTANCE OF EMPATHY

In many instances the most helpful response interns can give one another is to offer empathic understanding. On numerous occasions I have observed interns being overwhelmed by suggestions from instructor and peers. Often, what the intern needed most was for a peer to acknowledge how tough the case was and how frustrated, sad, angry, etc., the intern felt. This is so important that before offering their peers suggestions or feedback about a case, interns are well advised to ask themselves if they really understand how their peer is feeling and what he or she needs most at the moment.

When an intern is in need of empathy and support, the relief that comes when these are provided by a peer is almost palpable. It is sometimes as if a great weight has been removed from the intern and he or she is at last able to breathe again. Until that happens, all of the well-intentioned technical suggestions are likely to be of little benefit. Interns are in a unique position to provide empathic understanding and support to one another because they are most closely in a position to feel what their peers are experiencing. Instructors and super-

visors easily get caught up in the theoretical or technical aspects of a case and may forget to attend to the intern's affective needs. By remembering to attend to empathy, peers can meet an essential need for one another and in the process can both practice and directly observe the effects of this key therapy skill.

RECEIVING FEEDBACK

Along with considering ways to give feedback, it is equally important to think about how one receives feedback. The first thing to understand about receiving feedback is that it is not easy. This awareness will help you better understand your own experience at receiving feedback from supervisors or peers. It can also help you appreciate some of what clients experience in therapy.

Whenever you expose yourself to feedback from others you make yourself vulnerable. You run the risk of revealing weaknesses, errors, or personal qualities that you might wish others were unaware of or at least would not comment on. As an intern in the helping professions, the stakes are even higher because you have been charged with the responsibility for helping others. This makes it easy to feel that perceived mistakes, failures, or shortcomings mean you have somehow let down or perhaps even harmed the clients who have come to you for help.

The matter is complicated still further by the fact that the nature of therapy involves using the therapist's self, or at least the presentation of self, as part of the healing process. As a result, even the most well-intentioned suggestions or feedback can easily be experienced as intimations or outright assertions that there is something amiss with one's presentation of self. That will probably not be easy to cope with but it is part of the learning process and, not incidentally, it is part of what clients experience whenever they come to therapy and must explore who they are.

ACKNOWLEDGING IMPERFECTION

To help interns accept feedback from peers and supervisors, it is useful to remind and give permission to be something other than perfect and flawless. Although interns should do their best, that does not mean they can never make mistakes. Therapists and interns are only human and part of learning means there will be some things you do not know.

If you do not feel you have to be or appear perfect, it is easier to accept the possibility that others can offer suggestions or observations that will help you improve. I encourage interns to experiment with an attitude that says: "I hope others will recognize some things I do well, but I also hope they will recognize some things I am not doing as well as I could. If people identify my mistakes that will help me learn and I am grateful to them." If interns approach learning with this attitude they are much more likely to be open to suggestions from others. They are also more likely to be given helpful suggestions because people will recognize that suggestions are welcomed.

Most students have not been taught to hope that others will recognize their weaknesses. However, if one thinks about it, the alternative is actually rather absurd. By virtue of the fact that one is in school or internship training there is an assumption that one has not yet mastered a body of knowledge or skill. Therefore, the best way to learn is to identify areas of deficiency and seek to remediate them. If one seeks to hide areas of deficiency, how can growth and learning in those areas occur?

The best thing that can happen to you as an intern or student is to discover what you do not know or what you think you know or understand but in fact do not. If this sounds strange, ask yourself if you would rather go on to practice without knowing that you lack certain information or misunderstand key concepts.

One way to put this attitude into practice is to develop the habit of thanking people whenever they offer suggestions, corrections, or constructive criticism. I know of a person who travels around the world and speaks several languages with fluency that most people would envy. In spite of his proficiency, he makes a point of asking people who speak the language as their own to correct him whenever he makes a mistake. My friend explains his approach this way,

> I know it might seem impolite to correct me, and of course I appreciate compliments, but for me the sign of true friendship is when someone cares enough to correct my mistakes. That is the only way I can learn and I'd rather be corrected than go around thinking I'm speaking properly when I'm really making some glaring mistake.

My friend is quite sincere about this and he always makes a point of acknowledging his appreciation and thanking people when they offer corrections. That attitude is probably why he speaks so many languages so well. By acknowledging mistakes and being open to feedback he lets everyone become a teacher and he is able to learn much more rapidly than people who fear mistakes and do not accept suggestions.

VIDEO OR AUDIO RECORDINGS OF SESSIONS

In the models described earlier by Borders and by Wilbur et al., group case discussions often center around audio or video tapes of therapy sessions. Because these media enable the supervisor and class to observe the actual clients and treatment interactions, they can be extremely valuable tools for clinical training. If you have the opportunity to incorporate taped sessions in your training, several suggestions may be helpful.

One question that often arises is which part of the session to review in class or supervision. Since time limitations generally prohibit reviews of entire treatment sessions, it is necessary to select portions of the session for presentation. This poses an interesting paradox. Most interns want to present a positive impression of their clinical skills and work, so there is a temptation to choose only those points in a session where one feels particularly confident in one's work. This process has been addressed by Friedman and Kaslow (1986) who noted that beginning therapists may not fully share their work with supervisors or others because they fear looking silly or incompetent.

Though understandable, this is not necessarily the best way to learn. As an alternative, interns might choose to pick a few sections where they feel they were doing their best work (it is perfectly valid and important to want and receive some positive strokes) and a few other sections where they felt lost, confused, overwhelmed, on the spot, tense, frightened, etc. I know of one intern who took this suggestion to heart and had the courage to bring in a tape in which the client actually fell asleep during a session. For several minutes the tape consisted only of the client's snoring. Sharing this with the internship class and supervisor took courage on the part of the intern, but it took even more to then play another portion of the tape and reveal that for a few minutes there were two people, the client and the intern, snoring. (This really happened.) In your own work, you will probably not have an experience exactly like this, but you will feel sleepy at times and you will undoubtedly say and do things that you will immediately wish you could take back or try again. Do not be ashamed to acknowledge such mistakes or to share them with your peers so you and they can learn from the experience.

As you listen to tapes of your sessions or those of peers, you may find it interesting to attend to the tapes in various ways. When most beginning interns observe or listen to therapy sessions they focus primarily on the words people say to each other. This focus is consistent with how people interact during ordinary conversations, but one of the lessons of therapy is that the content, i.e., the words, of an interaction, often carries far less information than the process, i.e., the way the words are said, the position of the speakers, the sequence of the overall interaction, and a host of other nonverbal elements. When you participate, when you listen to tapes of sessions, and as you work in actual therapy interactions, learn to receive other elements than the words alone.

EXERCISE

I learned this exercise during a supervision workshop presented by Jesse Geller. The exercise involves listening several times to a brief taped portion of a therapy session. The first time through, you should simply play the tape and listen to it with no specific instructions. Then, play the tape again but focus very carefully on the words each person uses as they interact. Next, listen to the tape a third time, but this time focus on receiving not the words but the affect—the emotional messages and experiences of the people. What do you experience as you receive with your attention focused on different elements of the interaction? Most people report that they get something different out of the interaction each time through. It is also common to notice that in the third listening, in which the focus is on affect rather than words, people feel they begin to understand the client in a different way than they had before.

The previous exercise introduced you to the experience of receiving elements of an interaction other than words. In this case the focus was on affect, but it would also have been possible to emphasize such things as rate of speech, length of pauses, tone of voice, body position etc.

ROLE PLAYS

An alternative to working with recorded therapy sessions is to enact therapy sessions within the group. Because role plays may be a new experience, it may help to have a brief introduction about their purpose and function and how to make the most of them. Students who are interested in learning more about role plays as part of the therapy process may wish to consult writings on the subject of psychodrama or Gestalt therapy techniques.

Role plays involve class members taking the roles of clients, trainees or other staff members and acting these roles as they portray a situation or interaction of interest. Role plays can be particularly helpful in developing basic helping skills and in learning to deal with difficult clients or staff. Role plays can also help interns become more aware of their therapeutic style and, in some instances, about significant issues in their own lives. Field instructors can also use role plays to learn about issues and techniques of supervision. Cohen and Ruff (1995) describe five different role play scenarios and offer suggestions for accompanying discussion.

Role plays are most productive when participants are aware of several principles. The first of these is that the goal of the role play is not necessarily to provide an exact replication of the "real" situation or people. While realism may be useful, role plays also exist as experiences in themselves and need not be perfectly accurate for learning to occur. Indeed, there are times when the deviation from reality provides important clinical insights about what is happening and how things might change. Thus, although several of the suggestions that follow offer hints about how to enhance the realism of role plays, keep in mind that realism is not the goal that matters; experiencing, understanding, and learning are the real goals.

A second key to successful role plays is for the people involved to not just imagine or act their role, but temporarily to "become" the person they are portraying. Role players should not just talk about what they are doing. They should try to get out of their own mind, feeling, and behavioral set and into that of the person they portray. Feel what that person feels, hold or move your body as that person might, use the tone and volume of voice that person might use. Experience what life has been like for the person you are playing. Experience what this moment and interaction mean for them and how their body feels.

This process of "becoming someone else" not only facilitates role plays; it is also an excellent way to develop or enhance empathy. By trying to get inside someone else's skin, we understand that person at a much deeper level than if we merely discuss them as some abstract object of clinical interest. This was brought home to me when I worked with a man in his late thirties who had lost both arms and hands below the elbow. To increase my awareness of what life was like for this man, my supervisor induced a light hypnotic trance, suggested that I too had lost my arms and hands, then created images of otherwise mundane activities, such as opening doors, dressing, shaking hands, going to the bathroom, etc. The images progressed from these activities to the more profound awareness of wanting to hug a child, caress a lover, wipe away a tear. The point of the exercise was not to evoke pity for this client. Rather, it was to help me get some sense of an important aspect of the client's life that I had never experienced myself.

In some form, this kind of learning experience applies to all of our interactions with clients. We have never experienced exactly what another person has, yet we must try to get a sense of what it is like to be that person. In your role plays, do your best to make this happen. As you do your best to portray an individual in a role play, it is also important to be open to suggestions about how to adjust your actions to more closely approximate the person you are representing. If you are unsure of how to play a role, ask for suggestions. Similarly, if you are directing a role play, you may need to give feedback to your players about how they need to act, move, speak, etc. For example, if two students who are good friends are trying to role play a relationship between people who despise each other, it may help to suggest that the friends not think about each other as friends but instead try to imagine someone else whom they detest. I once observed an instructor deal with a similar situation by asking the students in the role play to think of a time when they had been sick to their stomach and at the point of vomiting. When this image was so real the students were almost sick themselves, the instructor said, "Okay, now imagine that you feel that way whenever you are around this other person."

Suggestions for images and deep involvement in characters can enhance the accuracy and benefits of role plays, but there will probably be times when you find it almost impossible to portray certain clients or situations. During role plays it sometimes happens that interns who normally do very well in such exercises suddenly find they are blocked and cannot act like the person or cannot play a certain kind of behavior. This may be experienced as an inability to understand the character intellectually, or the participants might be aware of strong emotional reactions to a role.

Such experiences can help lead to valuable insights for the participants. When a person who is otherwise skilled at role plays is suddenly unable to portray a role or situation, this may be a clue that some unresolved issues are being touched. The exact nature of the issues may be unclear from the immediate experience, but it is a good sign that something important has been evoked and is worth exploring further. If you experience this kind of reaction, ask yourself if one of the characters, the situation, or the setting of the role play is somehow reminiscent of an experience or person in your own life? Is it difficult for you now to portray anything about a person, or are there only certain qualities that you are blocking on or feeling troubled about?

Through awareness of your own experiences in role plays, and by pursuing and trying to understand your reactions, you may learn more about yourself than about the specific situation or client that stimulated the role play. This can be very beneficial. If there was something in your own life that needed to be dealt with and that was related to the client's issues, your own issues might block not only the role play but also the actual work with the client. Experienced psychodramatists have observed that, as people deal more effectively with underlying issues, their ability to portray the related roles also improves. Thus, just as the initial difficulty may be an index of underlying issues, changes in your role playing can be an indication of progress in your self-awareness. As you become more aware of and able to deal with your own issues, your ability to interact therapeutically with clients is also likely to improve.

One final suggestion regarding role plays. As a general rule, role plays are more useful if they are not interrupted by frequent discussions or commentary. If you are involved in a role play, it will probably work best if you get into the role, stay with it, and see what happens. Try not to stop and ask for guidance or talk "about" the role. If you find yourself frequently interrupting the role, that could be a sign, as was just discussed, of some issues in your own life. On the other hand, many interns interrupt role plays because they are most accustomed to learning by talking "about" a subject, not by trying to experience something. After the role play, it is useful to discuss what you experienced or observed, but during the role play be very careful not to substitute intellectualization for experience.

ETHICS IN CLASSES AND GROUPS

The previous chapter introduced essential ethical principles for clinical practice and internship work. These included the principles of knowing your limitations, confidentiality, and the proscription against harmful dual relationships. Because

internship classes often include case discussions, reviews of tapes, and role plays, and because internship classes and groups deal with personal and sensitive issues, care must be taken to follow similar ethical principles within the classroom setting.

Case discussion is an activity that raises a number of ethical questions in internship classes. In most internship classes it is standard practice for interns to review clients and clinical experiences as part of the class. Sensitive to issues of ethics, interns rightly ask if bringing case material to class is a violation of their client's or placement's confidentiality.

This is admittedly a somewhat gray area, so a definitive answer cannot be given. There are, however, measures that can and should be taken to lessen the possibility of confidentiality breeches. The first step is for each member of the internship class to know about the principle of confidentiality and agree to keep whatever occurs during the internship class strictly confidential. This means students do not discuss class material with anyone beyond the confines of the class. Confidentiality is particularly important because, in addition to reviewing their cases, students and trainees must feel safe to acknowledge their own concerns, weaknesses, fears, and personal issues relating to their training. They must also be able to discuss cases and clients without fear that confidential information will go beyond the confines of the internship class or group.

Many institutional agreements with internship sites include a clause explaining that interns will be expected to discuss clients and clinical experiences with their instructor and during the class as part of their educational process. Interns are also instructed to tell clients from the outset that they may discuss the case with their instructor or supervisor and in the internship class. Interns are advised to tell clients that the client's identity will be protected in such discussions and that the discussion will be strictly for educational purposes.

Before recording therapy sessions or using audio or video tapes in class, one must obtain permission from the client. The ethical principles of informed consent and confidentiality require that if a clinical session is to be taped, all those involved in the session must give permission. Written "permission to record" forms should specify precisely the purpose of the taping, how the tapes will be used, the time period for which this use will be authorized, and what will happen to the tapes at the end of the time period. Clients must have the right to refuse recording clearly explained to them and they must not be coerced into giving permission. Clients must also be given information about the purpose of the taping and the confidentiality of the information on the tapes. Clients should also be informed that the tape will only be shared with the supervisor and class, that information will be kept strictly confidential, and that the tapes will be erased by a specified date or immediately after the class use.

Another step to preserve confidentiality is to advise interns that when they discuss cases in class or write about them in a journal they must take measures to protect the identity of clients. As discussed in previous chapters, interns may use a standard identification of simply Mr. or Ms. X to describe all clients. Interns are also instructed that if speaking about the details of a case might reveal the identity of the individual, even without explicitly saying his or her name, the intern should discuss the case with the instructor before raising it in class. This is particularly important if interns are working in a college counseling center or other setting where the identity of student clients might easily be discernible by other interns who also know the client. In such instances, particular caution is required and on occasion it is better not to discuss a case in class if confidentiality cannot be preserved. An example of this situation might be if an intern were working with a student body officer whose identity would necessarily be compromised in class simply due to the nature of the concerns being addressed in the case discussion. A similar situation might exist if tape-recorded therapy sessions would reveal a client's distinctive voice and the identity of the person might be known to others in the class. Under such circumstances, the need to protect the client's confidentiality outweighs the educational benefit to the class.

Case material and information about clients is not all that must be protected by confidentiality. During internship classes, interns themselves often bring up highly personal material that must be accorded the same respect and protection given to clients. Because clinical work is so demanding and often touches on issues from the intern's own life, it is vital that interns feel they can trust their classmates enough to feel it is safe to explore whatever arises. In other classes it might be acceptable for a student to tell a roommate something like "You'll never believe what another student said in class today," but that is absolutely unacceptable for students in an internship class. Confidentiality is essential to your role as a professional and the internship is the place to establish ethical practices that will be present throughout your career.

REFERENCES

Akamatsu, T. J. (1980). The use of role-play and simulation technique in the training of psychotherapy. In A. K. Hess (Ed.), *Psychotherapy supervision: Theory, research and practice.* New York: John Wiley & Sons.

Benshoff, J. M. (1993). Peer supervision in counselor training. *The Clinical Supervisor, 11,* 89–102.

Borders, L. D. (1991). A systematic approach to peer group supervision. *Journal of Counseling and Development, 19,* 248–252.

Cohen, M. B., & Ruff, E. (1995). The use of role play in field instructor training. *Journal of Teaching in Social Work, 11,* 85–100.

Friedman, D., & Kaslow, N. J. (1986). The development of professional identity in psychotherapists: Six stages in the supervision process. In F. W. Kaslow (Ed.), *Supervision and training: Models, dilemmas and challenges.* New York: Haworth Press.

Hayes, R. L. (1990). Developmental group supervision. *The Journal for Specialists in Group Work, 15,* 225–238.

Kadushin, A. (1985). *Supervision in social work,* 2nd ed. New York: Columbia University Press.

Wilbur, M. P., Roberts-Wilbur, J., Morris, J. R., Betz, R. L., & Hart, G. M. (1991). Structured group supervision: Theory into practice. *The Journal for Specialists in Group Work, 16,* 91–100.

Woit, J., & Brownlee, K. (1995). Reflecting teams in the classroom: An effective educational tool? *Journal of Teaching in Social Work, 11,* 67–84.

CHAPTER 5

SUPERVISION

When asked to name the best part of professional training, a colleague said without hesitation, "Supervision. From one of my supervisors I learned more about treatment and working with people than I had learned in three years of graduate school."

As such comments suggest, supervision can be a tremendous learning opportunity. This chapter discusses different approaches to supervision and elements that make for quality supervisory experiences. We also consider how personalities and theoretical orientation play a role in the supervisory experience and how interns and supervisors can manage differences that may arise in supervision.

HOPES AND FEARS

Berger and Buchholz (1993) observed that, in spite of the importance of the supervisory experience, it is rare for supervisees to receive instruction in the supervisory process or in what is expected of them. These authors suggest that giving supervisees an opportunity to voice their wishes and fears is one of the first steps in preparing for supervision. When I ask interns what their hopes are for supervision, they often speak about the qualities they would prefer in their supervisor. Most interns want supervisors to be a combination of teacher, role model, and mentor. Interns seek supervisors who will help

them learn about theories and techniques of therapy, assessment, and other clinical functions. Interns tend to prefer supervisors who give enough freedom to try new things but are careful to select activities that are not beyond the intern's abilities. Interns also want supervisors who are supportive and to whom they can turn for advice and encouragement. Finally, many interns want to get to know their supervisors as people outside of the internship setting.

These impressions are supported by research in which interns have been asked to identify preferred characteristics of supervisors (Baker & Smith, 1987; Gandolfo & Brown, 1987). Results from these studies indicate that the desired supervisor qualities vary somewhat depending on experience, but across experience levels there is a consistent desire for supervisors who are perceived as supportive and understanding. Within a supportive environment many interns feel it is valuable for their supervisor to help interns understand themselves and explore the interpersonal dynamics between interns and clients and between the intern and supervisor. Interns also express a need for direct observation and meaningful feedback and instruction about their work. Help with problem solving regarding their own cases, and opportunities to observe the supervisor in therapy, are also rated highly by interns.

Along with their hopes for supervision, interns also bring fears. Perhaps the two most common fears are: "I am afraid I don't have a clue what I'm supposed to do or how to do it" and "I am even more afraid someone will find out I don't know what to do." Similar observations have been expressed by other authors. Charny (1986) described a number of common fears of practitioners and emphasized the value of supervision that allows interns to voice their fears. Among the most frequent worries, Charny identified fears that patients will "flake out," that a supervisor will discover a trainee does not like a patient or that a trainee is feeling attracted to a patient, fears of being responsible for what happens to the patient, and fears of "not really helping." Charny contends that voicing and exploring these inner fears is much more conducive to learning than supervision that stays at the "I said then they said" level of discourse. Costa (1995) offers a similar recommendation and speaks of the value of "normalizing" the supervisee's anxiety.

Awareness of the needs and concerns of supervisees has also been stressed by those who take a developmental approach to supervision. Friedman and Kaslow (1986) suggest that a key question of beginning interns is, "What exactly is my job with these patients?" (p. 35). Friedman and Kaslow also recognize interns' concerns about competence and propose that interns who are just beginning may be plagued by self-doubts and anxieties. Quoting Barnat (1974, p.190), Friedman and Kaslow speak of the interns' "affirmation hunger" and suggest that it is particularly important for beginners to have affirming, accepting supervisors.

I find it helpful to acknowledge from the outset that fears are perfectly understandable not only for beginning interns but for experienced therapists as well. Any time we learn something new, there are usually elements of both excitement and fear. Instead of disguising fears, interns are encouraged to acknowledge them so the fear can be worked through together. In order for this to succeed, it is vital that interns feel "safe" and that they actually are "safe" when they take the risk to speak about fears. In other words, interns must know that they will not be punished with poor evaluations or low grades if they are honest enough to speak about their insecurities.

HOPES AND FEARS OF SUPERVISORS

Interns are not the only ones who have hopes and fears in supervision. Supervisors also have their own sets of wishes and trepidations when they accept interns. Words to describe the "ideal" intern would probably include: well-informed but eager to learn, gets along well with staff and clients, shows initiative, follows through reliably, and is attentive to detail. An intern should also be dependable, receptive to supervision, able to seek help when necessary but also willing to accept challenges, intelligent, creative, sensitive, and insightful.

The most common fear of supervisors is that an intern will do something that jeopardizes patients, the interns themselves, or the supervisor. In the clinical realm, supervisors get frightened when interns are not frightened. The supervisor's two worst nightmares are well-intentioned but overly confident

or careless interns and the occasional pathological intern who acts irresponsibly or is manipulative without concern for patients or the institutions.

Concerns of supervisors about intern actions are not without foundation. Harrar, VandeCreek, and Knapp (1990) have described the concepts of "Direct Liability" and "Vicarious Liability" (p. 39). These authors indicate that supervisors can and have been sued for the actions of supervisees. They also note that trainees are generally held accountable for the same standards of care as licensed professionals (see also Zakutansky & Sirles, 1993). Because the supervisor is responsible to ensure that interns meet professional standards of care, it should not be surprising that supervisors are intently concerned about the quality of work interns perform. For similar reasons, interns should not become defensive if supervisors insist on high standards of professionalism or if supervisors are occasionally critical of an intern's performance. It is not the primary job of the supervisor to make every intern feel happy and comfortable. Rather, the supervisor's main task is to ensure that all interns are competent and apply themselves diligently and reliably to their responsibilities.

Along with fears that interns will make harmful mistakes or are somehow unstable themselves, supervisors also have many of the same fears as interns, i.e., "Do I know what to do in my own clinical work or in my role as supervisor?" and "What if someone finds out or suggests that I don't know what to do?"

The supervisory role is at least as complex as the role of therapist and it is by no means easy. When a professional agrees to serve as a supervisor, he or she is accepting a position that will undoubtedly present a unique set of demands and vulnerabilities. Although some supervisors have received specific training in supervision, many have not. Surveys assessing supervisor training have shown that only 20 percent of respondents report having a supervision course or seminar, and 32 percent have no training at all in supervision (McColley & Baker, 1982). Further evidence that supervisors are often untrained in supervision comes from a survey of 151 APA approved internships. That survey indicated that only a third of the facilities provided training in supervision (Hess & Hess, 1983).

In recent years training in supervision has increased, but the nature and extent of such training has varied widely. Progress toward more structured training has included development of a comprehensive curriculum guide for training counseling supervisors (Borders et al., 1991), and establishment of standards for counseling supervisors (Dye & Borders, 1990; Supervision Interest Network, Association for Counselor Education and Supervision, 1990).

The combination of a complex task and relatively little training places supervisors in a position that is not greatly unlike the intern's. Each is expected to be competent in a role for which he or she is not necessarily fully prepared. Just as interns must learn to deal effectively with anxieties about their role, supervisors must deal with similar anxieties about their role and responsibilities. Although the lack of specific training in supervision is likely to be a hindrance for supervisors, that does not mean that supervisors have nothing to teach. It does, however, mean that in many cases both the supervisor and the intern will be in learning roles.

EXERCISE

It can be very useful for interns and supervisors to be open with one another from the outset about what some of their mutual and individual needs, fears, and concerns are. Just by acknowledging these things up front, a great deal of anxiety, crossed communication, and frustration can be reduced. To get this process started, listed below are some of the common needs of supervisors and interns. Interns and supervisors may wish to check this list, modify or add to it in any way you like, then discuss your individual and joint needs together.

Supervisor needs from interns: Honesty and integrity, ethical conduct, openness to suggestion, respect for the supervisor's experience, careful quality work, deep thought, hard work, and willingness to listen even if there is disagreement.
Others:_____

Interns needs from supervisors: Support, patience, knowledge of the field, guidance, accessibility, modeling, direct teaching of information, involvement, some autonomy, trust, openness, and willingness to listen.
Others:_____

CLARIFYING EXPECTATIONS

Clarifying from the outset what the expectations are for interns and supervisors is essential to preventing later confusion and to achieving the most beneficial learning experience (Freeman, 1993). Among the expectations that should be delineated as clearly as possible are: 1.) The frequency and timing of supervisor sessions. 2.) The content of supervisory sessions. (For example, will they consist of case reviews via notes, tapes, etc.; didactic instruction in topic areas; informal personal exchanges; or some combination of techniques?) 3.) The theoretical orientation or techniques that the intern is expected to learn and how specifically this learning will be demonstrated and assessed. 4.) The extent to which personal issues of the intern or supervisor will be addressed as part of supervision.

FREQUENCY AND TIMING OF SUPERVISION

In Chapter 2 it was suggested that formal agreements should be established regarding how often and when supervision sessions will be held. Once such agreements are formed, interns and supervisors must make their best efforts to set aside as much time as necessary for supervision and hold to that time. When schedules get busy, it is all too easy for people to begin to sacrifice supervision time for other "more urgent" tasks. This should be avoided. Except in very rare situations or absolute emergencies, nothing should be considered more urgent than supervision. Interns and supervisors should schedule other events, projects, meetings, etc., around supervision, not vice versa. If supervisors or interns begin to allow other things to take precedence over supervision, someone may need to gently call it to their attention, emphasize the importance of supervision, and explore ways of meeting reliably.

Exactly how frequently one should receive supervision depends on several factors, including the nature of the intern's activities, the level of the intern's experience or training, and the expectations of the placement site, instructor, or, in some cases, guidelines established within a profession (Jarvis, 1989). In the field of counseling, the Council for Accreditation of Counseling and Related Educational Programs (CACREP) has set a standard of "a minimum of one hour per week of individual supervision by a program faculty member supervisor, or a student supervisor working under the supervision of a program faculty member" (CACREP, 1988, p. 28). At the 1987 National Conference on Internship Training in Psychology, delegates agreed on internship policies for APA approved graduate programs. Because these guidelines are intended for internships that are advanced, typically "full-time" placements that come at the end of graduate course work in psychology, they will not apply to all disciplines or settings. They are presented here as but one example of how professions specify supervision requirements in their internship guidelines.

With regard to the matter of supervision frequency, these policies indicate that

> Supervised practice must include at least 900 hours, including 450 hours in direct provision of psychological services in intervention/treatment and assessment/diagnosis, and 300 hours in formal supervision (both group and individual). (Belar et al., 1989, p. 64)

Several paragraphs later, the same document indicates that:

> At the end of the predoctoral year the internship director must certify that . . . (c) the trainee received a minimum of four hours per week in regularly scheduled, formal, face-to-face supervision, at least three hours of which were on an individual basis. (ibid.)

Where specific professional standards are lacking or do not apply, as a general principle the more interns are involved in direct services with clients, i.e., therapy, assessment, etc., the more supervision they will need. Some programs suggest an initial ratio of one hour of supervision to every four to six hours of direct patient contact. This is ideal, but experience indicates that in practice it is relatively rare for supervisors of beginning interns to have sufficient time to meet this frequently. More common ratios are one hour of supervision for every eight to ten hours of clinical contact. In settings where interns are involved in three or four cases per day, this would amount to about one hour of supervision every two to three days. If supervision is less frequent than this, the time span between clinical interactions and supervision is too long and important details or impressions are likely to be forgotten.

To the extent that interns have greater clinical experience or, at the other end of the spectrum, are less involved in direct clinical services, the frequency of supervision may be lessened. However, this does not mean supervision is unnecessary. Even therapists with many years of experience recognize the value of supervision and schedule it for themselves as part of responsible practice. Thus, whether you are an absolute beginner and your internship consists primarily of observation, or if you have several years of training and are given greater responsibility and independence, you should still be sure to arrange for regular supervision.

CONTENT OF SUPERVISION

Most supervision involves a combination of activities. These may include such things as didactic instruction, case discussions, review of audio or video tapes, role plays, direct observation of sessions, joint therapy, and opportunities to observe the supervisor in therapy (Hess & Hess, 1983). On occasion, a single activity may comprise the entire supervisory session, but often several types of activities will be included. For example, a session might begin with a general discussion, then shift to review a taped interaction, followed by more discussion and perhaps some role play.

To help you understand the function of the activities of supervision, several are discussed here. The goal in reviewing these approaches is to enable you to take an active role in selecting activities for your own supervision. Thus, you might wish to ask your instructor directly to teach you about a specific topic that you have not studied before. Or, if you feel a need for something other than didactic approaches or discussion, you might suggest to your supervisor that you role play a case. You might also want to request the opportunity to observe your supervisor in therapy. Of course your supervisor will have the final say in what happens during supervision, but you should be involved in the process and make your needs and interests known.

How Supervisors Determine What to Do
Before describing specific approaches to supervision, it may be helpful to provide some insights into how supervisors determine what should happen in supervision. For a variety of reasons, including limited training in supervision, the lack of clear consensus on what the content of supervision "should"

be, and because people tend to do what they know best, the content and approach to supervision are likely to reflect and be closely related to the supervisor's own approach to treatment or assessment. This has been demonstrated empirically by Friedlander and Ward (1984) who found, for example, that Gestalt- versus psychodynamically oriented therapists differed in their supervision approaches and tended to use techniques of supervision that were similar to the therapy techniques of their orientation.

Supervisors also choose supervisory approaches that mirror their therapy approach because they believe this is a useful way to teach trainees their therapeutic orientation. For example, Frances and Clarkin (1981) described how techniques of supervision often parallel the techniques of therapy. In a review of therapy and supervision approaches for schools of therapy including psychoanalysis, behavior therapy, brief psychotherapy, and family therapy, these authors note that what goes on in supervision provides a model of what happens in therapy. Similar observations have been made by other authors. Martin and McBride (1987) assert that congruence between the supervisor's therapeutic orientation and approach to supervision is a desirable training technique. In their model of supervision, trainees learn the theory and techniques of an approach by experiencing them directly during the supervisory interaction. Thus, an intern studying under a cognitive therapist would be asked to explore cognitions related to a client. Similarly, an intern studying psychodrama might be asked to participate in a psychodrama relating to one of the intern's cases.

In addition to working from their own theoretical orientation, supervisors are also encouraged to study the broad literature on supervision. (For a comprehensive reference list, see Robiner & Schofield, 1990. For a review of cross-cultural supervision issues and research, see Leong and Wagner, 1994.) They should also understand the personal and developmental needs of their interns (Friedman & Kaslow, 1986; Stoltenberg, 1981; Tracey, Ellickson & Sherry, 1989), and consider the process of the intern's therapy work and the supervision itself (McNeil & Worthen, 1989). Based on these considerations, supervisors can then choose among many different techniques to best match the needs of specific interns with specific clients. This may include direct modeling of the supervisor's therapy approach, but it might also involve other activities that are not included in the normal treatment approach of the supervisor. The key point is that whatever activities are chosen for supervision, they should be based on an understanding of the supervisee, client, and situation, not simply on habitual and familiar approaches of the supervisor.

DIDACTIC SUPERVISION

One approach to supervision is similar to what instructors and students do in their academic classes. Didactic, or teaching, supervision is best chosen when an intern wants to learn, or a supervisor wants to teach, specific information about a theory, technique, diagnosis, or some other topic relevant to the intern's activities (Hess, 1980). The goal of a didactic approach is to get information across as efficiently as possible so the interns can learn and apply the information directly to their work. Didactic approaches tend to be particularly appealing to beginning interns because they feel a need for concrete, practical information to help them cope with the anxiety and ambiguity of starting something new (Ronnestad & Skovholt, 1993).

An example of didactic instruction would be a supervisor defining terminology from a certain school of therapy. Another example would be an intern asking a supervisor for instruction about the characteristics of a specific disorder. To supplement material taught directly by the supervisor, selected reading assignments or recommendations can also be given to interns. For example, an intern working with clients who have eating disorders might be assigned to review the recent literature on the disorders, then discuss the readings with the supervisor. Beyond the relevance of the readings to the intern's immediate activities, this practice also establishes a model that should be followed throughout one's career. Whenever a professional is working with an individual or group it is her or his responsibility to be as informed as possible about the nature of the problems, the options available for treatment and, where available, outcome data to help determine the most effective treatment.

If your supervisor does not initiate suggestions or assignments for readings, you may want to ask if there are any books or articles he or she would recommend. Supervisors sometimes take it for granted that the information they have studied is known by everyone and they forget that interns might not yet have studied it. A sincere request for references will typically produce useful resources that will help you to both understand your clients better and to appreciate where the supervisor may have acquired his or her knowledge or approach.

Perhaps the main drawback to didactic methods is that if they are relied upon too heavily, supervision can become merely another venue for lecture-based instruction. The temptations to rely on lecture in supervision are many. Lecture-based teaching and learning are familiar to both the intern and supervisor. Lectures allow supervisors to feel they have useful knowledge to pass on and that they are benefiting their interns by conveying that knowledge. Lectures are also safe for both the supervisor and the intern. The trouble is that by keeping supervision at the didactic level, more challenging issues, such as how interns feel about themselves or clients, how the supervisor and intern are interacting, how one deals with ethical dilemmas, and other challenging subjects can be avoided. Such avoidance can be quite tempting but it can also inhibit the benefits of supervision that deals with ambiguous material, that addresses challenging issues, and that encourages self-exploration (Ronnestad & Skovholt, 1993). If you become

aware that too much of your supervision is comprised of a traditional, passive learning model, you might consider suggesting an alternative approach.

CASE DISCUSSIONS

Although students are most familiar with didactic approaches from their classroom education, in clinical internships didactic activities usually comprise a relatively small portion of supervision. The most common activity of supervision is typically case discussion. As the name implies, case discussion means the intern describes a case to the supervisor and the two discuss what is going on.

Case discussions can take a variety of formats depending on the goals and preferences of the intern and supervisor. Perhaps the most common approach involves interns describing what is happening in a case, explaining their actions, and offering interpretations for what is happening. The supervisor typically listens, asks questions, and may offer alternative interpretations or suggestions.

THE SOCRATIC METHOD

A more formalized model of supervisory discussions and questioning has been described by Overholser (1991), who proposes Socratic questioning as a technique for supervision. As Overholser describes the technique, it involves three elements: "systematic questioning," "inductive reasoning," and "universal definitions." Overholser emphasizes that Socratic questions are not actually requests for information but are designed to encourage the supervisee's thinking. Four content areas are targeted by systematic questions. These questions focus on helping the intern define the problem, generate response alternatives, think critically about the case, and, finally, evaluate the success of responses once they are implemented.

The second element in Overholser's model, "Inductive Reasoning," is designed to help interns generate general inferences about a case from specific details or events of the case. "Universal Definitions," the third element of Overholser's model, refers to questioning designed to develop broader concepts about therapy in general. This can help interns understand such concepts as "resistance," "transference," and other important ideas of therapy.

Whether a supervisor intentionally uses Socratic questions or takes a less structured approach to case discussions, it is important for interns to understand that questions, suggestions, or instructions in supervision do not necessarily mean the interns are supposed to have "the right answer" or that they have "done something wrong." I raise this point explicitly because interns tend to bring expectations from academic settings to supervision. In supervision, questions are not synonymous with tests. Their purpose is not to elicit a "correct" answer but to stimulate the intern's thought and understanding. This means it is okay to not know an answer, because that means there is an opportunity to think and learn.

As an intern, if you are asked a factual question that you cannot answer, it is fine to acknowledge that you do not know and ask someone to explain the answer to you. If you are asked a question designed to stimulate your thinking, don't feel like you are on the spot or should have a quick response. Instead, take your time, think about the question and what you have been discussing, then explore your ideas with the other person. In supervision, this process of being asked questions that encourage you to think in new ways is part of developing your clinical knowledge and understanding. It is also an implicit element of professional work because it is not your task as a professional to know the answers beforehand. Rather, your task is to ask yourself the same kinds of questions your supervisor would ask so you can develop an understanding of your clients and make well-reasoned treatment decisions.

EMPATHY AND EXPERIENTIAL CONSIDERATIONS

Before concluding this review of questions and discussion in supervision, there are a few caveats that should be mentioned. First, when questions are used, supervisors should give careful thought to the focus of the questions. As noted earlier, Charny (1986) and others (Kaiser, 1992; Bogo, 1993) believe it is extremely important to focus not solely on the external events of therapy but also to consider the internal experience, concerns, feelings, etc., of the intern and the relationship of the intern to the supervisor. A questioning approach that emphasized the overt content of a therapy session might neglect the internal experience of the intern in the session.

Consistent with this attention to the intern's experience, it was also noted earlier that interns need supportive, affirming, and empathic supervisors. A supervisor who focuses exclusively on Socratic or other forms of questioning might not readily communicate the support and understanding interns need. The role of empathy in supervision has been studied empirically by Shanfield et al. (1992) who used a structured inventory to evaluate supervisor performance during videotaped supervisory sessions. Results of this research showed that the factors most closely related to ratings of supervisor excellence were the supervisor's empathy and attention to the immediate concerns and experience of the interns. By comparison, supervisors who intellectualized and offered general elaboration with little attention to intern concerns were rated as "low" in their facilitation of trainee learning. Shanfield et al. noted that their study was based on observational ratings and did not include assessment by the supervisors or interns themselves. Nevertheless, the fact that the ratings of the observers, who were all highly experienced supervisors, yielded such strong relationships between empathy and excellence in supervision, attests to the importance of supervisor

empathy. This finding is also wholly consistent with the previously discussed results of surveys of supervisee preferences for supervisors and with studies of the processes supervisees find most important at different stages of training (Rabinowitz, Heppner & Roehlke, 1986).

In light of research on the role of empathy in supervision, if an intern is working with a supervisor who does not provide the kinds of support the intern needs, the intern might consider telling this to the supervisor. The intern might also want to express this to the instructor or internship class. In many cases, supervisors may not be aware that they are not offering the needed support and this feedback is likely to be welcomed. As in any situation in which constructive feedback is offered, the intern would be well advised to offer suggestions about supervisory style in a positive rather than critical manner.

One final thought on this subject; just as it can be a mistake for questions to predominate in a supervisory interaction, it is generally advisable to use questions sparingly in treatment interactions. Beginning interns are often prone to asking too many questions of clients in an effort to "solve" the client's problems. If a supervisor establishes a model of supervision through questioning, interns might be inclined to emulate that approach in their therapy. This is inadvisable because, much as interns need support and affirmation, clients also need more than just questions to experience therapeutic gains. This principle might not be modeled well in questioning-based supervision. As Lambert and Beier (1974) reported, when supervisors are acting as counselors they tend to offer more empathic statements than when they are interacting with interns. Interns and supervisors should keep this in mind and recognize that the supervisory process is not necessarily an ideal model for therapy, but certain therapeutic principles definitely have a place in supervision.

TAPES AND ROLE PLAYS

Chapter 4 discussed the use of tapes and role plays during internship classes. If you have not read that chapter or section you may wish to peruse it now because it contains suggestions for how to use tapes and role plays most effectively. Since most of what was said in that chapter also applies to supervision, only a few of the key suggestions are reviewed here. For an interesting review of how tape recording came to be used in therapy research and supervision, see Hill and Corbett (1993).

Perhaps the most important suggestion for using tapes is to select sessions in which you felt good about your work and sessions in which you felt confused or ineffective (Ronnestad & Skovholt, 1993). The successful sessions can help build your confidence and can also provide opportunities to identify what went well and why. On the other hand, less successful sessions should also be reviewed in supervision so you can learn from your mistakes and expand your skills. If there is some reason why you do not feel comfortable revealing sessions in which your performance was not ideal, that feeling itself is worth exploring. You may want to consider the comments later in this chapter regarding how to deal with conflicts in supervision. If something can be done to increase your comfort in exploring weaknesses with your supervisor, I encourage you to do so. Unless you are free, encouraged, and safe to reveal both strengths and weaknesses, your opportunities for learning and development will be markedly reduced.

With regard to role plays and supervision, the previous chapter mentioned the importance of becoming deeply involved in the imagined role and situation. Interns may find this difficult in the context of supervision because the evaluative element of interacting with a supervisor can interfere with the ability to be open and involved. Much as you are encouraged to deal with issues concerning sharing of taped sessions, if your supervisor uses role play techniques in supervision and you feel restricted by the evaluative component, talk about your experience with the supervisor. This may help bring out underlying issues relating to your dual roles of supervisor-evaluator and intern-student. Understanding your own difficulties in role playing with a supervisor may also help you understand your clients in new ways. Students or supervisors who are interested in research on role plays in supervision may wish to consult Akamatsu's (1980) review of the subject.

LIVE SUPERVISION

As useful as recorded sessions and role plays can be, there is no substitute for directly observing therapy sessions. Several arrangements can be used for observing treatment (Bubenzer, West & Gold, 1991). One way is for the supervisor to be physically present in the room with the trainee. Another possibility involves the use of special observation rooms equipped with one way mirrors. These allow supervisors to remain unseen behind the glass as they watch and listen to therapy sessions.

By observing sessions as they occur, supervisors get a better sense of the process of treatment sessions. They can listen to what is said, watch the nonverbal behaviors of the trainee and client, note key moments in the session, and get a deeper awareness of the overall "feel" of the interactions. In some arrangements, supervisors can also instruct the trainee during the interaction. Using a technique known as the "bug in the ear," supervisors observe the session from behind a mirror and can speak to trainees through a microphone connected to tiny earplug-type speakers (Gallant, Thyer & Bailey, 1991; Gallant & Thyer, 1989). This enables supervisors to accomplish several things. For example, a supervisor can call the trainee's attention to certain behaviors or statements of the client. The supervisor might also point out the trainee's own behaviors or suggest specific things the trainee should say or do.

Direct observation can be one of the best ways for interns to learn therapy, but there are also some drawbacks to this process. Perhaps the greatest potential problem is that many interns, who already feel anxious about the role of therapist, are now placed simultaneously in the role of therapist and student (Costa, 1995). Friedlander et al.(1986) commented on the role conflict that can result for interns who are at the same time in the "subordinate" role of trainee and the "superordinate" role of therapist. This conflict can become acute when the intern receives instructions from a supervisor that contradict the intern's own sense of what should happen in therapy. One can imagine how this can play out when the bug-in-the-ear technique is used. If an intern is thinking about responding in a certain way but then is told through the bug to do something different, the intern must deal with the internal conflict while outwardly maintaining a composed demeanor for the client.

Because direct observation poses such problems, it is helpful for supervisors and interns to establish an agreement about how directly observed sessions will proceed. This agreement should clarify such things as what the expectations and goals for the therapy session are, when or if a supervisor will intervene, whether the intern is expected to follow unconditionally the supervisor's lead or is allowed some discretion, and what the process of debriefing after the session will entail.

My own preference is to give interns a great deal of leeway and freedom to follow their own instincts. It is especially important, as Gallant and Thyer (1989) emphasized, for supervisors to keep in mind that they are teaching the interns, not doing the therapy itself. Thus, although I occasionally offer suggestions, the intern is generally free to choose what to do. It is, however, essential to establish an agreed upon signal that tells the intern if I have identified something important and they must follow my lead. This is used only rarely, but it is vital that the intern understand and respect the importance of this option. If, for example, the supervisor detects an issue of particular sensitivity, or if there is a possibility of significant risk, the intern must trust the supervisor's judgment and save explanations for later. As noted earlier, the supervisor is ultimately responsible for the treatment and interns must respect that responsibility. It simply does not do for the intern and supervisor to get into a conflict during the session. This is particularly true if important issues are at stake in the client's treatment.

One additional comment applies not only to direct observation but to all forms of observing therapy. It is always easier for the observer to pick things up than it is for the therapist. This means supervisors must be patient and not overly critical with interns if the supervisor detects something in therapy that the intern may have missed. Calling things to the intern's attention is certainly useful, but the purpose must be to help educate the trainee, not to make the supervisor look good. The same principle applies when interns observe the work or are reviewing tapes of other interns.

OBSERVING THE SUPERVISOR IN THERAPY

Studies in which interns have been asked what their supervisors might have done differently have revealed that many interns desire more opportunities to observe their supervisor in clinical work (Gandolfo & Brown, 1987). Interns recognize that discussion about their own work can only take them so far. They also feel they can learn a great deal when they can watch their supervisor in group or individual sessions, read reports written by the supervisor, and observe the supervisor in other actions such as staff meetings, conferences, etc. One way to accomplish this is for the supervisor and intern to work jointly as cotherapists with clients. This is most commonly practiced in group or couples therapy but it can also be used with individual clients.

If cotherapy is arranged, the same caveats described for observation techniques must be addressed. The supervisor and intern should agree upon who will be the "primary" therapist and how to signal the intern if the supervisor needs to take the lead. It is also important to discuss the sessions afterwards to explore what happened and share impressions of the interaction.

Although most supervisors are open to cotherapy if it meets with the needs of clients, many are not aware that interns would like such an opportunity. As a result, interns may need to ask if they can observe the supervisors in different settings. If this sounds obvious, it is, but often we neglect to do the obvious because no one thinks to ask.

EXERCISE

Because many interns do not realize they can take the initiative to suggest learning opportunities that might be useful, take a few moments to think of what opportunities your internship is providing and what additional experiences you might find interesting. In relation to supervision, if you had the opportunity to observe your supervisor in different aspects of clinical work, what would benefit you the most to observe? In order to better understand your supervisor's perspective, now ask yourself if you were a supervisor being observed by an intern, what concerns might you have? Having considered these issues, you may want to speak with your supervisor directly about the kinds of learning experiences or opportunities for observation that you would find most helpful.

THEORETICAL ORIENTATION

Whatever the content or style of supervision, there are several major themes that have the potential to create conflict. One of the most common sources of confusion and conflict between interns and supervisors has to do with differences in theoretical orientation. Theoretical issues can be dealt with in many ways, but three of the most common approaches are:

A. The supervisor believes a particular theoretical and technical approach to therapy or assessment is best so the intern must learn, practice, and demonstrate knowledge and skill in that approach. Often, there is an accompanying expectation that the intern must also demonstrate a personal commitment to the approach and the philosophy or research that underlies it.

B. The supervisor has studied or developed an approach to therapy or assessment that works for him or her, and the intern is welcome to learn from what the supervisor has to offer. The intern may choose to use the techniques or theoretical perspectives, but that is his or her choice.

C. Because the supervisor believes no one knows what is best, the intern is free to try any approach to see how it works. The supervisor is available to help out if needed.

The advantage of the first approach, i.e., training under a supervisor who adheres strictly to a single orientation and expects interns to do the same, derives from the clarity of focus such training provides. Faced with many different schools and techniques of therapy or assessment, interns sometimes feel at a loss to know how to proceed. By choosing a single orientation and associated techniques, the intern can gain a sense of security in that approach. This basis can then give the intern enough confidence to pursue the chosen approach further or to explore other approaches.

Focusing on a single approach also has advantages for supervisors. No one can be expert in all things and many supervisors feel the best they can offer interns is to teach the approach the supervisor knows best. If interns have opportunities to train under different supervisors, and if each supervisor focuses on a single approach, the interns will be able to sample different approaches from supervisors who specialize in them. This is likely to give a much clearer impression of the different approaches than if each supervisor tries to teach from many different perspectives.

There are two main drawbacks to focusing on a single approach to treatment or assessment. The first is that if the supervisor's approach does not match well with the intern, there is a potential for conflict that will interfere with the learning experience. The potential for conflict is likely to be heightened if the supervisor demands not only knowledge and technical proficiency but "faith" in the theory as well. It is one thing to ask an intern to understand and be skilled in an approach. It is quite another to expect the intern to uncritically share the supervisor's commitment. I have encountered supervisors who judge interns more by their "belief" in the supervisor's model than on the intern's knowledge and skill. The reasoning in such instances has apparently been that the supervisor is certain his or her approach is superior, so any interns who are really worth their salt will also recognize the superiority of the supervisor's chosen model. For interns who are not as sold on the model or who also want to gain experience in other approaches, this attitude among supervisors can be quite detrimental.

The second problem with this model of supervision is that when a single approach is emphasized, interns sometimes develop the idea that the approach they are studying is superior to all others or works for all clients and all problems. This process of endorsing one approach to the exclusion of others may be part of interns' struggles to develop professional identity, but it is also possible for interns to find an identity in ways that keep them open to new learning and do not depend on denigrating others or exaggerating claims for one's own preferences.

The issue of teaching a single therapy or assessment approach to the exclusion of others is not simply a matter of personal preference. In their review of ethical issues of supervising counselors, Kurpius et al. (1991) point out that standard H10 of the AACD ethical standards states,

> members must present thoroughly varied theoretical positions so that students may make comparisons and have the opportunity to select a position. (p. 8)

Kurpius et al. also point to empirical evidence (Allen, Szollos & Williams, 1986) suggesting that good supervisors respect differences in values and experience and encourage experimentation with novel strategies.

An alternative to emphasizing a single therapy approach is for the supervisor to present interns with one or more models but allow the interns to experiment and choose what works best for them. This avoids some of the pitfalls just described but it also carries certain problems. For the intern who is searching for direction, the lack of clearly defined models can be frustrating. This is particularly likely if the intern has had relatively little prior training or experience and, hence, does not have a personal basis from which to begin to try things out independently. This model also poses problems for interns who are intentionally seeking training in a specific theory or technique of therapy or assessment. A supervisor who does not provide a well-defined model may not be able to meet the intern's desires for training.

The supervisor who operates under this model may feel that being tolerant allows the intern freedom to explore, but the intern may need more structure or may have freely decided to focus very intently on a single approach and may want to be trained by a supervisor who firmly believes in that approach. When this situation arises in supervision, the supervisor and intern should discuss it together. Fruitful topics of such discussions might include the intern's legitimate need for guidance or a wish to gain focused supervision from a committed role model. Other useful subjects might be the reasons why people, including interns and supervisors, need structure, and the consequences of imposing artificial structures on inherently ambiguous processes.

The principal advantage of this model is that it reduces the problem of ideological conflicts and allows the supervisor and intern to focus more on skills and less on adherence to a fixed philosophy. This approach also tends to facilitate more discussion of the relative pros and cons of different interventions. The intern who does not feel pressured to adopt a specific perspective is more free to question, experiment, and learn through experience. The supervisor's responsibility in this approach is to be present for the interns as they explore and experiment and to reassure interns that one can do effective work in a variety of ways.

In my experience, the third model, in which the supervisor takes a laissez-faire approach to training, is generally the least preferred of the three. With the exception of interns who have a great deal of experience and training, most interns need more structure and direction than a laissez-faire supervisor provides. In contrast to the problems posed by the potential for excessive dogmatism in the first approach described, the completely open supervision model suffers from the reverse difficulty. It is an exceptionally rare intern who will receive optimum benefit without at least some structure and model to work from. Whether or not the intern and supervisor agree or disagree on theory or technique, interns are usually helped by having supervisors who can articulate and demonstrate a coherent approach to treatment or assessment.

Supervisors who follow the more open approach may contend that it has advantages that outweigh any potential drawbacks. Perhaps the primary advantage is that it lets the intern learn by discovery rather than by following fixed rules. This requires the intern to think independently about what treatment or assessment should entail. A second advantage to not giving a specific model is that potential conflicts about theory and technique may be reduced. If a supervisor is truly open to allowing interns to experiment with different methods and to discover what works, there is less potential to impose the supervisor's own biases on the intern.

Whichever approach your supervisor adapts, you should consider the pros and cons of that approach as it relates to your own needs, the supervisor, and the setting. As noted before, different interns will have different needs and a supervisor who is ideal for one intern may not match at all with another. Do your best to understand the reasons for a supervisor's theoretical and supervisory approach and be willing to try new approaches whether or not you agree with them. At various times in my own training I believed certain therapy models were complete bunk until I had the opportunity to observe them and discovered that they had valuable lessons to offer.

SUPERVISION AND THERAPY—DIFFERENCES AND SIMILARITIES

Because clinical work and the internship experience can evoke deeply personal and often difficult material for interns, clinical supervisors must not only help interns acquire specific skills, they must also help interns manage the emotional and intellectual challenges and the personal issues that emerge in their training. This responsibility may place supervisors in a role that is very much like that of therapist for the trainee. This similarity of roles and processes is sometimes referred to as "parallel process" (Searles, 1955; Ekstein & Wallerstein, 1972) and has been described by Rubinstein (1992), Hebert (1992), Schneider (1992), Burns and Holloway (1989), and others.

While recognizing similarities between therapy and supervision, many of the authors just cited also acknowledge that interns did not sign up for their internship as clients and they have a right to work personal issues out on their own. Thus, for both supervisor and intern there is a dilemma about how to deal with the intern's personal issues. This dilemma becomes particularly acute if an intern's personal issues begin to interfere with the intern's clinical work or development (Bradley & Post, 1991; Lamb et al., 1987; Stadler et al., 1988).

DIFFERENCES BETWEEN THERAPY AND SUPERVISION

Among the more important differences between therapy and supervision are: the degree of choice involved in receiving therapy or supervision, the purpose and goals of therapy versus supervision, the role of the trainee as compared to client, the role of supervisor as compared to therapist, and the evaluative function of supervisors.

In therapy, clients have made a conscious decision to seek assistance with personal issues. They also have freedom in choosing who will be their therapist and under what conditions the therapy will take place. By comparison, interns are often required to receive supervision as part of their education and training. They may or may not have a say in who their supervisor will be but they are very likely not to have any say in whether or not they will receive supervision.

Thus, from the outset, consent and choice are two fundamental differences distinguishing the therapy process from supervision. One is voluntary and can be terminated at any time at the client's discretion. The other is essentially involuntary (unless a trainee wants to risk expulsion from the training program) and generally cannot be terminated without the risk of substantial consequences.

Another key difference between therapy and supervision is found in the purpose of the activity. Clients seek therapy primarily because they want to be helped personally in some way by the therapy. By comparison, as Wise, Lowery, and Silverglade (1989) have noted, when it is required by training programs, supervision of therapists is mandated not so much to help the therapist as to "protect the welfare of the client. . .". Wise et al. go on to say that ". . . this purpose precludes making the counselor's personal growth a primary focus" (p. 327). Such conclusions do not mean that trainees cannot grow as individuals through the process of supervision. They do, however, suggest that the supervisee's personal growth is not the primary goal of many supervision arrangements, particularly those that are required as part of training programs.

Closely related to the issues of choice and the purpose of therapy and supervision is the matter of dual roles for supervisors who would also engage in therapy with trainees. Because supervisors must perform many different functions with trainees, including teaching, mentoring, supporting, and, of critical importance here, evaluation, their position in relation to the trainee differs markedly from that of the therapist in relation to a client. Interestingly, several researchers have noted that although students are well aware of power differentials between themselves and their supervisors, supervisors may be relatively unaware of this issue (Kadushin, 1974; Doehrman, 1976).

A therapist may form positive or critical opinions about clients but, apart from certain institutional settings or extreme circumstances, the therapist is not in a position to take actions that would substantially impact the client's future outside of therapy. This is not the case for supervisees. Supervisors may well hold the key to the supervisee's professional future. The "key" metaphor has been underscored by Rubinstein, who stressed the importance of considering the context of supervision and the power of supervisors to influence the intern's future. Citing Berman (1988), Rubinstein drew a comparison between supervision and "total institutions" and suggested that supervisors who neglect the evaluative context run the risk of replicating

> the tendency of therapists working in total institutions to interpret the fears and suspicions of clients regarding intervention in their lives as transference feelings. (Rubinstein, 1992, p. 114)

The point of this comparison is that the evaluative power of a supervisor is comparable to that of therapists who determine whether or not patients or inmates are ready to be released from institutions. In the face of that power, interns may have good reason to choose information carefully and not be fully honest with their supervisors. Because the dual nature of supervisory and therapy relationships would create such dilemmas, Burns and Holloway (1989) state directly that,

> Although supervisors provide facilitative instructional environments, in their role as evaluators, they ethically cannot undertake counseling relationships with their trainees. (p. 48)

Similar ethical concerns have been voiced by Wise et al. (1989) and by Kurpius et al. (1991), who advised:

To be sensitive to the dual relationship issue, the promotion of the supervisee's self-exploration during supervision sessions would focus primarily on his or her interaction with the client and should not extend beyond raising awareness about the supervisee's helpfulness to the client. (p. 52)

However well-intentioned a supervisor might be, the inherent power differential between supervisor and trainee can cause trainees to be in, as Rubinstein phrased it, "permanent distress concerning the selection of contents through which they are to communicate with their supervisor" (Rubinstein, 1992, p. 110). One manifestation of this distress was a student-drafted "bill of rights" described by Haley (1976), which stated that teachers were not to investigate students' personal lives unless the teacher could demonstrate the relevance of the exploration to the therapy task and could show how the personal exploration would help change the therapist's behavior in a positive direction.

As the discussion above has demonstrated, there are a number of critical differences between therapy and supervision and it is essential for both supervisors and interns to be cognizant of these differences. Along with this list of differences, Rubinstein (1992) has also emphasized that most discussions of therapy and supervision similarities emphasize concepts from psychodynamic theories. Those concepts do not necessarily apply as well to supervision in behavioral and other less dynamically based approaches.

Keeping in mind the differences between supervision and therapy and the differences across different approaches to therapy, there remain certain conditions that are common to virtually all supervision and that have important similarities to the therapy process. Because these intrinsic conditions cannot be avoided, interns and supervisors need to be familiar with them and learn to recognize and understand how they influence the supervisory relationship and process.

EXPLORING THE NEEDS AND PERSONAL QUALITIES OF INTERNS

In a paper describing the importance of intern self-awareness, Hebert (1992) wrote:

> . . . becoming an effective counselor revolves around the need for interns to understand their presentation of self. An understanding of their needs, defenses, their favorite coping devices, and their psychological predispositions is crucial for providing effective professional services. (p. 124)

Of the many reasons for interns to be aware of their own needs, two stand out most prominently. First, insofar as the therapist's self is "a therapeutic instrument" (Hebert, 1992, p. 131) it is necessary for the therapist to understand and be able to adapt the instrument, i.e. the self, as needed to assist the client. Second, if therapists are not aware of their own needs, they are more likely to use the therapy session to satisfy those needs, sometimes at the expense of the client. Two common

needs that Hebert sees as affecting most interns are "the need to please and the need to allay self doubt" (p. 125).

If self-awareness is so important to therapists, and if lack of self-awareness can lead to trainees using therapy to satisfy their needs, how is a supervisor to promote self-awareness without serving as a therapist for the trainee? Hebert advocates self-examination on the part of interns. The goals of this self-examination are to increase the interns' awareness of such things as sources of their anxieties, the struggle between wanting to change and wanting to stay the same, stimuli that trigger tendencies toward self-blame, authoritarian posturing, and other characteristics that could influence therapy.

Although Hebert stresses the role of self-examination, he maintains that this examination should also involve the supervisor. Describing the responsibility of the supervisor, he states,

> The supervisor must show confidence in the intern's ability to change. Interns are attempting to accomplish a very difficult task and thus deserve the supervisor's respect. The change will occur in a supportive/challenging ethos that will impede the intern from utilizing exploitative maneuvers.

Hebert's description of the supervisor's role sounds not unlike descriptions of the therapist's role and the necessary ingredients for helping relationships (cf. Rogers, 1961, pp. 50–57). Thus, although it is apparent from his writing that Hebert is keenly aware of the vulnerable position of trainees vis à vis their supervisors, he sees the task of self-awareness as primary to the development of therapists. He concludes by saying:

> . . . it is the intern's self that all ingredients are filtered through. To avoid that filter is to risk the training of a counselor who is oblivious to his/her own exploitative tendencies. (Hebert, 1992, p. 131)

EXERCISE

This exercise has two parts. The first part asks you to explore any reactions you may have had to the ideas that have just been presented regarding supervision and therapy. Do you think it is important to explore the needs and "self" of the therapist? Do you have any hesitations or concerns about this process for yourself? What would your reaction be to addressing these issues in supervision and how would you like your supervisor to deal with this issue?

The second part of the exercise involves trying to identify any personal needs you are aware of that, if not managed well, could impede your functioning as a therapist. For example, you might consider such things as your own needs for affection, approval, power, etc., and ways in wihch these needs could influence your actions as a therapist. After thinking about these issues for yourself, you may wish to discuss them with a peer or perhaps with your instructor or supervisor.

RESISTANCE TO SELF-AWARENESS AND CHANGE

Recognizing the importance of self-awareness to therapy training and supervision, it should not be surprising that some of the same processes that accompany self-awareness and change in therapy also emerge in the supervisory process. At least three types of resistance stand out in supervision. The first, resistance to awareness, relates closely to the preceding discussion of interns' needs. Resistance to awareness refers to the challenges associated with becoming aware of personal qualities or needs that are not easily acknowledged or owned.

> In learning about human behavior we are learning about ourselves, about our defenses, our motives, our unflattering impulses. In dispassionately examining the sources of our most cherished attitudes and illusions, we are throwing open to question the way in which we order our lives. (Kadushin, 1985, p. 237)

Resistance to this process is perfectly understandable and is probably to be expected of most trainees. Hebert described this process well by acknowledging that:

> This is a predictable and altogether acceptable defensive response. All human beings make efforts to perpetuate some fiction about themselves and others. (Hebert, 1992, p. 129)

In spite of the apparent inevitability of self-awareness stress and accompanying resistance, supervisors and training programs often devote relatively little attention to helping trainees cope with the process effectively. This was documented by May and Kilpatrick (1989) who surveyed social-work programs and concluded that, "A large majority of schools agreed that preparation of MSW students for this stress is the schools' responsibility, but little is being done about it in a formal way" (p. 316). Although these authors focused on social-work programs, a similar conclusion would almost certainly emerge if one surveyed psychology, counseling, or other similar programs.

A second source of resistance has to do with the reality that in order to learn one must confess ignorance of what is to be learned. This is not easy for anyone and it can be especially difficult for students who feel their competence is being tested at every turn. Kadushin (1985) described this dilemma particularly well:

> The learning situation demands an admission of ignorance, however limited. In admitting ignorance, supervisees expose their vulnerability. They risk the possibility of criticism, of

shame and perhaps rejection because of an admitted inadequacy.

> Supervisees have the choice of being anxious because they do not know how to do their work or being anxious about confessing ignorance and obtaining help. (p. 238)

Because this paradoxical situation is inherent in the learning process, it can be very difficult for interns to resolve on their own. As such, it is extremely important for supervisors to be sensitive to it and make every effort to allow interns to acknowledge their limitations in order to make learning possible. At the same time, interns should resolve that it is better to risk acknowledging their limitations than to feign knowledge at the possible risk of harming clients or the agency.

A third source of resistance in supervision is resistance to change. In a review of this and other topics in supervision, Rubinstein (1992) paraphrases similar comments by Kadushin (1985) and Rothman (1973) and explains that:

> . . . change requires giving up old behavior patterns, which have helped the supervisee keep homeostasis in his or her personal life. Hence, a change of this kind evokes anxiety in supervisees, who are not sure they wish to change what has taken them so much time to learn. . . . (Rubinstein, 1992, p. 99)

When it appears that interns resist trying, learning, or sometimes even considering certain issues or techniques of therapy, the resistance is often because they feel that their established ways of being and doing things as people are being threatened. Although the overt content of the verbal defense may be couched in language about what is good for the client, the source of the resistance is often found in the intern's need to defend what has worked well for him or her as an individual or as a therapist.

An example of this process comes from my own experience in the early stages of training. At that time I was very resistant to "reflective" techniques in therapy. Although I wanted to develop the skills of therapy I was intent on not "sounding like a therapist." This desire gained support in my first practicum placement, in which the clinical staff followed a treatment model that was not at all consistent with the reflective approach. That same semester, during a classroom role play exercise in which students were to practice reflective techniques, I offered verbal protest but "went along" with the exercise at the insistence of the instructor. After the exercise I remained unimpressed with the technique but the instructor patiently suggested that we review a tape of the role play to identify which kinds of statements had elicited the most response from the client. Much to my surprise, the tape revealed that the reflective statements, which I had been so critical of before, turned out to have produced the most extensive and useful exploration for the client. Along with demonstrating the potential of reflective techniques, this experience showed how resistance to a technique can sometimes reflect our own desires to meet personal beliefs or needs more than actual knowledge about what does or does not help clients.

A somewhat different, though undoubtedly related, interpretation of resistance was described by Kadushin (1985). In a particularly thought-provoking discussion, Kadushin suggested that change can create a sense of betrayal because the supervisee is being asked to give up behaviors or ways of thinking that were learned from parents and other significant people in the supervisee's past.

> The ideas and behavior that might need changing represent, in a measure, the introjection of previously encountered significant others—parents, teachers, highly valued peers—and the acceptance of other models implies some rejection of these people. The act of infidelity creates anxiety. (p 237)

In these circumstances, resistance may take the form of arguing that a given concept or technique will or will not help clients, but the underlying issue is that accepting the new idea or approach carries with it the implication that one's parents or other role models were somehow "wrong." That possibility is resisted because, if it were accepted it would introduce a host of other issues and anxieties with which most trainees are ill equipped to cope.

As the discussion thus far should demonstrate, resistance is a fact of life in supervision. How, then, can supervisors and supervisees deal with resistance most effectively?

In my own thinking about this subject, several principles have been very helpful. First, resistance to awareness and change should not be confused with legitimate self-protection deriving from the situational context of supervision. Students who appear to resist self-exploration may be seeking to avoid self-awareness, or they may be protecting their privacy against an unwanted and potentially damaging intrusion by their supervisor. As Rubinstein pointed out, one must be careful not to assign attributions without carefully considering the situation in which the behavior occurs. Before assigning a student's behaviors to resistance, supervisors would be well advised to consider how their own behaviors as supervisors might be contributing to the student's apparent resistance. Supervisors should also realize that, just as interns may resist self-awareness, supervisors are not always the best judges of their own behavior. Seeking an outside consult can sometimes help supervisors become more aware of their actions. Asking the supervisees themselves can also be helpful, but it must be remembered that in extreme situations the very factors that lead to apparent resistance might inhibit genuine feedback about the supervisor's behaviors.

Just as supervisors should be aware of how their actions might induce resistance in students, attention should also be given to what supervisors can do to help students work through their resistance to achieve greater self-awareness and growth. The first step in this process is to help students understand the concept of resistance, its effects, and some of the possible manifestations. It may help to tell students directly that if they are to develop their skills they will have to develop self-awareness and change certain behaviors and this process is not always easy. It follows, therefore, that students will have to deal with resistance. Supervisors can then facilitate this process by acknowledging both its importance and the difficulty involved. Supervisors should also create safe and supportive environments that allow and encourage students to consciously express, identify, and explore their own resistance.

One final and extremely important point about resistance in supervision is that it provides a wonderful learning opportunity for interns to understand something of what the process of change is like for clients. Studying concepts in the abstract is never quite as meaningful as experiencing them firsthand. If interns have the opportunity to become aware of their own resistance in the course of supervision, that awareness may help them appreciate and honor the resistance client's display in therapy. Lacking such firsthand experience of their own resistance, interns tend to respond to client resistance as something that "interferes with therapy" or that shows clients to be "unmotivated." By comparison, after displaying and acknowledging resistance themselves, interns are more likely to go beyond the simplistic interpretation and appreciate resistance not as an obstacle to therapy but as a normal and important part of the therapy process.

EXERCISE

Considering the three types of resistance identified above (i.e., resistance to awareness, to revealing ignorance, and to change), think about your education and training up to this point and try to identify instances in which you may have responded with each type of resistance. Next, give some thought to the future and try to imagine situations that could evoke such reactions. Finally, because all of us are likely to show resistance in some areas, what matters most is that we learn to recognize and cope with the resistance productively. As you think of what might evoke resistance and how you would recognize resistance in yourself, give some thought to how you could learn to understand your resistance and be able to work with that resistance to allow yourself to change.

TRANSFERENCE AND COUNTERTRANSFERENCE

In much the same way as resistance in supervision parallels resistance in therapy, transference and countertransference can also be seen in both therapy and supervision. These terms, which have their origins in psychoanalytic approaches, have been defined in various ways by different authors (Schneider, 1992). For our purposes, it is enough to understand transference as a process in which clients, or in the case of supervision, supervisees, "replace" some other, typically earlier, person in their lives with the person of the therapist or supervisor, relating to the latter individuals in ways that are similar to their relationship with the original persons. For example, students may relate to supervisors much as they related to parents or other authority figures in their lives. If students happen to be older than their supervisors, it can also happen that the student will relate to the supervisors as they may to one of their own children.

Countertransference is somewhat the reverse of transference. Instead of the client relating to the therapist as if they were someone else, in the case of countertransference it is the therapist (supervisor) who relates to the client (supervisee) as if they were someone else. An example of this might be observed in a supervisor relating to a trainee as if the trainee were one of the supervisor's children or clients.

According to psychoanalytic explanations, both transference and countertransference take place unconsciously and are expressed behaviorally and emotionally. Schneider explains that, in supervision, "The supervisor, just by virtue of his/her serving as an authority figure, allows a transference relationship to develop and grow." (Schneider, 1992, p. 73).

As explained in regard to resistance, understanding transference and countertransference in supervision can help interns make the most out of supervision and gain greater awareness of processes they are likely to observe and experience in therapy. Recognizing and exploring transference reactions in supervision can also help interns develop greater self-understanding, which is critical to the therapist's development.

EXERCISE

Although transference is conceived to be largely an unconscious process, each of us has certain individuals in our lives who have represented authority figures in the past. Parents are perhaps the most likely to have filled this role, but others, such as older siblings, relatives, friends, or teachers could also provide such figures. The point of this exercise is not to circumvent the transference by dealing with it before it arises. Rather, it is to introduce a process of reflection and an understanding of transference that may be useful if or when transference does occur in supervision or therapy. To help you understand how transference might affect your own experiences with supervisors, consider this question: If you were to anticipate a transference reaction toward a supervisor based on someone from your own past, who would the most likely person be? Why?

SUGGESTED GUIDELINES REGARDING THERAPY AND SUPERVISION

Having explored some of the similarities and differences between therapy and supervision, we have seen that it is not easy to provide absolute demarcation between the two activities. On the one hand, as part of the training process, it is important for trainees to explore personal needs and dynamics in order to understand how these might influence their work with clients. On the other hand, trainees are in a vulnerable position relative to supervisors and they should have a right to choose how much personal information they wish to disclose.

Without expecting to resolve this issue completely, a number of authors refer to criteria that can help determine when or if the fine line between therapy and supervision has been crossed. The core of this criterion is the purpose of the activity in question. Burns and Holloway (1990) concluded their review of the topic by stating:

> . . . it might be entirely appropriate to use counseling skills (such as facilitative conditions) when the intent is to enhance trainee's understanding of their own reactions, behaviors and attitudes toward the client. However, it may not be appropriate to use such techniques with the intent to solely affect counselor change outside of the counseling role. (p. 56)

In his discussion of the importance of intern's personal needs, Hebert (1992) established a comparable criterion by asserting that

> . . . psychotherapeutic efforts may coexist as long as the focus is upon the relevance that various intern personal characteristics have for their work with clients. As long as the emphasis is continuously placed upon the impact of an intern's presentation of self upon therapeutic efforts, that in itself should serve to mitigate its moving into the realm of psychotherapy. (p. 124)

The theme that is common to these statements is that the focus of supervision must remain on the intern's actions in therapy. As long as their actions do not violate ethical standards, what trainees do outside of therapy is not the concern of supervisors and should be left for the trainees to address on their own.

In my work with interns, I find that personal issues relating to an intern's clinical work can and sometimes should be identified by supervisors but the process of working through those issues should best be left for therapy with someone other than the supervisor. I encourage interns to consider personal therapy as a valuable experience in itself and as an important, perhaps essential, step toward professional development. The benefits of individual therapy will very likely carry over to the intern's clinical work and to supervision, but the supervisory work will not be confounded by the dual roles of supervisor/therapist or intern/client.

If an intern has access to a therapist, issues that arise in the intern's clinical work or supervisory relationship can be addressed in therapy. However, the goal of therapy should be to facilitate the intern's personal growth, not to serve as an opportunity to vent frustrations or second guess supervisors. For useful suggestions regarding personal counseling for interns as it relates to supervision issues and level of training, see Wise, Lowery, and Silverglade (1989). Later in this book, the stresses of clinical work are addressed in Chapter 9 and personal therapy is discussed in greater detail in Chapter 10.

EXERCISE

What are your personal attitudes toward seeking therapy or counseling for yourself? If you or your supervisor detect personal issues that are affecting your clinical work or training, would you be amenable to seeking therapy? If not, what are your concerns? What would the relative risks and benefits be if your supervisor began also to function as a therapist for you? How could you respond if you felt a supervisor was in some way stepping into the role of therapist and you were not comfortable with that?

CONFLICT IN SUPERVISION

FREQUENCY AND RESOLUTION OF CONFLICTS

Although most trainees have positive supervisory experiences, conflicts that interfere with learning are not uncommon. Moskowitz and Rupert (1983) surveyed 158 graduate students in clinical psychology and found that 38 percent reported major conflict that made it difficult to learn from supervision. The three areas of conflict most identified by students were: theoretical orientation and therapy approach, style of supervision, and personality issues. Each of these issues has been addressed already in this chapter, but the results of the Moskowitz and Rupert study provide useful information about different ways and results of dealing with conflict.

One of the most interesting findings of this research was that all of the trainees who responded indicated that when conflict was present they wanted the supervisor to identify it openly. In spite of the interns' desires, 83.8 percent of those who had experienced conflicts reported that the trainees, not their supervisors, had initiated discussion about the conflict. This finding suggests that if you experience a conflict in supervision and think it should be dealt with, you, the trainee, may have to be the one who raises the issue. It might also be helpful to indicate at the beginning of your internship that you hope any conflicts will be dealt with openly. This may not guarantee that a supervisor would initiate discussion of conflict, but at least it expresses your position up front.

With regard to resolution of conflicts, Moskowitz and Rupert's findings reveal that outcomes relate significantly to the nature of the conflict. Overall, more than half of those who experienced conflict and discussed it with their supervisors reported that the discussion lead to at least some improvement. However, 37 percent of the students who discussed conflicts indicated that there was no improvement or that the situation became worse. The most successfully resolved conflicts were those relating to supervisory style. In

90 percent of these cases discussion led to improvement; in none of the reported cases did conditions worsen following discussion. Conflicts relating to theoretical orientation also showed improvement with discussion, but the effect, 55 percent improvement, was less than with supervisory style. The most difficult conflicts to resolve related to personality issues, with only 36 percent of these showing improvement and 37 percent indicating that the situation became worse or led to a change in supervisors.

In addition to describing the outcomes of cases in which conflicts were discussed, Moskowitz and Rupert also note that although most students chose to discuss conflicts directly, 23 percent opted not to discuss the conflict. Students who did not discuss conflicts explained that they feared discussion might worsen the problem or lead to the student being blamed or negatively evaluated by the supervisor. In lieu of dealing directly with supervisors, this group of students indicated that they sought support from peers or from other staff members.

Two positive findings emerge from this research and should be emphasized. First, most interns do not report significant conflicts with supervisors. Second, most conflicts relating to supervisory style or theoretical orientation can be successfully resolved through discussion. At the same time, however, it must also be recognized that conflicts between supervisor and trainee are by no means infrequent and discussion of the conflicts does not always lead to improvement.

GUIDELINES FOR DEALING WITH CONFLICT

Because conflicts in supervision are not uncommon, several principles may help interns and supervisors deal with conflict more effectively. The first principle is to approach conflicts as opportunities for learning rather than situations that interfere with learning. In the process of managing a supervisory conflict, you may be able to discover such things as how you react to conflict, what kinds of issues or interactions tend to promote conflict, and how you can more effectively cope with conflicts. In raising these possibilities, the intent is not to offer the simplistic aphorism that "everything is a learning experience," nor do I want to suggest, as one supervisor was fond of telling interns, "conflict builds character." I do, however, want to suggest that one of the biggest blocks to resolving conflicts is the underlying idea that "conflicts should not happen and I should not have to deal with this." If you take an attitude of learning from a conflict, rather than an attitude of anger, fear, or avoidance, you are more likely to deal effectively with the situation.

A second general principle is to identify what a conflict is really about before raising it with your supervisor. Are you at odds over issues of theory or technique? Do you feel that the supervisor is not giving you sufficient support? What sorts of transference or countertransference issues might be present? Are logistics, such as timing of supervision, a problem? In thinking about the key subject of a conflict, recognize that often the surface content of a conflict does not necessarily reflect the "real" nature of the difficulty. For example, people who work together might get into a conflict over who should have the bigger office. In reality, the conflict is probably not about office size but about who wants or deserves more rewards or prestige and why.

After identifying the conflict, next ask yourself as honestly as you can what role you are playing in it. This does not mean that you should engage in self-blame, but it does mean that you should explore your own actions and reactions in order to better understand your part in what is happening. If self-exploration is difficult, or if you find that it is hard to really know what your role is, you may want to get an outside perspective. If you do decide to get another perspective, do not approach the interaction by expecting the other person to reassure you that the conflict is all the other person's fault. There is a crucial difference between support and uncritical agreement. When you discuss a supervisory conflict with a third person, ask the other person to support you emotionally and to appreciate the difficulty of the conflict, but ask them also to listen critically and try to help you understand things that you may not be aware of on your own.

For example, you might go into a discussion convinced that a supervisor places too many demands on your time. In listening to your description, someone else might hear that perhaps the supervisor is paying you a compliment by relying on you. It is also possible that you have a role in the conflict because you do not tell the supervisor when you are overbooked. The purpose of getting another opinion is to understand what is happening, not to prove you are right.

Trying to see the situation from the supervisor's perspective is another valuable step toward resolving a conflict. Is your supervisor doing or saying things for reasons that might not be immediately evident to you but that might make perfect sense from his or her position? Is your supervisor aware that a conflict exists? If so, would he or she define the conflict differently than you? Asking yourself these questions may help you resolve a conflict without speaking directly to your supervisor about it. If you do discuss the matter, this forethought will serve as preparation that should make the discussion more productive.

One more important element of dealing with a conflict is to ask yourself what it is you want to be different and what you would like to have happen to be satisfied. This might be a change in the way you and your supervisor interact, or it might be a modification of some arrangement such as the hours you work, your caseload, or a similar matter. By thinking about what your own desires are, you will be more clearly able to articulate both the present situation and your wishes for change. This clarity can help both you and your supervisor identify specific steps for dealing with and resolving, the conflict.

Finally, although the ideal may be that conflicts can be resolved to the mutual satisfaction of everyone, there are times when this is not the case. Under such circumstances the best solution may be to negotiate a change in supervisors or placements. This does not have to be a negative experience for the people involved. Sometimes, after efforts have been made to resolve a situation, it becomes apparent that people just do not match and the most constructive way of dealing with the situation is to arrange for an alternative. In such situations it is a good idea to enlist the involvement of a neutral third party, such as another supervisor or an instructor who can help mediate and find alternatives that are mutually satisfactory.

EVALUATION

Lazar and Mosek (1993) observed that students who receive grades in field placements often feel they have little clear understanding of why they received a specific grade. To remedy this situation, interns, instructors, and supervisors should discuss grading and evaluation from the outset and should agree upon and understand the rationale and methods to be used.

One of the things that should be understood is the relationship between evaluations performed by supervisors and the grades assigned by instructors. In most placements, supervisors will conduct some form of evaluation designed to identify the intern's relative strengths and weaknesses. Ideally, evaluations provide useful feedback that can help interns learn where they are doing well and identify areas in which they need improvement.

When interns will also be receiving academic grades, they should know the relationship between the evaluations from site supervisors and the academic grades that will be assigned by the academic instructor. If the evaluation from supervisors will play a role in the instructor's grade system, interns should know how that will occur and what other factors may contribute to their grade.

It sometimes happens that students in internships present as being "grade motivated." This means students may focus on how they think they will be graded rather than on the basis of what they are learning or how they are performing. It is essential for interns to understand that the internship experience is fundamentally different from the rest of their academic work. In a typical class, lacking knowledge or skill may mean one's grade is lowered, but otherwise little of any real consequence happens. By comparison, at internships, an intern's lack of knowledge or skill has real consequences and those consequences apply not only to the intern but to the clients, supervisor, and the agency with whom the intern works. Thus, it is important for interns to go beyond the grade mentality and focus instead on learning. This means evaluation, i.e., the process of giving and receiving feedback about the quality of one's performance, must be embraced. When evaluation is accepted as an essential part of learning, mistakes, successes, and feedback can be understood for what they really should be—learning opportunities—rather than points added or subtracted from an ultimately meaningless grade book.

PRINCIPLES OF EVALUATIONS

Kadushin (1985) has offered a series of principles that can be extremely helpful in the process of evaluation. Those principles are summarized below. As you read this list, you may wish to consider the evaluation procedures followed by your placement site. You also may wish to discuss these elements with your instructor or supervisor.

1. Evaluation should be a continuous process rather than an occasional event.
2. The supervisor should discuss the evaluation procedure in advance with the supervisee.
3. The evaluation should be communicated in the context of a positive relationship.
4. The evaluation procedure should be a mutual, shared process.
5. Evaluations should be made with some recognition and consideration of reality factors that might be determinants of the worker's performance.
6. The principle, if not the exclusive, focus of evaluation should be the work performance of the supervisee rather than any evaluation of the worker as a person.
7. The evaluation should review both strengths and weaknesses, growth and stagnation, and should be fair and balanced.
8. A good evaluation is not like a final game score but rather a review of how the game was played.
9. The evaluation should suggest tentativeness rather than finality and should focus on modifiable aspects of the worker's performance: this is the way the worker performs at this particular time; the expectation is that she will develop and mature.
10. Evaluations should be formulated with some consistency. Both intra- and inter-supervisor consistency is desirable.
11. It is desirable for the supervisor to indicate a willingness to accept evaluation of his own performance from the supervisee.
12. Involvement of staff in establishing criteria is likely to ensure more relevant criteria, to intensify commitment to the evaluation process, and to clarify expectations with regard to evaluation.
13. Since the worker does his work in an organizational context which might impede as well as facilitate satisfactory performance, some effort should be made explicitly to identify organizational difficulties over the evaluation period. (pp. 340–345)

Consistent with Kadushin's suggestions, the responsi-bility for evaluating an intern's performance should fall to the intern and the supervisor. Both individuals should be committed to thorough, honest, accurate, critical, and constructive examination of the intern's strengths and weaknesses. One way in which this can be promoted is for supervisors and interns to complete evaluations of the intern separately, then bring the evaluations together and compare their impressions.

In reviewing performance as part of the evaluation process, multiple aspects of the intern's performance should be addressed and the evaluation should be based on multiple observations and data sources. Thus, a single event or observation should not form the basis of an entire evaluation and, wherever possible, several forms or sources of information should be used. Multiple sources might include written material, direct observations, impressions of more than one individual, etc.

Based on a review of job analyses and other research relating to the tasks of counseling psychologists, Hahn and Molnar (1991) suggested that intern evaluation systems should address each of the following domains:

> (a) individual therapy, (b) couples therapy, (c) group therapy, (d) assessment (vocational and psychological), (e) crisis intervention, (f) case conceptualization, (g) teaching or structured group and workshop presentations, (h) use of supervision, (i) professionalism, (j) consultation, and (k) supervision (e.g., doctoral practicum students). Written communication skills are an important aspect of professional training that can be evaluated within several of these domains. (p. 422)

Because the guidelines proposed by Hahn and Molnar are specifically directed toward graduate level programs in counseling psychology, evaluations for other disciplines or levels of training will undoubtedly differ. Whatever elements are chosen for evaluation, if the elements of an intern's performance are evaluated separately, efforts should be made to avoid "carry over" or "halo" effects that might influence an evaluation in one area positively or negatively based on performance in some other activity.

Avoiding "halo effects" in evaluations is not always easily accomplished. This was demonstrated empirically by Borders and Fong (1992), who found low correlations between supervisor global ratings of their supervisee's counseling and external judges' ratings of supervisee behaviors in actual counseling sessions. Based on their results, Borders and Fong suggested that the evaluations of supervisors may have been influenced not only by supervisee performance in counseling per se, but also by how the supervisees responded during supervision sessions. Borders and Fong further suggested that supervisors may adjust their expectations and evaluation criteria depending on the experience and developmental levels of their supervisees.

Comparable findings were reported by Lazar and Mosek (1993), who found that grades were impacted both by the quality of the intern's performance and by the nature of his or her relationship with the supervisor. Based on this finding, Lazar and Mosek recommended that using a Pass-Fail grading system would be a preferred approach for field placements and supervisors.

Along with considering the specific areas to be evaluated and the sources of information for evaluations, the form of evaluation and the "reference" by which interns will be evaluated are also important considerations. Common models for evaluation forms reference performance according to criteria such as "expected levels," "average," or "standard." Individuals are then evaluated as either falling below, meeting, or exceeding these reference points to varying degrees. The use of such scales has the advantage of offering succinct and convenient feedback in a variety of areas of performance. However, whenever such scales are used there should be clarification about what the reference terms mean (Hahn & Molnar, 1991). Do "expected" or "average" levels refer to expectations or averages for interns at similar levels of experience, or do they speak to levels expected of professionals employed by the agency?

Appendix D of this book contains an evaluation form that I ask supervisors to complete for our interns. Sections of the evaluation form address areas such as basic work behaviors (punctual, reliable, etc.), knowledge of clients and treatment issues, response to supervision, interactions with clients, and interactions with coworkers. Space is also provided for more specific comments and supervisors are encouraged to offer constructive criticism. The evaluation form is offered primarily as an example of some of the issues that can be addressed in an evaluation process. Depending on the nature of the internship and the goals of the intern, instructor, or supervisor, other areas will undoubtedly need to be addressed and some areas currently mentioned may be deleted.

In addition to rating scales, it is also helpful for supervisors to give more specific behavioral feedback to interns. Being told one is below or above expectations can offer a general sense of how one is evaluated, but it does not provide information about what is being done well or how performance could be improved. Thus, supervisors should offer, and interns should request, specific suggestions for continued growth. An example of such feedback would be, "Tom demonstrates very good listening behaviors and develops rapport quickly with clients. He is less skilled at determining when and how to offer effective confrontations when clients have violated program rules." Another example might be, "Tom needs to work on writing more succinct reports with less jargon and more specific recommendations for the treatment team." In comparison to the rating scale approaches, comments such as these focus more on the individual's own strengths and weaknesses without comparison to an external standard of performance.

Finally, insofar as evaluations are meant not only to rate past performance but also to guide future development, it is a good idea for evaluations to be part of a process of developing goals and action plans for the intern. This means that areas of relative weakness are not simply acknowledged and forgotten. Once identified, areas needing improvement should be addressed with specific strategies for how the intern can make the necessary changes or acquire the needed skill or knowledge.

EVALUATION OF SUPERVISORS

Just as evaluation is an essential part of internship training for interns, evaluation should also provide useful feedback to supervisors. As with intern evaluation, this process should not be limited to a single event at the end of the experience but should be part of an ongoing communication process. Throughout this chapter it has been suggested that interns communicate with their supervisors about any concerns they may have or ideas for how supervision might be improved. If that advice is followed, much of the work of evaluation will be incorporated as a natural part of the supervisory process. Nevertheless, it can still be helpful for interns to give more structured feedback at the end of an internship.

Sleight (1990) observed that in comparison to the availability of models for supervisee evaluation, relatively few examples have been published pertaining to supervisor evaluation. Kadushin (1985) made a similar observation and suggested that although well-intentioned supervisors often engage in self-evaluation, self-evaluation alone may not be sufficient to produce substantial changes in supervisor behavior. A further drawback of self-evaluation is that supervisor self-ratings are not necessarily consistent with ratings that would be assigned by their interns.

Gandolfo and Brown (1987) noted that supervisors and supervisees may have different ideas about the elements of good supervision and these may vary across levels of training. In a study of supervisee ratings of actual versus ideal supervisory experiences, Gandolfo and Brown found differences in regard to the focus of supervision, the format of supervision, the roles of supervisor and supervisee, the "evaluation and atmosphere" elements of supervision, and supervisor characteristics. Comparable findings were reported by Baker and Smith (1989), who examined differences between student ratings of supervision as compared to social-work field-faculty ratings.

The evidence of different perceptions of supervision suggests that supervisors and interns alike stand to benefit from increasing the use of formal evaluation procedures. Kadushin (1985) offers a brief model of items from instruments for this purpose. Efstation, Patton, and Kardash (1990) have developed an inventory specifically designed to measure the "working alliance" in supervision. Efstation et al.'s Supervisor Working Alliance Inventory (SWAI) includes forms for both the supervisor and the supervisee to complete and addresses several factors, including the emphasis on promoting understanding of clients, rapport between the supervisor and client, and identification with the supervisor.

Based on a review of the literature and comments of students, I have developed an evaluation tool that has been useful for interns and supervisors. That form is presented in Appendix I. As with the form described earlier for evaluation of interns, the supervisor evaluation tool is offered here primarily to serve as an example. Modifications may be needed to better fit specific needs of the supervisor or interns. Ultimately, what matters most is not the precise detail of any form but the process of the evaluation itself and the spirit in which it is performed. Interns who will be involved in evaluating the performance of their supervisors would do well to revisit the guidelines offered by Kadushin and presented at the start of this discussion of evaluation.

PLANNING FOR FUTURE SUPERVISION

Supervision is an important part of internships but the value of supervision does not end when your internship concludes. In closing this chapter, I want to encourage you to consider supervision as an essential part of a therapist's work for the entirety of your professional career. Clinical work can be extraordinarily complex and there will be many times when you are not able to understand a client or situation on your own. At such times, one needs to seek supervision and be open to the ideas and insights of a colleague. If you have positive experiences in supervision as an intern, the benefits will probably be evident and continuing supervision as a professional will simply be a matter of remembering its value and making arrangements with a fellow professional. If your supervisory experience as an intern was not as positive, it might take some time for you to be willing to try supervision again. That is understandable, but do not let one or two unpleasant experiences dissuade you from something that has the potential to be among the most valuable learning opportunities.

In a very real sense, the decision to enter the helping professions is also a decision to accept and seek supervision. The challenge is to find the right supervisor to meet your personal and professional needs, then work with that person to ensure that you both make the most of the experience.

REFERENCES

Akamatsu, T. J. (1980). The use of role-play and simulation technique in the training of psychotherapy. In A. K. Hess (Ed.), *Psychotherapy supervision: Theory, research and practice.* New York: John Wiley & Sons.

Allen, G., Szollos, S., & Williams, B. (1986). Doctoral students comparative evaluations of the best and worst psychotherapy supervision. *Professional Psychology: Research and Practice, 17,* 91–99.

American Association for Counseling and Development (1988). Ethical standards of the American Association for Counseling and Development (3rd Revision, AACD Governing Council, March 1988). *Journal of Counseling and Development, 67,* 4–8.

Baker, D. R., & Smith, S. L. (1987). A comparison of field faculty and field student perceptions of selected aspects of supervision. *The Clinical Supervisor, 5*(4), 31–42.

Barnat, M. (1974). Some characteristics of supervisory identification in psychotherapy. *Psychotherapy: Theory, Research and Practice, 11,* 189–192.

Belar, C. D., Bieliauskas, L. A., Larsen, K. G., Mensh, I. N., Poey, K., & Roelke, H. J. (1989). The national conference on internship training in psychology. *American Psychologist, 44,* 60–65.

Berger, S. S., & Buchholz, E. S. (1993). On becoming a supervisee: Preparation for learning in a supervisory relationship. *Psychotherapy, 30,* 86–92.

Berman, E. (1988). Ha'libun ha'meshutaf shel yechasey madrich-mudrach ke'heibet shel hadracha dinamit. [The joint exploration of the supervisory relationship as an aspect of dynamic supervision.] *Sihot-Israel Journal of Psychotherapy, 3,* 13–20.

Bogo, M. (1993). The student/field instructor relationship: The critical factor in field education. *The Clinical Supervisor, 11,* 23–36.

Borders, L. D., Bernard, J. M., Dye, A. H., Fong, M. L., Henderson, P., & Nance, D. W. (1991). Curriculum guide for training counseling supervisors: Rationale, development, and implementation. *Counselor Education and Supervision, 31,* 58–80.

Borders, L. D., & Fong, M. L. (1992). Evaluations of supervisees: Brief commentary and research report. *The Clinical Supervisor, 9*(2), 43–51.

Bradley, J., & Post, P. (1991). Impaired students: Do we eliminate them from counselor education programs? *Counselor Education and Supervision, 31,* 100–108.

Bubenzer, D. L., West, J. D., & Gold, J. M. (1991). Use of live supervision in counselor preparation. *Counselor Education and Supervision, 30,* 301–306.

Burns, C. I., & Holloway, E. L. (1989). Therapy in supervision: An unresolved issue. *The Clinical Supervisor, 7*(4), 47–60.

Charny, I. W. (1986). What do therapists worry about: A tool for experiential supervision. *The Clinical Supervisor, 4,* 17–28.

Costa, L. (1995). Reducing anxiety in live supervision. *Counselor Education and Supervision, 34,* 30–40.

Council for Accreditation of Counseling and Related Educational Programs (1988). *Accreditation procedures manual and application.* Alexandria VA: Author.

Doehrman, M. J. G. (1976). Parallel processes in supervision and psychotherapy. *Bulletin of the Meninger Clinic, 40,* 3–104.

Dye, H. A., & Borders, L. D. (1990). Counseling supervisors: Standards for preparation and practice. *Journal of Counseling and Development, 69,* 27–29.

Efstation, J. F., Patton, M. J., & Kardash, C. M. (1990). Measuring the working alliance in counselor supervision. *Journal of Counseling Psychology, 37,* 332–339.

Ekstein, E., & Wallerstein, R. (1972). *The teaching and learning of psychotherapy.* New York: International Universities Press.

Frances, A., & Clarkin, J. (1981). Parallel techniques in supervision and treatment. *Psychiatric Quarterly*, *53*(4), 242–248.

Freeman, S. C. (1993). Structure in counseling supervision. *The Clinical Supervisor*, *11*, 245–252.

Friedlander, M. L., & Ward, L. G. (1984). Development and validation of the Supervisory Styles Inventory. *Journal of Counseling Psychology*, *31*, 541–557.

Friedman, D., & Kaslow, N. J. (1986). The development of professional identity in psychotherapists: Six stages in the supervision process. In F. W. Kaslow (Ed.), *Supervision and Training: Models, Dilemmas and Challenges*. New York: Haworth Press.

Gallant, J. P., & Thyer, B. A., (1989). The "Bug in the Ear" in clinical supervision: A review. *The Clinical Supervisor*, *7*(2/3), 43–58.

Gallant, J. P., Thyer, B. A., & Bailey, J. S. (1991). Using bug-in-the-ear-feedback in clinical supervision: Preliminary evaluations. *Research on Social Work Practice*, *1*, 175–187.

Gandolfo, R. L., & Brown, R. (1987). Psychology intern ratings of actual and ideal supervision of psychotherapy. *The Journal of Training and Practice in Professional Psychology*, *1*, 15–28.

Hahn, W. K., & Molnar, S. (1991). Intern evaluation in university counseling centers: Process, problems and recommendations. *The Counseling Psychologist*, *19*, 414–430.

Haley, J. (1976). *Problem solving therapy*. San Francisco: Jossey-Bass.

Harrar, W. R., VandeCreek, L., & Knapp, S. (1990). Ethical and legal aspects of clinical supervision. *Professional Psychology: Research and Practice*, *21*, 37–41.

Hebert, D. J. (1992). Exploitative need-fulfillment and the counseling intern. *The Clinical Supervisor*, *10*(1), 123–132.

Hess, A. K. (1980). Training models and the nature of psychotherapy supervision. In A. K. Hess (Ed.), *Psychotherapy Supervision: Theory, Research and Practice*. New York: John Wiley & Sons.

Hess, A. K., & Hess, K. A. (1983). Psychotherapy supervision: A survey of internship training practices. *Professional Psychology: Research and Practice*, *14*, 504–513.

Hill, C. E., & Corbett, M. M. (1993). A perspective on the history of process and outcome research in counseling psychology. *Journal of Counseling Psychology*, *40*, 3–24.

Jarvis, P. E. (1989). Standardization versus individualization in the clinical internship. *Professional Psychology: Research and Practice*, *20*, 185–186.

Kadushin, A. (1974). Supervisor-supervisees: A survey. *Social Work*, *19*, 288–298.

Kadushin, A. (1985). *Supervision in social work*. New York: Columbia University Press.

Kaiser, T. L. (1992). The supervisory relationship: An identification of the primary elements in the relationship and an application of two theories of ethical relationships. *Journal of Marital and Family Therapy*, *18*, 283–296.

Kurpius, D., Gibson, G., Lewis, J., & Corbet, M. (1991). Ethical issues in supervising counseling practitioners. *Counselor Education and Supervision*, *31*, 48–57.

Lamb, D. J., Presser, N. R., Pfost, K. S., Baum, M. C., Jackson, V. R., & Jarvis, P. A. (1987). Confronting professional impairment during the internship: Identification, due process, and reme-

diation. *Professional Psychology: Research and Practice*, *18*, 597–603.

Lambert, M. J., & Beier, E. G. (1974). Supervisory and counseling process: A comparative study. *Counselor Education and Supervision*, *14*, 54–60.

Lazar, A., & Mosek, A. (1993). The influence of the field instructor-student relationship on evaluation of students' practice. *The Clinical Supervisor*, *11*, 111–120.

Leong, F. T., & Wagner, N. S. (1994). Cross-cultural counseling supervision: What do we know? What do we need to know? *Counselor Education and Supervision*, *34*, 117–131.

Martin, G. E., & McBride, M .C. (1987). The results of implementation of a professional supervision model on counselor trainee behavior. *Counselor Education and Supervision*, *27*, 155–167.

May, L. I., & Kilpatrick, A. C. (1989). Stress of self-awareness in clinical practice: Are students prepared? *The Clinical Supervisor*, *7*, 303–309.

McColley, S. H., & Baker, E. L. (1982). Training activities and styles of beginning supervisors: A survey. *Professional Psychology*, *13*, 283–292.

McNeil, B. W., & Worthen, V. (1989) The parallel process in psychotherapy supervision. *Professional Psychology: Research and Practice*, *20*, 329–333.

Moskowitz, S. A., & Rupert, P. A. (1983). Conflict resolution within the supervisory relationship. *Professional Psychology: Research and Practice*, *14*, 632–641.

Overholser, J. C. (1991). The Socratic method as a technique in psychotherapy supervision. *Professional Psychology: Research and Practice*, *22*, 68–74.

Rabinowitz, F. E., Heppner, P. P, & Roehlke H. J. (1986). Descriptive study of process and outcome variables of supervision over time. *Journal of Counseling Psychology*, *33*, 292–300.

Robiner, W. N., & Schofield, W. (1990). References on supervision in clinical and counseling psychology. *Professional Psychology: Research and Practice*, *21*, 297–312.

Rogers, C. R. (1961). *On becoming a person*. Boston: Houghton Mifflin Company.

Ronnestad, M. H., & Skovholt, T. M. (1993). Supervision of beginning and advanced graduate students of counseling and psychotherapy. *Journal of Counseling and Development*, *71*, 396–405.

Rothman, B. (1973) Perspectives on learning and teaching in continuing education. *Journal of Education for Social Work*, *9*, 39–52.

Rubinstein, G., (1992). Supervision and psychotherapy: Toward redefining the differences. *The Clinical Supervisor*, *10*(2), 97–116.

Schneider, S., (1992). Transference, counter-transference, projective identification and role responsiveness in the supervisory process. *The Clinical Supervisor*, *10*(2), 71–84.

Searles, H. F. (1955). The informational value of the supervisor's emotional experiences. *Psychiatry*, *18*, 135–146.

Shanfield, S. B., Mohl, P. C., Matthews, K. L., & Hetherly, V. (1992). Quantitative assessment of the behavior of psychotherapy supervisors. *American Journal of Psychiatry*, *149*(3), 352–357.

Sleight, C. C. (1990). Off-Campus Supervisor Self-Evaluation. *The Clinical Supervisor*, *8*(1), 163–171.

Stadler, H. A., Willing, K. L., Eberhage, M. G., & Ward, W. H. (1988). Impairment: Implications for the counseling profession. *Journal of Counseling and Development, 66,* 258–260.

Stoltenberg, C. (1981). Approaching supervision from a developmental perspective: The counselor complexity model. *Journal of Counseling Psychology, 31,* 63–75.

Supervision Interest Network, Association for Counselor Education and Supervision, (1990). Standards for Counseling Supervisors. *Journal of Counseling and Development, 69,* 30–32.

Tracey, T. J., Ellickson, J. L., & Sherry, P. (1989). Reactance in relation to different supervisory environments and counselor development. *Journal of Counseling Psychology, 36,* 336–344.

Wise, P. S., Lowery, S., & Silverglade, L. (1989). Personal counseling for counselors in training: Guidelines for supervisors. *Counselor Education and Supervision, 28,* 326–337.

Zakutansky, T. J., & Sirles, E. A. (1993). Ethical and legal issues in field education: Shared responsibility and risk. *Journal of Social Work Education, 29,* 338–347.

CHAPTER 6

WORKING WITH DIVERSITY

Learning to work with differences is one of the central challenges and opportunities of internship experiences. Because internship settings often involve people from economic, ethnic, and cultural backgrounds much different than your own, it will be important to have an awareness of how you have been influenced by your background and how others are influenced by theirs.

Until relatively recently, helping professions and techniques developed from, and were largely directed by, a predominantly Western European, college-educated, financially well-to-do, and male perspective. With a few exceptions, this perspective was taken for granted and was applied both in training and treatment. As a result, great numbers of people were left unserved or in many cases dis-served by our professions.

Evidence of this is found in studies reviewed by Ponterotto and Casas (1987), which showed that less than 1 percent of counseling programs included in a 1977 survey reported any required study of diverse cultures (McFadden & Wilson, 1977). More recent studies reveal greater attention to diversity training, but a 1986 survey found that only one-third of programs required courses in cross-cultural counseling (Ibrahim et al., 1986).

This limited training may help explain the general inadequacy of service deliveries to minorities (Rosado & Elias,1993). Lack of multicultural training may also help account for results from studies described by Sue and Sue (1990), which showed that more than 50 percent of minority clients terminated therapy after just one contact with the therapist.

REASONS FOR AND RESISTANCE TO DIVERSITY TRAINING

Proctor and Davis (1994) cite three critical reasons for addressing issues of diversity in clinical practice. These include traditional segregation that limits the knowledge of different ethnic groups by persons outside that group; the growing percentages of "nonwhite" persons in the population; and the historical and present negative tensions that exist between groups. Given such factors, professionals and interns who are not sensitive to cultural issues may be ill prepared to deal with clients of cultural backgrounds or ethnicity different than their own.

Although Proctor and Davis focused primarily on ethnic differences, the same principles apply to working with persons of differing economic means, religious beliefs, genders, sexual orientations, and, in some cases, geographic regions of the country. To the extent that our personal experience has not afforded contact with people who differ in significant ways from ourselves and those we grew up with, and in the context of past and ongoing social tensions and prejudices, we may have difficulty understanding the experiences, strengths, needs, and perspectives of others.

During an internship this reality was brought home to a student whose initial response to a discussion of diversity was to say,

> I think too much is made about race and all the other differences. We are all just people and if we all just treat everyone alike there wouldn't be all these problems. I'm not prejudiced myself and I try to treat everyone the same.

This student's comments were made in all sincerity and from her perspective she believed she had achieved an understanding of how best to deal with differences. Several weeks into her internship, a journal entry revealed that she was beginning to gain deeper awareness of herself and others.

> I always thought that everyone was just the same and that I was not prejudiced at all. Working here I've started to understand that just because I think everyone is the same doesn't mean everyone else thinks that or everyone has had the same chances I have. I wonder what my life would be like if my family was as poor as the people I am working with. I always thought that people who were poor just didn't want to work hard. I think I was prejudiced and just didn't know it. Now I see this family working so hard and still not being able to afford the things I just take for granted. They can't even take the kids to the doctor. I'm beginning to understand why they seem angry. I'm getting angry myself. It isn't fair but these people have to live with that every day and I get to go home to my comfortable dormitory. I'm starting to realize how sheltered I've been. This is opening my eyes and it isn't easy.

This student was coming to understand that one cannot simply dismiss diversity issues by saying they are unimportant or "treating everyone alike." A much deeper awareness of ourselves and others is required and the internship is a good place to start developing that awareness.

As professional organizations have come to recognize the importance of diversity, ethical, and, in some cases, legal mandates for multicultural training have developed. In an extensive review of models and issues associated with multicultural training in the helping professions, Ridley, Mendoza and Kanitz (1994) concluded that

> . . . the issue of whether or not to include some form of MCT *(multicultural counseling)* is no longer open for debate. Graduate training programs must provide MCT. . . . With this proviso, concern is now focused on deciding what kind of MCT to offer. (p. 227)

While calling for such training, Ridley et al. caution that if the motivations for pursuing training in muticultural

counseling are not carefully considered, the results may be counterproductive. Reluctant conformity to organizational standards can lead to half-hearted, symbolic gestures that lack substance or sincerity. Cautions are also raised about the potential for "paternalistic attitudes" impacting training. Such attitudes run the risk of:

> . . . implicitly communicating the message to trainees that nondominant cultural groups are weak. This sets the stage for members of the majority group to pity individuals thus characterized and sanctions the pathologizing and disempowerment of minorities. Furthermore, this attitude fosters the image of the White counselor in multicultural counseling as a benefactor who is providing a charitable service worthy of gratitude on the part of the minority beneficiary. This structuring of power roles perpetuates the disparity of power between dominant and nondominant cultural groups existing in the larger social complex. (ibid., p. 236)

RESISTANCE

In spite of the evidence and arguments offered above, when the subject of differences is introduced, some students, and even more vehemently, certain faculty, protest that there is enough to learn about "basic" clinical skills without throwing additional variables into the equation. The argument is often made that we should focus on teaching basic skills first. Then, "if there is time at the end," we can consider how those skills apply to different groups.

A variation of this theme is the suggestion that "the core" therapy skills and theories should be taught in a required class while issues of differences should be offered as an elective for those who are interested. Dobbins and Skillings (1991) describe similar arguments from their students and note that "there are often institutional influences that foster the impression that multiculturality is somehow an ancillary specialty area" (p. 38).

Although such responses are presented as a logical rationale for why diversity issues should not or cannot be central to training, the arguments themselves illustrate the very problems that diversity training seeks to address. Indeed, such arguments sound remarkably like the "Avoidant" type of identity described by Rowe, Bennet and Atkinson (1994). In defining this type, which is discussed in more detail later in this chapter, Rowe et al. state:

> Whereas members of visible racial/ethnic minority groups have little choice concerning their awareness of racial identity, White Americans have the option of minimizing the impact of racial awareness by dismissing the issue in various ways. . . . Whether these individuals find these issues merely inconvenient or actually anxiety arousing, their preferred method of responding is to ignore, minimize, or deny the existence of importance of the problematic issue. (p. 136)

Rowe et al. go on to say:

> Life experiences that bring about dissonance, of course, will be trying to the denial system. But until the experiential factor is strong enough that avoidance is no longer a satisfactory resolution to the dissonance, the racial attitudes expressed will lack personal meaningfulness. (p. 136)

Another manifestation of the avoidance of racial issues can be found in what has been called the "color-blind" approach to treatment and training. Proctor and Davis (1994) note that this approach was once advocated as a way to account for therapist-client differences and treat people with equal regard as people. This is essentially the model that was initially advocated by the student described earlier who believed "if we all just treat everyone alike there wouldn't be all these problems."

In spite of the good intentions that may underlie such statements, the color-blind approach tends to ignore a major part of people's lives and contributes to "unrealistic, abstract views of clients and their problems" (Proctor & Davis, 1994, p. 316). Pretending not to see differences may make the person who does the pretending feel better, but it does not really make the differences go away or solve the problem of how to deal with related issues in therapy. Further, avoiding differences allows the person in power, in this case the helping professional or intern, to avoid the real social issues that persons of differing backgrounds must contend with on a daily basis. As Proctor and Davis state:

> Finally, color-blind practice is escapist, enabling professionals to avoid both the cognitive and affective components of America's racial turmoil. The color-blind professional is excused from confronting racial injustice and its impact on the client's social reality. (p. 316)

Perhaps the greatest difficulty with approaches that minimize diversity stems from the implicit assumption that ideas and techniques developed primarily by one group of people would or should be helpful for people with vastly different gender, ethnic, cultural, class, and educational experiences. There is a certain irony to the fact that a field that emphasizes introspection and empiricism has managed for so long to neglect the biases inherent in its own theories and techniques.

The magnitude of the oversight was described well by Pedersen (1987), who pointed out the reality that:

> In strictly numerical terms it is increasingly true that the Western viewpoint is the more exotic: The majority of people in the world accept a non-Western perspective. (p. 17)

Pedersen goes on to observe:

> Despite that numerical reality, many social scientists, includ-

ing psychologists, depend on textbooks, research findings, and implicit psychological theory based almost entirely on assumptions specific to European and American culture. These assumptions are usually so implicit and so taken for granted that they are not challenged even by broad-minded and insightful psychologists. (p. 16)

The negative effects of this self-centeredness are exacerbated by failure to appreciate the historical context of discrimination, injustice, and socio-economic inequities that have been perpetrated against people from minority cultures or orientations (Sue & Sue, 1990).

A REFORMULATION OF DIVERSITY

In a later writing, Pedersen (1991) offers what may be an antidote to the shortcomings of the traditionally dominant perspective. Pedersen asserts that multiculturalism is not peripheral to counseling but should in fact occupy a central role.

> By defining culture broadly—to include demographic variables, (e.g., age, sex, place of residence), status variables (e.g. social, educational, economic) and affiliations (formal and informal), as well as ethnographic variables such as nationality, ethnicity, language, and religion—the construct "multicultural" becomes generic to all counseling relationships. (p. 7)

From this understanding, Pedersen observes that:

> Culture has frequently been seen as a barrier to counseling rather than as a tool for helping counselors be more accurate and as a means of facilitating good counseling. (p. 9)

Although Pedersen acknowledges that there are pitfalls to broad definitions of culture, he contends that:

> Multiculturalism should complement rather than compete with traditional theories of counseling. Taking the broad definition of culture, it is difficult for a counselor to be accurate and skilled, according to any theory, without in some way accounting for the ever-changing cultural salience in his or her client's perspective. (p. 9)

I concur with Pedersen's ideas and stress that by emphasizing diversity in teaching interaction skills we are not "creating" additional variables. Instead, we are raising fundamental issues that have previously been artificially subtracted from the picture. Rather than protesting the apparent addition of information, instructors and supervisors, along with our students, should be studying how and why a topic so fundamental to education and clinical work has been ignored or demeaned in the past. Understanding diversity is not a "luxury," it is an essential.

If a counselor is unable to work with those whom she or he is different from, with whom will that counselor be able to work. (Speight et al., 1991, p. 30)

STEPS TOWARD WORKING WITH DIFFERENCES

Acknowledging diversity is the easy part. The more difficult and exciting challenge is to find a way to work effectively with people from many different backgrounds. One of the goals of this chapter is to help interns become more aware of their own backgrounds and perspectives and the ways in which their assumptions about themselves, others, and the treatment process relate to their work.

Atkinson, Morton, and Sue (1989) have pointed out that most discussions of counseling with "minority clients" assume that the counselor is from the majority group while the client is from a minority group. This assumption tends to overlook the possibility that it may well be the counselor who is from a minority group and the client from the majority. Another problem with the "majority-minority" distinction is that it overlooks cultural differences that exist within each of those groups. As an alternative to majority-minority distinctions, Atkinson et al. prefer the phrase "cross-cultural counseling," which they suggest "refers to any relationship in which two or more of the participants are culturally different" (p. 9). Similar to Pedersen's broad definition of multiculturalism, this terminology encompasses situations in which the counselor is from a minority group and the client from the majority. Cross-cultural counseling also includes counseling

> in which the counselor and client(s) are racially and ethnically similar but belong to different cultural groups because of other variables such as sex, sexual orientation, socioeconomic factors and age (White male-White female, Black straight person-Black gay, poor Asian American-Wealthy Asian American). (Atkinson, Morten & Sue, 1989, p. 9)

Anyone who has had the experience of moving from one region of the country to another or from an urban to a rural community knows firsthand that great differences exist in the cultural experience among people with apparently common ethnicity. Similar differences are encountered among people from different religions, educational backgrounds, sexual orientations, and positions of socioeconomic advantage. Failure to appreciate and adapt one's approach in response to such differences can only decrease the chances of successful interactions taking place. On the other hand, awareness and conscious effort to adjust services or treatment to meet cultural and personal differences is a first step toward improving the chances for successful interactions.

The title of the present chapter, "Working with Diversity," was selected to reflect a belief that the issue of "cross-cultural" counseling is part of the broader matter of dealing with differences in counseling. In a way, the goal is to work through resistance to cross-cultural counseling by pointing out the undeniable reality that counselors must learn to work with people who are different from themselves. If that premise is accepted, then it follows that working with differences includes working with cultural differences. It also follows that counselors and interns must come to grips with issues such as racism, sexism, economic and social class, and other realities that cannot be ignored if they wish to fully understand diversity and the experience of people from different backgrounds.

Echoing Pedersen's discussion of multiculturalism and emphasizing the importance of "internalized culture," Ho (1995) stated the matter well:

> Those who do not know the culture of others do not really know their own. (p. 21)

Ho adds that

> . . . without multicultural awareness, self-understanding would be limited and incomplete, let alone other-understanding. This is why multicultural awareness figures prominently in any counseling process—more so than counselors have hitherto envisioned. (p. 21)

KNOWING THE DIVERSITY WITHIN US

A number of authors (Locke, 1992; Sue & Sue, 1990; Wintrob & Harvey, 1981) have recognized that awareness of self is a vital element in learning to work with clients from different backgrounds than the therapist. As Wintrob and Harvey (1981) identified the issue,

> . . . an understanding of the therapist's feelings about his or her own social class, racial, ethnic, and religious characteristics and points of convergence with or divergence from a patient is critical to therapeutic effectiveness. (p. 111)

Consistent with these ideas, as a step toward developing your own ability to work with differences, it can be extremely beneficial to think at length about your personal experience and perspective. Unless you have given careful thought to who you are, it is difficult to be sensitive to differences or similarities with clients. In a moment, I will offer an exercise designed to promote greater awareness of one's own ethnic and cultural background.

TERMINOLOGY MATTERS

Before proceeding, a brief word is in order about terminology. Most students, interns, and many practicing therapists are not aware of the meaning of certain critical and often used terms associated with multicultural counseling. Johnson (1990) reported that the terms *race*, *culture*, and *ethnicity* are often used interchangeably and without appreciation of their different meanings. Similar observations and concerns have been expressed by Dobbins and Skillings (1991), who offer an informative review of the history of distinguishing people on the basis of "race." These authors explain that the concept of "race" carries with it a deceptive impression that there are clear and meaningful biological differences that can be used to establish distinctions between people. As Dobbins and Skillings phrased the matter, "there is an erroneous presumption of biopsychosocial precision"(p. 39). Such erroneous understandings of race are accompanied by equally inaccurate assumptions that specific sets of cultural norms and values are associated with all members of a given "race."

Recognizing the lack of biological meaning and the tendency to confuse culture with race, Johnson notes that "Racial classifications draw attention to group factors, ignore the individual, and contribute to the maintenance of destructive racial stereotypes."(p. 43). Dobbins and Skilling draw the same conclusions regarding racial distinctions.

> For professional purposes, confusion of biological features and cultural predispositions draws attention away from more salient determiners of behavior such as values of the neighborhood, spirituality, the extended family and one's economic situation, which have very little to do with gene pools. (p. 39)

Dobbins and Skilling go on to state,

> . . . in addition to overlooking more relevant sources of variance between groups, racial categories imply a sameness to all members within the stated group. This type of thinking is simply inaccurate. (p. 39)

To avoid the inaccuracies and confusion associated with racial labeling, Johnson advocates ". . . use of the more contextually sensitive constructs of ethnicity and culture when referring to interpersonal processes. . . . The use of the term, race, should be reserved for demonstrating the vestiges of racism as well as for documenting progress in eradicating it" (p. 48). Dobbins and Skillings also suggest that labels which are used to describe people

> . . . should reflect some aspect of the person's background. In this sense the term *Black* is less preferred than the term *African American*, or if one can be even more precise, *Nigerian American, Irish American,* or *Native American*. (p. 43, italics in the original)

Following these recommendations, except in discussions that relate specifically to racial terms in the context of racism, or when referring to writings in which other authors have referred to race, in this book I will avoid racial distinctions and will refer instead to differences in ethnicity, culture, or background, with culture defined broadly as discussed before by Pedersen.

EXERCISE: KNOWING YOURSELF IN RELATION TO DIVERSITY

This exercise is designed to help you become more aware of your own cultural and personal background and characteristics. Because this understanding is a first step toward understanding how you will interact with others, it is perhaps more important than anything else that is in this chapter. I encourage you to spend substantial time on the exercise and discuss it with your peers and instructor.

Listed below are certain personal and cultural characteristics that have profound influences on how people understand the world and interact with others. For each characteristic, begin by describing yourself, then take some time to seriously consider how each aspect of yourself taken separately, and how all the aspects taken together, affect your understanding of yourself and others. Also give some thought to how these characteristics shape the assumptions you bring to your training as an intern. One way to enhance this understanding is to imagine how things you may have taken for granted about yourself are due at least in part to your ethnic or cultural background. For example, you might ask yourself, "Because I have pink/brown/red/yellow, etc., skin, I have experienced . . ." Or, "Because my family's economic status was . . . I have experienced. . ." Another approach to enhance your understanding is to imagine how your life might be different if you had other characteristics. For example, you might consider, "If I were of a different culture." "If my parents were very (poor/rich) I might . . ." "If I were a new immigrant I might experience . . ." As a final yet critical step to this exercise, discuss your own responses with a peer or other person. If you have the opportunity, try to discuss this with several people who are much different from you. Learning how they have answered the items and contrasting those answers with your own can be extremely enlightening.

1. My gender is ____ and this is how it influences my experiences and how I understand and relate to others.
2. My age is ____and this is how it influences my experiences and how I understand and relate to others.
3. My physical appearance includes the following qualities (Describe these as accurately as you can and try to avoid oversimplifying or using racial terms):
Skin:
Hair:
Facial Features:
Build:
Other Features:

This is how those features influence my experiences and how I understand and relate to others:

4. The nationality and cultural background of my parents and grandparents are:
   My father's mother
   My father's father
   My mother's mother
   My mother's father
   My father
   My mother

   This is how the culture of my family influences my experiences and how I understand and relate to others:

5. With regard to economic resources, the family I was raised in was _____.
   This is how that background influences my experiences and how I understand and relate to others:

6. The religious orientation of my mother is_____.
   The religious orientation of my father is_____.
   This is how that background influences my experiences and how I understand and relate to others:

7. My mother's educational background is _____.
   My father's educational background is _____.
   This is how that background influences my experiences and how I understand and relate to others:

8. My own educational background is:

   This is how that background influences my experiences and how I understand and relate to others:

9. My physical health and abilities are:

   This is how that background influences my experiences and how I understand and relate to others:

10. My Sexual Orientation is:

    This is how that background influences my experiences and how I understand and relate to others:

11. Other characteristics that have influenced my experiences and understanding of others are:

CONFRONTING OUR BIASES AND ACKNOWLEDGING OUR IGNORANCE

In the second edition of their book on counseling with people from different cultures, Sue and Sue (1990) wrote:

> As mental health professionals, we have a personal and professional responsibility to (a) confront, become aware of, and take actions in dealing with our biases, stereotypes, values,

and assumptions about human behavior, (b) become aware of the culturally different client's world view, values, biases, and assumptions about human behavior, and (c) develop appropriate help-giving practices, intervention strategies, and structures that take into account the historical, cultural, and environmental experiences of the culturally different client. (p. 6)

Some interns come to training believing they have everything it takes to treat almost any client who comes to them. Others are not so confident but very few are really aware of just how limited their own experiences or theories are. Carrillo, Holzhalb, and Thyer (1993) phrased this well when they noted that:

> Many students are unaware of their biases or are unaware that they may hold firm beliefs that may be discriminatory to others. They may believe they are without prejudice and are fully tolerant and empathetic toward all groups regardless of race, ethnicity, gender, age or other characteristics. . . . Another common posture of students is that their commitment to work with oppressed populations is evidence of their lack of any common human misconception to which the rest of humankind is vulnerable. Either stance limits growth and change and seriously compromises professional effectiveness. (p. 264)

In recognition of the importance of both cultural awareness itself and therapists' awareness of their own cultural awareness, a number of instruments have been developed to assess the beliefs, knowledge, and skills of therapists and counselors in relation to working with persons of different ethnicities and cultures (e. g., Sodowsky, et al., 1994). Reviews of these instruments have been offered by Ponterotto et al. (1994) and Carrillo, Holzhalb, and Thyer (1993).

Based on principles incorporated in the instruments alluded to above, the exercise that follows is designed to encourage self-exploration of one's preparedness to work with others from different backgrounds. In this exercise you are invited to consider carefully and honestly the kinds of clients with whom you feel you have sufficient experience, knowledge, or understanding to interact in a way that will be genuinely helpful.

If you are like many of our interns you may find that after completing the exercise you are unsure of whether or not you should try to interact with anyone other than yourself. If that feeling emerges, do not despair. The first step toward learning is acknowledging ignorance. Following the exercise, concepts and suggestions are offered to help build your awareness and abilities to work with differences.

EXERCISE: KNOWING WHAT YOU KNOW AND DON'T KNOW ABOUT OTHERS

Listed below are some of the many characteristics that distinguish individuals and groups from one another. Consider these and try to identify where your knowledge, understanding, or experience would enable you to understand accurately and relate to their experiences, concerns, thoughts, emotions, needs, etc., in a helpful way. For each group you indicate you feel you know well enough to work with, give the reasons why. For example, what experiences, training, or personal knowledge do you have relating to this group?

Age Groups:

Genders:

Appearance (i.e. skin color, facial features, etc.):

Ethnic or cultural background:

Generations lived in this country:

Economic status:

Education Level:

Religion:

Sexual Orientation:

Physical Abilities or Disabilities:

THE HISTORICAL CONTEXT MUST BE ACKNOWLEDGED

Part of knowing what you do not know about other groups or individuals is acknowledging your knowledge or ignorance of their history. However tolerant, open, understanding, empathic, etc., therapists or interns might believe themselves to be toward others, those qualities cannot erase long histories of racial, class, gender, and other oppression. If a client, intern, or both are from a group that has experienced historical or ongoing discrimination or oppression, that fact will unavoidably influence the clinical interaction. Similarly, clients and interns from the dominant group in society will hold certain stereotypes, prejudices, and misconceptions that will influence their actions and interactions. These realities simply cannot be avoided and they must not be denied.

During discussions of this subject one often hears statements such as, "What happened to 'those people' in the past is not my fault and I can't change it. We need to get on with what is happening today." The problem with such statements is that they suggest it is possible to somehow erase all that has gone before and all that is in fact still going on, without dealing with the cognitive, emotional, economic, social, and other effects the past and present realities have created.

A colleague who teaches multicultural education suggests that, in regard to history, "We do not have to feel guilty for the past, but we must accept responsibility for the present." (Hardiman, personal communication.) Her point is that those who feel overwhelmed with sorrow and guilt for what

their ancestors did to others, as well as those who would prefer to ignore the past completely, need to find a realistic, constructive, and, importantly, a personal way to deal with the reality of the past within the context of the present.

I hasten to add to my friend's counsel that for students learning to be therapists, her message is one therapists must internalize for themselves, not preach to their clients. As someone who will deal with clients different than yourself, and often clients whose ancestors may have been perpetrators or victims of injustice, you must come to grips with your own reactions to your own connection to that history. But you must not come to grips with this so you can say to your clients, "Look how I dealt with this; you should deal with it this way too." Rather, you must deal with your own reactions so you can accept and understand what your client is experiencing without needing to deny or defend if some of their history or struggle is directed toward you. You must also deal with your own connection and struggle so you will not need to project your own struggle on to your client.

Having advised that one must be aware of the historical context in working with difference, it is unfortunate but true that very few interns or professionals are well informed about the historical treatment of persons from minority groups. Most students know little about the history of struggles for civil rights, women's rights, economic justice, or other long-fought battles to achieve fairness and respect for all peoples. If you are interested in learning more about these topics, (and I believe that as part of your training you should be interested), the following resources may be instructive.

REFERENCES TO MULTICULTURAL HISTORY

The listings below are only a sampling of the many excellent sources available. They represent works I have found useful or challenging or that have been recommended to me by scholars in the field of diversity education. I recognize and apologize for the fact that space does not allow me to list more references here or provide representative material for all groups. I am also aware that some readers will disagree with the perspectives offered in some of these sources. That is inevitable. One simply cannot cite a reference for every issue or group and it is impossible to select works on any subject that will please everyone. (Parenthetically, it may be that the way one reacts to this list will relate to, and provide some insights into, the stages and models of identity development that are discussed later in this chapter.) My hope here is that by citing a few interesting and thought provoking examples, readers will be encouraged to read these sources and go on to consult material relevant to their personal background or that of their clients.

In addition to the nonfiction works cited below, I also strongly recommend studying poetry and fiction as well as other cultural works including art, music, etc. As I once explained to a professor from the department of philosophy who had asked me what my syllabus references to "listening to music" had to do with a course entitled "Imaging the World": "You can read all you want about a country and still not get a feel for what life is like, where the culture comes from, or the spirit of the people. But if you listen to two or three selected songs, it suddenly starts to make sense."

SUGGESTED READINGS

Acuna, R. (1988). *Occupied America: A history of Chicanos.* New York: Harper and Row.

Bell, D. (1987). *And we are not saved: The elusive quest for racial justice.* New York: Basic Books.

Billingsley, A. (1992). *Climbing Jacob's ladder: The enduring legacy of African-American families.* New York: Simon & Schuster.

Chan, S. (1991). *Asian Americans: An interpretive history.* Boston: Twayne Publishers. (Note: This is one of a series of books about various immigrant populations.)

Duberman, M. B., Vicinus, M., & Chauncey, G. (Eds.). (1989). *Reclaiming the gay and lesbian past.* New York: New American Library.

Fuchs, L. H. (1990). *The American kaleidoscope: Race, ethnicity and the civic culture.* Hanover, NH: Wesleyan University Press.

Jaimes, M. A. (Ed.). (1992). *The state of Native America: Genocide, colonization and resistance.* Boston: South End Press. (Note: This is one of a series of books about "Race and Resistance.")

Kanellos, N. (1994). *The Hispanic almanac: From Columbus to corporate America.* Detroit, MI: Visible Ink Press.

Sanders, R. (1988). *Shores of refuge: A hundred years of Jewish emigration.* New York: Henry Holt and Company.

Takaki, R. (1993). *A different mirror: A history of multicultural America.* Boston: Little, Brown & Company.

Woloch, N. (1994). *Women and the American experience.* New York: McGraw Hill.

THE CURRENT CONTEXT MUST BE ACKNOWLEDGED

Awareness of the historical background of different people should be accompanied by equal awareness of the current social context relating to perceived racial, gender, cultural, and other differences. Racism, sexism, and economic injustice are not things of the past. They are ongoing, daily, and destructive realities in the lives of millions of people. Those who have not experienced that reality for themselves may not understand how it affects clinical interactions. As a result, they may be unaware that clinical interactions occur in a context that is far more complex that simply "two people talking together." Sue and Sue framed the matter in strong terms by stating:

> Thus, the world view of the culturally different client who comes to counseling boils down to one important question:

"What makes you, a counselor/therapist, any different from all the others out there who have oppressed and discriminated against me?" (p. 6)

A counselor or intern who is unaware that clients may harbor such questions is likely to experience frustration, failure, and hostility without understanding the underlying causes. Furthermore, interns who are unaware of the cultural context may misinterpret the meaning of their client's actions and may ascribe erroneous diagnoses or causal explanations to clients. In other words, professionals or interns who do not appreciate the history and daily experience of clients from different cultures are not simply not part of the solution, they may unintentionally be part of the problem.

STRENGTHS MUST BE RECOGNIZED ALONG WITH PROBLEMS

Much of the recent literature on multicultural counseling has focused largely on issues of injustice and inequality between different groups. As emphasized throughout this chapter, it is essential for interns to understand these issues, consider them in their clinical work, and work to influence them in society. At the same time, however, it is important also to recognize that stereotypical images may prevent one from seeing beyond repression to understand and appreciate the cultural richness and heritage of different groups.

It is not uncommon for interns to have at least some sense of the disadvantages faced by other groups but little or no awareness of the personal and cultural strengths of others. The role of family, religion, school, art, music, etc., may be much different for members of one group than for another. These and other institutions and traditions are essential to understand because they can help one appreciate the client's experience and can provide invaluable resources to help the client deal with his or her presenting difficulties.

Some of the most profound experiences interns describe have occurred when they have been invited into the other cultures of their clients. One young intern was working in a center serving refugees from Southeast Asia. After working with a client in a vocational training program for about a year, the intern was invited to attend a traditional celebration. The intern's journal reflected his reactions:

> I had the most amazing experience tonight. Until now I've really only seen one side of my clients. They have always been poor and struggling and I've been the one helping them try to get work. Tonight I was the only person like me in the room and everyone else was Vietnamese. I was the minority. I felt out of place and like I was the one who was dressed funny. But everyone treated me with so much warmth and caring. There was all kinds of wonderful food (and a little not-so-wonderful to me), and music and entertainment and everyone was laughing and having a great time. I couldn't help but think how different the images from tonight were from the things I have always thought up 'til now.

Appreciating the richness of a client's ethnic and cultural experience is essential for many reasons. If one sees only the negative side or disadvantage of a person's background, one is likely to feel pity, guilt, or other such emotions. But, if that is all one feels, it will be difficult to accord the person genuine respect for who they are as an individual. It will also be difficult to identify personal and cultural resources the person can draw from to help deal with their situation.

This does not mean we must return to the "color-blind" or "people are all alike" approach. Rather, it means we must understand to the greatest extent possible the challenges and resources of clients and how these stem from and relate to the client's ethnic and cultural background and the larger social context in which they occur.

ETHNIC IDENTITY DEVELOPMENT

While many authors have addressed how established cultural differences can conflict with therapy expectations, others have addressed the challenges that individuals from nondominant cultures face when they attempt to embrace their own ethnicity or cultural background. In recent years, increasing numbers of writers have argued for the importance of reclaiming one's ethnic heritage. Parham (1989), for example, expanding on concepts introduced by Cross (1971, 1978), described a theory of "psychological nigrescence," which

> hypothesizes the changes in racial identity that a Black person can experience at various points in the life-cycle process. (p. 187)

Parham's model details a progression through stages he identifies as "pre-encounter," "encounter," "immersion/emersion," and "internalization." Parham stresses the importance of understanding

> . . . how individuals' racial identity attitudes influence their mental health as well as how racial identity attitudes influence the dynamics (i.e. relationship) of the therapeutic process itself. (p. 215)

Parham cites research suggesting that

> . . . development of pro-Black attitudes may be indicative of healthy psychological adjustment, whereas attitudes that denigrate oneself as a Black person and simultaneously promote wishes to be White may be psychologically maladaptive. (p. 215)

According to Parham, counseling and therapeutic relationship issues will vary depending on where individuals are along the stages of identity awareness.

Models similar to Parham's have been developed to describe Chicano identity development (Ruiz, 1990). They have also been developed within a more broadly applicable framework proposed by Sue and Sue (1990). The "Racial/Cultural Identity Development Model (R/CID)" of Sue and Sue is presented as "a conceptual framework to aid counselors in understanding their culturally different client's attitudes and behaviors" (p. 95). This model views people as trying to "understand themselves in terms of their *own culture,* the *dominant culture,* and the *oppressive relationship* between the two cultures" (p. 96; italics in the original).

Much like the models described by Parham and Ruiz, the R/CID model of Sue and Sue identifies five stages of identity development. The first stage represents a denial of one's own culture and the final stage reflects full awareness of one's own culture and its relation to the dominant culture. Sue and Sue label these stages "conformity, dissonance, resistance and immersion, introspection, and integrative awareness." They suggest that each stage is characterized by certain beliefs or attitudes, and understanding the stages and their attitudinal correlates can help counselors better understand and communicate with their minority clients. Sue and Sue organize these key attitudes in terms of how individuals from minority groups view themselves, others of their same minority, others of other minorities, and individuals from the majority group.

The attitudes described by Sue and Sue are similar to issues addressed by Smith (1991), who identifies patterns of ethnic identity conflicts experienced by members of both majority and minority groups. Among the conflicts identified by Smith are:

- Ethnic awareness versus ethnic unawareness
- Ethnic self-identification versus nonethnic self-identification
- Self-hatred versus self-acceptance
- Self-acceptance versus other-group acceptance
- Self-rejection versus other-group acceptance
- Other-group rejection versus self-acceptance
- Other-group rejection versus self-rejection
- Ethnic identity integration versus ethnic identity fragmentation or diffusion
- Ethnocentrism versus allocentrism (p. 184)

According to Smith's model, these conflicts occur as phases within each stage of development and can be experienced by majority as well as minority groups.

Each of the theories described above takes a somewhat different approach to understanding ethnic identity development, but they share the message that therapy interventions must take into consideration the individual's cultural background and identity development in relation to that background. Depending on where individuals are in their development and the specific attitudes and beliefs that correspond with that development, different issues will need to be addressed in the counseling relationship. Sue and Sue gave particular attention to this and stressed that understanding identity development is critical because the way minority individuals relate to counseling and counselors is likely to be influenced not simply by minority-group membership but by where the person is in their own development in relation to that membership.

ONE'S OWN PREJUDICES AND BIASES MUST BE ACKNOWLEDGED

Learning about historical or current social conditions and studying concepts of ethnic identity development can help interns better understand the experiences of clients and others, but if the process is simply external and intellectual, interns may not become aware of their personal biases or prejudices. Corvin and Wiggins (1989) have stressed the importance of going beyond intellectual understanding to confronting one's own intrinsic racism. This message was echoed with particular relevance to interns by Kiselica (1991) who described his own experiences in a multicultural internship.

> Questioning my ethnocentrism provoked me to recognize and confront my own racist behaviors, and this was a painful but necessary experience for me to grow even more as a person and professional. . . .
>
> By confronting my Eurocentrism, racist behaviors, and stereotypical thinking, I had a better sense of myself and how my foibles might impede the counseling process. By remaining cognizant of these imperfections during actual counseling sessions, I was able to prevent them from becoming barriers in my efforts to establish rapport with culturally different clients. (p. 29)

As Kiselica's description and the reports of other interns reveal, confronting one's own prejudice and racism is not an easy or pleasant task. Nevertheless, if one is to work with diverse clients it is essential to be aware of personal biases and work to understand and overcome them.

A MODEL OF "WHITE" IDENTITY DEVELOPMENT

A moment ago we addressed the issue of identity development among members of ethnic groups that are not dominant in a society. Now, we must also consider identity development among the dominant group. Because members of dominant groups tend to take their own position as a given and compare all other groups or perspectives to themselves, understanding one's own cultural identity development can be a surprising experience.

Building on a model developed by Hardiman (1982), Corvin and Wiggins (1989) describe an "antiracism" training model that focuses primarily on stages of "white" identity development. Corvin and Wiggins assert that most whites

tend, largely unconsciously, to accept their own background as inherently superior to others and view diversity as inherently inferior. To understand and go beyond this position, Corvin and Wiggins propose a four-stage model of white identity development. The first stage, labeled "Acceptance," typifies people who do not consider themselves racist, but nevertheless have an implicit "assumption of Whiteness as 'the norm'"(p. 108). People at this stage make overt statements such as "people are people," without realizing that this denies cultural differences and in the process reinforces unexamined assumption of white norms. As awareness of white cultural racism begins to grow, the second stage, "Resistance," is entered. In this stage the individual acknowledges racism as a problem, but the individual's personal racism is not yet fully acknowledged or recognized.

In my work with students, an example of this second stage of development was provided by a young woman whose family owned an apple orchard in eastern Washington State. Describing the migrant workers who perform much of the labor in the orchards the woman said,

> I'm not a racist, but I have to say the Mexicans that work for us really are a problem. You just can't rely on them. They're dishonest, they're drunk half the time and they don't even take care of basic things like bathing. You should see the way they live.

As she continued it was evident that this student believed she was simply making observations of "fact," not prejudicial statements. However, when I began to ask pointed questions about the treatment of workers by orchard owners, the limited wages the workers are paid, exposures to pesticides, the failure of owners to provide adequate sanitation facilities, and the inherently racist treatment that the workers receive in the region, she became rather defensive. At one point, when asked if she thought the workers wanted to live in the conditions she had described, the student said with a critical tone,

> A lot of them could afford to live better if they wanted but they send most of their money back to their families in Mexico.

When it was suggested that she was now criticizing people for making sacrifices for their families, something that might otherwise be considered courageous and admirable, she became quiet for a moment, then said hesitantly,

> That's true isn't it. I never thought of it like that before. Maybe . . . maybe I am a little prejudiced. I'll have to think about this more.

The third stage in the model of Corvin and Wiggins, labeled "Redefinition," involves the individual's discovery of his or her own identity, including greater awareness of personal values, some of which are racist. This stage also includes understanding the relative luxuries and advantages that have come from being white and reflecting on how those advantages relate to membership in the white system. In the process of reflecting on their own role and values, individuals become better able to direct energies both toward personal change and toward working to change systems. With awareness of systemic and personal racism, and a commitment to change that racism, the final stage of "Internalization" is realized. In this stage, individuals are aware of the complexity of their own "racial identity," have internalized a multicultural perspective, and have made a commitment to work with others to bring about change and influence racist systems.

Corvin and Wiggins view their stage model as a "diagnostic tool for assessing where one is in White identity development and where one has yet to go in combating racist behavior" (p. 113). From this premise, they recommend specific training goals and learning activities designed to meet individuals at each stage of identity development.

Developmental models of white racial identity have been offered by other writers as well, most notably by Helms (1984 & 1990). Such models have also been criticized. Rowe, Bennet, and Atkinson (1994) point out that most developmental models of White racial identity have tended to parallel models of identity development for minorities, but it is likely that the identity of majority culture members may be much different than that of minorities.

> . . . the attitudes that racial/ethnic minorities develop about Whites are forged from a recognition that Whites represent the society oppressing them. White attitudes about themselves and other racial/ethnic groups are not forged under such conditions. Attitudes that most Whites develop about their own group and other racial/ethnic groups are reinforced by the stereotypes of the dominant society. Thus the system of oppression impacts the racial attitudes of both Whites and racial/ethnic minority person, but is experienced differently. (ibid. p. 131)

These authors also assert that the developmental sequence and directionality of white identity models is "imposed," i.e., movement from a racist to nonracist identity is assumed in developmental models but is by no means a biological or social given. As an alternative to the developmental model, Rowe et al. propose that white identity can better be described according to "types," which are then defined according to the kinds of racial attitudes that tend to go together. One example is the "avoidant type," which characterizes people who prefer to avoid ethnic issues in general, including the ethnicity of others as well as their own. Other types include, "dominative," which is characterized by a "strong ethnocentric perspective, which justifies the dominance of racial/ethnic minority peoples by the majority culture" (p. 137), and "conflictive," which opposes overt discrimination but would also be likely to oppose programs designed to reduce covert discrimination.

According to this model, racial attitudes and identities change not because of a developmental process but:

> . . . as a result of experiences that cause dissonance in the person's cognitive structures or schemas. (p. 135)

Whether or not one agrees with a developmental pattern or finds the model of Rowe et. al. more appealing, both approaches provide useful perspectives from which to view ethnic awareness and identity among members of the majority culture. Further, because it is important to be aware of both one's personal cultural identity and that of clients, interns are encouraged to reflect on models of majority and minority identity. The exercise that follows invites you to explore your own ethnic and cultural identity and your reactions to where others might be in their identity development or type.

EXERCISE: PERSONAL CULTURAL IDENTITY

The discussion above described models of identity for individuals from majority and minority cultures. In order to make this more real, this exercise is designed to explore two issues. First, in relation to the models described above, where would you place yourself along the stages of development or how would you describe your identity type? Second, if you were interacting with a person from a culture or ethnicity different from your own, which stages of their development or which identity type might be easiest, and which most difficult for you to deal with and why? Again, this exercise will be most effective if you discuss your reactions with peers whose ethnicity or cultural experiences are different than your own.

ASSUMPTIONS, MODELS, AND TECHNIQUES OF TREATMENT

As if it were not enough to challenge students to better understand their own background and those of others, we must now confront another difficult reality: Many of the fundamental principles that underlie the leading techniques of treatment and assessment are antithetical to the values and practices of people from different cultures.

We need not look far for an example to illustrate this. The structure of the typical therapy interaction is, if one thinks about it, a rather strange arrangement. Two or more individuals who have not formerly known one another get together and talk about the most intimate details of one of the individual's lives. The strangeness is compounded by the assumption that part of the purpose of the interaction is to help one of the people become aware of, understand, and modify things that are not even accessible to that person's own consciousness. Strangeness can be transformed into harmfulness when the assumptions of a therapy model imply that an oppressed person's problems are the sole result of intrapsychic processes, with no attention to the social pressures and challenges the person faces (Priest, 1991).

Even for people who are from the dominant culture and social classes, the structure and theories of psychotherapy are often a difficult adjustment. For those from other cultures, therapy may seem inherently foolish, crazy, or perhaps even harmful. If an intern who takes the dominant models and theories of treatment for granted sits down with someone from another culture and expects them to find the interaction perfectly normal, the intern and the client are probably in for a rude awakening.

Various authors have described how Western European models of therapy conflict with values and traditions of other cultures. For example, Pedersen (1987) listed ten common assumptions reflecting cultural bias in counseling. Included among these were assumptions about what constitutes normal behavior, the emphasis on individualism and independence, neglect of support systems, linear thinking, neglect of history, and a focus on changing individuals rather than systems.

Sue and Sue (1990) identify comparable issues, noting that even fundamental assumptions about counseling such as verbal and emotional expressiveness, the value of insight, cause-and-effect orientations, and the process of communication itself may differ across cultures. Sue and Sue also address the possibility that not only the techniques of counseling, but also the goals of counseling, may not be compatible across cultures. They delineate four conditions that may apply to culturally different clients.

The ideal situation is one in which the therapist uses culturally appropriate treatment processes to help the client achieve culturally appropriate treatment goals. In contrast to this condition are situations in which processes are culturally appropriate but the therapy goals are not; situations in which the goals are culturally appropriate but the processes are not, and, finally, but all too commonly, situations in which neither the goals nor the therapy processes are culturally appropriate.

A somewhat different approach to this issue has been proposed by Ibrahim, who emphasizes the importance of "world-views" in understanding cultural differences in counseling. Ibrahim and Kahn (1987) developed an instrument to assess world-views in relation to assumptions about human nature, social relationships, nature, time, and activity orientation. Ibrahim suggests that a first step in counseling should involve understanding the client's world-view and cultural identity in order to better match treatment approaches to the client.

While the models described above are proposed as general guides to cross-cultural counseling, examples of differences in cultural assumptions and world-views have also been discussed in relation to specific cultural groups. For example, Heinrich, Corbine, and Thomas (1990) review differences among Native American people and their reactions to counseling. Recognizing that there are more than three hundred different nations and equally as many different cultures among Native Americans, these authors explain that many Native Americans who are treated by psychotherapists may experience the therapists' expectations for self-disclosure to be "intrusive and inappropriate." On the other hand, differences in attitudes toward time, a cultural value of silence, and models of health may be misinterpreted by therapists as indications of resistance, defensiveness, or noncompliance.

Comparable cultural differences and resulting possibilities for misunderstandings have been described for Asian-American clients. In a comprehensive review, Leong (1986) discussed studies suggesting that Asian clients may prefer less ambiguity and more structured therapy interactions, may exhibit lower levels of verbal or emotional expressiveness, and are more likely to view counseling as "a directive, paternalistic, and authoritarian process" (p. 199).

EXERCISE

In light of the four possible conditions identified by Sue and Sue, and some of the cultural differences just described, select one or two of your preferred therapy models or techniques and consider how these might conflict with the values or traditional practices of people from other cultures. How might the goals you take for granted in therapy conflict with the cultural values of someone from a different background? If possible, after thinking about this for yourself discuss the matter with someone from a different culture to hear their impressions and ideas.

THE CULTURALLY SENSITIVE COUNSELOR

It would be possible to go on to list potential clashes between therapy assumptions and cultural values for Hispanic clients (Ponterotto & Casas, 1987), African-American families (Wilson & Stith, 1991), and many other cultural groups. The question this literature raises is: How can one possibly know everything there is to know to work with people from different cultural backgrounds? As Speight et al. (1991) acknowledged:

> Counselors-in-training have the insurmountable task of memorizing recipes for each of the cultural, racial, and ethnic groups (including the "exotics"). How many pages would such a cookbook require to address each of these groups? (p. 30)

Several responses to this issue have been proposed. One approach that is often recommended is to seek a "match" between client and counselor. According to this approach, counselors would come from the same cultural background as the client and would, presumably, be aware of, and sensitive to, the client's cultural experience.

The matching model has a number of merits but it is not without problems. One difficulty is that it is seldom possible to have on staff members of all the various cultures that might be served by a given agency. A second problem is that, as discussed earlier in this chapter, "categorization" of individuals is neither a simple nor necessarily desirable process. Speight et al. pointed out that,

> The problem with the matching model . . . is that individuals cannot be categorized so simply. For instance, who would be the best counselor match for a Puerto Rican lesbian, an African American gay man, or a multiracial woman? And what if age, religion, language, physical/mental challenge, acculturation level, generational status, identity development, or socioeconomic status were factored into the matching model? (p. 30)

Ho (1995) makes a similar point, cautioning that efforts to focus on group characteristics could make counselors vulnerable to

> activating automatically expectations and judgments about clients from that group—that is, to apply knowledge about a group to make judgments about individuals. . . . But there is a danger of overgeneralization and even stereotyping. The form and extent of a client's sharing of the patterned regularities must be investigated empirically and not taken for granted. (p. 7)

Faced with such complexities, interns and experienced therapists alike may be tempted to throw up their hands and declare that it is not possible to serve everyone. The issues are simply too complex to solve so let's go on just as we have before and "treat everyone alike." Understandable though this reaction might be, it is possible to deal more constructively with the complexity of cultural issues and to enhance substantially one's ability to work with individuals from different cultures.

Sue and Sue (1990) emphasize three key points about cross-cultural counseling. The culturally skilled counselor is first:

> . . . one who is able to relate to minority-group experiences and has knowledge of cultural and class factors. Second, counselors need to recognize that working with individuals from different cultures does not dictate the same approach, but one that is differentially consistent with lifestyles. In counseling *equal treatment may be discriminatory*. Third, it is important to systematically look at racial and ethnic differences as they relate to (a) the counselor's own approach and values, and (b) their various schools of counseling. (p. 165)

From this premise, Sue and Sue proceed to systematically identify and describe characteristics of culturally skilled counselors. These characteristics include: an awareness of one's own assumptions and biases, an understanding of the world-view of clients, and the ability to develop culturally appropriate intervention techniques. The first two characteristics, i.e., awareness of one's assumptions and understanding world-views, have already been addressed in this chapter. Next, we explore some ideas about culturally appropriate intervention techniques.

CULTURALLY SENSITIVE INTERVENTION APPROACHES

Throughout this chapter it has been emphasized that diversity exists not only across cultures but also within cultures. As such, one should be careful about offering specific recommendations for therapy approaches with members of specific cultures. I have found that a more useful approach is to describe a model for how one might develop and evaluate specific counseling techniques for specific cultures.

CULTURE-SPECIFIC COUNSELING

In spite of all that has been written about the differences between and within cultures, attempts to teach students to work with individuals from other cultures have tended to focus on how the predominant counseling and psychotherapy approaches can be adapted to serve people from other backgrounds. While it is probably preferable to adapt therapy to match clients rather than trying to force clients to match the therapy, adapting established methods may still fail. Nwachuku and Ivey (1991) point out that:

> The problem with adaptation of existing methods is that they begin with traditional theoretical assumptions, which are culturally biased. (p. 70)

As an alternative, Nwachuku and Ivey describe a model for generating "culture-specific" counseling theories and methods. Instead of adapting dominant therapy models to a culture, culture-specific approaches begin by trying to understand the culture's existing ways of helping.

> Culture-specific counseling asks such questions as "How does a particular culture view the helping relationship?" "How do they solve problems traditionally?" "Are there new specific counseling skills and ways of thinking that make better sense in the frame of reference of the culture than typical Euro-North American systems?" (p. 107)

In order to answer these questions, Nwachuku and Ivey begin by asking individuals from the specific culture to examine their own culture and describe the culture's values and helping styles. Based on this information, they develop training materials to teach counselors about the cultures, cultural values, behaviors, and traditional helping methods. Their research demonstrates that this approach modifies both the thinking and behavior of trainees to bring them more in line with the cultural norms. Nwachuku and Ivey suggest that similar procedures could be used to develop cultural specific training for other cultures.

EXERCISE: EXPLORING CULTURE-SPECIFIC STRATEGIES

As a way to enhance your own awareness of culture-specific counseling strategies and the helping models within cultures, select your own culture and, in consultation with others, reflect on what its traditional helping models are. Try to identify some principles or techniques that would help you advise others about what to consider in working with your culture. Then, select a culture with which you are relatively unfamiliar, and ask a member of that culture to explore with you what that culture's helping models and goals are. Again, with the person from that culture, try to identify principles or techniques that would help you advise others about what to consider in working with the other person's culture.

RESOURCES

As noted at the outset, the issue of cultural diversity in therapy was long neglected. Fortunately, in recent years, numerous books, special issues of journals, and individual articles have been written about working with clients from different populations. In addition, journals are now being published that focus specifically on diverse populations. Examples include the *Journal of Multicultural Counseling and Development*, *Journal of Black Psychology*, *International Journal of Intercultural Relations*, *Journal of Gay and Lesbian Social Services*, *Journal of Multicultural Social Work*, and many others.

In the space available here, it is not possible to review all of this literature. I have, however, organized a list of some of the most outstanding works addressing different groups. This list is presented below and additional sources cited in this chapter are included in the references at the end of the chapter. You are encouraged to review this list, the reference list for the chapter, and to pursue specific references that apply to clients with whom you work.

SPECIAL ISSUES OF JOURNALS

American Journal of Social Psychiatry (1983) Spring Vol. 3(2). Special Issue: The psychiatric care of "minority" groups.

Counseling Psychology Quarterly (1992) Vol. 5(3). Special Issue: Transcultural psychology: Perspective on theory, research and practice.

Counseling Psychology Quarterly (1989) Vol. 2(2). Special Issue: Counseling women and ethnic minorities.

Elementary School Guidance and Counseling (1989) Apr. Vol. 23(4). Special Issue: Cross-cultural counseling.

Journal of Counseling and Development (1991) Sep-Oct Vol. 70(1). Special Issue: Multiculturalism as a fourth force in counseling.

Journal of Counseling and Development (1990) March/April Vol. 68(4). Special Feature: Gender issues in counseling.

Journal of Counseling and Development (1989) Nov/Dec Vol. 68(2). Special Feature: Counseling persons with disabilities: 10-year update.

Journal of Counseling and Development (1989) Sept/Oct Vol. 68(1). Special Issue: Gay, lesbian and bisexual issues in counseling.

Journal of Counseling Psychology (1994). Special Section: Asian Americans seeking counseling.

Journal of Mental Health Administration (1992) Fall Vol. (19)3. Special Issue: Multicultural mental health and substance abuse services.

Journal of Psychology and Christianity (1992) Win Vol. 11(4). Special Issue: Multicultural counseling.

The Counseling Psychologist (1993). January Volume 21(1). Feminist counseling and therapy.

The Counseling Psychologist (1991) April Vol. 19(2). Special Issue: Counseling lesbian women and gay men.

The Counseling Psychologist (1989) April Vol. 17(2). Special Issue: Psychological nigrescence.

Women and Therapy (1990) Vol. 9(1-2). Special Issue: Diversity and complexity in feminist therapy.

BOOKS

Atkinson, D. R., & Hacket, G. (1995). *Counseling diverse populations*. Dubuque, IA: William C. Brown.

Atkinson, D. R., Morten, G., & Sue, D. W. (Eds.). (1993). *Counseling American minorities: A cross-cultural perspective, 4th ed.* Dubuque, IA: William C. Brown.

Locke, D. C. (1992). *Increasing multicultural understanding: A comprehensive model.* Newbury Park, CA: Sage.

Lonner, W. J., & Malpass, R. (1994). *Psychology and culture.* Needham Heights, MA: Allyn and Bacon.

Marsella, A. J., & Pedersen P. B. (Eds.). (1981). *Cross-cultural counseling and psychotherapy.* New York: Pergammon Press.

Meyers, H. F., Wohlford, P., Guzman, P. L., & Ecnemendia, R. J. (Eds.). (1991). *Ethnic minority perspectives on clinical training and services in psychology.* Washington, DC: American Psychological Association.

Pedersen, P. P., Draguns, J. G., Lonner, W. J., & Trimble, J. E. (1981). *Counseling across cultures (revised and expanded edition).* Honolulu, HA: The East West Center—University Press of Hawaii.

Sue, D. W., & Sue, D. (1990). *Counseling the culturally different: Theory and Practice, 2nd ed.* New York: John Wiley & Sons.

REFERENCES

Atkinson, D. R., Morten, G., & Sue, D. W. (Eds.). (1989). *Counseling American minorities.* Dubuque, IA: William C. Brown.

Carrillo, D. F., Holzhalb, C. M., & Thyer, B. A. (1993). Assessing social work students' attitudes related to cultural diversity: A review of selected measures. *Journal of Social Work Education, 29,* 263–268.

Corvin, S., & Wiggins, F. (1989). An antiracism training model for white professionals. *Journal of Multicultural Counseling and Development, 17,* 105–114.

Cross, W. E. (1971). The Negro to Black conversion experience: Towards a psychology of Black liberation. *Black World, 20(9),* 13–27.

———. (1978). The Cross and Thomas models of psychological Nigrescence. *Journal of Black Psychology, 5(1),* 13–19.

Dobbins, J. E., & Skillings, J. H. (1991). The utility of race labeling in understanding cultural identity: A conceptual tool for the social science practitioner. *Journal of Counseling and Development, 70,* 37–44.

Hardiman, R. (1982). White identity development: A process oriented model for describing the racial consciousness of white Americans. *Dissertation Abstracts International, 43,* 104A. (University Microfilms No. 82–10330).

Heinrich, R. K., Corbine, J. L., & Thomas, K. R. (1990). Counseling Native Americans. *Journal of Counseling and Development, 69,* 128–133.

Helms, J. E. (1984). Toward a theoretical model of the effects of race on counseling. *The Counseling Psychologist, 12,* 153–165.

Helms, J. E. (Ed.). (1990). *Black and white racial identity: Theory, research and practice.* Westport, CT: Greenwood.

Ho, D. Y. F. (1995). Internalized culture, culturocentrism, and transcendence. *The Counseling Psychologist, 23,* 4–24.

Ibrahim, F. A. (1991). Contribution of cultural worldview to generic counseling and development. *Journal of Counseling and Development, 70,* 13–19.

Ibrahim, F. A., & Kahn, H. (1987). Assessment of world views. *Psychological Reports, 60,* 163–176.

Ibrahim, F. A., Stadler, H. A., Arredondo, P., & McFadden, H. (1986). *The status of human rights issues in counselor education: A national survey.* Paper presented at the annual meeting of the American Association for Counseling and Development, Los Angeles, CA.

Johnson, S. D. Jr., (1990). Toward clarifying culture, race, and ethnicity in the context of multicultural counseling. *Journal of Multicultural Counseling and Development, 18,* 41–50.

Kiselica, M. S. (1991). Reflections on a multicultural internship experience. Special Issue: Multiculturalism as a fourth force in counseling. *Journal of Counseling and Development, 70,* 126–130.

Leong, F. T. L. (1986). Counseling and psychotherapy with Asian-Americans: Review of the literature. *Journal of Counseling Psychology, 33,* 196–206.

Locke, D. C. (1992). *Increasing multicultural understanding: A comprehensive model.* Newbury Park, CA: Sage.

Marsella, A. J., & Pedersen P. B. (Eds.). (1981). *Cross-cultural counseling and psychotherapy.* New York: Pergammon Press.

McFadden, J., & Wilson, T. (1977). Non-white academic training within counselor education, rehabilitation counseling, and student personnel programs. Unpublished manuscript.

Nwachuku, U. T., & Ivey, A. E. (1991). Culture-specific counseling: An alternative training model. *Journal of Counseling and Development, 70,* 106–111.

Parham, T. A. (1989). Cycles of psychological nigrescence. *The Counseling Psychologist, 17,* 187–226.

Pedersen, P. B. (1987). Ten frequent assumptions of cultural bias in counseling. *Journal of Multicultural Counseling and Development, 15,* 16–24.

Pedersen, P. B. (1991). Multiculturalism as a generic approach to counseling. *Journal of Counseling and Development, 70,* 6–12.

Ponterotto, J. G., & Casas, J. M. (1987). In search of multicultural competence within counselor education programs. *Journal of Counseling and Development, 65,* 430–434.

Ponterotto, J. G., Rieger, B. P., Barrett, A., & Sparks, R. (1994). Assessing multicultural counseling competence: A review of instrumentation. *Journal of Counseling and Development, 72,* 316–322.

Priest, R. (1991). Racism and prejudice as negative impacts on African American clients in therapy. *Journal of Counseling and Development, 70,* 213–215.

Proctor, E. K., & Davis, L. E. (1994). The challenge of racial difference: Skills for clinical practice. *Social Work, 39,* 314–323.

Ridley, C. R., Mendoza, D. W., & Kanitz, B. E. (1994). Multicultural training: Reexamination, operationalization, and integration. *The Counseling Psychologist, 22,* 227–289.

Rosado, J. W., & Elias, M. J. (1993). Ecological and psychocultural mediators in the delivery of services for urban, culturally diverse Hispanic clients. *Professional Psychology: Research and Practice, 24,* 450–459.

Rowe, W., Bennet, S. K., & Atkinson, D. R. (1994). White racial identity models: A critique and alternative proposal. *The Counseling Psychologist, 22,* 129–146.

Ruiz, A. S. (1990). Ethnic identity: Crisis and resolution. *Journal of Multicultural Counseling and Development, 18,* 29–40.

Smith, E. J. (1991). Ethnic identity development: Toward the development of a theory within the context of majority/minority status. *Journal of Counseling and Development, 70,* 181–188.

Sodowsky, G. R., Taffe, R. C., Gutkin, T. B., & Wise, S. L. (1994). Development of the multicultural counseling inventory: A self-report measure of multicultural competencies. *Journal of Counseling Psychology, 41,* 137–148.

Speight, S. L., Myers, L. J., Cox, C. I., & Highlen, P. S. (1991). A redefinition of multicultural counseling. Special Issue: Multiculturalism as a fourth force in counseling. *Journal of Counseling and Development, 70,* 29–36.

Sue, D. W., & Sue, D. (1990). *Counseling the culturally different: Theory and practice, 2nd ed.* New York: John Wiley & Sons.

Westwood, M. J., & Ishiyama, F. I. (1990). The communication process as a critical intervention for client change in cross-cultural counseling. *Journal of Multicultural Counseling and Development, 18,* 163–171.

Wilson, L. L., & Stith S. M. (1991). Culturally sensitive therapy with black clients. *Journal of Counseling and Development*, *19*, 32–43.

Wintrob, R. M., & Harvey, Y. K. (1981). The self-awareness factor in intercultural psychotherapy: Some personal reflections. In P. P. Pedersen, J. G. Draguns, W. J. Lonner, and J. E. Trimble, Eds. (1981). *Counseling across cultures: Revised and expanded edition*. University Press of Hawaii: Honolulu, Hawaii.

CHAPTER 7

CLINICAL WRITING

Clinical writing is different than other writing you have learned. The purpose, style, subject matter, and format of clinical reports require a new set of skills that very few students are trained in during their undergraduate education. This chapter and the next are designed to help you understand the process and content of clinical writing so you can begin to develop skills that will serve you throughout your academic and professional career.

One way to approach this topic is to assume that students have mastered basic writing skills and need only to focus on the unique aspects of clinical writing. My experience suggests this assumption is sometimes valid, but more often than not, students have trouble with clinical writing because they have yet to develop their writing skills in general. Based on that experience, along with discussing clinical writing, this chapter offers suggestions for improving your overall writing skill. If your writing skills are already well established, you may want to skim the initial portions of the first chapter and spend more time on the later material. Most students will be well advised to read all of the chapters carefully. As Fischer (1985) has observed, many of the principles of writing good reports are "*commonsensical . . . but not yet commonplace.*"

WRITING CAN BE LEARNED

It is sometimes said that writing is a gift and cannot be taught. That statement is false. Writing, like any other skill, can be taught and learned by most people. This does not mean we will all win Pulitzer prizes, but it does mean most students can learn to write reports that are accurate, clear, and in a style that is consistent with professional standards. If you are fortunate enough to have developed good writing skills already, this chapter will help you adapt those skills to clinical writing. If writing has never been a strong point for you, take heart in the following anecdote.

The summer before my first year of graduate school, I spent two months hiking and climbing in the mountains near my family home in Colorado. Much of that time I hiked alone and often went for several days without speaking, hearing, reading, or writing a word. The experience was therapeutic but it also posed a problem when graduate school began. Among the requirements for all first-year students was a course in psychological assessment. The course involved learning to administer, score, and interpret the major psychological tests. The course also involved writing two lengthy assessment reports each week.

As an undergraduate I was an average writer but received no specific training in clinical writing. After spending so much of the summer away from language, I found the task of writing in graduate school extremely difficult. In a time before word processing, I worked days on each report, typing, erasing, retyping, starting over, and finishing at 2:00 or 3:00 A.M. on the morning reports were due. To make erasures easier, I used specially treated "erasable" paper. To save money on "white-out" liquid I was tempted to buy a gallon of white interior latex wall paint and use it instead. At one point, when my manual typewriter kept skipping spaces between letters, I literally pitched it out our second floor window.

In spite of my best efforts, on embarrassingly frequent occasions reports were returned with huge red Xs or NO! covering the entire first page. With innate clinical skill I sensed that these messages were a sign of dissatisfaction on the part of my professor. I was right. Indeed, midway through the semester I was told that if my writing did not improve I would have to retake the course or might even be dismissed. Faced with this disheartening news I asked what I could do to improve my skills. The instructor replied that he did not know. He could teach assessment, but he could not teach writing. I would have to learn to write somewhere else.

The standard resolution to such stories is to conclude: "Looking back on the experience it was probably very good for me." Without offering that cliché, I can say that as the result of my own difficulties in writing I may have learned some things that will help readers of this book develop their skills more efficiently. I begin with simple rules that apply to all writing.

FOCUSING READING TO LEARN WRITING

One of the best ways to improve your writing is to change the way you read. Most of the time when people read they are interested primarily in the content of what they are reading. They want to know the news of the day, learn what the journal article concludes, or discover how a story turns out. This emphasis on content is a fine way to gather information but it is not likely to improve your writing. In order for reading to help improve your writing you must focus on the structure and style that are used, not just on the information. In other words, the focus of reading changes from "what" the writing is about to "how" the piece is written.

A useful analogy may be to think about how a person who plays the violin will listen to a violin concerto much differently than a casual spectator with no aspirations of playing themselves. The casual spectator merely enjoys the melody. The person learning to play attends closely to the technique of the musician. Similarly, people who do not play golf themselves may watch only to see how far and straight the ball goes. By comparison, a person who wants to learn the sport

would do well to ignore the ball and focus instead on the player's motions.

If you want to learn how to write clinical reports, a good place to begin is by reading reports others have written. When you do this, remember to change your focus. Merely reading the content of other reports will tell you little about how to write about clients you might see yourself. What really matters is the structure and style that are used in the reports. The specific content will change from client to client, but the structure and style can be used again and again.

As an exercise to illustrate the distinction between content and style, consider the sentence pairs below. You will note that the contents of each pair are essentially the same, but they differ in style and structure. The differences are intentionally subtle and you are not told which is "better." Your task is to note the differences and give some thought to how they communicate information. You may also want to try rewriting the sentences yourself to see if you can improve them in some way. I will discuss these sentences further in a moment.

EXERCISE

Sentence Pairs
1. A. During the interview the client said that he had never before been seen in therapy by a therapist.
    B. The client indicated no previous experience in therapy.
2. A. Test results suggest the presence of mild to moderate depression, anxiety and concerns about family matters.
    B. According to the results of the test there is evidence of depression in the mild to moderate range, along with anxiety and apparent concerns about issues relating to family.
3. A. William Smith is an affable, energetic, 75-year-old male, who arrived neatly attired in a dark gray suit, spoke openly about his presenting concerns, and expressed a willingness to "do whatever it takes to get going again." Mr. Smith stated that he came to therapy out of concern that his sex life has begun to decline from a frequency of five to three times per week.
    B. William Smith is a 75-year-old male with a presenting problem of decreased sexual performance. At the time of the interview he was well dressed and groomed and appeared to be well motivated.

PRACTICE AND FEEDBACK

Writing, like any other skill, is learned through practice, but practice alone is not enough. One also needs feedback and constructive criticism. Without such feedback there is a risk of practicing mistakes rather than learning new skills. As an intern you have access to at least three sources of feedback about your writing. Your peers, supervisor, and course instructor can all offer input about both the style and content of your clinical writing. I encourage you to take advantage of each of these resources because they will offer different perspectives and because you may find it easier to work with one person rather than another. In my own experience, when my instructor was unable to help with writing, fellow graduate students were the most valuable source of feedback. Indeed, had it not been for their help, I might not have completed my degree. Later, supervisors at several internship placements offered further assistance. The importance of feedback continues to this day as colleagues, editors, and students offer their comments and criticisms.

Just as you must read differently to improve your writing, you must also seek and accept a different kind of feedback. When people ask for comments about what they have written, they often ask with the hope of receiving positive statements. "Looks fine to me," "Very good," "Nice work," etc., can help us feel good, but such comments do nothing to improve our writing. In order to make feedback productive you must be willing to invite and accept blunt criticism and suggestions. Compliments are important, but we learn more by discovering mistakes and correcting them. One student expressed this well when he circulated a draft of his report to several peers with a cover note that said, "Do me a favor and be as critical as you can. Rip this apart. I mean it. I need your honest criticism and suggestions."

Because people are used to asking for and giving only general and positive comments, you may need to take the initiative to ask for more specific and critical suggestions. The most important step is to go beyond global "grade"-like statements and solicit comments about specific parts of what you have written. For example, rather than simply asking people to read your work and tell you what they think of it, ask someone to read each sentence or paragraph and tell you how the writing could be clearer or more succinct. Invite your readers to suggest alternative ways of expressing what you have written. You may even ask them to write the same information in their words, then compare your work and theirs to see how each might be improved. I often instruct students to exchange their reports and offer one another criticism. With students' permission I read reports aloud in class anonymously and ask for constructive group feedback about how the writing could be improved. Throughout the feedback process, you must be willing to wrestle with difficult phrases or passages until they come out the way you want. You may also have to throw out some of your favorite passages in order to make the overall writing work. This process of writing and revising helps develop the skills of the writer and of those who give feedback.

As a way of helping your reader give you the most useful suggestions, you may find the following instructions helpful.

Please read this as carefully and critically as you can. I am not asking for you to tell me if it is good or bad. I want you to suggest how you think it can be improved. I welcome your comments and will appreciate whatever criticism you have to offer. As you read, please mark any sentences or phrases that are unclear, awkward, poorly worded, ambiguous, uninteresting, or in some other way lacking. If you have suggestions for how sentences or passages could be improved, please feel free to write them. If there are problems with organization please note them and suggest alternatives. If any information is omitted or is not expressed clearly, please identify what should be added or expressed differently. Finally, if there are any other changes that you think would help, I would welcome your ideas. Thank you in advance for your help. Honest criticism is very hard to find and I value your assistance.

Instructions such as these facilitate feedback in two ways. First, they give permission for your reader to be critical. Second, they suggest specific areas for the reader to focus on and ways of giving feedback about those areas. The next task is perhaps the most difficult. Having asked for honest criticism, you must be open enough to really accept the criticism you receive without getting your feelings hurt or becoming defensive.

REWRITING

Before any of the chapters in this book were ready for publication they each went through perhaps as many as twenty revisions. This comes as a surprise to some readers, but it merely reflects a basic yet often unappreciated fact about the writing process: writing skill develops through rewriting (Zinsser, 1980).

There are two ways in which quality writing depends on rewriting. First, in order to develop your skills as a writer you must gain practice through revising whatever you write. Writing is like anything else you want to learn. You have to try, make mistakes, try again, make more mistakes, try again in a different way, make more mistakes, and so on, until your skills develop. This process of repeated revision helps you learn more efficient ways of writing and gradually enables you to write better first drafts.

Unfortunately, many students have not had experience rewriting because writing assignments in academic settings seldom require revision. The typical written report is submitted for a grade at the end of a semester but there may be no requirement or opportunity to receive useful feedback and a chance to rewrite the paper. As a result, students may have some practice in writing first drafts, and they may receive an evaluation of their writing skills, but such assignments do little to teach students how to write. Students do, however, learn the bad habit of expecting to write something once and then be done with it. This experience often creates resistance when students are eventually told they must rewrite a report or paper.

It would be much better if every writing assignment in college and graduate school involved at least two drafts and feedback from multiple sources. This would develop the habit of revision and would improve writing skills far more than the predominant single-draft practice (Baird & Anderson, 1990).

Along with improving writing skills, rewriting is important because even the most accomplished authors realize their first drafts can always be improved. No matter how much skill one develops as a writer, rewriting will always be part of the process. Understanding and embracing this reality may be just as important as the development of writing skill itself.

COMMON WRITING PROBLEMS

As an instructor and supervisor I have read several thousand papers and reports by students. This experience has taught me that most of the problems students have in writing can be grouped into a few categories. These include problems relating to clarity, choice of wording, grammar, transitions between topics, and organization. Students who do not write well produce sentences that lack clear meaning. Their writing often contains words that were chosen carelessly or mean something the student did not intend to say. Poor writers also have difficulty structuring the overall sequence of topics and connecting smoothly from one topic to another. These problems are all remarkably common and can lead to papers that are painfully difficult to read. The good news is that most of the errors can be corrected.

I have found several books to be particularly useful in helping students learn to write. Three books that address issues common to all writing are: *On Writing Well* by William Zinsser (1980); the *Harbrace College Handbook,* by Hodges et al. (1990); and the classic, *The Elements of Style* by William Strunk, Jr., and E. B. White (1972). Two excellent works geared specifically to clinicians are Norman Tallent's *Psychological Report Writing,* (1988) and Constance Fischer's *Individualizing Psychological Assessment* (1985). Tallent has conducted extensive research on clinical reports and writing, and, although his title addresses psychologists specifically, the book contains information that is useful to professionals and interns from many disciplines. Fischer's book, in addition to providing one of the clearest descriptions I have found of the assessment and report writing process, offers extremely valuable writing tips and a host of examples of common student writing errors and how they can be corrected. One other source that can help beginning clinical writers find suitable wording for reports is *The Clinician's Thesaurus 3* by Edward Zuckerman (1990).

CAUTION: TASTES, SUPERVISORS, AND INSTRUCTORS VARY
The next section reviews the suggestions of the authors mentioned above as well as insights gained from my own experience as a clinician, supervisor, and instructor. Before offering those suggestions, a brief caveat is in order. Although I will present examples and explanations of what I consider good and bad writing, be aware that different instructors and supervisors may have opinions and preferences that vary from what is said here. If your instructor or supervisor offer alternative expectations or suggestions, there is no need to become frustrated by such differences. Instead, try various approaches and examine their differences. As you continue your training you can develop a style that works best for you.

KEYS TO GOOD WRITING

SIMPLIFY YOUR WRITING BUT NOT YOUR CLIENTS
Strunk and White instruct the writer to "Use definite, specific, concrete language. Prefer the specific to the general, the definite to the vague, the concrete to the abstract" (p. 15). In a similar vein, Zinsser's first principle of writing well is "simplicity." As he describes it: ". . . the secret of good writing is to strip every sentence to its cleanest components" (1980, pp. 8–9). I strongly endorse these principles but would add that the clinician's task is to simplify writing without simplifying the client. In other words, you must strive to write as simply and directly as possible, but you must also communicate accurately about your client.

The following examples demonstrate how simplicity and directness in writing can contribute to improved clinical reports.

EXAMPLE 1

A. At various occasions during the interview Mr. Johnson exhibited signs of nervousness and distress.
B. In response to questions about his family, Mr. Johnson began to shift in his chair, stammered slightly, and appeared to avoid eye contact.

Note how the first example may sound like it uses "clinical language" and form, but it actually speaks in very general terms. Words like "various occasions" and "signs of nervousness" do not really tell what the client did or when. By comparison, the second example directly describes Mr. Johnson's behavior and when it occurred. This lets the reader better visualize the client and connects specific behaviors with specific stimuli. Thus, by following the principle of preferring "the definite to the vague, the concrete to the abstract," the sentence is improved both stylistically and clinically.

For a second example we can return to a sentence pair presented earlier in the discussion of focused reading.

EXAMPLE 2

A. William Smith is an affable, energetic, 75-year-old male, who arrived neatly attired in a dark gray suit, spoke openly about his presenting concerns, and expressed a willingness to "do whatever it takes to get going again." Mr. Smith indicated that he came to therapy out of concern that his sex life has begun to decline from a frequency of five to three times per week.

B. William Smith is a 75-year-old male with a presenting problem of decreased sexual performance. At the time of the interview he was well dressed and groomed and appeared to be well motivated.

Which of the two descriptions, A or B, do you prefer? Why?

This example is more subtle and might be subject to more dispute, but for most situations I would prefer the description offered in A. There are several reasons for this preference. First, although the second example is clearly more succinct, that quality alone does not necessarily mean it is more direct or that it better represents the client. Describing a "presenting problem of decreased sexual performance" does not tell the reader what the problem is. For some, decreased sexual performance might mean going from having sex twice a month to once per month. As the alternative version shows, for this man decreased performance has a much different meaning. A second reason I prefer example A is that it gives the reader a better sense of who the client is as a person. Again, this comes about because the description is more specific. "Neatly attired in a dark gray suit" paints a clearer picture than "well dressed and groomed." Similarly, using the direct quote that the client would "do whatever it takes. . ." brings the reader closer to the client than saying he "appeared to be well motivated."

Fischer (1985) offers advice consistent with this example.

> Early in a report I provide physical descriptions of the client, in part so that the reader can picture the client throughout the written assessment. I try to describe the client in motion rather than statically, so the reader will be attuned to the ways the person moves through and shapes and is shaped by his or her environment. (p. 37)

Please note that although I would prefer the description offered in A for most situations, there are advantages to example B and there are instances in which it would be preferable. The main advantage of B is brevity. If time is at a premium and there is little need to convey a sense of the person beyond the clinical data that follow, the description can be shortened. Your task as a clinician and as a writer is first to make a choice about what matters, then determine how best to include that in your report.

OMIT NEEDLESS WORDS

One way to simplify your writing is to leave out words that are not needed. To appreciate this, compare the sentence you just read with the heading that preceded it. The heading, "Omit needless words," was borrowed directly from Strunk and White (p. 17). It conveys the main idea in three words. By comparison, the sentence that followed took seven

words, i.e. "leave out words that are not needed" to say the same thing.

Zinsser observes that: "writing improves in direct ratio to the numbers of things we can keep out of it that shouldn't be there" (p. 14). Strunk and White state:

> Vigorous writing is concise. A sentence should contain no unnecessary words, a paragraph no unnecessary sentences. . . This requires not that the writer make all his sentences short, or that he avoid all detail and treat his subjects only in outline, but that every word tell. (p. 17)

To illustrate this point, let us return again to the examples offered in the discussion of focused reading.

EXAMPLE 1

1. A. During the interview the client said that he had never before been seen in therapy by a therapist.
   B. The client indicated no previous experience in therapy.

What unnecessary words has the second sentence eliminated? The phrase "During the interview" is removed because it can be assumed that is when the client spoke. The phrase "said that he had never before been seen in therapy," ten words, is replaced by "indicated no previous experience in therapy," six words that mean the same thing. This cutting of words saves time and makes the report shorter but sacrifices no important information about the client. A similar process can be applied to a second example from our earlier discussion. Read the two examples and identify where and how needless words are omitted.

EXAMPLE 2

A. Test results suggest the presence of mild to moderate depression, anxiety and concerns about family matters.

B. According to the results of the test there is evidence of depression in the mild to moderate range, along with anxiety and apparent concerns about issues relating to family.

Strunk and White offer similar examples of how everyday expressions contain many needless words. For instance, "This is a subject that . . . ," versus, "This subject . . ."; "I was unaware of the fact that . . ." versus, "I was unaware that . . ." Common speech also unnecessarily places prepositions after many phrases or uses prepositions when other phrases would work better. Compare "Wake me up at seven" versus "Wake me at seven"; "Find out about . . ." versus "Learn . . ." Within the helping professions clinical verbiage can complicate very simple matters. For example, "The subject was engaged in walking behaviors" versus "He was walking." Or, consider, "He produced little verbal material" versus "He was quiet."

Just as dietary fat clogs your arteries, verbal fat will clog your writing. As the examples above have shown, learning to trim unnecessary words or phrases is a key step toward improving your writing. Zinsser puts this very nicely when he says, "Be grateful for everything you can throw away" (p 18).

As with the earlier recommendation to embrace rewriting, responding to the instruction to shorten your writing will take some adjustment. Students have learned that excess verbiage helps stretch papers to meet the ten-page minimum so often imposed by faculty. Now the message is to shorten those ten-page papers to the fewest pages possible and make every word count. Tallent suggests that one can tell a report is too long if the person who has written it,

> . . . is unhappy over the length of time required to write it and experiences difficulty in organizing a multitude of details for presentation. It is too long when it contains content that is not relevant or useful, when the detailing is greater than can be put to good use. (p. 73)

Tallent offers examples of lengthy reports to illustrate his point. Following one such example he quips, "Just glancing at this report one may wonder if it is too long. On reading it, one may be sure that it is" (p 139). To avoid such statements about your own work, practice trimming away everything that is unnecessary. You will have much greater impact if you can express the most meaning with the fewest words, rather than the least meaning with the most words.

CHOOSE WORDS CAREFULLY

Along with limiting the number of words used, you must also be attentive to the meaning of the words you use. Careful choice of words is essential to all of your work as a clinician. In staff meetings, therapy sessions, and in your written reports the words you use will be crucial. As a clinician you cannot afford to be careless or haphazard about what you say or write. You must be aware of all the subtleties of language and learn to say exactly what you mean. This is especially true of written reports because once a report is written others may read it without you being present to explain, clarify, or correct mistakes. Careless use of words can also come back to haunt you if your records or reports are ever used in a legal proceeding.

Zinsser advises: ". . . you will never make your mark as a writer unless you develop a respect for words and a curiosity about their shades of meaning that is almost obsessive. . ." (p. 35). I agree and would expand this statement by substituting the word clinician for writer. You will never be a fully skilled clinician unless you are acutely aware of words, attend precisely to the words used by others, and think carefully about the words you use.

Tallent (1985) describes a series of studies in which various groups of mental health professionals were asked to indicate what they like and what they dislike in typical psychological reports. Among the factors most frequently criticized, the use of ambiguous wording was frequently cited as a problem. The use of vaguely defined clinical terms also receives criticism in the literature. Tallent cites a classic study by Grayson and Tolman (1950) in which clinical psychologists and psychiatrists offered definitions for the twenty words most commonly used in psychological reports. Reviewing the list of words and definitions, the authors of the study were struck by how loosely defined many of the words were.

Fifteen years after the original study by Grayson and Tolman, Siskind (1967) replicated the design and found similar results. Although the specific words included in such lists might differ if the study were performed again today, there is no reason to assume the definitional ambiguities would be any less now than they were in 1950 and 1967. For students and interns the matter of ambiguity can be particularly challenging because many of the words that sound the "most clinical" are in fact highly ambiguous. Students may be eager to use technical terms as a way of demonstrating their knowledge to supervisors. The trouble is that a great deal of what passes for clinical wording may sound scientific but often obfuscates rather than elucidates. Fischer advises:

> Say what you mean in concrete terms rather than dressing up the text in professionalese. (p. 125)

Tallent concurs:

> In our view words like *oral, narcissistic, masochistic, immature, compulsive,* and *schizophrenia* are often more concealing than revealing.
>
> Technical words do not cause, but readily lend themselves to, imprecise or incomplete thinking. There is the error of nominalism, wherein we simply name a thing or an occurrence and think we understand something of the real world. (p. 69; italics in the original)

Earlier in this book I made similar observations about the overuse of the word "inappropriate." It would be possible to identify other words or phrases, such as "manipulative," "dependent," or "just doing it for attention," which are used with similar frequency and with equal ambiguity. As an antidote to the use of such jargon, Fischer asserts that:

> Saying what one means, both in speech and in writing, requires one to anchor abstractions in concrete examples. Ask yourself how you would explain what you mean to a 12-year-old. If you can't figure out how to do that then you do not yet know what you mean—what your technical information comes down to in terms of your client's life. (p. 134)

EXERCISE

Read the three sentences below and ask yourself if the differences in wording might communicate subtle yet important differences in meaning.

A. Mr. Smith denied any abuse of alcohol or drugs.
B. Mr. Smith said he does not abuse alcohol or drugs.
C. Mr. Smith does not abuse alcohol or drugs.

In the first sentence of the exercise above we encounter another of the many misused clinical words. The word "denies" in this sentence is very important. In psychological language, "denial" is a form of defense and implies that a person is not being fully honest or that he or she is unconsciously repressing information. In this case, it might be that Mr. Smith "denies" alcohol abuse but we know or suspect that he does in fact abuse. It might also be that Mr. Smith is genuine and does not abuse alcohol or drugs. If that is the case, the second sentence would be better because it avoids the subtle intimation raised by the word "denies." The third sentence is still more clear about whether or not Mr. Smith abuses but it may suffer from a different problem. Do we really know the statement is true, or is it just something Mr. Smith has told us? The sentence as written implies that we know it to be fact, but if the source of information is Mr. Smith we should so indicate.

If this sounds like nitpicking, it is not. To appreciate why, ask yourself what might happen if you gave a report containing these sentences to other professionals who based clinical decisions on a misunderstanding of what you wrote. Do other readers conclude from the first sentence that Mr. Smith really drinks but does not admit it, or do they conclude that Mr. Smith does not drink? Do they conclude from the third sentence that we are sure alcohol and drugs are not a problem, or do they assume that is just what the client has told us? If the scenario of clinical misinterpretation is not convincing, imagine trying to explain the meaning while testifying in your own defense in a liability suit.

One way to reduce ambiguity in reports is to read questionable passages to colleagues and ask them to tell you if the passage is clear or not and what they think it means. In some cases I ask nonclinicians to read my reports and offer feedback. This is particularly helpful if a report might be read by family members or others who are not trained in the profession.

Another, and too often overlooked, tool is the dictionary. I encourage students to use both a standard dictionary and a dictionary of professional terms. The standard dictionary can help you understand what words mean and imply in ordinary usage. Be careful, however, not to assume that definitions offered in a normal dictionary carry the same meanings when applied in clinical writing. If a word has specific clinical meanings the professional dictionary will cite specific meanings within the clinical context. Time after time students use words that they think they know only to discover that the word means or implies something entirely different than they thought. One student used the word "limpid" to describe how a brain injured patient held his arm. Another spoke of a situation attenuating the client's anxiety when the situation in fact exacerbated the anxiety. I recently heard a colleague

repeatedly use the word duplicity when he clearly meant duplication.

If you do not know the meaning of any of the words used in the previous paragraph, did you look them up? If not, why? One of my students answered a similar question in class by saying, "I already took the GRE." That student did not get the point, nor did he get a letter of recommendation.

Misuse of clinical terms is also common. Students frequently confuse delusions with hallucinations, obsession with compulsion, schizophrenia with multiple personality, etc. Certainly one of the most commonly misused terms is negative reinforcement. Even if you are sure you know what this means, look it up in a textbook. In one upper-division undergraduate class, out of twenty students who said they were sure they knew the definition, only five were actually right. Again, if you fail to appreciate the importance of precise wording, consider that misunderstanding the meaning of negative reinforcement in a report could lead to interventions that are exactly the opposite of those that the writer intended.

CLARITY

Choosing words carefully is part of the larger issue of achieving clarity in writing and clinical work. This demand includes both clarity of individual words and clarity in syntax and organization. If the organization of a report is not clear the reader will have to search to find important information. If the syntax of a sentence is unclear the meaning may be misinterpreted. For example,

The therapist told the client about his problems.

Whose problems is the therapist talking about—the therapist's or the client's?

Strunk and White caution that: "Muddiness is not merely a disturber of prose, it is also a destroyer of life, of hope" (p. 72). In clinical work, this is not an overstatement. I know of a case in which one therapist told another he had an appointment to see a client "next Friday." As the conversation took place on a Wednesday, the listener assumed the appointment was two days away. The speaker, however, was referring to Friday of the following week. Because the client in question was experiencing a serious crisis, this was a difference of potentially grave consequence.

Although most people would agree that clarity is important in clinical reports, the difficulty lies in recognizing when our own reports are unclear. Because we think we know what we mean when we write something, we assume that what we have written adequately conveys our intention. Thus, we readily overlook passages that may be virtually incomprehensible or, worse, that may appear comprehensible but will be misinterpreted by others.

As suggested earlier, one way to limit misunderstanding is to have someone else read a report before it goes to the intended recipient. If this is not possible, it is often helpful to pretend you know nothing of the case yourself, then read the report out loud. Reading aloud brings out aspects of writing that we do not recognize when we read silently to ourselves. If time permits, another extremely valuable technique is to set a report aside for several days and then read it again with an open mind. Along with helping to identify writing problems this also allows one to think more about the case before sending the report.

I cannot overemphasize how important clarity is to your writing. Clinicians simply must learn to be extremely careful about their words. You must know and say precisely what you mean. It is not enough to defend with "C'mon, you know what I meant." That may work in everyday discourse but it is unacceptable in professional work. If the reader does not know exactly what is meant, the responsibility falls on the writer, not the reader. Say what you mean and say it clearly. I feel so strongly about this that I have on occasion told students bluntly, "If you do not want to learn to use words carefully and accurately you should probably consider another profession."

KNOW YOUR AUDIENCE

The final recommendation about writing is to know your audience. Some instructors and articles about clinical writing dictate specific and fixed rules for the style and content to be included in clinical reports. I prefer an approach that offers suggestions but at the same time encourages you to choose and adapt your style and content with an awareness of your audience.

Fischer says repeatedly in her book: "reports are for readers, not for the author" (p. 115). Tallent stresses this principle as well and cites a report by Hartlage and Merck (1971) which showed that the utility of reports is primarily weakened by, as Tallent describes it, a ". . . profound . . . lack of reflection by report writers on what might be useful to report readers, a simple failure to use common sense" (Tallent, 1988, p. 20). Hartlage and Merck observed that ". . . reports can be made more relevant to their prospective users merely by having the psychologists familiarize themselves with the uses to which their reports are to be applied" (p. 460).

For example, a report prepared for a fellow professional in your discipline may differ from a report prepared for an attorney, family members, or others with different backgrounds and needs. Similarly, if you believe certain aspects of a client are being overlooked by others, you may want to emphasize those in your report. The most important thing is for you to write with conscious awareness of how your style and content meet your clinical and professional purpose.

EXERCISE

As a way of enhancing your awareness of different groups to which your reports might be targeted, read the list of people below and write some of the concerns that you might keep in mind if preparing a report for each. For example, you might consider factors such as the readers' level of training or knowledge, how much time they have, and the style of reports they are accustomed to reading. How do these and other factors differ for each group?

The client
Family members of the client
Insurance companies
Clinical psychologists
Counselors
Social workers
Psychiatrists
Non-psychiatrist M.D.s
School teachers
Students
Attorneys
Judges
Professional journals
Newspapers
Others for whom you might write

Reviewing the list above should enhance your awareness of general factors to consider in writing, but you must also remember that, regardless of their profession or role, different individuals will have different preferences and needs. One school teacher may be well versed in diagnostic categories but another may know nothing at all about them. One psychiatrist may prefer reports that are as brief as possible and that convey "just the facts." Another may appreciate more detailed reports that convey more of a sense of the client as a person.

If you know for whom you will be writing before you write a report, it is sometimes a good idea to contact the person and ask what their preferences are for style and content and what they will be looking for from your report. After you write a report you can follow up and ask the recipient for feedback. Your role as an intern gives you a perfect opportunity to ask for such information and many people will be glad to offer their suggestions.

REFERENCES

Baird, B., & Anderson, D. (1990). A dual-draft approach to writing. *The Teaching Professor, 4(3),* 5-6.

Fischer, C. (1985). *Individualized psychological assessment.* Monterey, CA: Brooks Cole.

Grayson, H. M., & Tolman, R. S. (1950). A semantic study of concepts of clinical psychologists and psychiatrists. *Journal of Abnormal and Social Psychology, 45*, 216-231.

Hartlage, L. C., & Merck, K. H. (1971). Increasing the relevance of psychological reports. *Journal of Clinical Psychology, 27*, 459-460.

Hodges, J. C., Whitten, M. E., Horner, W. B., & Webb, S. S. (1990). *Harbrace college handbook* (11th ed.) New York: Harcourt Brace Jovanovich.

Siskind, G. (1967). Fifteen years later: A replication of "A semantic study of concepts of clinical psychologists and psychiatrists." *The Journal of Psychology, 65*, 3-7.

Strunk, W., Jr., & White, E. B. (1972). *The elements of style.* New York: Macmillan.

Tallent, N. (1988). *Psychological report writing* (3rd ed.) Englewood Cliffs, NJ: Prentice Hall.

Zinsser, W. (1980). *On writing well* (2nd ed.) New York: Harper & Row.

Zuckerman, E. L. (1990). *The clinicians thesaurus: A guidebook for wording psychological reports and other evaluations.* Pittsburgh, PA: Three Wishes Press.

CHAPTER 8

RECORDS AND PROGRESS NOTES

THE FUNCTION AND MAINTENANCE OF RECORDS

If you have not yet had occasion to see or work with clinical records, enjoy the experience while it lasts. Records will soon become part of your life. Although many professionals hold negative attitudes toward records and other paperwork, understanding the function of records and developing a systematic approach to their use and maintenance can help make record keeping a recognized and accepted element of sound practice (Casper, 1987; Kagle, 1993; Van Vort & Mattson, 1989).

Van Vort and Mattson (1989) emphasize that records serve several functions. These include: contributing to the quality of a client's current and future care; satisfying agency requirements; documenting care for the purpose of third-party reimbursement (i.e., payment for care by insurance companies); and protecting against legal actions. These functions are also identified in the American Psychological Association's Record Keeping Guidelines (APA, 1993).

For institutions, Casper (1987) notes that medical hospitals and other health care institutions must maintain adequate records in order to receive approval from auditing agencies.

All major auditing agencies, such as the Joint Commission on Accreditation of Hospitals (JCAH) and the Health Care Financing Administration (HCFA), have established standards for reviewing medical records as part of their periodic surveys of psychiatric facilities. (p. 1191)

The maintenance of clinical records is further mandated both by ethical standards and by state laws. The APA Specialty Guidelines for Delivery of Services by Clinical Psychologists (APA 1981) state: "Providers of clinical psychological services ensure that essential information concerning services rendered is recorded within a reasonable time following completion" (p. 646). Similar requirements exist for other professions and record keeping guidelines are codified in state laws. Because these vary from state to state, you should familiarize yourself with the law where you study or hope to practice.

The importance of records is also evident in requirements concerning the length of time records must be maintained. In this regard, the APA Record Keeping Guidelines (1993) note that the length and manner of maintaining records may be dictated by state laws. Where such laws exist they supersede the organization's standards. Where laws or regulations do not specify a time frame for maintaining records, the APA guidelines dictate that:

. . . complete records are maintained for a minimum of 3

years after the last contact with the client. Records, or a summary, are then maintained for an additional 12 years before disposal. If the client is a minor, the record period is extended until 3 years after the age of majority. (p. 985)

An important footnote to those guidelines recommends that future revisions of the APA practice code, on which the record keeping guidelines are based, should place a seven-year requirement for retaining complete records.

Beyond what ethical or practice guidelines may dictate, many attorneys with whom I have spoken have offered more succinct advice about how long to retain records: "Forever!" The reason is that, in addition to formal ethical and legal requirements, concerns about civil liability also dictate careful record keeping. In a brief but highly informative review, Soisson, VandeCreek and Knapp (1987) consider the legal importance of records in our litigious society. Based on their review of existing case law, Soisson et al. emphasize that well-kept records can reduce the risk of liability, while the lack of good records may in itself be used as evidence that care was substandard. This point is reiterated by Harris (1995) and by Bennett et al. (1990), who state: "In hospital practice it is often said, 'If it isn't written down, it didn't happen'" (p. 77).

For the reasons described above, it should be evident that an essential part of your responsibility as a professional will be to maintain quality records. In order to do that, you should understand what goes into records and some of the models for organizing and writing progress notes.

WHAT GOES INTO RECORDS

When I refer to clinical records in this text I am speaking of the totality of written information pertinent to the client's treatment. The general rule for determining what to put in records is: If something is important, document it and keep a record but think carefully about what you say and how you say it. Good records should include all present and previous relevant information about a client's history and treatment, progress notes, correspondence, releases of information, documentation of consultation, billing information, informed consent forms, and any other pertinent information.

Different institutions and agencies have different record keeping technologies. Typical physical materials involve either manila or metal folders subdivided into sections containing certain types of information. For convenience, subsections are often color coded and flagged with tabs identifying the contents. In order to ensure compliance with record keeping guidelines, most institutions have some form of periodic record review that assesses the content, organization, and clarity of records.

Kagle (1993), Casper (1987), and Van Vort and Mattson (1989) have described systems for encouraging improved record keeping and greater compliance with agency guidelines. These include such things as simplifying records, reducing redundancy, utilizing established forms to collect information, and making use of technologies such as computers and dictation systems. Some agencies have also hired time management consultants to help assess how much time is actually going toward record keeping and how this can be made more efficient.

Perhaps the most concise and informative discussion of how to organize and what to include in records has been provided by Piazza and Baruth (1990), who describe six categories of material that should go into records. In discussing the utility of their system, Piazza and Baruth note that it has been used successfully in a number of treatment settings and records kept according to the system have consistently passed state and national standards.

Within each of the major categories, Piazza and Baruth list more specific information that should be included. Under the category "Identifying or Intake Information," they suggest that basic personal data such as name, address, home and work phones, date of birth, sex, family members' names, next of kin, employment status, etc. should be recorded. Also indicated here should be information about the date of initial contact, the reason for referral, and the names of other professionals, e.g., physicians, other counselors, etc., who are seeing or have seen the client.

Most agencies use standard forms to gather the information in this category. In some instances the information is completed by the client; in other settings intake specialists or the therapists themselves discuss the information with clients and record the data as the discussion proceeds. Interactive computer programs have also become available to allow clients to enter this information themselves.

Taking this type of information is a straightforward process with most clients, but I would add that in some cases clients may not want to be called or written to at their home address. For example, I have worked with abused spouses who did not want their partner to know they were seeing a therapist. In these circumstances, one should mark the record in some way to indicate precisely where and how a client wishes to be contacted and billed. This must be done in such a way that the therapist, secretaries, records departments, or other clerical personnel cannot inadvertently call the client's home to schedule an appointment or send billing information that would reveal the client is seeing a therapist.

The second category described by Piazza and Baruth contains what they identify as "Assessment Information." This information is typically collected at the outset of treatment for the purpose of developing treatment plans. In some approaches to records, this information might also be included in the initial intake forms alluded to above. Within the heading of assessment information, five "domains" are considered by Piazza and Baruth to be essential. The first domain is "Psychological Assessment," which addresses the client's "motivation for treatment," emotional status and functioning, cognitive capacity, and history of previous difficulties or treatment. "Social and Family Assessment" is the second domain. This encompasses the client's early family and developmental history, including parents, siblings, family dynamics, and any family history of illness. It also includes the client's current family and social status and functioning.

Piazza and Baruth emphasize the importance of considering not only information about "dysfunctional" aspects of the client's life but also attending to the client's strengths and resources. Such information is particularly relevant to the third domain, "Vocational/Educational Assessment." Along with information about employment and academic history, this domain takes in avocational interests, as well as leisure and recreational activities. In considering a client's background, it is important to look beyond titles of jobs or education to consider specific skills and accomplishments. Thus, if a woman seeking employment identifies herself as "a homemaker," the counselor should explore the skills, such as money management, planning, organization, child raising, etc., that may have gone into that role. Clients may tend to overlook such skills but identifying them as resources can be immensely valuable in mobilizing the client's strengths as part of the therapy process.

The fourth and fifth domains are, respectively, "Drug and Alcohol Use" and "Health Assessment." As these categories are rather self-explanatory, they will not be discussed further here except to emphasize that many helping professionals pay too little attention to the role of physical factors. Physical illness and "lifestyle" characteristics such as smoking, drinking, sleep patterns, caffeine use, etc., may all be significant causes of, or contributors to, client's difficulties. I advise interns wherever possible to obtain the requisite information releases and establish close contacts with clients' physicians. I also suggest, as do Piazza and Baruth, that clients who have not had complete physicals within the past year be encouraged to see their physician for a thorough checkup. A number of concerns that present with psychological symptoms may be caused by or related to underlying physical illness. To assess this possibility you may wish to contact the physician before the client's visit and discuss the physician's findings after the client has been seen.

In gathering and considering any of the information described above, keep in mind that some patients may be unreliable sources of information. Therefore, it is advisable to obtain corroborating information from family or friends whenever possible. The importance of meeting with family members or friends at intake should be viewed as virtually an essential for clients who, because of the nature of their presenting concerns, e.g., schizophrenia, brain injury, certain personality disorders, etc., may not be able or motivated to provide accurate data about themselves.

Along with the information described thus far, as part of an initial assessment I strongly recommend that if a client has been or is being seen by other treatment providers or related professionals, you should, with the client's permission and signed release of information, seek copies of those records. If a client is reluctant to allow you access to such records, that may serve as a "red flag" that suggests you should inquire further about the client's reasons. You should also be cautious in deciding whether or not to accept the client for treatment if you cannot obtain past records. From the perspective of managing liability risks, it is not advisable to treat clients without access to information about previous treatment. The reason is that such information can significantly impact how you understand the client's present situation and how you provide treatment yourself. If you have not made an effort to gather information about past or other ongoing treatment, and if you do not document that attempt and information in your own records, you could face added problems if legal concerns arise.

With information from the first two categories, clinicians are able to formulate treatment plans. "Treatment Plans" constitute the third category within the record model of Piazza and Baruth. They suggest that each treatment plan should be agreed to and signed by the client and the therapist. At a minimum, treatment plans should include a statement of the problem, the goal of treatment described in behavioral terms, and the steps that will be taken to achieve the goal. As treatment proceeds, the client and therapist should periodically review the treatment plan to assess progress and adjust the approach or goals as needed.

In formulating treatment plans, you should be aware that managed care and other changes in health care are placing increasing demands upon professionals in the mental health field to demonstrate the rationale for, and efficacy of, the work we do with clients. In some cases, if you have not formulated a sound treatment plan from the outset, and if you do not document through progress notes that your subsequent work with the client followed your plan, you, the agency you work for, or the client may be denied compensation from the insurer. Thus, along with contributing to the quality of patient care, well-formulated and clearly documented treatment plans can also contribute to your financial well-being and that of your clients.

Ongoing "Case Notes" fit into the next category of information in Piazza and Baruth's model. Case notes (referred to more often in this book as progress notes) are discussed at length later in this chapter. At this point it will suffice to convey Piazza and Baruth's suggestions that case notes should include the goals for each session, indications of whether or not those goals were met, behavioral observations and clinical impressions, and a plan for the next sessions.

When a case is eventually terminated, the therapist should write a brief synopsis of the case and include it in a "Termination Summary." In addition to reviewing the origin, course, and result of treatment, if the client will be referred to another professional the termination summary should include mention of this or of other "aftercare" plans.

The sixth and final category within records is labeled simply "Other Data." This is the place to include such things as authorization for treatment, releases of information, copies of test results, and communications from other professionals. If you consult with other professionals about a case, you should make records of that consultation and include that here or in your case notes. Because this portion of records can become quite crowded with miscellaneous material, you may find it useful to organize the material with tabbed inserts.

WHAT STAYS OUT OF RECORDS

PROTECTING CLIENTS

Like all simple rules, there are caveats to the rule of documenting everything that is important. In the case of clinical records the caveat arises because your case records are not strictly confidential. This reality is clearly recognized in the APA Record Keeping Guidelines, which state:

> These guidelines assume that no record is free from disclosure all of the time, regardless of the wishes of the client or the psychologist. (p. 985)

Recognizing the possibility that records may be disclosed under special circumstances does not mean you can afford to be careless or that it is not your responsibility to protect records from disclosure wherever legally required and permitted. It does mean that, when you keep any sort of record about clients or their treatment, you should keep in mind the possibility that others might have access to those records.

Institutional settings are one example of where confidentiality of records may be limited. If your treatment records are, or will become part of, a larger record to which other staff have access, it is obvious that your records can be seen by others. Under these circumstances it would not be in the client's best interests to reveal in such accessible records information that was shared with you in confidence or that might be harmful to the client.

Gutheil (1980) stresses the distinction between "progress notes" and "process notes." The former contain empirical information that could be observed by others in the treatment facility and that can be shared in the general record. Process notes, on the other hand, reflect the process of psychotherapy, including personal material revealed by the client and the therapist's speculation about such material. The latter material should not go in a record that is accessible to others Harris, 1995).

A common practice is to keep separate personal notes about your therapy work. It is sometimes suggested that such personal records are guaranteed confidentiality, but this is by no means certain. As described in Chapter 3, any and all clinical records may be subject to court order. Clients also have the right to demand access to their own records. In recognition of this possibility, Soisson et al. (1987) suggest that records should not include statements about sexual practices or other sensitive information that the client might not want to risk being made available to others. Because clients may demand to see your records as well, it is also advisable to avoid recording your own emotional reactions or personal opinions about clients.

PROTECTING YOURSELF

Just as it is important to protect clients from the possibility that records may be viewed by others, it is also important to protect yourself. This is an area in which no clear-cut rules exist, but interns and clinicians would do well to ask themselves how what they put in records might later sound in a court proceeding. Gutheil goes so far as to suggest that trainees

> . . . deliberately hallucinate upon their right shoulder the image of a hostile prosecuting attorney who might preside at their trial, and that to this visual hallucination they append the auditory impression of the voice most suited to it. (p. 481)

Gutheil continues, saying

> Having achieved this goal-directed transient psychotic state, the trainee should then mentally test out in that context the sound of what he or she is about to write. (p.481)

This does not mean you should be frightened about everything you write or that you should expect a lawsuit around every corner. At the same time, however, being aware that your records and notes can be exposed and analyzed in litigation serves as a helpful reminder and incentive to ensure that the quality of your treatment and documentation are kept at the highest levels possible.

Two things to avoid in records are "raising ghosts" and taking blame. By "raising ghosts," I mean recording unfounded or unnecessary speculation in your notes. For example, if a client seems a bit down during a session but there is no reason from the client's history, statements, or actions to suspect suicide potential, it would be unwise for a clinician to record "Client was down today but I do not think suicide potential is high." If you mention suicide, you must also assess the potential carefully and document that you did so. If suicide risk is not elevated above normal, do not mention it at all. The same would apply to issues relating to dangerousness to others. Do not simply speculate about something so serious in your notes unless you followed up on that speculation during your session.

A second thing to avoid in records is taking blame. In other words, do not write in your notes that you made a mistake in treatment. This might feel honest and cathartic but it could get you into trouble later. If you are tempted to make such an entry, ask yourself what good it serves to write in your own notes that you made an error. You know it yourself and that is sufficient. Remember the advice your auto insurance company gives you if you are in an accident. If something unfortunate happens and you have to defend an action in court, allow your attorney to advise you but do not put confessions in your records beforehand.

Finally, never falsify records. If your records are demanded for a legal proceeding you will be asked under oath if your records represent a true and accurate description of your treatment and if they have been altered in any way since they were originally written. If you alter records and do not so indicate, you may be guilty of perjury. It is far better to be careful in your treatment and in your records to begin with, and then to be scrupulously honest if you are ever called to court. If at some point in your work with a client you realize that a previous record was deficient in some way, at the time you notice the deficiency you can make a note that you discovered something that needed to be added or changed in an earlier note. This does not mean you go back and actually change the note. It means you make a separate and later note that indicates the need to adjust, clarify, or correct the earlier note.

For example, suppose that two days after you wrote an entry you were reviewing the notes and reflecting on the earlier session. As you thought about the session you realized something should be added. At that moment, you could write the present date and time, then indicate the change or correction. This process demonstrates the value of periodic note review because you must catch such omissions before any trouble develops and legal implications arise. Corrections made after legal action or after an unfortunate event are not likely to carry as much weight in court because they tend to be seen as self-serving.

PROGRESS NOTES

EXERCISE

If you are working in a clinical setting, find out if you can obtain permission to review some of the patient records. Then read the progress notes kept in the records and ask yourself the following questions. Do you detect differences in style or content for different staff members? What notes stand out as particularly useful? What notes are not useful? What matters of style and information account for this difference?

THE PURPOSE OF PROGRESS NOTES

Progress notes are the core of most clinical records. They provide a record of events, are a means of communication among professionals, encourage us to review and assess treatment issues, allow other professionals to review the process of treatment, and are a legal record. Recently, progress notes have also seen increasing use by insurance providers seek-

ing to determine if a treatment is within the realm of services for which they provide compensation (Kagle, 1993). In writing progress notes you must keep all of these functions in mind.

When I write progress notes I find it helpful to ask myself several questions. First, as I write I review the events in order to again assess and better understand what happened. This helps me process and check my treatment. Next, I ask myself: If I read the notes several months or years from now, will they help me remember what happened, what was done, and why?

Because I may not be the only one to read my notes, I consider what would take place if something happened to me and another clinician picked up my clients. Would my notes enable him or her to understand the client and treatment? If I am in a setting where other professionals refer to the same record, I ask if the notes I write will adequately and accurately communicate to them. Included in this consideration is the matter of legibility. If my handwriting is so poor that others cannot read it, the notes will not do them or the client much good. Finally, and very importantly, I ask, "What would be the implications and impact if these notes were used as a legal document in a court of law?"

TYPES OF PROGRESS NOTES

Because clinical work entails many kinds of interactions and events, and because settings and record keeping requirements vary, there are several types of progress notes. One type is event based. Such notes describe a specific, and usually brief, event, then tell what was done about it. A second type of note describes more sustained interactions, such as therapy sessions.

Event-based progress notes can take many forms. Two of the most common are problem-oriented or goal-oriented notes. As these names suggest, problem-oriented notes refer to one or more specific problem areas that are being addressed in treatment (Weed, 1971). Goal-oriented notes focus on specified treatment goals, with each entry relating in some way to a goal. In systems that use problem- or goal-oriented notes, each therapist, or the treatment team as a group, identifies several key areas of focus in the client's treatment. For example, problems might be identified as: 1.) Initiates fights with other residents. 2.) Does not participate in social interactions. Expressed as goals these might be stated: 1.) Reduce incidence of instigating fights. 2.) Increase socialization. Once lists of the problems or goals are established, progress notes then refer to these by number or name.

The theory behind this approach is that it helps staff target their intervention to meet specific treatment needs or goals. Such notes may also help demonstrate to insurers that the treatment provided is systematic and is related to specific problems or goals for which compensation is being provided.

Along with differences in note types, there are also differences in where treatment notes are entered. Individual therapists typically keep their own progress notes for each client or group they see. These notes are primarily for the clinician's own use and are not generally shared directly with others. In contrast to the individual therapist notes, records are also kept for the clinical setting as a whole, with many professionals having access to, and making entries in, charts for individual patients. In the course of your work as an intern you may have occasion to write many types of notes so it is important that you understand each.

STYLE OF PROGRESS NOTES

In most progress notes style is not important; clarity, precision, and brevity are. Your goal is to record all of the essential information in as little space and time as possible. Because you may be writing and reading notes on many patients each day, you will want to save time by including only the essential details. By keeping your notes succinct, you will also save the time of others who may read them. This is especially important in settings where notes are shared among many professionals, each of whom has contact with many patients. When there are many notes to be read, every minute saved in reading and writing will add up. As long as the notes are kept accurately and all essential information is provided, the time saved in charting can be better spent in direct clinical contact or other activities.

One way to shorten progress notes is through the use of shorthand. If you are taking notes primarily for your own use, any system of shorthand will do as long as you can decipher it later. However, if you are writing notes in a record that is shared by others it is essential that any shorthand be understood by everyone and accepted by your institution. If there is a possibility of misinterpretation, you are better off writing things out in full. You should also be aware that different settings may have different standards for using shorthand or abbreviations and some may not allow any shorthand at all. If you take notes as part of your internship responsibilities, check to be sure before you write.

STRUCTURED NOTE FORMATS

STANDARD FORMATS

In an effort to standardize treatment notes, many agencies have developed or adopted specific guidelines for what should go where in notes. Treatment- or goal-oriented notes are often included as part of such standards. If your agency has such guidelines you must learn them, practice using them, and get feedback to be sure you are writing your notes correctly. As noted earlier, most agencies conduct periodic audits to ensure that record keeping meets agency guidelines. By making sure your records are up to standards you can save yourself and your supervisor problems later. As a check, it is a good idea for interns to initiate their own record and progress-note review with their supervisors. Supervisors tend to get busy and over-

look such details so it is a sign of responsibility if the intern takes the initiative to be sure notes are being kept correctly.

DART NOTES

I have found that some of the most widely used formats for treatment notes have significant problems, particularly when applied to psychological, as opposed to medical, settings. One example is the SOAP format, which is part of the Problem Oriented Medical Records (POMR) system (Weed, 1971). The SOAP format and its shortcomings will be discussed shortly, but first let me offer an alternative that most interns find very helpful as they learn to keep treatment notes.

This system actually evolved out of some joking surrounding my frustration with the SOAP format, which was at the time required of all notes for my internship placement. The acronym for my alternative system is DART, but it began as DIRT, which shows the humor behind its origin and which explains why it would probably never be adopted in hospitals. Humor aside, the letters represent useful concepts that will help guide most progress notes. If your agency does not require adherence to some other standard, the DART format is a good method to follow.

The DART system is particularly useful when you are writing notes about a specific client or event. The "D" in DART stands for a description of the client and situation. "A" is for assessment of the situation. (This "A" was originally "I," which stood for the clinician's impression, and which produced the initial acronym.) "R" is for the response of the clinician and client, and "T" is for treatment implications and plan. One way to think of this system is that when you write progress notes you must tell what happened, what you made of it, how you responded, and what you plan to do, or think should be done, in the future. This sequence of events is not only a useful way to conceptualize progress notes, it is also a useful way to approach a treatment interaction.

DESCRIPTION

The first part of any progress note should describe the basic "W" questions of journalism: When, Where, Who, and What. In practice, these words are not actually used in the progress notes but the notes must contain the information the words subsume. Usually, the information of When, Where, and Who can be conveyed in a single sentence. "When" refers to the date and time the event occurred. Some people prefer to put date and time at the end of a note, but I suggest you start the note with this information for ease of reference later. "Where" indicates the location of the event. If the location is always the same, such as a clinic office, this can be omitted. However, if many locations are possible, as in a school, hospital, or other large setting, it helps to note the exact location. Next you should indicate "Who" played a significant role in or observed the event you are noting. This practice of noting who was present can come in handy later if there is a need to get additional information about a specific event or client.

Once you have provided the basic information, you should describe "What" is prompting you to write the note. This may be something routine, such as "Mrs. Smith has shown little change during the past week. She continues to pace the hall and talk to herself." The information may be a significant change in a client's appearance or behavior: "During individual therapy today Joseph informed me that he has been very depressed and is thinking of killing himself." Obviously, the more significant the event, the more space will be dedicated to the corresponding progress note. One would certainly want to expand on the second notation.

Assessment

Having described what you observed, the next step is to record your assessment of what it means. This is the "Why" of the event. As you think about this part of your notes be aware that you do not always have to offer profound insights or explanations, nor do you always have to know what something means. Sometimes the most important notes are about behaviors that stand out precisely because their meaning is not exactly clear. For example, if a client who is normally rather quiet becomes very talkative and energetic, the meaning of the change might not be clear but one could note it, suggest some possible considerations, or ask others to offer their insights.

To help guide your assessment, as you consider the present event or behavior, think about how it relates to other knowledge you have about the client and treatment. How does the present situation relate to previous behaviors, to recent events, to the treatment plan, to other factors? Also remember that most events reflect a combination of both lasting and temporary factors within the individual and within the environment. Thus, you might observe a change in a client's behavior and note that this seems to reflect stresses over recent family conflicts and may also be a reaction to the overall level of tension in the treatment facility. The most important task is to give some thought to what you observed and try to relate it to your overall knowledge and treatment of the client. Again, this is not just good note taking, it is sound clinical practice.

Response

In good clinical work you must first take in what is happening and what the client is doing and saying. Then you must assess what this means. Your next task is to respond in some way. Your progress notes should also reflect this sequence. After describing and assessing a situation you should record what you did in response. The description of your response need not be lengthy but it must accurately note any important details.

Like your clinical response itself, your record should reflect a well-founded and rational treatment approach. Here it is sometimes helpful to consider how other clinicians might judge your response. It may also be useful to think about the legal implications. As a legal standard, if something is not recorded it is difficult to prove it was done. Learn to record scrupulously anything you do or do not do that might later be considered important. Be particularly conscientious about noting if you refer a client to someone else, if any formal tests or other measures are administered, if homework assignments are given or contracts are developed, and if and when you schedule future contacts. Also keep notes if you consult with someone about a case. Include both the fact that you consulted and a summary of the consultation process and results (Harris, 1995).

To the extent that the severity of a client's concerns or the riskiness of a clinical decision increases, records should be more detailed. Bennett et al. (1990) suggest that records should describe the goal of the chosen intervention, risks and benefits, and the reason a specific treatment was chosen. It is also advisable to indicate any known risks and reasons for considering them justified, available alternatives and why they were not chosen, and what steps were taken to maximize the effectiveness of chosen treatments. In some instances, documenting what you did not do and why you decided not to do it can be just as important as documenting what you did do. As further information it is often useful to note any information provided to, or discussed with, the client, and the client's response.

In essence, this process is tantamount to "thinking out loud" in the record. Gutheil advises "As a general rule, the more uncertainty the more one should think out loud in the record" (1980, p. 482). In this process the clinician is recording not only the action taken but the reasons for taking or not taking an action. If questions arise later, the explanation is already documented. In a legal context, Gutheil stresses that for liability reasons this process is important because it reduces the possibility of a ruling of clinical negligence.

Treatment Plan

Following the description of your immediate response, the final element of a well-written progress note is your plan for future treatment. This may be as simple as a note saying "Schedule for next Monday," "Continue to monitor condition daily"; or it might be more complex, as in "Next session we will explore family issues. Client will bring written description of each family member and we will complete family diagrams." Notes of this sort allow you to refer back to refresh your memory of what was planned. This might seem unnecessary to you now, but with large and complex caseloads such records are necessary to help you keep track of your clients and their treatment.

If you are working in an agency where a daily log is

maintained, it is often possible to leave notes there for other staff. For example, you might conclude a note by suggesting that the evening staff keep close watch on a patient. If something is really important be sure to highlight it in some way in your notes. Use stars, **BOLD WRITING**, or other methods to make the note stand out. If the matter is urgent or life threatening, do not leave the matter to progress notes alone; speak directly to someone responsible.

DART IN PRACTICE

In order to demonstrate how the DART notation approach might work in practice, suppose you were working in a school setting and a child came in with severe straplike bruises and welts across his back. You suspect the child may have been abused, so you discuss it with him. He seems to avoid answering but finally says he fell and hurt himself.

The sample notes below illustrate how you might record this using the DART format. In this example the DART initials are used to help organize the note and for ease of later location of information. As you read the example, identify how and what information is included in each of the main areas. You may find some information following one initial where it might also go with a different initial. In contrast to other systems, the DART model is not so concerned with obsessing about what went where in the notes. What matters most is that all the important information gets recorded accurately and in a useful manner.

D: 10/16/95 Monday: After recess at 10 am today Timothy North was taking his jacket off and in the process his shirt pulled up revealing straplike red welts across his back. At noon break I spoke with him while the other children were out. I said I noticed he had some red marks on his back. He looked away and shrugged without answering. I asked where he got them and he said he did not know. Then he said he had fallen down over the weekend. I asked if his parents knew and he said yes. That afternoon I met with the school nurse, Karen Jones, and Tim. The nurse looked at the marks and asked Tim similar questions; he again said he had fallen.

A: The marks do not look like they came from a fall. Karen Jones, school nurse, agrees. We are concerned about possible abuse. This child has come in with questionable bruises before, but none were this severe and he has always offered plausible explanations. Given the nature of the present marks, we believe the situation warrants notification of Child Protective Services.

R: I notified the school counselor, Alice Black, and we contacted Child Protective Services. The contact person at CPS is William Randolph, MSW. He asked if we thought there was imminent danger of severe harm to the child. We replied that we did not have enough information to know that. He suggested we schedule a meeting for Wednesday October 18th, at 4 pm. If further concerns arise before then, we will call and inform him.

T: We will keep watch on Tim and check for further signs of injury. Future action will be determined at Wednesday meeting.

Signed, Joyce Jefferson, MSW, Date, 10/16/95
cc: Karen Jones, Alice Black, William Randolph.

SOAP NOTES

As noted earlier, one of the more common standardized note taking methods is the SOAP format. The letters in SOAP stand for Subjective, Objective, Assessment, and Plan. Although the concepts behind Problem-Oriented Medical Records, from which SOAP developed, are quite valuable, my experience with the SOAP format suggests that for use outside medical settings the terminology is ambiguous. That ambiguity can readily lead to needless debate about whether an entry should have been placed in the S, O, or A section. I have also noted that efforts to conform to rigid SOAP guidelines tend to produce contorted writing that may obscure rather than clarify what happened.

Many of the guidelines suggested for using the DART format will also apply to SOAP notes, but there are subtle differences. If you are interested in knowing more about SOAP, see the original work by Weed (1971) or a more general review of medical records by Avery and Imdieke (1984). Most settings that use SOAP or any of the other standard note formats will also have training material or workshops that will teach you more about how notes are to be written.

EXERCISE

If you are not already writing clinical notes you may wish to develop your skills by choosing a recent interaction with a friend or client and document it as if you were writing a progress note in a clinical record. If your supervisor is amenable, review the note with her or him and request feedback about how the note could be improved.

TIME-SEQUENCED NOTES

In contrast to the DART and SOAP approaches, which are used primarily to record specific events or interactions, a therapist's personal case notes from individual sessions typically follow a different format. The most common form of notation for therapy sessions is referred to here as "time-sequenced" notes. In time-sequenced notes, the therapy session is described as it progressed, with individual elements described sequentially in the order in which they occurred in the session. Some therapists make these notes during the therapy session itself. Others wait until the end of a session to record what happened.

The sequential approach is often used for records of therapy sessions because there are simply too many elements to address each separately following a more structured format. Sequential notes also enable the clinician to observe the order of events as they occur within a session. This can provide extremely useful clinical information. For example, it is probably not mere coincidence if a client begins by describing family conflicts then shifts the topic to problems at work. Sequential notes follow this shift and enable the clinician to notice it in the record even though it might have gone unnoticed during the session itself. An example of an abbreviated sequentially ordered progress note from a therapy session is given below. Note the use of an informal shorthand to save time.

> 2/7/95 2-3 pm. JA began session by revu of lst wks sesn. Said he had thought about it & did not understnd why he had cried about father. We explored this more. JA cried again, rembrd fishing trip and fathr takng his fish away. Felt humiliated. Realized this was typical pattern. Gave recent example of visit during Xmas. His father was critical of JA's job, an argument developed and JA returned home early. We explored pattern of seeking approval and fearing rejection. JA realized that anger is also there. This comes out in marriage as well. JA is often angry w wife if she disapproves of anything he does. He described two examples, when he cooks and in child care. He is not comfortable with own behavior but is having hard time chnging. Agreed to explore this more nxt sessn.

In a one-hour session there would obviously be more that could be recorded, but in this example the therapist has chosen to note the events and topics he or she considered most important. This will vary from therapist to therapist and is also closely tied to theoretical orientation. Analytically trained therapists, for example, would be likely to make much different notes than those recorded by a behavioral therapist.

Although such time-sequenced notes are quite common, one should realize that merely describing the events of a session may not be sufficient to satisfy the demands of an insurance company and may not contain all the information that would be useful in legal proceedings. Thus, in addition to using this type of notes to record the key events of a session, it is a good idea to include other information relating to treatment plans and of the sort described in the DART format. This would be especially important if a critical issue, such as suicide, violence, or other matters of unusually serious concern emerged. As noted before, in response to these issues one would need to document carefully how one had assessed the situation and what was done in response. The guidelines described earlier in this chapter would help ensure that all critical information is recorded.

PROCESS OR PROGRESS NOTES

Process notes are yet another type of note with which you should be familiar. Process notes refer to notes in which the therapist includes personal reflections on the unconscious dynamics of a patient, the transference or countertransference issues in therapy, and other such matters. As contrasted with "progress notes," which focus more on the externally observable, empirical events of treatment, process notes delve into the psyche of the therapist and patient. Professionals trained from a psychodynamic perspective will be quite familiar with process notes and may consider them essential to treatment.

While many professionals value process notes, concerns have been raised that such notes may not satisfy insurance company desires for clearly described treatment goals and procedures. Process notes may also be problematic if they are used in legal proceedings (Harris, 1995). A skilled attorney might make interesting uses of a therapist's personal reflections or feelings as recorded in progress notes. It should also be remembered that legally, clients themselves have access to their notes. If a client reads a therapist's private speculations on the client's libidinal attachments, latent desires, or other potentially sensitive matters, the client might not understand the purpose of such notes or the terminology involved.

Given these concerns, many professionals have chosen to reduce substantially or eliminate the types of introspective and theoretical contemplation that were once standard in process notes. What you choose to put in your notes is, of course, up to you, but keep in mind the benefits as well as the risks and, again, be aware that your notes may be read by other persons, some of whom may be on the opposite side in litigation.

SIGNING NOTES

The final step in writing progress notes is signing them. As an intern you should check with your supervisor to be sure you understand exactly how notes or other documents are to be signed and how you are to identify yourself with your signature. For example, some institutions require interns to sign notes and identify themselves as "Psychology Intern" or "Social Work Student." It may also be necessary for your supervisor to cosign any work that you write. This might include daily progress notes or it may only apply to more lengthy reports. Because different agencies or institutions will have different policies, the only sure way to know you are following procedures is to ask from the beginning.

Along with being sure to list your status correctly, you should also consider the legibility of your signature. Mine happens to be almost totally illegible. With experience, secretaries, students, and colleagues all learn more or less how to decipher my scratchings, but those who have less experience and do not know me well are often at a loss. This can present a problem for progress notes because it sometimes happens that there are questions relating to notes and people need to know who wrote them. If no one knows who you are and they cannot read your signature, it is going to be difficult to find you. My solution to this is to always print my name above my signature. Because most people will be less familiar with interns than with regular staff, it will be especially important for you to be sure people can read your writing and that you have identified your status clearly.

DICTATION

Whether you write or dictate your progress notes, the content and structure of your notes should follow the guidelines offered thus far. This may sound easy, but, for most people, dictation takes some getting used to. The typical approach of beginners is to write their notes first, then read them onto the recorder. That is not exactly a model of efficiency. If you work in a setting where dictated notes are an option or requirement, the following suggestions may help.

Dictation is like writing; both take practice to develop. When people begin dictating it may help to work from a brief written outline. This is not as lengthy or redundant as writing the entire entry beforehand, but it does provide some structure and a reference point. It is also possible to use a general outline, such as the DART format, and then make notes about the specific details for each client or event.

When you are dictating you should keep in mind that the people who will transcribe your record have only what they hear on tape as a basis for what they will write. Remember to speak clearly, spell out unfamiliar names or terms, and verbally indicate where punctuation, paragraph breaks, or symbols go. With the advent of digital recording systems, one can now speak quite rapidly because the person transcribing the note can easily stop or move back or forward to keep up. If a slower, tape-based system is in use, you may need to speak more slowly so the typist can keep up. Whatever system you use, you can save the typist time by using the pause button on the recorder when you stop to think. Also, do not be afraid to make corrections if you realize that you said something that was incorrect or left out a detail earlier in your report. Rather than rewinding and starting over, if you realize you made an error or omission you can say something like, "I just realized I left out a sentence. Could you go back to just after . . . and insert. . . ." When the correction is made you can continue from where you left off.

In most large institutions, dictated notes are transcribed by staff who you may never meet face to face. Because I find this structure rather unfriendly, I make it a point to get to know the people who will be typing my notes. Building relationships with records, secretarial, and other staff is not only rewarding interpersonally, it can also help prevent and more easily resolve a host of problems. Good secretarial work can be extremely valuable, so it is important to respect and support the people you work with. One way to show your respect and build a relationship is to visit with folks when you begin your internship and stop by from time to time later to say hello. It also helps to conclude your records by thanking the person who is doing the typing and acknowledging that person's work.

Future directions for dictation involve "voice recognition" systems, in which one speaks directly to a computer which then prints the text of what is said. These systems are growing in sophistication and can already manage very complex clinical terminology and editing functions. However, such systems require one to speak clearly and relatively consistently. This may take some getting used to, but with practice one can learn to interact effectively with such systems.

EXERCISE

To gain practice in dictation, think of an interaction that occurred in class or with your peers. Use a tape recorder and dictate your notes as if they were to be given to a secretary for typing. Then, either type the notes yourself from the tape or, if a friend is willing, ask him or her to try to type from your notes. Your friend can offer feedback about how fast you spoke, if you misspelled a technical term, if you were clear about punctuation, etc. Remember, dictation is a skill that takes time to learn. Do not be embarrassed about hearing your own voice or about how your notes will read on the first try. With practice you will find that dictated notes go much faster and can be just as informative as written notes.

PROGRESS NOTES AND SUPERVISION

I have described the importance of progress notes for meeting agency standards, ethical guidelines, and legal documentation. In addition to these functions, progress notes can also provide useful material for clinical supervision. The general subject of supervision was discussed earlier, in Chapter 5, but a few additional comments are warranted in the context of notes.

It is a good practice for interns and supervisors to make reviews of progress notes a regular part of the supervision process. This review serves several functions. As noted earlier, reviewing notes with supervisors helps to ensure that the intern's records are up to agency standards. Because record keeping is an important but often overlooked part of clinical training, supervisors may wish to offer advice about the content or the style of an intern's notes. Reviewing notes also allows interns the opportunity to ask about any issues pertaining to record keeping and note taking. Beyond the clerical aspects of note taking, reviewing notes and records helps supervisors observe what interns consider to be significant about a case or therapy session. Supervisors can monitor the intern's records of both the content and process of therapy sessions and the notes can be referred to as needed to supplement or guide case discussions.

USING YOUR NOTES

Having devoted this chapter primarily to how to keep records and progress notes, it should not be forgotten that the primary purpose of notes is to assist the treatment of your clients. It is surprising how often therapists take notes at the end of sessions but then do not refer to them again before the next session with their clients. This can easily happen as therapists with busy schedules shift from seeing one client to the next with little time in between. Understandable though this may be, the quality of treatment may be lessened as a result.

I confess to having been guilty of this myself on occasion. I recall an instance in which a client said he had given a great deal of thought to what was said last week, and I found myself internally struggling to recall just what it was we had discussed. It has also happened that I "assigned homework," i.e., suggested that a client do or write something between sessions, which I then forgot to discuss. Client's have called me on this and in some cases have expressed their displeasure over what appears to be a lack of concern or attention.

Beyond a matter of courtesy or simple forgetfulness, many clients may actually consider such oversights unethical. In a survey of ninety-six adults, some of whom had experience as clients and others who had not, Claiborne et al. (1994) found that of statements about sixty possible hypothetical events that might occur in therapy, the statement, "Your therapist does not remember what you talked about in the previous session" was ranked fourth highest among events considered to be ethically inappropriate. The mean ranking for this item on a scale of 1 to 5, with 1 being "completely inappropriate," was 1.32. Clearly, at least in this sample, recipients of clinical services placed a high value on therapists being aware of the content of previous sessions.

Given this finding, it certainly behooves the therapist to take the few minutes before a session to review the notes from the last visit. With heavy caseloads and busy schedules, unless one takes good notes and then makes use of them, oversights and lapses of memory are almost sure to occur. On the other hand, if progress notes are used well the clinician will be more aware of the sequence of events across sessions. This will lead to better therapeutic care and will result in higher levels of satisfaction on the part of clients.

OTHER GUIDELINES

Before concluding this discussion, let me offer a few additional suggestions. This book has emphasized repeatedly that you must know your limits and be open to learning. This applies to records and notes as much as any other aspect of your internship. If you do not know how to write a note, or if you are unsure of the wording to use, ask for help. If you are describing an interaction with a client, do not write notes to impress everyone with your skills. As an intern, humility is a virtue and hubris can get you into trouble. Remember simplicity and objectivity.

Another principle of note taking is to be constructive. This is especially important if you are writing notes in a record that is accessible to others. Although part of your task is to assess and try to understand what you observe, this is not done for the purpose of ascribing blame. Your goal is to facilitate treatment, not to be critical of clients or staff. For example, it would not be constructive to write a note such as "Dennis is up to his old tricks again. Found him masturbating in front of the television. Sometimes I think we should cut the thing off." This may sound shockingly callous, but I read precisely this note in staff records. Interns learn by example, but some examples are best not followed. Imagine the impact of such a note if read by an outside professional, a family member, or in a court of law.

For similar reasons, if you are working in an institution where many staff members record notes in the same book, using the record to question or attack the conduct of other staff is not a good idea. Consider, for example, "The night shift is still not following through with last week's treatment plan. How is he supposed to get better if we are not consistent?" This note may stem from legitimate frustration, but a formal progress note may not be the best place to air those feelings. I have read record books that sounded more like a name-calling war between staff than a mutual discussion of treatment. Such notes cannot really be helpful to the clients or the staff. If you have concerns, address them with your supervisor, but keep the progress notes objective.

Finally, from the outset of your career, develop good note taking and record keeping habits. Make yourself write notes immediately or as soon after an interaction as possible. Schedule the time you need for note taking and do not sacrifice this to other distractions. Keep your notes as thorough as they need to be, follow any required format, and establish a process of review to ensure that everything is kept up to date.

Faced with the many demands of clinical work, it is all too easy to become careless, or to let other tasks take precedence over note taking (Kagle, 1993). If you need ten minutes for note taking between therapy sessions, schedule that in and do not allow it to be taken up instead with phone calls or other distractions. Unless they are urgent, save those other matters until the notes are finished. You will be surprised how much gets forgotten or lost even by the end of the day. The longer you wait to record your notes, the less accurate and valuable they will be. When it comes to clinical record keeping, a little compulsivity is not a bad quality to develop. Well-kept notes will not only enhance your clinical treatment, they can also make the difference between whether or not an insurance company pays for services. In our litigious society well-kept progress notes may also save you untold legal problems if you are ever called upon to produce them in court.

REFERENCES

Albeck, J. H., & Goldman, C. (1991). Patient-therapist codocumentation: Implications of jointly authored progress notes for psychotherapy practice, research, training, supervision and risk management. *American Journal of Psychotherapy*, *45*, 317–334.

American Psychological Association: Committee on Professional Standards (1981). Specialty guidelines for the delivery of services by clinical psychologists. *American Psychologist*, *36*, 640–651.

———— (1993). Record keeping guidelines. *American Psychologist*, *48*, 984–986.

Avery, M., & Imdieke, B. (1984). *Medical records in ambulatory care*. Rockville, MD: Aspen Systems.

Bennett, B. E., Bryant, B. K., VandenBos, G. R., & Greenwood, A. (1990). *Professional liability and risk management*. Washington DC: American Psychological Association.

Casper, E. S. (1987). A management system to maximize compliance with standards for medical records. *Hospital and Community Psychiatry*, *38*, 1191–1194.

Claiborne, C. D., Berberoglu, L. S., Nerison, R. M., & Somberg, D. R. (1994). The client's perspective: Ethical judgments and perceptions of therapist practices. *Professional Psychology: Research and Practice*, *25*, 268–274.

Cohen, R. J. (1979). *Malpractice: A guide for mental health professionals*. New York: The Free Press.

Gutheil, T. G. (1980). Paranoia and progress notes: A guide to forensically informed psychiatric recordkeeping. *Hospital and Community Psychiatry*, *31*, 479–482.

Kagle, J. D. (1993). Record keeping: Directions for the 1990s. *Social Work*, *38*, 190–196.

Harris, E. A. (1995). The importance of risk management in a managed care environment. In M. B. Sussman (Ed.) A perilous calling: The hazards of psychotherapy practice. (pp. 247–258). New York: John Wiley and Sons.

Piazza, N. J., & Baruth, N. E. (1990). Client record guidelines. *Journal of Counseling and Development*, *68*, 313–316.

Soisson, E. L., VandeCreek, L., & Knapp, S. (1987). Thorough record keeping: A good defense in a litigious era. *Professional Psychology: Research and Practice*, *18*, 498–502.

Van Vort, W., & Mattson, M. R. (1989). A strategy for enhancing the clinical utility of the psychiatric record. *Hospital and Community Psychiatry*, *40*, 407–409.

Weed, L. L. (1971). *Medical records, medical education, and patient care: The problem-oriented record as a basic tool*. Chicago: Year Book.

CHAPTER 9

STRESS AND THE HELPING PROFESSIONS

When helping professionals tell others about their work, two common responses are: "That must be so difficult, listening to people's problems all day. I don't know how you do it.", or "Uh oh, I'd better be careful. You're not going to psychoanalyze me are you?"

Although these comments typically come from people who are not involved in the field, both responses raise legitimate questions and concerns for interns. What does happen to people who work in the helping professions as a result of their work? How do we balance our professional roles with our personal lives away from work? And how can interns manage the demands of internships, school, family, friends, and work without falling apart?

This chapter discusses the stresses that interns and helping professionals experience and the ways those stresses affect our lives and work. The goal of the chapter is to help you understand, and be able to recognize how you may be affected by, the challenges of your training and work. The next chapter offers suggestions for how to deal with those challenges in ways that enhance your growth as a person and as a professional.

EXERCISE

Before reading further, take a moment to write down some of your own thoughts about each of the following questions. If you do not have any actual clinical experience yet, answer the questions as you think you might be affected when you are working in a clinical setting.

1. In what ways do you think your work as an intern affects you emotionally now? For example, how do you feel at the end of an internship day? How do you feel on days when you are not at your internship?
2. How does your internship influence your ideas about the clients you work with? About people in general? About people who are close to you? Society?
3. How does your internship affect you physically? What kinds of physical demands or limitations do the activities of your work impose upon you? Do you experience any physical responses to working with stressful clients, colleagues, or supervisors?
4. How does your internship affect your close personal or social relationships?
5. Having considered how your internship is affecting you now, how do you think you would be affected if you were a full time professional in your field?
6. What personal qualities do you think will help you in dealing with the stress of your work? What personal qualities do you think may make it difficult for you to deal with the stress of your work?
7. How will you be able to recognize if you are being affected adversely by your work?

8. How might you cope with a situation in which you come to recognize that you are under excessive stress and your professional effectiveness or personal wellness is being harmed?

However you answered the questions above, it is certain that you will be affected by your work. You simply cannot interact with people and not be changed in some way. What is more, you do not always have control or even awareness of just how you will be changed. As Guy (1987) observed in his book, *The Personal Life of the Psychotherapist:*

> Since their personality is the "tool" used to conduct this clinical work, who a psychotherapist "is" undergoes constant challenge, review, and transformation. One would certainly hope that the resultant changes are largely positive, improving the therapist's satisfaction with life and relationships. Regrettably, . . . it may also be that certain changes have the potential to hinder interpersonal functioning in and outside of work. (p. 105)

Similar observations are offered by Kottler (1986):

> The process of psychotherapy flows in two directions, obviously influencing the client, but also affecting the personal life of the clinician. This impact can be for better or worse, making the helping professions among the most spiritually fulfilling as well as the most emotionally draining human endeavors. Some of us flourish as a result of this work. We learn from those we try to help and apply what we know and understand to ourselves. And some of us become depleted and despondent. Over time we may become cynical or indifferent or stale. (p. ix)

When one realizes that the work of therapy inevitably affects the therapist personally, and when one realizes that the therapist's own awareness and wellness are key elements of the treatment process, it is surprising that many undergraduate and graduate programs pay relatively little attention to this issue (Sowa, May, & Niles, 1994; Sussman, 1995). Fortunately, awareness of this subject appears to be increasing and there is a growing body of literature dealing with the effects of the helping professions on helping professionals and interns.

CLIENT AFTER CLIENT, DAY AFTER DAY

Consider this scenario. You are a beginning professional working in a mental health center. On a Monday morning at eight o'clock your first client is a 25-year-old woman who is married to a physically and verbally abusive spouse. The woman has two children, a third on the way, recently suffered the death of her mother, and just found out that she will be laid off from work. The client is basically a caring, hard-working person who finds herself in a terrible situation and feels there are limited ways to get out of, or through it. You feel very

deeply what it must be like for this client and determine to work with her.

Your next client is a fifteen-year-old boy whose parents are getting a divorce. He has been experimenting with drugs and is afraid he is getting hooked on crack. He has also just been arrested for breaking into a car with some friends and taking a stereo. He has never been in trouble with the law before and his court date is coming up next week. The boy is seeing you for help in dealing with the crack problem and with the upcoming court date.

The third case of the day is a man who was ordered by the court to seek therapy following an arrest for drunken driving. He makes it clear that he doesn't really want to be in treatment, has no intention of quitting drinking, and accepts no responsibility for his past actions or for change. He says he will come to meet with you only until the court-ordered time period is up.

It's now just eleven o'clock on Monday. You will see four more clients today and there are four more days to go until the weekend. Let's throw in as a background issue that your clinic's future is uncertain because federal and local funding for mental health have been reduced and third-party payments from insurers are also being lowered. What is more, there was a recent client suicide and a series of staff meetings is taking place to review the incident. Finally, several of the staff members do not get along well with each other, so there is a steady state of tension among the staff at the clinic. How are you doing? Oh yes, I forgot to mention that this weekend you will be on crisis duty.

If this sounds like an atypical scenario, concocted just to present the worst-case picture of professional life, it is not. In fact, in many instances the actual cases and institutional issues are even more challenging than those presented here.

HOW COMMON IS STRESS AMONG HELPING PROFESSIONALS?

Given the kinds of demands just described, it should not be surprising to learn that at one time or another most helping professionals will find themselves working under significant stress. Pope, Tabachnick, and Keith-Spiegel (1987) surveyed members of the Psychotherapy Division of the American Psychological Association and found that only 38.8 percent of those surveyed said they never engage in clinical work when too distressed to be effective. Of the remaining respondents, 48.5 percent said they only rarely worked under such conditions and 10.5 percent said they sometimes did. This left only .6 percent who indicated they fairly often or very often worked when too distressed to be effective. While it is encouraging to note the small percentage of therapists who acknowledge that they often work when they may be ineffective, this research also suggests that on some occasions more than half of the therapists surveyed said they have worked when their own distress might have impaired their therapeutic effectiveness.

Further evidence of the stresses of clinical work comes from a survey by Ackerley et al. (1988). In a sample of 562 licensed, doctoral-level psychologists practicing primarily in mental health agencies, results from the Maslach Burnout Inventory (Maslach & Jackson, 1986) showed that nearly 40 percent of the sample were "experiencing high levels of emotional exhaustion," and just over 34 percent were experiencing "high levels of depersonalization" (p. 629). Based on a survey that included comparatively greater proportions of clinicians in private practice, Skorupa and Agresti (1993) reported that 25 percent of respondents scored in the moderate range of emotional exhaustion, and 15 percent scored in the high range. Skorupa and Agresti also found that the presence of burnout symptoms was positively correlated with the amount of client contact hours per week. In general, higher numbers of contact hours were associated with higher ratings of physical exhaustion and depersonalization. On a positive note, these results also showed that psychologists who expressed more concern about the risks of burnout tended to demonstrate more knowledge of burnout prevention techniques and generally lower levels of burnout symptoms.

For most interns who are new to the field and full of energy and dedication, the stress of clinical work may not be an immediate concern. But such stresses should not be ignored. Boxley, Drew, and Rangle (1986) reported that 66 percent of the internship sites they surveyed reported having worked with "impaired" interns during the previous five years. The annual rate of trainee impairment was found to be 4.6 percent. This figure translates into approximately one in twenty interns who have difficulties sufficient to meet the definition of "any physical, emotional or educational condition that interferes with the quality of the intern's professional performance" (p. 50). Comparable findings have been obtained by Olkin and Gaughen (1991), who surveyed clinically oriented masters programs in a variety of mental health fields. Their results showed the mean percentage of "problem students was 4.8 percent" (p. 283). A problem student was defined as "having problems of such a nature or severity that s/he (a) comes to the attention of the faculty, and (b) requires some response from the faculty" (p. 282).

As the definitions used by Boxley et al. and by Olkin and Gaughen indicate, not all of the cases of impairment identified as "impaired" or "problems" were due solely to stress. Nevertheless, the findings from these studies suggest that preparing interns to deal with stress and personal issues should receive greater attention than it has in clinical training (Bradley & Post, 1991; Lamb et al., 1987; Stadler et al., 1988).

SOURCES OF STRESS

In a follow-up to the Pope et al. study, Guy, Poelstra, and Stark (1989) sought to identify the sources of stress reported by a sample of 318 practicing psychotherapists. This research revealed that therapists must contend both with stresses directly related to their clinical work and with stresses stemming from issues in their personal lives. When asked to identify sources of personal distress they had experienced in the past three years, 74.3 percent indicated at least one major source of distress during that time period. Of these, 32.9 percent identified job stress, 23.2 percent illness in the family, 20.4 percent marital problems, 17.9 percent a death in the family, 15.9 percent financial problems, 15.7 percent midlife crisis, 14.7 percent personal illness, and 10.9 percent "other." When asked if their personal distress resulted in decreased quality of care provided, 36.7 percent said yes and 4.6 percent said the distress resulted in inadequate care. The results did not show that any specific source of stress was found to predict either decreased or inadequate treatment care. However, it was noted that older clinicians were more likely to claim that personal distress had no impact on patient care. It was also found that respondents who reported job stress or marital problems were the most likely to maintain that their quality of care had not been reduced due to the stress. In their discussion of these findings, Guy et al. expressed concern that some therapists, particularly those experiencing job and marital stress, may tend to deny the effects of this stress on their clinical effectiveness.

While the studies just described provided data pertaining to experienced and practicing clinicians, other research has included interns and practicum students and has focused in more detail on specific, job-related stressors. Following research by Deutsch (1984) and Hellman, Morrison, and Abramowitz (1987), Rodolfa, Kraft, and Reilley (1988) surveyed experienced clinicians, interns, and practicum students working at Veterans Administration Hospitals and Counseling Centers. Their results identified client behaviors, therapist experiences, and therapist beliefs that were rated as stressful by clinicians, interns, and practicum students.

CLIENT BEHAVIORS

In the Rodolfa et al. findings, among the most stressful client behaviors were physical assault on the therapist, suicide attempts, and suicidal statements. Compared to more experienced professionals, interns and practicum students were more likely to rate as stressful such client behaviors as blatantly psychotic speech, homosexual and heterosexual flirting, premature termination, and clients' lack of motivation.

Fremont and Anderson (1986) looked at client behaviors from a slightly different perspective, asking senior staff members, interns, and practicum students to identify the behaviors of clients that were most likely to make the counselor angry, frustrated, or irritated. Respondents identified a number of incidents, which were then grouped into five categories. These included client resistance, impositions on the counselor, verbal attacks, the counselor becoming overly involved in client dynamics, and a more general category of other incidents. Specific incidents cited included clients failing to show up for appointments, clients continually blaming others or refusing to work on their own issues, clients asking for special privileges, or unnecessarily calling the therapist at home at odd hours. As in the Rodolfa et al. findings, concern was also expressed about clients verbally attacking or threatening physical harm to the therapist. Freemont and Anderson noted that for some of the issues, most notably resistance, the experience level of the counselor influenced their reaction, with more experienced counselors reporting less anger in response to resistance.

THERAPIST EXPERIENCES

In addition to exploring client behaviors, Rodolfa et al. examined therapist experiences and found the items rated most stressful included an inability to help clients feel better (see also Farber & Heifetz, 1981), receiving criticism from supervisors, professional conflicts, and seeing more clients than usual. As with client behaviors, compared to the professionals, interns and practicum students rated different therapist experiences as more stressful. For example, interns and practicum students assigned higher stress ratings to such experiences as lack of client progress, inability to help clients feel better, criticism from supervisors, and presenting a case in staffing. As these findings indicate, along with the other challenges faced by helping professionals, trainees also report the additional stress of supervision and related issues.

THERAPIST COGNITIONS

Stress-producing ideas represent a third area addressed by Rodolfa et al.. Using a version of an instrument originally developed by Deutsch (1984), Rodolfa et al. found that certain beliefs are associated with greater stress among interns. These beliefs include: the belief that therapists should always work at peak levels of competence and enthusiasm; the belief that therapists should be able to handle all client emergencies and should help every client; and the belief that lack of client progress is the therapist's fault. Failure to take time off also contributed to the reported stress, as did the belief that therapists should be models of mental health themselves.

EXERCISE

You have just read examples of stress-producing ideas that are common among interns. Take a moment to think about your own beliefs about your internship and clients. Do any of these beliefs unnecessarily add to the stress you experience in your internship or training? If so, how might you change the ideas and your corresponding level of stress? This would be a fruitful topic to discuss with other interns and with your instructor or supervisor. In these discussions, ask how your peers or mentors have dealt with these issues in their own work.

Rodolfa's findings regarding therapist beliefs and stress are consistent with the results of other research. For exam-

ple, Hellman, Morrison, and Abramowitz (1987) studied the relationship between therapist flexibility, boundary maintenance, and stress. Of particular interest in this study was the distinction between "fusion" and "boundary maintenance." As they defined this issue, "The boundary dimension reflects attempts to establish highly structured interaction by emphasizing space and time boundaries and adopting clear and explicit roles. The fusion dimension reflects a tendency to blur personal boundaries with the environment" (p. 22).

The issue comes down to one of maintaining a degree of professional distance in which one is able to empathize with clients but not lose, or fear the loss of, one's own identity in the process. Results of the Hellman et al. study indicated that therapists who were flexible reported less stress overall than therapists who were identified as rigid or dogmatic. With regard to the fusion/boundary questions, therapists who maintained higher personal boundaries reported less stress from client behaviors such as suicidal threats, passive-aggressive behavior, and negative client affect. Based on these findings, Hellman et al. suggested that the stresses created by patient behaviors may be reduced for therapists who are able to maintain a degree of flexibility and a degree of professional distance. They go on to suggest that for therapists who have greater fusion tendencies or are more rigid in their thinking and approach, working with certain kinds of clients may be unusually stressful.

In thinking about these conclusions, particularly those pertaining to boundaries and fusion, it is important to recognize that the key must be to maintain a therapeutic balance. Although different theoretical approaches place different emphasis on the importance of emotional empathy with clients, if one's primary need is to maintain inflexible boundaries it will be difficult to empathize with a client. Indeed, if carried to an extreme, the clearest way to eliminate therapeutic stress is to create boundaries so strong that one no longer interacts with clients at all. The trick is to find ways that enable you to empathize with, understand, and care about your clients, while still maintaining your role as a professional and your personal identity and life outside the therapy session.

THE EFFECTS OF STRESS

It should be evident from the discussion thus far that there are numerous possible sources of work-related and personal stress in the lives of interns and helping professionals. This raises questions about how such stresses may affect us as individuals and how stress impacts our work with clients.

PHYSICAL EFFECTS

The mental and emotional toll are probably what come to mind first when one thinks of the demands on helping professionals, but in many ways the physical costs can be just as high. I have talked to therapists who spend eight-to-ten hours per day seeing clients, one after another, in windowless offices, sometimes taking only ten minutes for lunch in the middle of the day, then starting right back up again with no other break. This simply cannot be healthy and it cannot be sustained for long before the effects begin to appear. As one of these therapists said: "Every job has its occupational hazards. For us it's hemorrhoids." He might have added clogged arteries, atrophied muscles, weight gain, low back pain, and other physical ailments.

Psychotherapy and related activities are not aerobic exercises. In fact, if one watches tapes of therapy it is startling how little many therapists move during certain sessions. A great deal of mental energy may be spent, but physical motion is minimal. This lack of motion contributes to what a colleague calls "hypo-kinetic disorders," i.e., physical illness caused by inactivity.

Commenting on this aspect of therapy Guy (1987) remarked that other occupations may be relatively sedentary, but:

> Few require that the individual stay riveted to a chair for 50 minutes at a time, without the opportunity to stand up, stretch, or walk around. If a therapist fails to appreciate the need for regular, extended breaks to allow for sufficient physical activity, his or her only exercise is likely to be an occasional brief stroll to the water cooler and restroom between appointments. Day after day of such a sedentary pattern creates a physical fatigue which can negatively impact both the professional and personal functioning of the individual. (p. 82)

Along with the problems stemming from limited activity, physical problems can also develop from patterns of storing stress through muscle tension. Early in the first month of a summer practicum placement, I developed extreme pains in the area between my left shoulder and neck. The pain tended to subside during the night then became progressively worse as each day went on. For several weeks I tried warm and cold packs, took an occasional anti-inflammatory, and even tried laying on a tennis ball while rolling it around under the shoulder. All of this was to no avail until one day, while working with a particularly difficult client, I realized that as the client spoke my left shoulder was rising up. Although I was trying to stay relaxed while working with the client, my shoulder was evidently taking the tension. This insight lead me to focus on my physical reaction to other clients. I discovered that whenever a session was difficult, my shoulder went up. With that awareness, I was able to self-monitor and relax my shoulder and other muscles as well.

In my case the physical tension was stored in my shoulder. Other interns and colleagues have reported neck pain, aches in their jaws, headaches, tension in their forehead, and pain and tension in other areas. Physical consequences are by no means limited to muscle tension. To the extent that the role of intern creates additional demands, the risk of stress-related illness is increased. It is not uncommon for students to report severe stomach pains and other signs of physical reactions to stress. One colleague even believed he was having a heart attack the night before his dissertation defense. It turned out to be a combination of stress, altitude, and anxiety, but the experience helped remind him to be more attentive and take better care of himself physically as well as emotionally.

THE EFFECTS ON SOCIAL RELATIONSHIPS

As mentioned at the beginning of this chapter, every helping professional is probably familiar with being introduced to someone who responds with something like "You're not going to psychoanalyze me are you?" or, "Uh oh, now I better watch what I say."

This has happened so many times by now that it no longer troubles me. Still, I have been tempted on occasion to follow the advice of a colleague who says he never tells people he's a psychologist. Instead, he claims to be a mortician.

In response to those who are concerned that helping professionals are continually evaluating people, the honest answer is probably "yes and no." The answer is "no" because we tend to interact much differently in social settings and personal relationships than we do in our professional roles. If, for example, a patient in a session expresses a political viewpoint contrary to our own, we are not likely to challenge that in the session. On the other hand, if someone said the same thing at a party we might fly off the handle. Clearly, how one acts and interacts with people in a clinical setting is often very different than how one acts in other settings and roles.

At the same time, however, all people, helping professionals included, form impressions of one another. Indeed, many interns and professionals may try too hard to avoid doing this outside their office, sometimes to their detriment. This would perhaps be analogous to auto mechanics who spend all day working on other people's cars at the shop, but when their own cars break down they act as if they do not have any idea what to do about it. If your clinical training helps you to understand people in new ways, as long as you do not use that knowledge to the detriment of others, there is nothing unethical about carrying that understanding over to other aspects of your life.

Just as other people's apprehensions about therapists and therapists' own apprehensions about their role can be confusing and sometimes seem threatening, the reverse problem can also occur when people in social interactions seek advice from a therapist outside the clinical setting. There are many variations to this situation. For example, sometimes people will ask your opinion about a general subject because they believe you may have some training or education that is relevant or because they respect your intelligence and want to hear what you have to say on the matter. This is typically a sign of respect for you or your profession and it is generally benign. The challenge in such cases is to avoid pontificating or speaking as though you have knowledge if you really don't.

On the other hand, there are also times when people will begin a statement with something like "You're a therapist . . ." followed by a discussion of their children, spouse, parents, friends, boss, or someone else who is not present at the time.

Although it may be flattering to be consulted for your expertise, you should also realize that social situations in which your "clinical advice" is sought can be fraught with mixed roles, hidden agendas, and incomplete communication. As a general rule, it is wise not to offer any form of clinical advice or interpretation under such circumstances. In most instances of this type you are hearing only one part of the story, have not been formally contracted to fill the role of therapist, are often in a public setting such as a party, and do not have the environment, time, permission, or pay to do real therapy work. The problem is, how do you do refuse to give the desired advice or interpretation without being rude to the person who is asking the question?

When faced with this problem I try to empathize with the person's concern and their request for information. Then, having acknowledged their concerns, I indicate that out of care for them and any others who may be involved, I believe it is not a good idea to give clinical advice outside the clinical setting. For example, I might say something like, "That does sound like a difficult situation, and I can understand you wanting some help in figuring out how to deal with it. But for lots of reasons I generally find it best to avoid giving clinical advice or delving into personal issues too deeply when I'm not actually doing therapy with someone. I hope you can understand."

Many people will let the matter drop at this point and the conversation can naturally shift to something else. Others will pursue the question further, either by asking if you could see them clinically or could recommend someone else who could. This request can readily be dealt with through referral to your supervisor or another professional you know.

Another situation that many interns find awkward involves coincidental encounters with clients in nonclinical settings such as the grocery store, movies, or elsewhere. Although this has received relatively little research attention, a study of college therapists found their most common responses to incidental encounters with clients were surprise, uncertainty, and, to a lesser degree, discomfort (Sharkin & Birkey, 1992). In comparison, Pulakos (1994) reported that although clients who encountered therapists also mentioned awkwardness among their reactions, they ranked feelings of confidence and surprise higher than feelings of discomfort. For a discussion and exercises relating to therapist reactions to incidental encounters, see Arons and Siegel (1995).

EXERCISE

You may find it informative to give some thought to how you might feel and react to meeting a client in another setting. What do your reactions suggest to you about your role and the therapy process? You might also put yourself in the role of client and think how it would feel to meet your therapist in various public situations. Are there any settings where it would be more or less difficult to encounter clients? What are those and what do the possible difficulties tell you about yourself or your role?

Oddly enough, in encounters outside the office, the awkwardness seems to come because both clinicians and clients are worried that the other person will see them as "they really are." This feeling goes both ways, in the sense that just as each person may be afraid the other will see them in a different light, there may also be a tendency to not want to see a person as anything other than a client or therapist (Arons & Siegel, 1995).

For example, imagine that on a Saturday afternoon a therapist has been working in her garden, or perhaps painting the living room, and she goes to a store to buy some tools. Because she will get back to the same task when she returns, she does not change clothes or otherwise clean up. Thus, she happily heads to the store covered in mud or paint, wearing shabby clothes, hair uncombed or brushed, and otherwise lacking all the attire and grooming that might be her mode at work. At the store she runs into one of her clients who, as it happens, is similarly disheveled, having been doing similar tasks at her home. This could be a very positive experience for both therapist and client, but it may also feel uncomfortable as both realize they have now been seen and are known to be, in their "secret lives" outside of therapy, pretty much average human beings.

One intern told a humorous story that illustrated this concern perfectly. During a day off the intern was stricken with a rather nasty bout of indigestion that was accompanied by an equally nasty case of flatulence. While shopping for medication at a nearby pharmacy, the intern encountered a client from his clinic. The intern was at first anxious about what to say, but after a brief chat with the client he began to feel comfortable. Just as the intern and client were about to part company and continue about their business, the client happened to drop something from her purse. As the intern bent to pick the object up, the intern's flatulence made an untimely reappearance. Sheepishly, he returned the client's fallen object and explained, "Sorry. I'm battling the stomach flu." Much to his relief, the client simply smiled and said, "Don't worry about it. We're all human." To the intern's credit, he tactfully raised the issue in the next visit with the client and acknowledged that he had been terribly embarrassed. He then thanked the client for her understanding and they continued on to a productive session.

Along with the issue of revealing different roles outside of therapy, awkwardness in coincidental encounters is also created by the confidentiality of therapy and a sense of not knowing whether or how to greet and interact with the other person. This is further complicated if the client or therapist is in the presence of someone else and introductions seem called for. Given confidentiality concerns, the therapist cannot very well offer the introduction, "This is Eric Johnson; he's a client of mine in therapy."

As a preferred alternative, coincidental interactions with clients can be dealt with much as you would if you met a friend by coincidence in a similar setting. You might, for example, briefly ask how things are going, make small talk about the weather, etc. If others are present and introductions seem called for, names alone are sufficient; one need not provide more information.

One further note about incidental encounters is that in general it is a good idea to discuss them during the next therapy session. Pulakos (1993) noted that 71 percent of clients in her survey indicated such encounters were not discussed in the following session. In comparison, results of Sharkin and Birkey (1992) indicated that therapists reported discussing the incident 52 percent of the time. This apparent discrepancy suggests that perceptions of the importance of such encounters may differ between therapists and patients. I prefer to at least acknowledge such encounters during the subsequent session. If the encounter seems to trouble the client, that may be useful material to address in therapy. If the encounter is unusually difficult for you as a therapist, this might be worth exploring with your supervisor.

Before concluding the topic of social relationships, one more thought is offered regarding your professional role and social relationships. Whether you like it or not, whenever you interact with other people they may form opinions about both your personal qualities and your presumed qualities as a professional. What is more, based on their interactions with you, some people will form opinions about your profession as a whole. This does not mean that you should always try to present a certain impression in public. (It is okay to go out with paint or mud on your clothes on weekends.) It does not mean that all helping professionals must at all times be models of "perfect mental health." It does, however, mean that you should be aware of the image you create and what effects it might have on others and on your professional role.

For example, if at a party you begin to tell stories about clients, you may preserve confidentiality by not revealing personal data, but the very fact that you are discussing clients publicly may be troubling to others and might be disturbing to the clients themselves if they knew you were doing so. Even if no other person could possibly identify a particular individual based solely on a story told at a party, merely knowing that clients' lives are talked about publicly could prevent some people from seeking therapy or from being as open as they might need to be in therapy.

Apart from directly discussing clients, if in your life away from therapy you exhibit problems with substance abuse, controlling your anger, or other issues for which people might seek therapy themselves, questions may be raised about your credibility. If these or other behaviors are problems, you may want to consider seeking therapy for yourself to work on them.

THE EFFECTS ON CLOSE RELATIONSHIPS AND FAMILIES

Beyond the social awkwardness that can come with our professions, problems of greater consequence can arise in relationships with spouses, significant others, and family members (MacNab, 1995; Maeder, 1989). The stresses interns and helping professionals face have contributed to the breakup of many couples, and it is not at all uncommon for therapists to find themselves doing exactly the things they advise their clients not to do. We often work long hours and may not take enough time for recreation or private time with our families or significant others. Tired of "communicating" in our work all day, we may resist talking about our own feelings or those of our partners. We may feel we do not need to hear our partner's problems on top of everything else we have been dealing with during the day. When concerned partners begin to express feelings about the relationship, we may deny the legitimacy of the concern or become defensive.

Kottler (1986) describes the transition from work to home in the following passage.

> We keep a vigilant eye on personal fallout to protect our family and friends from the intensity of our professional life. Yet with all the restraint we must exercise in order to follow the rules regulating our conduct during working hours, it is difficult to not be abusive, surly, or self-indulgent with our loved ones. All day long we have stifled ourselves, censored our thoughts and statements, and disciplined ourselves to be controlled and intelligent. And then we make an abrupt transition to go home. Much of the pressure that has been building all day long as clients have come in and dumped their troubles finally releases as we walk through the door. If we are not careful, our families will suffer the emotional fallout. (p. 38)

EXERCISE

To help you assess some of the effects of being an intern on your life and relationships you may want to complete the checklist below for yourself and with significant others in your life.

1. How many days each week do you finish the work day feeling drained and lacking in energy or motivation to do much else?_____
2. How many days each week do you finish the work day feeling like you have been successful and have enjoyed your work that day?_____
3. When was the last time you did something with just you and your significant other?_____
4. When was the last time you did something with just yourself and one or more good friends?_____

5. How often in the past month have you not done something with your significant other because of work conflicts or effects?_____

6. How often in the past month have you not done something with friends because of work conflicts or effects?_____

7. Do you feel you listen as well to your significant other or close friends as you would like?_____

8. Do others feel you listen as well to them as they would like?_____

9. What are you doing to take care of your physical health?_____

10. If you were a therapist and had yourself as a client, what would be your advice or exploration regarding self-care?_____

11. What forms of self-care are you not doing and why?_____

12. In a typical week, how often do you find yourself thinking about your internship or clients when you are in other settings?_____

13. How often in your personal life do you experience anger or other feelings to a greater degree or with greater frequency than you would like?_____ Could this be related to stress at work?_____

14. How is your intimate relationship with your significant other?_____ Could work be affecting that?_____

After completing the checklist, I strongly encourage you to review your answers with significant others in your life. If areas of concern are identified, you may want to evaluate together how your internship and personal life are affecting one another. A superb resource for further information about this and other topics of this chapter is the previously mentioned book, *The Personal Life of the Psychotherapist* by James Guy (1987). See also Sussman's book, *A Perilous Calling: The Hazards of Psychotherapy Practice* (1995).

Should you or a partner feel your relationship is being adversely impacted by your work or training, you may want to consider seeing a therapist. One intern I instructed maintained that his clinical training was having only positive influences on his life and relationships. However, when he completed the previous exercise and discussed it with his partner, he was surprised to discover that, from the partner's perspective, the relationship was, in fact, suffering a great deal. As a result, the couple decided to begin therapy together. Sometime later they confided to me that entering therapy was one of the best decisions they ever made.

BURNOUT

When the stresses of work become too great, the phenomenon of "burnout" may result. The term "burnout" is attributed to Herbert Freudenberger, who introduced it to describe a pattern of responses shown by people who work in committed activities and begin to exhibit declines in personal involvement, effectiveness, or productivity (Farber, 1983b; Freudenberger 1974). Since its introduction, burnout has been written about and studied in a variety of populations, including school teachers, police officers, nurses, physicians, business executives, and others believed to work in high-stress positions (Farber, 1983a; Golembiewski & Munzenrider, 1988). Due to the kinds of stresses that have been described in this chapter, helping professionals and interns are also at particularly high risk of burnout.

SYMPTOMS OF BURNOUT

In a review of theoretical writing and empirical studies, Farber (1983b) noted that burnout has been defined in several different ways. Some authors and studies emphasize the emotional features; others address physiological symptoms of burnout. The most commonly mentioned symptoms include emotional distancing from clients and staff, decreased empathy, cynicism, decreased self-esteem, physical exhaustion, sleep disturbances, stomach pains, and other stress-related physical complaints. Farber observed that in spite of differences in emphasis by different authors, "there is general consensus that the symptoms of burnout include attitudinal, emotional and physical components" (p. 3).

Maslach's (1982) description of burnout placed special emphasis on the importance of estrangement from clients and colleagues. Similarly, Pines and Aronson (1988) have focused on the withdrawal process that is characteristic of burnout. They note that professionals who are nearing or in burnout typically seek to withdraw, either physically, emotionally, or mentally. This strategy is perhaps best understood both as a response to the other symptoms of burnout and as a symptom itself.

When therapists begin to experience the unpleasant symptoms of burnout, they seek ways to lessen those symptoms. If other methods are unavailable or fail, physical, emotional, or mental withdrawal provide ways of distancing themselves from clients or work and thereby reducing stress. This is a perfectly understandable response but it can adversely affect professionals and their clients. Withdrawal can also lead to further frustration and negative feelings as therapists recognize their lessened effectiveness and satisfaction but are unable to find more creative or constructive solutions.

STAGES OF BURNOUT

Many authors who study burnout have emphasized that it is important to view burnout as a "process" rather than an "event." That is, one does not suddenly become burned out in a single day. Rather, progressive stages are typically passed through on the way to burnout. Edelwich and Brodsky (1980) describe how people may pass through stages from initial enthusiasm through stagnation, frustration, and, ultimately, apathy. Edelwich and Brodsky emphasize that there is an important difference between frustration and apathy, with burnout associated only with the latter stage. As long as people are frustrated, they are still involved, caring, and struggling to make a change. In the frustration stage there is still a possibility of making changes and returning to the more positive stage of enthusiasm. By comparison, when someone becomes apathetic, that person is burned out and, according to Edelwich and Brodsky, the prospects for positive change are substantially lessened.

In the context of the withdrawal process that Pines and Aronson described, apathy may be understood as a result of avoidant learning. That is, therapists who are burned out have learned that when they try their best to do clinical work, and when they empathize closely with clients, they are often frustrated either by the inherent limitations of the task, the client's lack of change, organizational factors, or other elements that block success or pose excessive demands. This process produces a form of aversive conditioning in which therapists learn that one way to avoid the negative consequences is to withdraw from the process. If the empathic sharing of a client's emotional suffering is aversive, the therapist may withdraw emotionally. If efforts to make cognitive sense of client issues or organizational processes do not yield positive results, the therapist may withdraw mentally and just go through the behavioral motions of the job. If the work setting itself becomes associated with unpleasant experiences, the therapist may withdraw physically from that setting. Understanding this connection is clinically valuable because by identifying the ways in which a person is withdrawing one may gather clues about the key factors that are contributing to their burnout.

MEASURES OF BURNOUT

For both research and clinical purposes, attempts have been made to operationalize the concept of burnout through the development of instruments designed to measure it (Arthur, 1990). Two of the most frequently used instruments are the Maslach Burnout Inventory (MBI) (Maslach & Jackson, 1981) and the Staff Burnout Scale (SBS) (Jones, 1980). Maslach's inventory contains three subscales that address emotional exhaustion, depersonalization, and personal accomplishments. Emotional exhaustion is considered to be the result of the physical and emotional strains of sustained stress. Depersonalization is seen as an attempt to cope with the strain by distancing oneself from clients and peers and by treating others as objects rather than people. Finally, as a result of the sustained stress and attempts to cope with it, people's personal accomplishments decline. In combination with exhaustion and depersonalization, this can lead to a diminished sense of self-efficacy and possibly depression (Lee & Ashforth, 1990).

In comparison to the MBI, the Staff Burnout Scale focuses on many of the same issues, but emphasizes the phys-

iological and behavioral dimensions. The SBS produces an overall score for burnout but items can also be grouped into four factors. These are: dissatisfaction with work, psychological and interpersonal tension, physical illness and distress, and unprofessional patient relationships.

Along with their usefulness in helping to identify the symptoms of burnout, these instruments and studies help explain how and why burnout develops. This understanding is especially important to interns and therapists who, because they may be at risk, need to recognize the signs of burnout and need to be able to cope effectively with its potential causes.

CAUSES OF BURNOUT

Causes of burnout have been attributed to factors within the individual, inherent features of demanding jobs, organizational structure and managerial approaches. Broader social concerns, including worker alienation, have also been identified as contributing to burnout (Farber, 1983b). In addition to these general factors, several authors, including Farber (1983a) and Pines and Aronson (1988) have emphasized that the training and demands of helping professions contribute in unique ways to burnout. In most cases, all of the factors work in combination to contribute to burnout. Understanding their relative importance is useful because, as Pines and Aronson point out,

> How individuals perceive the cause of their burnout and attribute the "blame" has enormous consequences for action. If they attribute the cause to a characterological weakness or inadequacy in themselves, they will take a certain set of actions: quit the profession, seek psychotherapy and so forth. However, if they see the cause as largely a function of the situation, they will strive to change the situation and make it more tolerable, a totally different set of remedial actions. (p. 5)

Reviewing some of the more commonly identified contributors to burnout may help you recognize if you or someone you work with begins to develop signs of burnout. From that basis you may be more able to cope effectively with the situation. To draw again from Pines and Aronson,

> . . . the first and most important step would be to change the focus from "What's wrong with me?" to "What can I do about the situation?" (p. 5)

INDIVIDUAL FACTORS

Some of the personality characteristics that have been associated with burnout were alluded to earlier in this chapter as part of the discussion of stress and therapist characteristics. Among the characteristics often mentioned are lack of clear boundaries between self and work, extreme degrees of empathy, exceptional levels of commitment, and a fragile self-concept (Carroll & White, 1982).

Carroll and White also identify poor training as a contributor and note that training deficits can lead to burnout in two ways. First, inadequate training for a job leaves one feeling unprepared, vulnerable, insecure, and fearing failure. Second, even those who are adequately trained in the skills of their job may not be trained to cope with the stresses of the job. Thus, some people may face burnout because they were not adequately trained for the skills demanded in their job. Others may burn out because they have no training in coping with the emotional demands of the job.

Much as inadequate training can contribute to burnout, in the helping professions the training process itself can pose added risks. Pines and Aronson (1988) have described how people who become helping professionals do so out of feelings of concern for others but then encounter problems and suffering that they simply cannot alleviate completely. This can lead to feelings of hopelessness and helplessness that are incompatible with the motives and dedication that attracted the therapist to the position to begin with. This inherent feature of the helping professional's work is often a key factor in their burnout.

Consistent with the previously described results of Rodolfa et al. (1988), Farber (1983a) identifies both the challenges of therapy itself and the supervision process as particularly important stressors for trainees. Farber notes that the ambiguity of therapy, the difficulty of learning a complex new skill, and the mixed role of teaching and evaluation in supervision all make the training process highly anxiety provoking for most interns. These are complicated still further by the development of "psychological mindedness" among trainees.

> As part of learning psychotherapy, residents and interns are required to understand the inner dynamics of patients, and as a result, necessarily become more psychological-minded themselves, more aware of their own unconscious processes, motivations, and difficulties. (p. 101)

This process is essential to therapy training and can have positive results, but Farber notes that it also has the potential to lead to overidentification with clients. As interns become aware of their own dynamics while simultaneously beginning to fill the role of therapist, they must cope with two sets of issues that are fraught with ambiguity and anxiety. Either alone might be difficult enough, but the combination can be overwhelming. Because this is so important, it will be addressed in more detail in the following chapter.

ORGANIZATIONAL FACTORS

In contrast to approaches that emphasize the individual's characteristics as contributing to burnout, organizational and managerial factors have also been studied. Pines (1982) observed that in studies in which two different treatment centers were compared, higher levels of burnout were observed in one than the other even though the two were very similar in clients served, location, staffing, and other variables. This difference suggested that organizational factors were involved in contributing to or reducing burnout in the different centers. A similar conclusion was reached by Arches (1991) who surveyed social workers and found that "lack of autonomy and the influence of funding sources are major contributors to burnout" (p. 202).

Pines identifies four broad qualities of work environments that can contribute to burnout. She describes these as psychological, physical, social, and organizational factors. Pines and Aronson (1988) note that it is equally important to look for features that help prevent burnout. Such positive features include organizational flexibility, staff autonomy, variety, supportive colleagues, opportunities for breaks in times of stress, limiting the hours of stressful work, and, where necessary, reducing staff-client ratios.

Managerial style has also been identified as a possible cause or preventive element in burnout. Murphy and Pardeck (1986) note that burnout is probably best prevented by a managerial style that falls somewhere between authoritarian and laissez faire. They explain that the authoritarian approach does not provide sufficient autonomy or self-direction to staff, does not involve staff in decision making, and tends to give instructions without explanation. At the opposite extreme, laissez-faire approaches suffer from problems by failing to provide staff with sufficient direction, guidance, or support.

The alternative recommended by Murphy and Pardeck is a version of participative decision making based on Likert's (1967, 1978) "System 4" management philosophy. In essence, this system involves personnel from different departments working together to provide input into organizational decisions. Murphy and Pardeck suggest that this approach helps workers cope with the complexity of social service jobs and organizations by promoting greater awareness and cohesion across disciplines, and by increasing feelings of involvement in the overall mission of the organization.

As a final comment on organizational factors and burnout, some authors have drawn a distinction between job satisfaction, job changing, and burnout. This is a useful distinction because the literature suggests it is possible to be satisfied with a job yet still be burned out. This research also helps explain the connection between financial compensation, satisfaction, and burnout.

In a study of how seven job features related to satisfaction among social workers, Jayaratne and Chess (1983) looked at comfort, challenge, financial reward, promotions, role ambiguity, role conflict, and workload. Their results revealed that the facets of challenge, financial rewards, and promotional opportunities were all related to satisfaction, with financial reward being the best predictor of job turnover. Job-related stressors did not appear to affect satisfaction or turnover, but might still contribute to burnout. In other words, it is possible for workers to report overall satisfaction with their work and want to stay on the job but still experience the symptoms of burnout. It is also possible for workers to change jobs, not because they are burned out but primarily for financial reasons. Finally, financial compensation is a useful predictor of whether or not someone is likely to change jobs, but does not appear to be strongly related to burnout.

Jayaratne and Chess emphasize that this does not mean helping professionals do not want or deserve fair financial compensation. Low pay does have direct costs and consequences in worker turnover, but merely adjusting pay is not likely to be a lasting solution to burnout that is caused by factors other than economic considerations.

THE STATE OF THE WORLD

Along with the stresses relating to clinical activities, the nature of field placements and clinical work often bring interns into contact with aspects of life that can be difficult to deal with emotionally and that seem intractable or unsolvable. Kurland and Salmon (1992) comment on this and observe that:

> Social work practitioners enter into their work with idealistic motivation; however, they may not have the skills needed to face the enormous problems that seem to defy solution. (p. 241)

Kurland and Salmon go on to suggest that as a result of this experience, workers may:

> . . . soon fall prey to the perceived hopelessness of the situations and of these monumental social problems unless the teachers, supervisors, and consultants are able to help them go on. (p. 241)

This encounter with deep social ills is often the source of the most profound challenge that not only interns but experienced practitioners must contend with. How, if we care about others and are drawn to the professions out of a desire to help, can we go on in the face of problems that seem so huge and that do real and lasting harm to so many people? There is no easy answer to this, and when we are unable to cope with the situation, burnout or other symptoms may result.

RECOGNIZING AND UNDERSTANDING YOUR OWN SITUATION AND BURNOUT

The literature reviewed above is interesting from a theoretical perspective, but what really matters is how it relates to you personally. My experience suggests there is great variability in the extent to which individual interns and internship settings reflect both the negative and the positive features that have been identified. Some interns are extremely dedicated and sensitive to their clients but are also remarkably fragile and susceptible to burnout. At the opposite extreme, I occasionally encounter interns who seem virtually immune to burnout because they so distance themselves that they do not

empathize or connect with their clients. Somewhere in the middle, one finds interns who exhibit a healthy balance of sensitivity to clients and dedication to the field, but who are also able to keep a degree of objectivity and detachment that allows them to do good clinical work without excessively carrying the burdens of their clients' difficulties.

Similar variability can be found across internship settings. In the best settings, interns can feel the excitement, caring, staff support, and dedication to the profession and to clients. In other settings, there is a pervasive air of resignation, domination, or hostility.

Interns and their supervisors must be aware of both the individual factors and the situational factors that can lead to burnout. If interns are showing the symptoms that were described earlier in this section, that is a signal to explore what is happening and what can be done about it. As a relatively simple starting point for that exploration, and as a way to help prevent burnout by understanding it before it develops, you may find it useful to answer the following questions.

PERSONAL AND ENVIRONMENTAL BURNOUT PRONENESS OR PREVENTION

SELF-EVALUATION EXERCISE

In light of the material you have just read about burnout, answer each of the questions below.

1. What personal characteristics do you have that could contribute to burnout?
2. What personal characteristics do you think might help you prevent burnout?
3. What features of your current internship setting or possible future settings do you think would contribute most to burnout for you?
4. What internship setting features could help prevent burnout?

BURNOUT AS A COPING MECHANISM

Before concluding this discussion of burnout, there is an additional perspective that should be introduced. In much of the literature and in professional discourse on the subject, burnout is commonly viewed as a situation that is solely negative and thereby something that is to be prevented or avoided. There is a fundamental problem with this approach because it overlooks the value and importance of burnout as a potential learning and growth experience for the individual. If burnout is viewed in only negative terms, there may be a tendency for interns or professionals to deny their experience lest they acknowledge that they too are vulnerable to experiencing something that, because of its negative image, may be stigmatizing. The response may be, "I can't be burned out. Burnout is a sign of weakness or failure, and that just can't be me." Organizations may exhibit similar responses if employees begin to show signs of burnout. "No, our employees aren't burning out. That would mean there is something wrong with our organization and we know that can't be true."

As an alternative to viewing burnout in this way, interns, supervisors, and organizations would benefit more from a perspective that views symptoms of burnout as valuable information that something is not working optimally and could be improved. It should also be emphasized that symptoms of burnout do not necessarily mean the source of the problem is limited to the workplace. Other factors in the individual's life can contribute to burnout as well.

Roberts (1987) has suggested that in considering the effects of stress on helping professionals we must take into account the overall quality of relationships and demands in their lives. As Roberts points out, all individuals have some limits to the energy, resources, and abilities they can use to manage stress. As one's energy declines, or as normally effective resources fail to cope adequately with stress, the quality of coping responses declines. Thus, when people exhibit symptoms of burnout, that is a signal that the overall level of stress in their life is somehow exceeding their coping abilities and resources. From this perspective, burnout is viewed not as a failure but as an effort to cope in a different way.

In a particularly insightful and useful observation, Roberts explains that:

> Burnout is perceived as an appropriate coping mechanism under the circumstances given the history of choices, experiences, and resources of the individual. The arena in which this form of coping (burnout) would surface—work, family, or friends—would likely be that one which offers the least resistance or least consequence to the expression of burnout. (p. 116)

In other words, just as the causes of burnout are not limited to the work setting, one can show signs of burnout outside the work setting as well. According to Roberts, burnout is a form of coping and we are most likely to resort to it where it is safest to do so. This means we must be attentive to burnout not only on the job, but in our relationships, school, and other aspects of our lives. In many cases, burnout may hit relationships well before work because relationships are safer environments. Because it might be safer in some ways to burn out in our relationships rather than our jobs, the relationship and our partners suffer.

The key point is that if we recognize signs of burnout wherever they appear, we can interpret those signs as a signal that our alternative coping mechanisms are being overwhelmed. This may not be a pleasant realization, but from it we can begin to explore where the stresses are in our lives and why our other coping mechanisms are not managing them. Thus, instead of viewing burnout in solely negative terms, we can approach it as a signal and opportunity for learning more about ourselves and our situation. How to deal with that awareness is the topic of the next chapter.

REFERENCES

Ackerley, G. D., Burnell, J., Holder, D. C., & Kurdek, L. A. (1988). Burnout among licensed psychologists. *Professional Psychology: Research and Practice, 19*, 624–631.

Arches, J. (1991). Social structure, burnout, and job satisfaction. *Social Work, 36*, 202–206.

Arons, G., & Siegel, R. D. (1995). Unexpected encounters: The Wizard of Oz exposed. In M. B. Sussman (Ed.), *A perilous calling: The hazards of psychotherapy practice.* (pp. 125–138) New York: John Wiley and Sons.

Arthur, N. M. (1990). The assessment of burnout: A review of three inventories useful for research and counseling. *Journal of Counseling and Development, 69*, 186–189.

Boxley, R., Drew, C., & Rangle, D. (1986). Clinical trainee impairment in APA approved internship programs. *The Clinical Psychologist, 39*(2), 49–52.

Bradey, J., & Post, P. (1991). Impaired students: Do we eliminate them from counselor education programs? *Counselor Education and Supervision, 31*, 100–108.

Carroll, J. F. X., & White, W. L. (1982). Theory building: Integrating individual environmental factors within an ecological framework. In W. S. Paine (Ed.). *Job stress and burnout: Research, theory, and intervention perspectives.* (pp. 41–60) Beverly Hills: Sage Publications.

Deutsch, C. (1984). Self-reported sources of stress among psychotherapists. *Professional Psychology: Research and Practice, 15*, 833–845.

Edelwich, J., & Brodsky, A. (1980). *Burnout: Stages of disillusionment in the helping professions.* New York: Human Science Press.

Farber, B. A. (1983a). Dysfunctional aspects of the psychotherapeutic role. In B.A. Farber (Ed.) *Stress and burnout in the human service professions.* (pp. 97–118) New York: Pergamon Press.

Farber, B. A. (1983b). Introduction: A critical perspective on burnout. In B.A. Farber (Ed.), *Stress and burnout in the human service professions.* (pp. 1–23) New York: Pergamon Press.

Farber, B. A. (1990). Burnout in psychotherapists: Incidence, types, and trends. *Psychotherapy in Private Practice, 8*(1), 35 –44.

Farber, B. A., & Heifetz, L. (1981). The satisfactions and stresses of psychotherapeutic work: A factor analytic study. *Professional Psychology, 12*, 621–630.

Fremont, S., & Anderson, W. (1986). What client behaviors make counselors angry: An exploratory study. *Journal of Counseling and Development, 65*, 67–70.

Freudenberger, H. J. (1974). Staff burn-out. *Journal of Social Issues, 30*(1), 159–165.

Golembiewski, R. T., & Munzenrider, R. F. (1988). *Phases of burnout: Developments in concepts and applications.* New York: Praeger.

Guy, J. D. (1987). *The personal life of the psychotherapist.* New York: John Wiley & Sons.

Guy, J. D., Poelstra, P. L., & Stark, M. J. (1989). Personal distress and therapeutic effectiveness: National survey of psychologists practicing psychotherapy. *Professional Psychology: Research and Practice, 20,* 48–50.

Hellman, I. D., Morrison, T. L., & Abramowitz, S. F. (1987). Therapist flexibility/rigidity and work stress. *Professional Psychology: Research and Practice, 18,* 21–27.

Jayaratne, S., & Chess, W. A. (1983). Job satisfaction and burnout in social work. In B.A. Farber (Ed.), *Stress and burnout in the human service professions.* (pp. 129–141) New York: Pergamon Press.

Jones, J. (1980). *The staff burnout scale for health professionals.* Park Ridge, IL: London House Press.

Kottler, J. A. (1986). *On being a therapist.* San Francisco: Jossey Bass.

Kurland, R., & Salmon, R. (1992). When problems seem overwhelming: Emphases in teaching, supervision, and consultation. *Social Work, 37,* 240–244.

Lamb, D. H., Presser, N. R., Pfost, K. S., Baum, M. C., Jackson, V. R., & Jarvis, P. A. (1987). Confronting professional impairment during the internship: Identification, due process, and remediation. *Professional Psychology: Research and Practice, 18,* 597–603.

Lee, R. T., & Ashforth, B. E. (1990). On the meaning of Maslach's three dimensions of burnout. *Journal of Applied Psychology, 75,* 743–747.

Likert, R. (1967). *The human organization.* New York: McGraw-Hill.

———. (1978). An improvement cycle for human resource development. *Training and Development Journal,* (July), 16–18.

MacNab, S. S. (1995). Listening to your patients, yelling at your kids: The interface between psychotherapy and motherhood. In M. B. Sussman (Ed.), A perilous calling: The hazards of psychotherapy practice. (pp. 37–44) New York: John Wiley and Sons.

Maeder, T. (1989). *Children of psychiatrists and other psychotherapists.* New York: Harper & Row.

Maslach, C. (1982). Understanding burnout: Definitional issues in analyzing a complex phenomenon. In W. S. Paine (Ed.), *Job stress and burnout: Research, theory, and intervention perspectives.* (pp. 29–40) Beverly Hills: Sage Publications.

Maslach, C., & Jackson, S. E. (1986). *Maslach Burnout Inventory manual,* 2nd ed. Palo Alto, CA: Consulting Psychologists Press.

Murphy, J. W., & Pardeck, J. T. (1986). The "Burnout Syndrome" and management style. *The Clinical Supervisor, 4*(4), 35–44.

Olkin, R., & Gaughen, S. (1991). Evaluation and dismissal of students in masters level clinical programs: Legal parameters and survey results. *Counselor Education and Supervision, 30,* 276–288.

Pines, A. (1982). Changing organizations: Is a work environment without burnout an impossible goal? In W. S. Paine (Ed.). *Job stress and burnout: Research, theory, and intervention perspectives.* (pp. 189–212.) Beverly Hills: Sage Publications.

Pines, A., & Aronson, E. (1988) *Career burnout: Causes and cures.* New York: The Free Press.

Pope, K. S., Tabachnick, B. G., & Keith-Spiegel, P. (1987). Ethics of practice: The beliefs and behaviors of psychologists as therapists. *American Psychologist, 42,* 993–1006.

Pulakos, J. (1994). Incidental encounters between therapists and clients: The client's perspective. *Professional Psychology: Research and Practice, 25,* 300–303.

Roberts, J. K. (1987). The life management model: Coping with stress through burnout. *The Clinical Supervisor, 5*(2), 107–118.

Rodolfa, E. R., Kraft, W. A., & Reilley, R. R. (1988). Stressors of professionals and trainees at APA-approved counseling and VA medical center internship sites. *Professional Psychology: Research and Practice, 19,* 43–49.

Sharkin, B. S., & Birkey, I. (1992). Incidental encounters between therapists and their clients. *Professional Psychology: Research and Practice, 23,* 326–328.

Skorupa, J., & Agresti, A. A. (1993). Ethical beliefs about burnout and continued professional practice. *Professional Psychology: Research and Practice, 24,* 281–285.

Sowa, C. J., May, K. M., & Niles, S. G. (1994). Occupational stress within the counseling profession. Implications for counselor training. *Counselor Education and Supervision, 34,* 19–29.

Stadler, H. A., Willing, K. L, Eberhage, M. G, & Ward, W. H. (1988). Impairment: Implications for the counseling profession. *Journal of Counseling and Development, 66,* 258–260.

Sussman, M. B. (1995). *A perilous calling: The hazards of psychotherapy practice.* New York: John Wiley and Sons.

Welt, S. R., & Herron, W. G. (1990). *Narcissism and the psychotherapist.* New York: The Guilford Press.

CHAPTER 10

SELF-CARE

By definition, helping professionals seek to improve the quality of lives of the people they work with. Paradoxically, relatively little has been written about, and very few training programs give sufficient attention to, how helping professionals and interns care for themselves (Reamer, 1992). This is unfortunate. Taking care of yourself is one of the most important, yet sometimes one of the most difficult, tasks you will face as an intern or professional.

The previous chapter described some of the stresses of internships and professional activities. This chapter explores the importance of self-care and suggests strategies for keeping yourself healthy while you strive to assist others. Among the areas addressed are the cognitive, emotional, behavioral, physical, relationship, and financial elements of self-care.

Some may find that this chapter raises issues that "just aren't talked about" in school or training. Others may resist or possibly even resent suggestions about staying physically healthy. The discussion of financial considerations may also come as a surprise. I am sensitive to such concerns, but I am convinced it is important to address precisely those issues that are normally ignored in academic training but are of critical importance in life and work beyond academia.

This does not mean I am suggesting that all interns or professionals must agree with or follow these suggestions, nor do I wish to imply that I am offering the "best" or the "correct" approach to self-care. On the other hand, I cannot emphasize too strongly that the work of helping professionals and the experience of internship training are unique and at times highly demanding. As such, self-care can be vital not only to personal health but also to your effectiveness at your internship. Whether or not you agree with specific ideas or suggestions of this chapter, I hope it will stimulate your thinking about how you personally cope with stress and take care of yourself as you attempt to help others care for themselves. For additional information about this topic, see Sussman (1995), especially the chapter by Grosch and Olsen on preventing burnout.

TIME MANAGEMENT

When interns are asked to list the sources of stress in their lives, having too much to do and time management are consistently identified among the primary concerns. This is not at all surprising. In the desire to do a good job on the internship, and as one tries to balance school, work, family, and other demands, it is easy to feel that events control you. The problem is that if you do not manage your time well, you will eventually make inadequate notes, not take the physical and mental breaks you need, will take work home, and will probably regret it in the long run. If you do not take care of your time, it is symptomatic that you are probably not taking care of yourself in other ways as well. As a colleague of mine says, "If you're too busy to take care of yourself, you're too busy! Something's gotta change."

Interns are not alone in feeling time-related stresses. Many experienced therapists feel overworked, and many professionals do not manage their time well. Especially common are the habits of not allocating sufficient time between sessions and not taking enough breaks from work to stretch, relax, etc.

One way to deal with this is to do what Fiore (1989) has described as "unscheduling." The idea of unscheduling is to begin by planning your time to do the things you need for self-care. Once you have set aside the time you need to take care of yourself, you then schedule work and other activities around that. This might sound selfish to some, but the point is that if we do not take care of ourselves we will eventually be unable to care for others. By scheduling time for self-care first, we are forced to rethink our priorities.

One of the reasons many professionals have trouble managing their time is that they have not seriously examined how their time is actually spent. When I conducted an informal survey of colleagues in clinical practice, very few had kept precise track of how they spend their time and how long it takes to complete various tasks. In a discussion of fee structure as it relates to professionals' time, Callahan (1994) noted that many therapists in private practice have a false understanding of how much they earn for their efforts because they have not accurately assessed the time they spend in different tasks, such as note taking, correspondence, phone calls, etc., outside of therapy.

EXERCISE: TRACKING WHERE TIME GOES

To help develop your time awareness and management skills, during the next two weeks keep careful track of all the activities you do each day for the full 24 hours. From 12:00 midnight each day to 12:00 midnight the next day, make a note of when you start and stop different activities. This may feel like a nuisance or a waste of time, but in fact it is just the opposite. This is a way for you to begin to understand how *not* to waste time.

Keeping track of what you do will allow you to get a better sense of where your time goes and how long different activities actually take. For example, if you keep case notes for each session during a week, by recording how long it takes you to write a case note for each client you will become more aware of what that requires. You can then build that time into your schedule. In this process, try to be aware not only of where your time goes now, but also of ways in which you are not spending time that you probably should be. For example, are you taking time to stretch, to get out of the office, to recover between sessions? If your record reveals that comparatively little time is going to self-care, you may want to "unschedule" more of your time.

Along with budgeting time on a weekly basis for your regular activities, give some thought to anticipating special time demands, such as preparation for exams, papers, and conferences. As you look toward these events, be sure to allow additional time in your schedule to prepare for them. Avoid the temptation to simply take that added time out of what you have set aside for self-care.

Putting time in our schedule books is actually the easiest part of time management. Sticking to the time you schedule is the hard part. I advise trainees to include in their schedules a certain degree of "open time" that allows them to deal with unanticipated circumstances. I also advise trainees to make certain time inviolable. Except in extreme circumstances, do not let clients or staff intrude on this protected time. Do not use your note-taking time to instead make phone calls, do not let sessions run longer than they are scheduled, and do not treat time for exercise as "low priority" that can easily be sacrificed.

SAYING "NO"

Keeping certain time for yourself requires the ability to say "no." Interns are often overloaded with classes, other jobs, and families. The task of meeting all these demands is exacerbated by the fact that many interns, who are caring and dedicated people, have difficulty turning down worthy projects. In many cases, the underlying principle that guides decisions is to think first of the needs of others, then of one's own needs, and almost never of the real limitations of time and the physical demands for rest or sleep. If someone at school needs a hand with a class, the intern offers to help. If volunteers are needed for a community service project, the interns are the first to help. If extra work needs to be done at the internship, the interns volunteer.

All of these activities are to be commended, and it is admirable that interns are willing to step forward. But it is also important for each of us to learn how to set priorities and make decisions. There is nothing wrong with setting realistic limits and standing by them. There will always be more work to be done than one person can do and you do not have to feel like you must do it all.

SAYING "YES"

Learning to say "no" is an important side of self-care and time management, but learning to say "yes" is just as important. When I work with overstressed students or colleagues, the problem is not simply that they have a hard time saying "no" to extra work. It is also that they have a hard time saying "yes" to things they enjoy doing. A colleague who was working from 7:00 A.M. to 7:00 P.M. five days a week and half days on Saturday told me that one of his favorite things to do was go sailing. When I asked how long it had been since he had been sailing, he said he had gone once this year and two or three times each of the past two years. If sailing was indeed a favorite pastime, he was certainly not allocating a proportionate amount of time to it.

Rather than agonizing over every opportunity or request to do one more thing, I encourage you to sit down on your own, or perhaps with significant others, and think carefully about how you want to spend your time. It has been pointed out that the amount of time we give to things is one indication of how important we think they are. Yet, when people examine where they are really spending their time and why, they realize that some things are getting far more time than their real importance warrants.

EXERCISE: SETTING PRIORITIES

The previous exercise asked you to examine how you presently spend your time. When you have examined where your time has gone, give some thought to where you would like it to go in the future. Begin by making a list of things that are important to you, then identify how much time you would like to devote to them. As you do this, do not start with what you are doing and work from there. Instead, start by listing what is important to you, then see how you are actually spending your time. You may discover that there are significant discrepancies between what you say matters and how you are spending your time. Having identified what is important and how you want to spend your time, try to plan a schedule that would allow you to do more of what you have identified as top priorities.

CLOSING SESSIONS

One other common problem regarding time management has to do with keeping enough time for case notes, phone calls, etc., between appointments with clients. The advice to keep sessions within the scheduled time period is often particularly difficult for interns to follow.

If clients are still talking about an issue when the session is about to end, interns tend to allow or encourage them to keep going. It also happens that some clients do not raise important issues until just before the session ends. This can happen for many reasons. Perhaps the issue is particularly sensitive and the client spent the entire session trying to gather courage to discuss it. Raising it at the end of the session provides a safety valve of sorts. Another possibility is that a client is testing a therapist to see if the therapist will let him or her have "extra time" as a sign that the therapist really cares. Whatever the reason, if sessions run over, that is information the therapist should be aware of and seek to understand. Allowing overruns to occur repeatedly and without examination may mean that useful information is being overlooked.

There are several ways to bring sessions to an end constructively. The easiest and most direct is for the therapist to be aware of the time and as the end of the session approaches, state, "We need to finish for now." If the client has just raised an important issue, the therapist might observe, "I think what you just spoke of is important and is something we should probably address in the next session. For now, we need to conclude for today." If a client continues talking, the therapist can rise and begin to move toward the door. These methods will be well received and effective in most cases. If a client repeatedly runs sessions overtime, this is something the therapist may need to address. Here again, stating things directly in the form of a process observation can be helpful. "I have noticed that in the last few sessions we seem to raise important issues right near the end and then to run overtime. I want to be sure to give enough time to such things, but it is important to be aware of the conclusion of our sessions. I wonder if there is a way we can address this more effectively?"

In describing these techniques, it must be added that the therapist should, of course, use judgment. There are times when it is essential to run a little over. If a client reveals that he or she is in some danger, if a critical issue absolutely must be resolved, or if some other matter demands immediate attention, the therapist may elect to extend the session. This decision, however, should be made very rarely; if it is made repeatedly for the same client, this should be recognized and addressed.

It is not only clients who extend sessions past time. It also happens that clients are ready to conclude sessions on time but it is the intern who, perhaps wanting to feel needed or to "solve the client's problems," overextends the session. This tendency is not only contrary to sound time management, it can also interfere with therapy. The simple reality is that the work of therapy is seldom "finished" by the end of any single session. There will always be more to do and it is often a very good thing to end a session with work still left to do. Clients are able to continue thinking about things on their own and therapists need to be able to give them that opportunity. Interns must learn that sessions do not always end as neat or tidy packages and clients do not, and probably should not, always leave a session feeling that everything has been resolved.

A colleague of mine uses the concept of "holding the question" to help interns understand that not everything is resolved in each session. Holding the question means accepting that some things are best pondered and one should not expect an immediate answer to every question. Holding the question gives clients time to think about things between sessions. Because life does not always give neatly packaged solutions and we must be able to deal with that fact, developing the ability to hold the question is, in itself, highly therapeutic for clients as well as professionals.

COGNITIVE SELF-CARE

The normal stresses interns experience can often be exacerbated by beliefs interns hold about themselves, their clients, the therapy process, and about broader topics that might best be labeled cognitions about the world. To the extent that these ideas create stress, recognizing and coping effectively with them can be a valuable element of self-care.

COGNITIONS ABOUT SELF

It is not uncommon for interns to approach their training or placements with unrealistic expectations about their knowledge, efficacy, or feelings toward clients. For example, interns might believe they must not make any mistakes. Or, they might fear that others will recognize their lack of experience. It is also common for interns to want to be liked, perhaps even loved and supported, by all of their clients and coworkers.

Deutsch (1984) studied a number of ideas rated by clinicians as stressful and found that the three ideas considered most stressful all dealt with therapists' needs for perfection. Other stressful ideas included the belief that the therapist is responsible for client change, that therapists must be constantly available to clients, and that therapists should be models of mental health themselves.

Those familiar with Rational Emotive Therapy will recognize that many of these fears closely parallel the "irrational beliefs" described by Ellis (Ellis & Harper, 1975). According to Ellis's model, people create unnecessary stress themselves by holding irrational ideas about the world and basing their actions and feelings on these ideas.

For interns, unrealistic expectations about themselves or clients add to the challenges of an already demanding position. At the same time, however, it is quite realistic and to be expected for interns to have some anxiety about their abilities as therapists. Engaging others in a relationship and seeking to help them make difficult changes is indeed a great responsibility. That responsibility is all the more daunting when opinions vary about how to bring about change and there are no clear rules about what is defined as helpful. Interns who do not have some fear about their abilities or about the therapy process are themselves sources of stress and anxiety for their supervisors.

What is required is a "healthy balance" between anxiety and confidence. Interns who feel they must be perfect at everything will easily become paralyzed and will be afraid to move treatment forward. On the other hand, interns who believe they are already expert are prone to making dangerous mistakes that may, in fact, harm their clients. With this in mind, part of cognitive self-care involves checking one's cognitions about oneself as a person and professional. Interns should ask themselves if they have unrealistically high expectations about what their abilities should be or are. They should also share their ideas with their instructor or supervisor. If your beliefs about what your skills are, or should be, are extreme in either a positive or negative direction, there is a need for personal work.

Self-care also involves keeping a healthy perspective about anxiety itself. Some interns become anxious about being anxious. It is as if they believe that good therapists must be calm and confident at all times and any hint of anxiety is a sign of weakness or incompetence. Such concerns are understandable, but even the most accomplished professionals will acknowledge that they sometimes wonder if they really know what is going on with a client or in the therapy process.

Experienced therapists are able to cope with this uncertainty because they have learned to trust the process of treatment even though they are sometimes anxious about it. Skilled therapists also know to listen to how they are feeling because that information can often provide important insights about what is happening in the session.

In your own training, try to be aware of any beliefs or ideas that place unrealistic expectations on yourself. It may also be helpful to discuss these ideas with your peers, instructor, or supervisor. Do not be ashamed to admit that there are times when you are unsure about what to do. Experienced supervisors will certainly understand this and would much rather an intern talk about such feelings than keep them inside and proceed without seeking assistance. The most important self-care cognition is probably: "I do not have to be perfect, but I do need to get help when I need it."

COGNITIONS ABOUT CLIENTS

Just as unrealistic expectations for oneself can contribute to stress, inaccurate or unrealistic cognitions about clients are also a common source of stress for interns. Fremont and Anderson (1986) suggested that counselors carry a set of assumptions about how clients "should act and how counseling should progress" (p. 68). When these assumptions are not met, counselors may become angry or frustrated. Among the assumptions identified by Fremont and Anderson are that:

1. The client is in counseling to get better or to make some changes in behavior. It is part of the client's role to work on personal problems and to follow counselor suggestions.
2. The client should not become too dependent. Some degree of dependency is expected, but it should not interfere with the counselor's private life.
3. The client is expected to appreciate the counselor's expenditure of psychic energy. It is unacceptable for the client to reject this notion, especially with a show of anger or hostility.
4. The client should not successfully manipulate counselor behavior. (p. 68)

In spite of, or perhaps because of, the assumptions just described, in the course of your training you will probably find yourself thinking clients are heroic, lazy, dangerous, suicidal, seductive, distancing, helpless, whiny, crazy, unmotivated, manipulative, passive/aggressive, logical, motivated, creative, suffering, or a host of other things. When you experience such feelings, it may be helpful to keep in mind several ideas.

First, the most stressful of all cognitions about clients is probably, "Clients should be different than they are." This cognition can take many forms. You may think, "This client should be more open in therapy," or "This client should not be so angry," or "This client should not be so depressed," or, "This client should be more appreciative of the service we provide."

However you finish the sentence, believing clients should be different is a good way to create unnecessary and unproductive stress for yourself and your clients. This is not to say that clients would not benefit from change. It is to say that wanting clients to be different, and becoming upset because they are not, is not treatment. *Our task is not to identify how clients "should be," then wish that the clients were different than they are. Our task is to help our clients determine what they want to be, then help them achieve that goal for themselves.*

A second point to remember is that many interns add to their stress by overgeneralizing beliefs about specific clients to all clients. For example, some interns worry about the possibility of suicide with virtually all of their clients. Because suicide is such a serious action, and because it is possible that any person could take his or her own life, this concern is understandable. At the same time, however, most clients, even most depressed clients, do not commit suicide. Thus, if you actively worry about suicide for every client, you will do a lot of worrying and most of that worrying will be unnecessary.

The process at work here is part of learning any new skill. When we first learn to speak, we apply new words to anything that approximates whatever was initially associated with the word. Children who learn the word "dog" call everything that has four legs, fur, and a tail, a dog. Gradually they learn to differentiate between dogs, cats, and other creatures. Similarly, when students learn about new symptoms or diagnoses they tend to see those symptoms or try to apply the diagnosis to every patient they see. A large part of training involves moving from such overgeneralization to more specific applications and more precise understanding. As this happens, you will develop a better sense of when you can relax and when you really do need to be anxious about clients.

COGNITIONS ABOUT THERAPY

Closely tied to the idea that clients "should be different" are ideas about the therapy process in general. As noted above, one such cognition is the belief that clients "should not be resistant" to change. Interns and beginning therapists often become upset with clients who "obviously need to change" but resist the therapist's best efforts to "get them to do something different." In such situations, the problem, and the source of the therapist's stress, is not really the client. Rather, it is the therapist's belief that change is, or should be, easy for

people. The reality is that change can be very difficult, sometimes takes a long time to happen, and people (including interns and therapists) tend to resist change because it is unfamiliar and uncertain. When therapists do not recognize and work with client resistance, they are likely to become frustrated with the client and with themselves. On the other hand, when resistance is understood and recognized as an expected and normal part of the treatment process, a therapist or intern is more able to respond to it effectively.

Another cognition that adds to stress is the belief that the helping professional is responsible for the client's life. Clients come to you or your agency because they want your help in understanding or altering something about themselves or their lives. You charge money for your time, and you have supposedly been trained in ways of helping, so there is at least some implied burden on you to do something useful. At the same time, as we have just discussed, clients often resist change and do not cooperate in the therapeutic work. This makes it easy to blame the client when progress is not achieved or does not come as rapidly as you or they might hope. Blaming clients for not changing is one way therapists deal with their own frustrations at not feeling successful or validated. But this response is ultimately an attempt to meet the therapist's needs, not the client's.

To deal more effectively with resistance, it helps to think of your role as a catalyst for change but not as the primary agent of change. You cannot, and should not, take full responsibility for solving your clients' problems for them. You must instead recognize that you play an important role in helping clients cope with their situations, discover resources within themselves, and make the changes they need to make for themselves. Ultimately, however, the clients themselves must make those changes; we cannot do it for them.

COGNITIONS ABOUT THE WORLD

Even when interns are away from the internship and clients, experiences in therapy can contribute to cognitions about the world that add to therapist stress. One of the ways this happens is through the development of a rather distorted sense of what constitutes "normal." If an intern spends much of the day dealing with people who are experiencing serious problems in their lives, or who are hostile, or severely disabled, the experience may cause the intern to begin to believe that most people have such problems. In some instances, this process can actually create or reinforce racial or other stereotypes.

One of our interns, who worked for a semester in a juvenile detention center, said, "I can't believe what those kids are like. I used to think I wanted to have children, but now, if they could turn out like these kids, forget it." By comparison, an intern who worked with abused children found herself "hating those parents, and wondering if there are any decent people out there." Another intern worked with patients on an Alzheimer's Disease unit of a nursing home. When she had the opportunity to do some intelligence testing with an elderly person who was not demented she marveled at how intelligent the man was for his age. In fact, he was only in the average range for his age group, but relative to the people she had been working with, he seemed to her to be a genius.

Internship experiences also affect how interns think of systems. For example, an intern who worked in a social service agency became first angered, then frustrated and depressed by the inefficiency of the agency and lack of dedication on the part of many employees. Another intern, also frustrated by systemic flaws, despaired of the helping professions entirely and concluded that she should "change my major, quit trying to help anyone, and just make money."

In each of these cases, experiences with a selected population or system led interns to hold ideas about the world that were distorted by the internship experience. The potential effect of such ideas was revealed by the intern who said her experience caused her to wonder if she really wanted children of her own, and by the individual who wanted to leave the field entirely.

Interns should remind themselves that they are dealing with real people, real suffering, and sometimes with real dysfunctional systems. That is part of life, but it is not all of life. If you find yourself getting "soured" on life or your work, it can be extremely beneficial to seek experiences or information that will present "the other side" of the picture from what you encounter at your placement. Using a sports metaphor, Grosch and Olsen (1995) refer to the value of "cross training," i.e., varying one's jobs and activities to include variety and other perspectives as a way of staying fresh. For example, the interns described above might look for examples of youth who are contributing to their community; parents who are doing a thoughtful, caring job of raising their children; or senior citizens who are mentally alert and involved in programs that keep them healthy. Others might benefit by identifying systems that are successful and that are staffed by dedicated and competent people. Such systems do in fact exist, but you may not have the fortune to find them on your first or second field placement.

The point of this is to help interns come to grips with the reality of human suffering and shortcomings while not losing sight of the equally important reality of human joy, kindness, and health. It is essential for interns to understand that they have the potential to help change dysfunctional systems for the better. If everything worked perfectly already, there would be little need for human service professions. On the other hand, great strides have been made toward making things better and in each case these advances have occurred because one or more individuals dedicated themselves to a goal. As a student, and as an intern, you have the opportunity to develop knowledge, experience, and insights that can help you make a real difference in the world. The task will not be easy, and it will probably not be completed in any one person's lifetime, but you can have an effect and people's lives (including your own) can be more fulfilling thanks to your efforts.

EXERCISE: COGNITIONS REVIEW

Based on what you have read thus far and on your own experiences, review your own beliefs about your role as an intern, the treatment process, clients, or the world as a whole. What beliefs do you hold that may be causing unnecessary stress? What beliefs help you deal constructively with the stresses of your work or training? When you have written your own thoughts, discuss this with your peers and supervisor to get their ideas and feedback. If certain ideas are impacting you adversely, consider developing an active strategy to confront and change those ideas and their effects.

PHYSICAL SELF-CARE

Individuals must determine for themselves how they define physical health. In my practice as a medical psychologist, I work on a daily basis with people who suffer the psychological and physical effects of poor physical self-care. I am also involved in various efforts aimed at preventing illness and promoting better physical wellness. Perhaps because of this background, and because I know firsthand how physically draining internships and clinical work can be, I strongly encourage interns to care for their bodies as well as their minds. It is certainly not my intent to sound "preachy" in discussing this topic, but insofar as this book is intended to help interns develop skills and habits that will serve them throughout their careers, and having seen the physical and emotional toll this line of work can take on people, I feel an obligation to at least raise the issue and perhaps offer some new perspectives.

PHYSICAL EXERCISE

As described earlier in this chapter, the sedentary nature of clinical work, and the tendency to internalize stresses, place unusual physical demands on the body. Physical activity can help overcome some of the effects of sedentary work and can help one deal with stress more effectively.

When the subject of physical activity arises, some interns have no problem because exercise is already part of their daily routine. Others indicate that they are interested in exercising but cannot find time. Still others respond as if I have suggested they do something abhorrent.

For those in the first group, one need only encourage continuing what is already in place and jealously guarding the time for daily exercise. For those who would like to exercise but do not find the time, it may be useful to reread the discussion of time management. For individuals who respond negatively to exercise, allow me to offer just a few thoughts based on what has worked with students and with clients wanting to change their physical activity.

The first point is to not feel one must start a rigorous exercise program right away. Take some time to think about what is or would be healthy for you. As you consider this, do not think in terms of heavy workouts or strict diets when you think of physical self-care. Those terms do not really sound much like care, so it is not surprising that they are aversive. As a more appealing and realistic alternative, you are more likely to succeed if you start small and consider your own needs and values. Without launching directly into a full workout regimen, one can find opportunities to incorporate less strenuous forms of exercise throughout one's day. It is possible to increase fitness by doing little things such as taking stairs instead of elevators, parking a little farther from the office, or, better still, walking or biking to work. While at work, one can get in the habit of getting up and stretching between sessions. Similarly, if your work for the day involves long hours of reading, writing, or computer work, a watch or other timer can be set as a reminder to take a break to stretch the body and rest your eyes.

The changes just described can actually make a noticeable difference in health, but there may also be a need to structure some regular forms of aerobic activity during your week. When you reach this point, you may ask, as do many people, "So how much exercise do I HAVE to do?" Specialists in the area of physical wellness suggest that a more successful way to ask the question is "How little physical activity will let me realize noticeable health improvements?" This reframing removes the sense of obligation, and perhaps along with it, a degree of resistance. The alternative question also emphasizes that in terms of reducing risk for such illnesses as coronary vascular disease and others, relatively little exercise can produce significant benefits (T. Evans, Nov. 1994, personal communication).

It will probably not come as new information to the reader, but the minimum recommendation for exercise is twenty minutes of cardiovascular activity three times per week. This means one does not have to be a marathon runner, triathlete, aerobics addict, or really be dedicated to any "sport." One simply needs to find at least a half hour a few days a week to do something that will get one's limbs and muscles moving and encourage oxygen and blood to circulate. In the process, you will also have a chance to get out of the office and enjoy a different setting and activity for a while. For many people, even those who once thought of exercise as tantamount to self-imposed torture, the break they schedule for exercise is a highlight of the day, something they look forward to beforehand, enjoy while doing, and appreciate throughout the day. Ideally, exercise should not be something we do "to ourselves." It should be something we do "for ourselves" to release tension and improve our overall well-being.

MASSAGE

For some people, physical exercise may not feel like self-care, but most would agree that therapeutic massage is pretty close to the epitome of self-care. Perhaps the best thing about massage for helping professionals is that it allows you to put

yourself quite literally into someone else's hands and let them take care of you for awhile. This is something many of us, particularly in the helping professions, do not do.

An example of the benefit of massage is quite immediate for me as I write this chapter. In the final stages of preparing this book I was putting in extraordinarily long days of writing, beginning at 5:00 A. M. and staying at it until I could go no further, often continuing until well past midnight. After many months of previous work, this intense effort had gone on with little respite for the better part of three weeks and the effects were beginning to tell. Realizing I needed a break, but under pressure to meet deadlines, the idea of a massage came to me and seemed so appealing I almost called 911-MASSAGE. Fortunately, a massage therapist I knew was able to schedule an appointment for that same day. I explained my situation, lay down on the table, and let her do the work. During the entire massage I only thought about work once, and that was to make a brief mental note to add a word about massage to this chapter. It is not an exaggeration to say that an hour-and-a-half later, I felt like a new person. I still had several long days ahead, but the massage had helped me weather a point of near exhaustion and recharged the batteries to help me get through.

In addition to being a great way to release stress and help one relax, massage is also a good way of monitoring where and how you may be physically internalizing the emotional stresses of your work. Many of us tend to keep the accumulated emotions of our work somewhere in our bodies; headaches, backaches, and other pains may be the result. A skilled massage therapist will locate those places and, while helping to work them out, may give you some clues about where you keep stresses in your body.

MONITORING STRESSES IN THE BODY

Unfortunately, few of us have the time or money to afford a massage every day. Lacking that luxury, we need to learn to deal with physical tensions as they arise during the course of our work. One useful suggestion is to periodically run a "mental body check," noticing any signs of physical tension or other sensations that arise. Perhaps the easiest way to do this is to start at the top of your head and do a quick run-through of your posture, muscle tension, and other internal sensations. It may help to do this as you breathe in and out, thinking of letting go of any tension as you exhale.

With practice, this self-check and relaxation can be done in a very short time and in a way that is not noticeable to others. I try to do such checks several times during each therapy session, meeting, class, or other event. This helps to keep physical tensions from building and can reveal useful clues about how I am reacting to what is happening. When I work with clients, I also make it a point to observe their physical posture and apparent tension levels. This awareness can provide extremely valuable clues to what is going on clinically.

HEALTHY EATING AND HABITS

Along with encouraging a healthy amount of exercise and relaxation, a word about healthy eating is also in order. Just as internships can limit the time available for exercise, internships often have an adverse influence on how, when, and what interns eat. Many interns are unaware of this until they think about it and realize that, in fact, the internship has affected their eating in several ways.

Some interns find that eating is one of they ways they use to cope with the stresses of the internship. A common experience is to come home from the internship and feel a need to eat something to help settle down after a demanding day. Interns may also find themselves so rushed at their placements that they seldom take time to relax and enjoy a meal that is really good for them. Instead, "lunch" consists of a bag of chips and a soft drink or coffee (their third cup of five or more per day) from the vending machine or espresso stand.

The issue here is not so much what one should or should not eat. Rather, the goal is to increase awareness of how one is being affected by, and attempting to cope with, the challenges of the internship. Poor dietary habits can be intrinsically harmful over the long run, but they can also serve as a signal to help you recognize whether or not you are taking care of yourself. The same point can and should be made about other habits that are also related to stress and coping.

The use of alcohol, cigarettes, or other drugs is closely tied to stress and helping professionals are no less vulnerable, perhaps even more so, to abusing these substances. Hughes et al. (1992) reported that, among a large sample of resident physicians surveyed, emergency medicine and psychiatry residents reported higher rates of substance use than residents in other specialities.

In my clinical work, and as an instructor and supervisor, I have come in contact with students, supervisors, and colleagues who had significant substance abuse problems. In most cases, these same individuals denied that they had a problem even though virtually everyone who knew them was aware of, and concerned about, the situation. In addition to the damage and difficulties substance abuse causes the individuals themselves, the profession also suffers harm as members of the public look cynically at helping professionals who do not appear able to deal well with problems themselves.

Once again, the goal here is to help interns become aware of signs that may indicate they are not coping well with personal or professional stresses. If you find your own use of legal or controlled substances increasing—if it sometimes feels you just have to have a drink, smoke, pill, or something else to cope with the stress of work—perhaps it is time to examine how work is affecting you or how these habits themselves are affecting your work.

EXERCISE: PERSONAL PHYSICAL HEALTH-CARE REVIEW

As a step toward developing physical self-care habits, you may wish to conduct a simple personal physical health care review. This review involves taking stock of activities relating to exercise, diet, and harmful habits. Write each of these headings on a sheet of paper, i.e., exercise, diet, and habits. Then, beside these headings, list the things you think are conducive to self-care, and the things that might be harmful in some way. Ask yourself how your internship work or other activities relate to what you have written. Finally, give some thought to how changes in your self-care might benefit your internship, school, or other activities and how changes in those activities could affect your physical care.

EMOTIONAL SELF-CARE

Two brief anecdotes illustrate the need for attending to one's own emotional self-care as an intern or clinician. The first happened to a young intern during his predoctoral internship at a psychiatric hospital. On the last day of work before a holiday, the intern was riding his bike home from an evening group meeting. As he rode, he thought of the contrast between the home where he would spend the coming week and where the patients would be. Quite unexpectedly, as the lights of the hospital faded behind him and he turned down a darkened road, he began to cry. In fact, he began sobbing so hard he had to stop his bicycle and sit beneath a street light, crying to himself for almost half an hour. He had been working at the hospital for four months and knew some of the patients very well, but until that moment, the full reality of their situation had not really struck him. When the realization hit, all of the emotions stored for months came out at once.

A second incident occurred more recently and demonstrates again how emotional effects of clinical work can "sneak up" on us. As mentioned earlier, in addition to teaching, I practice as a psychologist in medical settings. For a variety of reasons, including a difficult course load, challenging cases, seemingly endless and pointless political struggles within the institution, and numerous other factors, I was going through a series of rough weeks at just the time I was teaching the internship class about the topic of self-care. One day in class I advised the interns to monitor their own emotional status. That same evening, a relatively small dispute with one of my children resulted in my shouting at, and criticizing, the child far more harshly than the situation called for. My wife noticed this and asked if perhaps the stresses at work were a factor in the reaction. Of course I denied this vehemently (after all I *am* writing a book on the subject), but after some reflection I realized she was right. Things at work had piled up and, although I did not think they were affecting me, I was carrying far more emotional tension than I realized.

It is probably not possible or desirable to try to be emotionally unaffected by one's clinical work, but it is vital that we learn to deal with those effects constructively. During a workshop on self-care and managing the stresses of work, a number of colleagues offered very useful suggestions, several of which are shared below.

SELF-CHECKS

Perhaps the most important principle of self-care is to be aware of, and acknowledge, how we are affected by our work. One counselor said she makes a habit of doing a brief emotional self-check that is comparable to the physical self-checks described earlier. At the end of each session, after the client leaves, she takes a deep breath, closes her eyes, and asks herself how she feels emotionally at that moment and how she felt emotionally during the session. This process serves several functions. It helps her to be aware of what she is experiencing, and it can provide new insights into what happened during the session. It also reminds her to relax.

"CLEANSING RITUALS"

Another colleague, a psychologist who often works with extremely challenging cases, makes use of what he calls "cleansing rituals" to help clear his mind and emotions between sessions. For example, if a session has been very demanding emotionally, he sometimes splashes a bit of cool water on his face afterward. This offers a refreshing break and it reminds him to be clear before meeting with his next client. He also uses stretching as a way to relieve both physical and emotional tension. After each client, he makes a practice of taking several deep breaths while he stretches his back and legs. With each breath out he imagines letting go of any stresses he might have stored during the session. With each breath in, he reminds himself to be patient and open to the next client's experience. He does not leave the office to invite the next patient in until he feels he has sufficiently processed the interaction with the previous individual.

A different type of cleansing process was described by a social worker specializing in domestic violence. She uses the act of opening the door to her office as a signal to clear her mind for the next client. After finishing her case notes, she puts the client's folder away and says to herself that she will leave the client there until the next visit. This helps to prevent her from "taking her clients home." Using the opening door as a cue helps her meet the next client where that client is, rather than with emotional baggage left over from the previous session. At the end of the day, she uses the closing of her office door behind her as a reminder to leave the work of the day at the office. This allows her to go home to her family without carrying all of the day's accumulated feelings away from the office. Describing this practice she noted that if she did not have some way of keeping what she deals with at work separate from her home life, she doubts she would last three months in practice.

There are many other possibilities for emotional self-care and you can probably find ways that work best for you. Whatever approach you develop, it is worth developing some form of reliable practice that you can do between clients, meetings or other activities, and at the end of the day to finish the work and leave it where it belongs.

SUPPORT

Self-care activities can go a long way toward helping clinicians cope with the emotional demands of their work, but the support of other interns or clinicians is also important (Berger, 1995). If you find yourself feeling overwhelmed by work, or if you are carrying emotions from your sessions, you may want to spend some time talking with you peers or supervisor about what you are experiencing. Unfortunately, this advice is easier to give than to follow.

It is often very hard for interns or clinicians to acknowledge that they are having a hard time. The vulnerable moment in which one asks a friend or peer, "Can I talk to you?" can be extraordinarily frightening. Yet that moment can also begin a dialogue that will be of invaluable help. In my own career, there have been a number of times when I recognized that I needed help and had the good sense to ask for it. There have also been occasions when I needed help but was unaware of it or denied the situation. Fortunately, close colleagues who knew me well recognized that things were not right and gently offered an ear. At other times, I have done the same for them. In your own training, try to be aware of when you need support, and try to be sensitive to when other interns or professionals could use support from you.

LETTING OFF STEAM

The process just described involves a serious interaction that occurs in private with another peer or colleague. As helpful as these exchanges are, sometimes it is also incredibly helpful to just let off steam with people who know what the job is like. This is different than talking over one's day with a spouse, and it is different than clinical supervision. The goal is simply to relax and have fun; to do something with your colleagues that has as little to do with work as possible. Even if you are not "the social type" it is important to do things with your peers and away from work.

If you do participate in such activities, without taking away the fun, keep in mind three precautions: First, be careful about the locations you choose and issues of confidentiality if the conversation is about clients. Everyone in your group may know about a given client, and there may be interesting or funny stories to share, but if the setting is public and the talk gets too loud, others may easily overhear you. Whether or not they personally know the individuals involved, merely hearing professionals talking, and perhaps even laughing, about clients in public could cast a negative image.

A second concern is that there is a fine line between constructive stress release for staff and destructive derision of clients. It is one thing to say "You'll never believe what . . . did today . . .," followed by an anecdote that is funny without being demeaning. It is quite another to say the same opening with a harsh or critical tone, followed by a negative story about "how bad" the client is in some way. The same principle applies to stories about colleagues. Never forget that clients and colleagues, no matter how frustrating, are people who are doing their best to get by. If it helps for you to laugh, by all means do so. But be sure you are laughing as much at yourself and the wonderful, sad, and confusing thing it is to be human.

Finally, many TGIF activities tend to take place in settings where alcohol is served. This is not necessarily a problem, but it is important to keep in mind that alcohol can very easily become an external mood controller that one gradually comes to depend on for dealing with stresses. As noted before, if this starts becoming a pattern for you or your peers, it is a good idea to explore how well you are coping with stress and what alternatives to alcohol might be more constructive.

EXERCISE: EMOTIONAL COPING

Having read the suggestions about coping with the emotional stresses of your work, this would be a good opportunity to do an emotional self-check of your own. As part of this check, identify things you currently do to help care for your own emotional reactions to your work. Also identify things that might be helpful but that you do not currently practice. If you find there are some things you could and perhaps should be doing differently to take care of yourself, develop a plan to implement changes. As a first step in this process, you may want to discuss this issue with a peer and perhaps explore ways of working together to help one another.

PERSONAL THERAPY

The discussion thus far has encouraged you to reflect on your own self-care practices. This is based on the premise that those who are most aware of themselves are most likely to grow from, and in, their roles as interns. By contrast, those who are not aware of their own needs, issues, strengths, weaknesses, etc., are most likely to be adversely influenced by their work. Because all of us are limited in our ability to know ourselves, and because we tend to be so exquisitely creative and effective in defending ourselves from awareness, we need outside information. One way to get such information is through therapy.

Based on a review of literature relating to therapy for professionals and trainees, Norcross, Strausser, and Faltus (1988) noted that personal therapy is considered to be a desirable experience by the majority of training programs and practitioners surveyed. Further, studies of factors contributing to professional development indicate that clinicians rank personal therapy second only to practical experience as the most important influence.

The benefits of therapy were demonstrated in research conducted by Andy Carey, Heather Stewart, and myself. Our survey of more than 500 counselors and clinical psychologists demonstrated that the majority of respondents, 79 percent of the sample, reported they had participated in personal therapy or counseling. Of that group, 93 percent categorized the experience as from mildly to very positive. Results also showed that on an instrument designed to assess cognitions about clients, the therapy process, and the role of the therapist, 13 out of 38 items yielded statistical significance when therapists with personal experience in therapy were compared to those without such experience (Baird & Carey, 1992; Baird, Carey & Giakovmis, 1992).

Comparable findings were obtained by Pope and Tabachnik (1994), who reported results from a survey of 800 psychologists. Of those who responded, 84 percent reported having been in therapy on at least one occasion. The most common reasons identified for seeking therapy included (in descending order of frequency): depression or general unhappiness, marriage or divorce, relationship issues, self-esteem and self-confidence, anxiety, career, work or studies, family of origin, loss, stress, and a variety of less frequently mentioned concerns. Among those who had been in therapy, 85.7 percent described their therapy experience as having been "very or exceptionally helpful." The chief benefits mentioned were self-awareness or self-understanding, self-esteem or self-confidence, and improved skills as a therapist.

In spite of the apparently widespread belief and empirical evidence that therapy is perceived as beneficial for trainees and professionals, this is an admittedly controversial subject. While not recommending that therapy be *required* for all students or interns in training, the evidence suggests that personal therapy can be a valuable experience for interns and therapists. In addition to helping us become more aware of ourselves, personal therapy also gives us a better awareness of what clients experience when they are in therapy.

Having said that, to be honest I must now add that in the early days of training I might have thrown a book such as this away if it suggested that therapy should be recommended for therapists or students. My feeling at the time was that one went into the field because one was pretty well put together to begin with and wanted to use this fortunate status to the benefit of others. That idea seemed at the time to make good sense and it was certainly very comforting to believe I was so well-adjusted as to be able to help others without further work on myself. The fact that this belief was held by someone who was then still in his very early twenties did not seem at all surprising. Indeed, it only served to support a belief that healthy personal adjustment and effective psychotherapy were not necessarily so difficult.

That is how I once felt. As I gained experience, and after a number of challenging events in my personal life, the awareness gradually emerged that "even therapists," (perhaps "especially therapists"), have issues that need to be worked through. This realization led me to enter a group therapy experience with other professionals. The results were enlightening. Not only did I receive invaluable assistance in recognizing and working through some of my own issues, I also came to know firsthand how therapy can be helpful and how helpful it can be.

EXERCISE

If you have previously experienced therapy or counseling, this might be a good time to reflect on that experience and how it has affected you as an individual and in your work with others. If you have never been in therapy, you may want to consider if you would be willing to seek therapy at some time. If you find yourself open to the idea, what benefits would you hope to receive? If you are opposed to the idea of entering therapy for yourself, give some thought to the reasons for that. You may also want to consider what alternative methods you will establish and practice for coping with how your work affects you personally and how your own issues affect your work.

POSITIVE EFFECTS ON THERAPISTS

Thus far, we have focused primarily on coping with the stresses and potentially negative emotional and physical impacts that face helping professionals and interns. The intent has been to apprise you of some of the personal challenges you may face in your role as an intern or professional. As important as it is to understand the challenges, it should not be forgotten that if stress were the only effect of this work not many people would go into it. Therefore, it is equally important to recognize and value the positive effects of what you do (Berger, 1995).

EXERCISE: POSITIVE EFFECTS OF CLINICAL WORK

List the positive emotional effects you derive as a result of your internship training.

List the positive cognitive effects you derive as a result of your internship training.

List any other benefits you derive from the internship.

As you look toward the future, what benefits would you expect to achieve in each of these areas as a professional in the field?

Finally, if you have the opportunity, discuss this question with those who have worked in your profession for some time. Ask them about both the benefits and the stresses and how they have managed to balance the two.

I have asked numerous interns and experienced therapists about the positive effects they experience from their work. The most frequent response describes a sense of satisfaction in doing something to help others. As one clinician said, "Every now and then you work with a client and it is just clear that you have been helpful to them. That really feels good to me, to know I made a difference like that." Berger (1995) reports similar statements from senior therapists describing factors that sustain their work.

Other rewards include the opportunity to continue learning, the pleasure of working with colleagues who share similar backgrounds and goals, the intellectual challenges of clinical work, and personal growth (Guy, 1987). Many professionals enjoy the relative autonomy and responsibility of the work, while others have emphasized the variety of tasks and clients they deal with. Your own list of benefits may have included those just described or others. Whatever you identified, it is important to recognize the positive elements of your work. If the positive elements begin to decline or are outweighed by the negatives, your motivation, effort, and effectiveness will eventually begin to suffer.

Being aware of the benefits of your training or profession can also influence the quality of your work itself. For example, if one of the benefits for most therapists is the satisfaction that comes when a client makes progress, it is easy for the therapist to become dependent on the client's changing, not for the client's own benefit, but because the client must change in order for the therapist to feel good. Helping professionals must maintain a delicate balance between appreciating the rewards that come from feeling one has helped another person, while not becoming dependent on that reward or allowing it to interfere with what one must do to, in fact, be helpful.

FINANCIAL SELF-CARE

The final self-care topic to be addressed here has to do with financial matters. Given the focus of this chapter on managing the stresses that come with internships and clinical work, it must be acknowledged that financial concerns are among the top-ranked sources of stress for persons in virtually all lines of work, including the helping professions. I have known more than a few colleagues whose personal lives and clinical work were significantly impacted by issues related to financial management. This can become especially important for those in private practice, as clinical and ethical issues regarding termination, referral, billing, etc., can easily become confused with the therapist's personal financial situation at the time.

In this book I would not pretend to offer advice on topics such as how you should invest your money, whether mutual funds are superior to money markets, or what the best retirement plan should be. Instead, the goal here is to suggest a way of thinking that may help reduce the stresses that so often accompany money matters. Much of what I have to offer in this regard is described well in the book *Your Money or Your Life,* by Dominguez and Robin (1992). Unlike many books that offer strategies to "get rich quick," Dominguez and Robin set out to help people determine when they "have enough." Their approach is centered around the simple yet profound truth that "Money is something we choose to trade our life for" (p. 54).

From this awareness, it is possible to examine carefully not only the costs of spending money but also the costs of earning it. When one translates dollars earned and spent into life energy sacrificed, three questions naturally follow. Dominguez and Robin suggest we ask:

1. Did I receive fulfillment, satisfaction and value in proportion to life energy spent?
2. Is this expenditure of life energy in alignment with my values and life purpose?
3. How might this expenditure change if I didn't have to work for a living? (p. 112)

Asking these questions of ourselves, seriously thinking about them in the short term as we go to work and make purchases, and weighing them in the long run as we set goals and plan our lives, can have enormous impact on the way we live. I know colleagues who establish a practice or take a position with an agency, then purchase homes and cars that demand virtually all of the income available. These purchases are then followed by luxuries such as sailboats, condominiums, or various other "toys" for grownups. To meet those expenses, the individuals increase their practice or take on another position. In the end, they spend so much of their time earning money that they have almost no time to do anything but work to pay for the things they've bought. As Dominguez and Robin remind us, the monetary cost that is paid in dollars is in fact paid in life energy. What we take out of life to put into "things" can never be reclaimed.

Failure to think carefully about personal values and their relationship to financial matters can easily interfere with all other aspects of self-care. In extreme cases, as noted earlier, financial concerns can also interfere with sound clinical practice. Given this possibility, interns may wish to think seriously about the role of money in relation to their eventual goals and current practices. It can also be exceptionally valuable to ask yourself what your purpose in life is and how your career and other activities fit within or compete with that purpose. Finally, you may find it enlightening to ask yourself what it means to have "enough" and if you are using your life energy, whether that is measured in time or dollars, wisely.

REFERENCES

Baird, B. N., & Carey, A. (1992, April). *The Therapist Cognition Survey: Development, standardization, and uses.* Paper presented at the meeting of the Western Psychological Association, Portland, OR.

Baird, B. N., Carey, A., & Giakovmis H. (1992, April). *Personal experience in psychotherapy: Differences in therapists' cognitions.* Paper presented at the meeting of the Western Psychological Association, Portland, OR.

Berger, M. (1995). Sustaining the professional self: Conversations with senior psychotherapists. In M. B. Sussman (Ed.), *A perilous calling: The hazards of psychotherapy practice.* (pp. 302–321) New York: John Wiley and Sons.

Callahan, T. R. (1994). Being paid for what you do. *The Independent Practitioner.* (Bulletin of the Division of Independent Practice, Division 42 of the APA.) *14*(1), 25–26.

Deutsch, C. J. (1984). Self-reported sources of stress among psychotherapists. *Professional Psychology: Research and Practice, 15,* 833–845.

Dominguez, J., & Robin, V. (1992). *Your money or your life.* Penguin Books: New York.

Ellis, A., & Harper, R. A. (1975). *A new guide to rational living.* North Hollywood, CA: Wilshire Books.

Fiore, N. (1989). *The now habit: A strategic program for overcoming procrastination and enjoying guilt-free play.* New York: St. Martin's Press.

Fremont, S., & Anderson, W. (1986). What client behaviors make counselors angry? An exploratory study. *Journal of Counseling and Development, 65,* 67–70.

Grosch, W. N., & Olsen, D. C. (1995). Prevention: Avoiding burnout. In M. B. Sussman (Ed.), *A perilous calling: The hazards of psychotherapy practice.* (pp. 275–287) New York: John Wiley and Sons.

Guy, J. D. (1987). *The personal life of the psychotherapist.* New York: John Wiley and Sons.

Hughes, P. H., DeWitt, C. B., Jr., Sheehan, D. V., Conrad, S., & Storr, C. L. (1992). Resident physician substance use, by specialty. *American Journal of Psychiatry, 149,* 1348–1354.

Norcross, J. C., Strausser, D. J., & Faltus, F. J. (1988). The therapist's therapist. *American Journal of Psychotherapy, 42,* 53–66.

Pope, K. S., & Tabachnick, B. G. (1994). Therapists as patients: A national survey of psychologists' experiences, problems, and beliefs. *Professional Psychology: Research and Practice, 25,* 247–258.

Reamer, F. G. (1992). The impaired social worker. *Social Work, 37,* 165–170.

Sussman, M. B. (1995). *A perilous calling: The hazards of psychotherapy practice.* New York: John Wiley and Sons.

CHAPTER 11

ASSAULT AND OTHER RISKS

On the first day of my graduate internship at a VA hospital, the new interns took a tour of the various wards, met the staff, and got a chance to talk with some of the patients. As soon as we came through the door on one of the wards, a man with wild, long, gray hair and wide, glaring eyes approached us rapidly. For some reason, perhaps because my appearance resembled his, the patient headed straight toward me, brought his face just a few inches from mine and shouted some unintelligible words. Not knowing what else to do, I said "hello." At that he smiled, then turned and walked away, mumbling to himself. That patient was acting very strange, but he was not dangerous. Indeed, he had been diagnosed with schizophrenia for some twenty years, but he had never assaulted anyone.

Later in the same internship year, I was working with another patient whose behavior was by no means as unusual as the schizophrenic patient I just described. This man was in the hospital for treatment of depression and alcohol abuse. Throughout his stay he had the habit of leaving the grounds on passes, visiting a nearby tavern, and returning to the ward in a highly intoxicated and belligerent state. After a series of these incidents, the staff decided he would not be allowed any spending money for a period of two weeks. When the patient, who was about six foot four and weighed over two hundred pounds, asked for money and a pass so he could go off grounds to purchase a watch, it was expected that he would in fact use the money to buy alcohol. I was given the

task of explaining that because of past actions he would not be given any money.

Needless to say, the patient was not happy to learn he could not have his money that week. He argued and tried to bargain but I insisted that he would have to wait a week. When no further progress was made in the discussion, I rose to leave. As I turned to go, the patient jumped over the chair, threw his hands toward my throat, and backed me against a wall. He then tried to choke me and smash my head against the wall. I was able to keep his hands away from my throat long enough for help to arrive, but it was a close call to say the least and it left me bruised and shaken.

The possibility that you will be assaulted during an internship will depend heavily on the setting in which you work and the clients with whom you interact. It will also depend on your own behaviors. I have included this chapter because it is important that interns have an awareness of the risks involved in clinical work and give some thought to how they can lessen or cope with those risks. I have also included this chapter because the subject is too often neglected by academic programs and training sites. Indeed, Gelman (1990) reported that only 1 out of 95 field learning agreements formally informed students of the potential risks of working in the field setting.

This finding, and the importance of preparing students, receives support from the research of Tully, Kropf, and Price

(1993), who noted that although 26 percent of students in the field placements they studied had experienced "some type of violence" at their placement, only 39 percent of all students surveyed had received any training on the subject from their field instructors. Of the students who had received training in dealing with assault or violence, most perceived it to be inadequate. Among field instructors in the same study, 94 percent identified a need for further training to deal with issues related to physical or verbal assault, but only 8 percent had actually received such training themselves. Based on these findings, Tully et al. noted that violence in treatment settings seems to be increasing, and, "Without experience and training, students may be unable to manage or contain potentially dangerous situations with clients" (p. 192). To remedy this situation they recommend that "curriculum materials on violence and safety issues be integrated into the curriculum or included in field placement seminars" (p. 191).

Although it may be frightening to think about the possibility of an assault, the intent of this chapter is to help reduce that possibility by giving you some suggestions for preventing and responding to risks. The message is: do not be afraid but do be careful and prepared.

Before continuing, one important caveat must be presented. The discussion that follows is intended to increase your awareness of how you can guard against violent assault by patients or clients. This should not be taken as teaching you how to identify or predict violence. As will be explained shortly, research on the prediction of violence suggests that the accuracy of such predictions tends to be low, even among those who believe they are able to assess violence well. Thus, while you seek to improve your understanding of violence among patients, keep in mind the limitations to your own knowledge and the research within the profession.

THE RISKS OF ASSAULT

If the people we work with were all reasonable, self-controlled individuals, we would probably not encounter them in many of the settings where we work. While most clients, even those with serious mental illness, are not dangerous, behavior can be unpredictable. Those who work with clients who have been committed to psychiatric hospitals should be aware that in most states the criteria for involuntary commitment specify that the individual must be considered dangerous to themselves or others. Thus, in any setting where clients are involuntarily committed, the possibility of violence must be taken seriously. Further, there are some clients who, in addition to, or as part of, their mental illness, are simply mean and dangerous individuals.

Studies have yielded varying estimates of the probability that a therapist will be assaulted. The previously mentioned study by Tully et al. is one of the few I am aware of that have addressed violence in relation to field placements

for interns or practicum students. Research on this topic as it applies to practicing professionals is more plentiful and consistently points to the fact that the risk of violence is real and should be considered in the training of students.

Thackrey and Bobbitt (1990) reported that among participants in a workshop at a VA medical center, 59 percent of clinical staff, and 28 percent of nonclinical staff participating indicated that they had been attacked at least once. Similar findings have been reported from a study in which 116 British psychologists were surveyed (Perkins, 1990, reported by Hillen, 1991). Of this group 52 percent said they had been assaulted at least once by a client, and 18 percent had been assaulted in the year preceding the study. Higher percentages were reported by Tryon (1986), who found that 81 percent of respondents to a national survey of psychologists had experienced a physical or verbal attack at work. Results such as these have lead some authors to conclude that over the course of a career, it is likely that most therapists will have to deal with some form of assault (Whitman, Armao & Dent 1976).

These findings should not be taken to mean that most patients are dangerous individuals. In fact, most patients do not pose a high risk of assault. The conclusions of Whitman et al. derive more from the fact that during one's career as a clinician the number of patients encountered is very high. As a result, even though only a small proportion of patients are likely to be assaultive, over the course of time there is a good chance that a clinician will encounter numerous patients who are potentially assaultive. In spite of the very real risk of assault during one's career, training for dealing with assault is seldom adequate (Thackrey & Bobbit, 1990).

COPING WITH AGGRESSION

Coping with the possibility of client aggression involves a combination of knowledge and associated behavioral skills. Before discussing these, let me say again that whenever you encounter a situation that is beyond your abilities or that poses significant risks, you must inform your supervisor and instructor. This is particularly important in the case of potentially violent clients. If you have reason to believe a client you work with may be likely to harm himself or herself, or may be dangerous to others, you must let your supervisor know so that appropriate action can be taken to prevent either the client or someone else from being harmed. Do not try to deal with such situations by yourself unless there is absolutely no alternative. If you have no other alternative, even as you deal with a volatile situation yourself one of your primary goals should be to obtain assistance as soon as possible.

With the awareness that you must contact your supervisor if you think a client or situation may be dangerous, some of the factors to consider in assessing, preventing, and coping with violence include: 1). Understanding that strange and unusual behavior may be distressing but is not necessarily a sign of dangerousness. 2.) Understanding developmental differences in clients and recognizing why clients of different ages may act aggressively. 3.) Understanding and recognizing motivational factors that contribute to aggression. 4.) Understanding and recognizing situations in which clients may become assaultive. 5.) Recognizing individuals who may be more likely to be dangerous. 6.) Early prevention of violence through establishment of relationships and expectations. 7.) Prevention of violence that appears imminent. 8.) Coping with assault in such a way that harm to yourself, the client, staff, and setting are minimized. 9.) Dealing with the emotional aftereffects of an assault. 10.) Debriefing to understand why violence occurred and how it can be prevented in the future.

STRANGE BEHAVIOR AND STRANGE PEOPLE ARE NOT NECESSARILY DANGEROUS

People with mental illness are sometimes described as "disturbed," but a more accurate description would be to say someone is "disturbing to others." There is something very troubling about individuals who say and do things that we do not understand and that do not fit the norm. When a man on the street corner is talking to voices that we cannot hear, when a woman sits staring and snarls at a vision we cannot see, or when someone wears bizarre clothing and dances down the middle of a busy street, most of us become uneasy.

There are probably two reasons for this. First, we are afraid that if people are acting strangely in one way, all of their behavior may be unpredictable and possibly dangerous. Second, and equally important, we do not know how to respond to people who act so differently than we do.

In your experience as an intern you will probably encounter individuals who are at least in some ways not like the people you spend time with in your life away from the internship. Depending on how different the clients and setting are from what you are familiar with, you may feel uneasy both about the clients and about yourself. This is normal and is nothing to feel bad or ashamed about. As you gain experience, you will gradually feel more comfortable and by the end of your internship you will take it for granted that you work in a setting and with people who may have once seemed strange or intimidating.

One of the most important things internships teach us is that people who are different than we are do not necessarily pose a threat to us. The first lesson about dealing with the possibility of violent patients is that most clients are no more violent or dangerous than anyone else. In spite of what may seem to be extremely bizarre behavior, in most clinical settings, unless an individual has a history of violence, it is a relatively rare client who poses a significant risk.

UNDERSTAND DEVELOPMENTAL DIFFERENCES

A five-year-old throwing a temper tantrum, a twenty-one-year-old starting a fistfight, and a seventy-year-old Alzheimer's patient may all engage in assaultive behavior, but the reasons for the assault and the consequences for the individual and the staff members are very different. Although much of the material in this chapter applies well to clients of all ages, developmental differences require that we adjust our thinking and behavioral responses to match the age and developmental level of each client.

EXERCISE

Take a moment to think about the three clients just mentioned, i.e. the five-, twenty-one-, and seventy-year-old. How do these individuals differ and how do those differences influence what you would think and do about possible aggression? Among the factors you might want to consider are: the individual's peer group and peer group norms regarding violence, the message that violence communicates for each person, the physical and mental capacity of the person to inflict serious harm to people or property, the person's understanding of and attitudes towards the consequences of a violent act, and the person's motivation. Many of these considerations will be addressed in a moment, but exploring them first yourself will deepen your appreciation of the causes of aggression in clients.

UNDERSTAND AND RECOGNIZE MOTIVATIONAL FACTORS

Apart from conditions in which a patient's consciousness is markedly distorted, either through illness, injury, or substances, violent acts happen for a purpose. Like all behavior, violence is a way of attempting to influence a situation or people. Understanding the purpose behind violent behavior can help you identify the best way to prevent the violence from happening and respond effectively if violence does occur.

When students are asked why people behave violently, the most common response is that people become violent because they are angry. This is often true, but it does not explain why violence is chosen as a behavior instead of some other response to anger. Focusing on anger as a cause of violence also ignores several other important motivational factors. These include violence as a response to fear, as a response to frustration, and as a way of controlling people. Dubin (1989) emphasizes that many patients who become violent are in

> . . . a desperate and panic-stricken struggle to prevent their imagined annihilation, either through the destruction of their physical selves or, even more frightening at times, through the destruction of their self esteem. (p. 1280)

Dubin goes on to observe that

> Paradoxically, clinical staff who are anxious and frightened by a patient whose behavior is escalating toward violence may react with an authoritarian or counteraggressive response that increases the patient's feelings of helplessness. (p. 1280)

If someone is angry and may become violent, it helps to first try to determine why they are angry, then consider why violence is a possible response. Often, one can ask the client directly by saying something like, "I can see that you're upset about something and seem pretty angry. Can you tell me what's going on that has you so upset?" This message, which is not threatening or authoritarian, acknowledges that the clinician recognizes the client's present state and is interested in trying to understand it better.

If it appears the client might become violent, it is probably not advisable to say directly that you are afraid they will be violent. It may, however, be worth asking how they are feeling at the moment. The purpose of this is to bring the client's feelings out so you can explore with them what to do with those feelings. If a client responds to your question by shouting at you or making threatening comments, a possible response would be to say calmly, "I understand that you are upset and I want to listen to what you have to say." This is much more likely to be effective than a response that commands the client to "Calm down," when the client is obviously not interested at the moment in being told what to do or in calming down.

One of the reasons it is important to try to begin a dialogue with a client who is angry is that we may not understand what the client is upset about. Some clients become angry because they feel insulted by another client or a staff member. Others may respond with anger to frustrations at work or elsewhere in their lives. For another group of clients anger is a habitual response to any situation in which they feel insecure. The initial task facing the clinician is to try to understand the client, not to make a judgment about whether or not the anger is an "appropriate" response to a situation. That process may be useful later when the client is in a condition that makes exploration possible, but in a highly agitated emotional state people are not likely to be open to exploring in the abstract whether or not their anger is justified.

As part of the process of trying to understand why a person may appear angry, it helps to recognize that what appears as anger may not necessarily be a result of anger. As mentioned earlier, sometimes violent behavior is the result of fear, not anger. For example, I have seen clients become violent when they were pressured extremely strongly to deal with something. A case that comes to mind involved a wheelchair-mobile head-injured patient who struck a staff member who was attempting to transfer the patient to a toilet against the patient's wishes. Through talking with the client about the incident later, he revealed that he was not so much angry as frightened that he could fall. When he did not feel anyone was listening or giving

him an alternative he panicked and struck out. Had his therapist recognized his emotional status and acknowledged it, the client might have been able to express his fear verbally and thereby deal with the situation differently.

While most beginning clinicians find violence that grows out of anger or fear understandable, when violence is used as a means of intentional intimidation or manipulation it tends to be more difficult to understand and deal with. Some clients have learned in their lives that violence is a way to get what they want and they do not really care if it hurts others or even themselves in the process. For these patients, violence may come as a response to anger or frustration, but it may also be a calculated means of achieving a desired end.

One example would be a client who in a group therapy session stated "If I do not get moved to a different ward by next week, I'm going to hit someone. It's as simple as that." Upon hearing such a message, the clinician must determine if this is merely bravado on the part of someone who knows no other way of getting people to listen, or if it is an intentional threat by someone who habitually uses violence as a lever over others. One way to determine which is the case might be to say: "From what you just said you want to move to another ward. You also said you would hurt someone if you did not get moved. From my perspective I want to understand why it is you want to move so I want you to tell me about that. But I'm also concerned that you were threatening to harm someone if you did not get what you wanted." If the client responds by reiterating threats, the therapist might reply "I am glad to listen to what you have to say, but I don't think threats or hurting someone will get you what you want and I'm concerned about that. Maybe we need to talk about both the request for changing wards and the reasons you feel you needed to threaten." If, in response to this, the patient reiterates the threat rather than responding to the opportunity to voice concerns, it is reasonably likely that the threat was a manipulative device rather than a request for people to listen. The trick then becomes how to deal with the situation without the patient resorting to violence as a further manipulative response to your attempts to intervene.

Throughout this book I have emphasized that whenever you are confronted by a situation that is beyond your abilities or that appears to pose a risk you must seek help. If you find yourself faced with a client who threatens violence as a manipulative tool, your best choice as an intern is to seek assistance from someone who has more training, as well as has more knowledge and authority in the setting.

SITUATIONAL FACTORS AND VIOLENCE

Along with considering the client's developmental stage and motivations, one should also evaluate immediate situational factors and conditions that might increase the potential for violence. Important situational factors include similarities between the present situation and previous incidents, recent or immediate stress, the presence or absence of certain prescription medications (some of which may decrease assault potential, while others may increase it), alcohol or other drug intoxication, the patient's cognitive functioning, the power differential between the patient and responding staff, and obvious signs, such as gestures, weapons, etc., that reveal violent intentions.

SIMILARITIES TO PAST SITUATIONS

One of the fundamental principles of psychology is that previous behavior is the best predictor of later behavior. If a person has a history of violence that follows certain patterns, one should be attentive to those patterns and any similarities to the present situation. For example, if a patient's history of violence is exclusively confined to assaults on women, the risk factor for women would be higher than that for men. While there are no guarantees that men are immune to assaults from such patients, women staff members should obviously use particular care in dealing with the patient. Other factors to consider would be patterns in locations of assaults, timing, weapons used, or specific stimuli that appear to have triggered assaults in the past. Recognizing such factors may enable one to control them and thereby prevent or at least anticipate and deal more effectively with the risk of violence.

STRESS

Stress is a situational factor that is often connected with violence. In general, whether or not a person has a history of violence, the level of stress he or she has been experiencing may increase the likelihood of a violent act. Before or during interactions with patients, we should keep in mind what stresses they have been under and how they have coped with stress in the past. If a patient has a history of responding violently when stressed, we should be particularly careful. We should ask what alternatives the patient has other than violence. Is this patient able to deal with difficulties in any other way than through violence? Has he or she had success in the past doing so? To the extent that a patient has a history of violence, lacks alternative behaviors, and is under stress, the potential for violence is likely to increase.

Situational factors also come into play when one is asked to make predictions about the potential for violence in the future. A client may seem to be coping relatively well, but if several unfortunate events happened simultaneously, such as a fight with a significant other, getting fired at work, a traffic accident, or some other event, the client might be overwhelmed and act out violently in response.

CONTROLLED SUBSTANCES AND MEDICATIONS

Along with the situational factors just mentioned, certain intoxicating drugs can also increase the likelihood of aggression. The so-called "war on drugs" notwithstanding, the most commonly used and abused drug is alcohol. Alcohol has dis-

inhibiting effects that may make some individuals feel invulnerable and lessen their awareness of fear or pain. Other drugs, such as amphetamines, tend to produce excitation, feelings of invincibility, and, in some cases, paranoia. This combination of energy, invincibility, and paranoia is extremely volatile. Another drug, PCP, or angel dust, is well known for its ability to precipitate sudden and lasting psychoses, with violent, almost unrestrainable outbursts typical of the acute phase of intoxication. Trying to reason with someone who is influenced by any of the substances just mentioned may bring little or no success and the potential for violence must be considered as a relatively high risk.

Among the prescription medications that may reduce the potential for violence, antipsychotic, antimanic, and antiseizure medications have long been used to help control violent behavior both in inpatient settings and in the community. For patients who have been prescribed medications to help control their behavior, the risk of assault may be increased if a patient has not been taking his or her medications. For this reason, one of the questions mental health crisis response teams routinely ask is "Are you taking your medications?" If a client has not been taking medications as prescribed, the potential for unpredictable behavior goes up.

While appropriately prescribed psychotropic medications may help reduce the risk of violence, there is evidence that some medications have the potential to increase the risk in certain patient groups. Haller and Deluty (1990) reported a significant relationship between the prescription of anxiolytics, and the severity of patient assaults on staff. They suggest that such medications may produce a disinhibiting effect for some patients. This finding should not be considered conclusive at this point, but it does offer further evidence that one should be aware of medication effects when assessing the potential for violence.

PATIENT MENTAL STATUS

Related to the effects of both prescription drugs and illegal substances is the more general question of the patient's state of consciousness and awareness. Is the patient capable of reasoning effectively and controlling his or her own behavior? Although it is possible to reason with many patients who appear to be at risk for violence, in some patients, conscious awareness is so clouded that reasoning is not possible or practical. For example, some patients with brain injuries, illness, or other neurological impairments may not be in control of their own behaviors or capable of understanding what people say or do to them. These patients may act violently not out of an intention to hurt people, but because they are confused and frightened and do not understand their situation or the people who are trying to treat them.

As noted earlier, patients exhibiting certain psychiatric symptoms may also pose a risk of violence that is closely connected to their state of awareness. Patients in an acute phase of mania are not likely to listen well to calm discussion. Paranoid patients may well interpret whatever is said to them as a sign of trickery. The problem each of these conditions poses for treatment staff is that we cannot assume our normal approaches to talking or reasoning with a patient will have any effect. Unfortunately, in some instances, the patient's mental and behavioral functioning may be so severely out of control that only physical or pharmacological measures will be able to prevent them from hurting themselves or others. Failure to recognize or acknowledge such situations may place the helping professional or the patient in jeopardy of being injured.

Some patients, particularly those suffering from certain neurological conditions or drug intoxication, may not be able to control their behavior regardless of the situation or consequences. There are, however, times when patients who seem to be out of control will be able to regain control if they recognize that they will not benefit from violence. To the extent that a patient is capable of functioning cognitively, and if they can recognize that they are in a less powerful position, the potential for aggression is likely to go down. Even highly agitated and threatening schizophrenics will often become cooperative without a struggle if enough staff members confront them with an overwhelming physical presence and provide an alternative to violence. It is therefore in the patient's best interest for staff to be aware of the influence of this factor in dealing with potentially or actively violent patients. Approaching a truly dangerous situation with too little power may indirectly encourage a patient to act aggressively. Having insufficient support also tends to increase the likelihood of injuries to staff or clients if an altercation does ensue.

WEAPONS

Finally, regardless of a patient's history or other situational factors, if present behavior suggests they may be dangerous (for example, if someone is armed with a weapon), we should be careful. This seems obvious, but there is a true account of a patient who entered a clinic carrying a gun and demanding to see a therapist. The therapist was called and was warned that the man had a gun, but he nevertheless came out to talk with the patient. As soon as he entered the waiting room, the therapist was killed by a blast from the gun (Annis & Baker, 1986).

It is unclear that this tragedy could have been prevented, but one can imagine a similar situation in which a therapist either overestimates his or her ability to manage things or fails to accurately assess the client's intentions. Without wishing to blame the victims in such cases, it is instructive to learn that if a person looks menacing and has the means to cause damage, the risks must be taken very seriously. If someone overtly threatens violence, either by saying he wants to hurt someone or through physical signs such as clenching fists, holding a weapon, or through some other sign, extreme caution should be exercised and help summoned. Your task as an intern is to learn, but you should not lay down your life or be injured in the process.

RECOGNIZE POTENTIALLY DANGEROUS INDIVIDUALS

Unfortunately, it is extremely difficult to assess dangerousness with any useful accuracy. In part, this is due to the "low-base-rate" phenomenon (Meehl, 1973). What this means, in essence, is that because only a small percentage of individuals engage in violent assault, even a highly accurate test is likely to produce a substantial number of misdiagnoses of dangerousness. This also suggests that in most clinical settings, if one spends a great deal of time worrying about the possibility of every patient becoming violent, that worry, for the most part, will be unnecessary and unproductive.

The low-base-rate problem would limit diagnostic accuracy even if we had a highly valid means of assessment, but we still do not have such objective instruments and we still know relatively little about who is likely to be violent and under what circumstances. Lacking objective tests of dangerousness, we may be inclined to use our own subjective judgments. But subjective judgments of dangerousness are notoriously inaccurate, even for experienced clinicians.

Some studies suggest that our ability to identify the dangerous personality is not very good and clinicians predictions of which patients will or will not exhibit violence are often less accurate than chance guesses would be (Janofsky, Spears & Neubauer 1988; Monahan, 1988). More recent studies have countered this conclusion, suggesting that mental health professionals may in fact be able to predict violence more accurately than chance. Mossman (1994) utilized quantitative techniques for studying "receiver operating characteristics" and reviewed more than forty studies of violence prediction. Based on this review, he concluded that although professionals may be able to better chance in predicting violence, the best predictor of all appears to be the patient's past behavior.

> Past behavior alone appears to be a better long term predictor of future behavior than clinical judgments and may also be a better indicator than cross-validated actuarial techniques. (p. 783)

The message from this research is that we may be able to do somewhat better than simply guessing, but we should be very suspect about trusting our subjective impressions of who is or is not likely to be dangerous. At the same time, however, we may be able to reduce the uncertainty somewhat by considering a few things that are known about dangerousness. In discussing this information the goal is not to give you the impression you are competent to diagnose dangerousness. Rather, it is to provide a framework that will help you structure your thinking about dealing with patients and the issue of dangerousness. With this information you may be able to assess clients and situations more carefully and reduce at least some of the risks.

What do we know, if anything, about predicting dangerousness in individuals? First, as mentioned earlier, previous behavior is the best predictor of future behavior. Thus, if a patient has a history of violent assaults, that patient presents a greater risk than someone with no record of assaults (Mossman, 1994; Klassen & O'Connor 1989). This seems like common sense, and it is, but we often forget to find out about patients' histories before interacting with them. The obvious way of reducing this risk is to include questions about previous violence or criminal acts as part of an intake history. This information can be corroborated by family members or friends if they have accompanied the patient to the intake. Wherever possible, it behooves the clinician to review intake notes and case history before interacting with clients.

If we are aware of past violence we sometimes fall into a different trap and intentionally disregard or discount the information. In my own experience of being assaulted by a patient, my mistake was to not fully consider that the reason the patient in question was not being allowed to have a pass was his belligerent behavior upon returning from previous passes. In the case of the patient who shot and killed the psychiatrist, case notes showed that the patient had previously made direct threats to kill his doctors.

The potential to ignore or discount past behavior may be due to carelessness, but it may also reflect our need to believe we are somehow more able than others to deal with people. Overestimating our own capacity, we confidently reason that merely because a patient is violent with others does not mean he or she will be violent with us. In some cases, this may be true, but most of the time when we make this assumption it is based more on our own ego than on real data and it may take us into dangerous situations.

This was well illustrated by a situation in which a patient who had assaulted several different people during the previous two-month period was being transported between wards by a nurse. The nurse had been well informed of the case but had never worked with the patient before. In spite of the patient's recent actions and the nurse's lack of personal experience with him, she felt that the patient would not harm her. Upon leaving the locked ward, the nurse, against policy, released restraints that had been holding the patient's hands to a belt around his waist. Seconds after he was released, the patient viciously attacked the nurse. Fortunately, her life was saved due to the quick intervention of several workers who had witnessed the events from a nearby window.

There is a place for compassion, but there is also a place for caution, and the two are by no means mutually exclusive. If excessive self-confidence leads us to do something foolish, we are not acting out of compassion, we are acting out of egotistical needs and neither our best interests nor those of clients will be best served.

If a patient has a history of violence, we should ask what the consequences have been and if the patient has learned anything from those consequences that would either increase or decrease the likelihood of further violence. For some patients, violence has worked very well as a behavior choice. Although we tend to think of the down sides of violence, it can also bring a person power, status, money, self-esteem, protection, momentary release of tension, and a host of other desirable consequences. We forget this at our peril. If someone has learned from experience that violence works, there is an increased likelihood that this person will resort to it again. There are also those for whom violence may have brought on negative consequences, but they failed to learn from experience. This diminished ability to learn from experience is characteristic of the sociopathic or antisocial personalities.

An example of how patients can learn that the consequences of violence are not necessarily undesirable came during a group discussion in a unit for patients who had committed crimes but were ruled to be suffering from mental illness. When confronted by a staff member for behaviors on the unit, a patient in the group responded by threatening to kill the staff member, then boldly stated, "And when I do, they won't do anything about it because I'm already in a nuthouse." In dealing with this patient, one would obviously want to use exceptional caution.

Finally, although there is great variability among patients in different diagnostic groups, certain diagnoses and symptoms may suggest an increased potential for dangerousness. In considering these groups it must be emphasized that the majority of patients in each group are not likely to be violent. In other words, although there may be an increased potential for someone with a given diagnosis to act aggressively as compared to someone with a different diagnosis, just knowing a diagnosis provides little basis for concluding that a patient is dangerous. With the exception of known violent patients, the vast majority of patients in any given diagnostic group are not likely to be violent.

With the preceding caveats in mind, symptom and diagnostic factors that may increase the risk of assault include: patients for whom assault is a presenting problem (Klassen & O'Connor, 1989); patients with personality disorders (Haller & Deluty, 1990); patients exhibiting delusions or hallucinations; and patients with manic disorders (Janofsky, Spears & Neubauer, 1988).

EARLY PREVENTION OF VIOLENCE

The best way to deal with violence is to prevent it from happening. The importance of accurately assessing client and situational variables has been discussed above. Next we consider how the things we say or do can lessen or increase the potential for violence.

Ultimately, the best prevention of violence is good clinical work. If you are skillful at understanding clients and building therapeutic relationships, the likelihood of becoming the target of violence is lessened. This does not mean that people who are assaulted are therefore at fault or are, by definition, poor clinicians. It does mean that the way you interact with clients in any given situation will influence their behavior in later situations. It also means that by building positive relationships and a system of interacting that gives clients alternatives to violence, clinicians can reduce clients' potential to resort to violence.

This principle was modeled by a special education teacher who had some of the toughest, most disruptive students in the school together in one classroom. When other teachers heard of the combination of students in the class, they offered their condolences and remarked how awful it must be for the teacher. In fact, her classroom was surprisingly peaceful. This teacher's secret was not in some overpowering discipline technique. Instead, she treated the students in a way that showed she respected and cared for them, and that she expected the same treatment in return. She emphasized their accomplishments, got to know each one as an individual, and when discipline was needed she was firm, fair, and consistent. She also made it a point to touch each student in some way and to speak to each one by name every day. As a result of these activities, she did not have to deal with dangerous situations because she built a positive atmosphere that prevented dangerous situations from developing or escalating.

The setting of your internship or clinical work may not be identical to the classroom situation just described, but there will be parallels that relate to prevention. Whatever the setting, it is valuable for clinicians to ask themselves if they are paying enough attention to developing the positive side of relationships, setting and modeling expectations of respectful behavior, and setting limits and clear consequences for violent or aggressive behavior.

PREVENTION OF IMMINENT VIOLENCE

The first rule of interacting with clients who appear to be agitated is to remain calm and in control. Even if you are afraid a client is about to become violent, showing that you have that fear is unlikely to help the situation and may increase the chances that the client will become violent. This is easy to say, but the threat of violence automatically evokes our physiological flight-or-fight response. The rush of adrenaline and other sympathetic nervous system changes may help us to respond physically, but it tends to impede our ability to think clearly and calmly. In order to help you keep your wits in spite of fear, practice stepping back physically and mentally to evaluate the situation as objectively as you can.

As you think about a dangerous situation, try to assess quickly what you might do if attacked. Scan the room, consider your options, and as you speak, move to where you will be the least vulnerable. As you consider safety and protection, try to understand what the client's motivations might be for violence. Running through the earlier discussion of motivation may be helpful and can suggest some possible responses to each of the different motivations. In the things you say and do, try to acknowledge the client's distress but do not validate physical aggression as a response to that distress.

For example, if a client is responding out of fear, you can seek to lessen the fear. Giving the client physical space, holding your hands low and relaxed, speaking calmly, and reassuring them that they are safe may help to lessen their fear, and their potential for violence. It may also help to say something like "I can see you are upset and I would like to help. What can I do?" This statement lets the client know you are aware of their condition, and, by asking what they want to do, it offers them a sense of control that may lessen their fear.

In all cases of possible violence, it is important to speak clearly and simply. This is especially important if you determine that the client is confused or disoriented. Short, direct sentences that give specific information are desirable. Sometimes you may need to orient a person to who and where they and you are. For example, to a patient who is disoriented you might say, "Mr. Smith, you are in a hospital. I am your therapist. Let's sit down and talk." Note how short the sentences are and how they each express only a small bit of information at a time. They also give specific instructions because in this instance the patient's own thought processes may be so disrupted that he cannot determine what to do on his own.

Along with remembering what you should do in dealing with clients, it is also important to know what not to do. Some suggestions for things to avoid include arguing with a client, making threats that the client knows cannot be carried out, and challenging or daring the client to be violent. You may be able to argue with coworkers and friends without getting in a fight, but this does not always apply to your relationships with clients. Similarly, when you are not in a clinical setting you might become angry if you are insulted or threatened physically, but you must not respond to that with violence against a client. While it may be useful to remind clients if there are known and sure consequences for violence, it is probably not a good idea to invent threats that have little probability of being carried out. Such empty threats may only serve to remind the client that they can aggress without consequences. Further suggestions about dealing with individuals who are armed and clearly intent on violence have been offered by Burgess, Burgess, and Douglas (1994).

RESPONDING TO ASSAULT

Although the best way to deal with violence is to prevent it from happening, even the best prevention efforts are not perfect. Therefore, we need to give some thought to what might happen if we are assaulted and how we would respond in order to minimize the harm to ourselves, the client, other persons, and property. Among the factors to consider in responding to assault are clothing, office layout, communications, dangerous and protective implements, and assault response training.

CLOTHING

If you are working in a setting where assault might be a possibility, it is important that you dress in such a way that your clothing cannot become an impediment to movement or a weapon that can be used against you. Take a moment to check out your personal attire and ask how it could aid or harm you if you were assaulted. Among the clothing elements that can increase risk are items worn around the neck. Ties, scarves, or strong necklaces all provide tempting and dangerous items for people to grab and possibly strangle you with in a struggle. If something is around your neck it can be extremely difficult, perhaps impossible, to release yourself, and you will have only a short time to get free before losing consciousness.

If ties and scarves present an attractive target to grab, so do large earrings, particularly the loop kind. Regardless of your personal fashion tastes, think of a client grabbing a piece of jewelry or clothing and pulling hard. Then decide if that is really something you want to wear to your work or internship setting. If a dress code requires you to wear ties or other dangerous items, you may want to discuss the safety implications of this with your supervisor or the setting director. If all else fails, wear a clip on bow tie. Who knows, you may start a trend.

While avoiding items of clothing that may harm you if attacked, you should also consider how your clothing might assist or impede your ability to avoid or escape an assault. For example, footwear should be of a sort that enables you to move quickly and have a steady base of support in a struggle. This means high heels and slick soled shoes are not recommended. Similarly, tight clothing is generally recommended against because it too may restrict your movement.

Finally, it is important to avoid clothing that might be deemed "provocative" in some way. While recognizing that in an ideal world people should probably be able to dress however they like, in reality, at your internship, you must recognize the institutional needs and client characteristics and exercise good judgment about your appearance and the impression it creates. If you do get assaulted, you do not want to become the target of criticism that you invited the assault by the way you dressed.

OFFICE LAYOUT

Escape routes are the first thing to think about in considering your office layout. If you were attacked or threatened with an attack, how readily could you exit without having to contact the patient? Similarly, if a client is feeling pressured or cornered, could they escape without having to "go through" you. The earlier discussion of situational assessment noted that dangerous patients should not be seen alone. If this cannot be avoided, try to find a room with two doors such that the therapist or patient can exit easily or help can enter in the event of an emergency. If a room has only one door, be sure that the door cannot easily be locked in a way that would trap you inside and prevent assistance from entering quickly.

Also involved in office layout is the matter of space between client and therapist. When working with potentially dangerous people, leave sufficient space to give you time to react if they move to attack you. Although I generally avoid seeing a client "across the desk," the desk can provide an element of protection and sometimes the space will help a client feel less pressured, thereby further reducing the likelihood of attack. Make sure, however, that the desk cannot easily be turned over, trapping you beneath it.

Visibility is another factor that can increase safety but is often overlooked. If people can see into your office to be sure things are okay, the chance of assault decreases and the opportunities for quick help increase. You should also be sure you are situated in such a way that you can see who is coming and going or who might be about to enter your office. Placing your desk against the far wall may seem like a convenient location, but if it means you must sit with your back to an open door it could leave you very vulnerable. A bit of interior decorating creativity can make for a much safer working environment.

COMMUNICATION

If you were attacked in your office or elsewhere in your workplace, how would people know you needed help? If you are working with someone who might be dangerous, it is vital that you have a way of letting others know if you are in trouble. There must also be a way for help to reach you quickly. This means you should establish an unmistakable and unambiguous signal that alerts people when help is needed. Some settings provide alarm buzzers on the therapists' desks, others have phone signals, and in some instances a secretary or other staff member checks every few minutes to see how things are going. Leaving your door open may be a viable option, as might telling the person in the next office to be aware that, if sounds of a scuffle emerge, help is needed. If your office is removed from others, it will be especially advisable to have a form of remote communications device, such as a buzzer or phone.

As you think about how to inform others that you need help, remember that research on bystander assistance indicates that ambiguity may substantially impede the likelihood of help being provided. If you need to send a person to get help, do not simply shout "Somebody get help." Chances are, no one will go. Instead, pick a specific person, call that person by name, and tell him or her exactly what to do. "Joe, go to the nurses' station and tell the first staff you can find that there is trouble in room 100 and we need help immediately. Go now and hurry." The importance of being specific applies not only to assault situations, but to any emergency situation you might encounter.

DANGEROUS AND DEFENSIVE IMPLEMENTS

To further enhance your safety, check your office for whatever potentially offensive and defensive implements may be there. It is not a good idea to have letter openers, spike-type message spindles, paper weights, etc., in locations were clients could easily reach them. On the other hand, it is a good idea to have potential shields, such as books, cushions, a wastebasket, chairs, etc., nearby where you can easily reach them. If you deal with dangerous individuals frequently, you should probably practice grasping a shield, or perhaps even carrying a clipboard, so it becomes a habitual and ready protection that can be used automatically if you ever need it. If you sit behind a desk, as mentioned earlier, the desk should be anchored so that it cannot be tipped over on top of you. It would not be a pleasant experience to have an angry patient overturn your desk and have it land on you, pinning you to the floor. This has actually happened to therapists. Again, the goal is to prevent unpleasantness by preparing for situations before they happen.

ASSAULT RESPONSE TRAINING

With all the precautions in place, you may still be wondering what to do if you are assaulted. Answering this question is not easy because every situation is unique and the resources you bring to a situation will differ from those of other interns. Recognizing these limitations, there are some suggestions that may prove helpful.

The first suggestion is that you seek some form of specific training in dealing with patient assault. Many hospitals, mental health centers, and other programs offer such training, which typically involves a discussion of legal and policy issues, assessment of dangerousness, how to prevent assaults, and various means of physically protecting yourself without harming clients. In a study of the effects of such training, Thackrey (1987) found that staff who completed a training course reported significant increases in confidence in their ability to cope with aggression, but they would not be described as "overconfident." These gains were maintained at eighteen-month follow up, suggesting that training can have lasting effects.

While such findings are encouraging, it is important to weigh the quality of the training being offered. I am familiar with a widely distributed video tape series that purports to teach therapists how to deal with assaultive or belligerent patients. In my judgment, much of the advice and modeling in this series is extremely naive and may actually be counterproductive.

If you do not have access to a quality program specifically designed around patient assault, some forms of self-defense training may be helpful. Techniques of aikido are particularly adaptable. The nonviolent approach of aikido and the philosophy that accompanies the techniques are useful training for interns and therapists. Other so-called "martial arts" may also be useful, but for your clinical needs focus on the defensive techniques more than the counterattacking, punching, and kicking skills. Knowing such skills may help boost confidence and could well help you in other situations, but obviously you should not use them to harm or intimidate clients.

If you do not have experience or training in dealing with assaults, your best approach is to use common sense, be creative, do not be heroic, but do resist harm. Common sense suggests that if you are assaulted you need to protect your vital areas, try to escape, and get help. At the same time, creativity can help you defend yourself. The comedian Steve Martin used to say that you could discourage robbery by throwing up on your money. He said it for laughs, but he is not far wrong. Try to rapidly assess the situation, identify options, and seek responses other than what the assailant expects. This may give you an element of surprise, and sometimes it can even stop the attack altogether.

I know one young woman who, as she was waiting to buy a newspaper in New York city, was handed a note by a would-be robber. The note instructed the woman to be quiet and give him her money or she would be killed. Thinking her would-be assailant was handing out handbills or other propaganda of some sort, the woman simply glanced at the note, said "No, not interested," and walked on. A few seconds later it dawned on her what the note had said. Upon realizing this, she turned to look back and saw her dumbfounded and unsuccessful assailant staring in disbelief at her and at his note.

The advice against heroics is meant to give you permission to run away if you must. If someone much larger or stronger poses a threat, you can try to deal with that threat verbally or in other noncombative ways, but if combat appears inevitable, you will probably lose. Under such circumstances it may help simply to tell the person that they do not need to fight with you because you will leave.

AFTEREFFECTS

If you do have the misfortune to be assaulted, it is extremely important that you deal effectively with the aftereffects. Tully et al. (1993) note that some institutions have developed "violence plans" designed to help victims adjust after an assault. These plans include such things as whom to notify, how to handle the assailant, documentation, and steps to help the victim deal with the emotional aftereffects.

The first thing to do if you are assaulted is to notify your supervisor so that necessary records can be made. If you are injured, you must get medical help and be sure that events are well documented. You may also have to fill out certain incident reporting forms or other paperwork so you can receive compensation for medical expenses.

If you are not injured, and after notifying your supervisor, go somewhere with your supervisor or a colleague and take time to deal with what happened. Immediately after an assault you will probably experience the physical effects of the crisis. You may find yourself shaking, feeling your heart racing, and perhaps feeling sick to your stomach. These are normal responses and nothing to be ashamed of or hide. You probably do not want to try to go right back to what you were doing as if nothing has happened. Give yourself some time to let your body and mind get back to normal.

You will also need to work through the emotions that follow an assault. For example, you might be afraid to go back to the site of the assault. Or, you may feel angry; you may want to "get back" at the client who assaulted you. Depending on the circumstances that lead to the assault, you may try to think back to what happened. How did things develop, what might have been done differently, what was done well under the circumstances? All of these questions and feelings may strike at once, and it is not uncommon to find yourself replaying the event again and again in your mind. This process can often take at least several days and as long as a couple of weeks or more to work through.

If the aftereffects of an assault continue and are troubling or interfering with your work, you may want to seek some form of counseling. You and your supervisor should also explore how the experience may affect your work and interactions with clients in the coming days and weeks. If the assault was seen by others, you may feel embarrassed about returning to work. A primary consideration in this process must also be the possibility of the assault recurring. If your supervisor does not raise this concern but it is on your mind, be sure to express it yourself. In order for you to feel safe in returning to your position, you will need to consider this possibility and be assured that steps have been taken to prevent another assault from happening. You will also need to have support to ensure that your clinical work will not be adversely affected by the experience.

To close this chapter, I want to reiterate that you should not be afraid about going to your internship or interacting with clients, but you should be cautious. Knowing your limitations, developing your clinical skills, and seeking assistance when necessary are the keys to safety in your internship and in your future clinical work.

REFERENCES

Annis, L. V., & Baker, C. A. (1986). A psychiatrist's murder in a mental hospital. *Hospital and Community Psychiatry, 37,* 505–506.

Burgess, A. W., Burgess, A. G., & Douglas, J. E. (1994). Examining violence in the workplace: A look at work-related fatalities. *Journal of Psychosocial Nursing, 32*(7), 11–18.

Dubin, W. R. (1989). The role of fantasies, countertransference, and psychological defenses in patient violence. *Hospital and Community Psychiatry, 40,* 1280–1283.

Gelman, S. R. (1990). The crafting of fieldwork training agreements. *Journal of Social Work Education, 26,* 65–75.

Haller, R. M., & Deluty, R. H. (1990). Characteristics of psychiatric inpatients who assault staff severely. *The Journal of Nervous and Mental Disease, 178,* 536–537.

Hillen, S. (1991). U.K. Study: Half of therapists attacked. *APA Monitor,* Nov., 22.

Janofsky, J. S., Spears, S., & Neubauer, D. N. (1988). Psychiatrists' accuracy in predicting violent behavior on an inpatient unit. *Hospital and Community Psychiatry, 39,* 1090–1094.

Klassen, D., & O'Connor, W. A. (1989). Assessing the risk of violence in released mental patients: A cross-validation study. *Psychological Assessment: A Journal of Consulting and Clinical Psychology. 1,* 75–81.

Meehl, P. (1973). *Psychodiagnosis: Selected papers.* Minneapolis, MN: University of Minnesota Press.

Monahan, J. (1988). Risk assessment of violence among the mentally disordered: Generating useful knowledge. *International Journal of Law and Psychiatry, 11,* 249–257.

Mossman, D. (1994). Assessing predictions of violence: Being accurate about accuracy. *Journal of Consulting and Clinical Psychology, 62,* 783–792.

Thackrey, M. (1987). Clinician confidence in coping with patient aggression: Assessment and enhancement. *Professional Psychology: Research and Practice, 18,* 57–60.

Thackrey, M., & Bobbit R. G. (1990). Patient aggression against clinical and nonclinical staff in a VA medical center. *Hospital and Community Psychiatry, 41,* 195–197.

Tryon, G. (1986). Abuse of therapists by patients: A national survey. *Professional Psychology: Research and Practice, 17,* 357–363.

Tully, C. T., Kropf, N. P., & Price, J. L. (1993). Is field a hard hat area? A study of violence in field placements. *Journal of Social Work Education, 29,* 191–199.

Whitman, R. M., Armao, B. B., & Dent, O. B. (1976). Assault on the therapist. *American Journal of Psychiatry, 133,* 426–429.

CHAPTER 12

CLOSING CASES

By their nature, internships are time limited. Interns should keep this in mind throughout their placement and should plan well in advance for when they will leave the internship (Penn, 1990). This chapter discusses some of the tasks that must be accomplished and issues that arise as one prepares for the completion of an internship. As in other chapters, I recognize that not all interns will be directly responsible for seeing clients or doing therapy. Nevertheless, I believe all interns need to learn about these issues to prepare for a time when they will have such responsibilities.

CLIENT AND INTERN RESPONSES TO TERMINATION

The short-term nature of internships or internship rotations prevents many interns from having the opportunity to work individually with clients from the beginning to the conclusion of treatment. A common pattern is for interns to work with clients who have already seen another therapist, then work with those clients until the internship or rotation ends, at which time the clients are transferred to yet another therapist (Geller & Nash, 1987). This situation is probably typical of many internships, but it presents a number of challenges for interns and clients. One of those challenges is the necessity of dealing with forced terminations, i.e., termina-

tions that happen before the work of therapy has been fully accomplished.

UNDERSTANDING CLIENT REACTIONS TO EARLY TERMINATION

In order for interns to deal successfully with termination, it is important to understand how clients and interns are affected by the termination process. Penn (1990) points out that clients may experience a variety of thoughts and emotions in response to termination. Clients may become angry over perceived abandonment or a feeling that their trust in the therapist has been betrayed. Anxiety is also common, as clients wonder if and how they will be able to manage without the assistance of the therapist. Many clients may feel a sense of loss for the therapy relationship and for the therapist.

In responding to these reactions, the therapist should keep in mind that the initial or surface presentation is likely to be only part of the client's overall reaction. Penn describes this well:

> Whatever the initial reaction of a patient to the forced termination, it is likely that his or her reaction is more complex and layered than first seems to be the case. A patient who is in touch with only sadness over the loss of the therapist may find it more difficult to acknowledge anger toward the therapist for causing that loss; one who is in touch with only the rage may be reluctant to feel the tender feelings and the sad-

ness behind the anger. Indifference can alternate with strong feelings of separation anxiety. (p. 381)

Siebold (1992) voiced similar appreciation of the complexity of termination:

> Following the announced ending of treatment, much of what the client raises may relate to termination, but as with many other factors in the client's life, feelings and associations are disguised, denied, or avoided. Time is needed for the person to take in, act out, and master the news. (p. 331)

As part of appreciating the complexity of reactions to termination, therapists should also be aware that the client's reaction to ending the therapy relationship will be closely connected to the client's previous relationship and termination experiences. McRoy, Freeman, and Logan (1986) note that clients' reactions to the termination process:

> . . . will be influenced by the level at which they have achieved mastery of the early separation-individuation crisis and the manner in which they deal with the polarized conflicts of dependence-independence, passivity-activity, trust-mistrust, and love-hate. (p. 49)

In other words, although the immediate termination is of the relationship between you and the client, each of you will cope with that termination based in large part on your experience of previous termination experiences in other relationships. Awareness of this fact can be an invaluable aid in helping the therapist make the termination experience part of the overall therapeutic process.

EXERCISE

Some of the reactions clients might have to termination are identified above. To further your understanding of client reactions, consider the following questions.

1. How might the client's personality and presenting concerns influence his or her cognitive, emotional, and behavioral reactions to termination? In other words, how will different types of clients cope differently with the termination experience?
2. What kinds of previous termination experiences might influence how a given client will cope with terminating an interaction with you?
3. How will the approach one takes to therapy influence the way clients cope with therapy termination?

UNDERSTANDING INTERN REACTIONS TO TERMINATION

Understanding the client's reactions to termination is only part of the puzzle. For termination to be constructive, interns must also understand their own reactions. As with clients, the effects of termination will vary depending on the intern's personality and the nature of their interactions with specific clients. Siebold (1992) has described common therapist reactions to termination and notes that "letting go can be as difficult for the therapist as it is for the client" (p. 331).

Among the many emotions interns may experience at termination, guilt is especially common. Having encouraged the client to trust, be open, and establish a therapeutic relationship, the therapist is now ending that relationship before the work has been fully accomplished. This may be particularly difficult for interns, who, because they are working with some of their first clients, are likely to establish especially close ties. Being forced to break those ties without realizing the fruits of their joint labor with the client can bring both guilt and frustration.

Closely linked to guilt feelings may be a sense of "omnipotence" on the part of the therapist or intern. If a therapist feels he or she is the only one who really understands a client, it can be all the more difficult to transfer that client for fear no one else will be able to help. The reverse of omnipotent feelings is seen in an intern's fears that the next therapist the patient sees may in some ways do a better job or will recognize mistakes that have been made. Owing to their relative inexperience, interns may be especially susceptible to concerns of this sort. The evaluation component of internship training is likely to heighten such concerns.

In contrast to feelings of guilt, loss, or concern about the client's well being, it also happens that interns experience a sense of relief at termination with some clients. As Siebold remarked: "Some clients you'd like to take with you, while others are a pleasure to leave" (1992, p. 330).

Siebold's observation of different therapist reactions to termination with different clients receives empirical support from a study by Fair and Bressler (1992). Their results showed that termination planning and emotional reactions differed for patients with DSMIII-R Axis I, (i.e., in this study, dysthymia, anxiety, or adjustment disorders), as compared to patients with Axis II diagnoses (i.e., for this study, borderline or narcissistic personality disorders). In general, student therapists reported less attention to termination planning, but greater emotional reactions to Axis II patients than to Axis I patients. This finding reveals the influence of client type on termination approach and the importance of interns reflecting on their own feelings about clients and the termination process. Whether or not one is "glad" to terminate a therapy relationship, it is still the therapist's responsibility to try to ensure a productive termination process.

Independent of reactions to specific clients, interns should also be aware of how transitions within their own life and their personal future can influence their management of termination with clients. Gavazzi and Anderson (1987) contrasted the feelings of loss that clients may experience with the elation or relief that interns may feel as they look towards completing an academic program or going on to other, perhaps more appealing, rotations. Interns who are glad "to be done with" a rotation, or who can hardly wait to start something new, may have a difficult time empathizing with clients who are experiencing loss, anxiety, anger, or other unpleasant reactions to termination.

EXERCISE

Given what has been said about interns understanding their own reactions to termination, the questions below are designed to help you consider your own thoughts about terminating the internship or your relationship with specific clients. These questions might provide valuable material for discussing termination with your supervisor or instructor.

1. What concerns do you have for your clients as you think about concluding your work with them?
2. How are you dealing personally and in therapy with the concerns identified in the first question?
3. Are you giving equal attention to termination for all of your clients, or are some receiving more of your energy than others?
4. How might your own thoughts about what lies ahead for you be influencing the way you are interacting with clients or others?

COMMON PROBLEMS IN TERMINATION

One of the reasons for reviewing client and therapist reactions is to help interns anticipate and avoid some of the problems that can contribute to or result from terminations that are not handled well. The key to many such problems is the failure of the therapist to approach the termination process therapeutically. To the extent that the therapist fails to use basic therapy skills, such as understanding the client, monitoring the therapeutic relationship, being aware of process as well as content, and watching for one's own issues, the termination process is likely to be difficult and possibly even counterproductive.

Therapists who fail to understand the possible origins and complexity of client reactions to termination are unlikely to deal with those reactions effectively. Confronted by a client's anger at termination, the therapist may become defensive; confronted by client anxiety, the therapist may be inclined to reassure the client with unrealistic promises. The potential for such responses is increased if therapists are also trying to deal with their own reactions (perhaps including guilt), or their needs to feel needed or competent.

Therapists who are conflicted about termination may also unconsciously pass some of their needs or fears onto the client. For example, Siebold (1992) describes how therapists who feel themselves to have been the only one able to help a client might unconsciously communicate this and thereby sabotage attempts to transition the client to another therapist. Therapists may also try to make the client into a "good" client, both to ease the work of the colleague who will take the case and to make it appear that the therapy to that point had been more successful.

In my supervisory experience I have noted that many interns subtly extract reassurance or perhaps even absolution from their clients. In an effort to ease the transition for themselves, interns might create opportunities for clients to tell them how much the therapy helped, or that the clients are happy for the intern's future opportunities. Such client statements might be perfectly legitimate, but if they are extracted covertly, or to meet the intern's needs rather than the client's, they are less likely to be therapeutic.

Another approach to minimizing the difficulty of transitions is to leave little or no opportunity for clients to express any negative feelings. Some interns wait until the end of a session to tell clients that this will be their last visit. A less blatant approach is to give clients advance warning but then occupy the remaining time or sessions by reviewing only the positive elements of therapy. Such practices may ease the termination process for the therapist, and perhaps for the client as well, but they do not allow clients to work through their full range of feelings about termination.

Throughout therapy, and especially at termination, therapists must remember that their job is to do what is necessary to help the client, not to meet their own personal needs in therapy. If this means learning how to deal with unpleasant and difficult material or interactions, therapists must do so. If a therapist shrinks from that responsibility at termination, this is an indication that the therapist probably has significant personal work to do in regards to termination and to his or her role as therapist.

TOWARD SUCCESSFUL TERMINATION OR TRANSFER

Although the focus of the discussion thus far, and, for that matter, in much of the literature, has been on the difficulties associated with termination, if properly managed, termination has the potential to be an extremely valuable therapeutic experience for clients and interns. Toward that end, our attention now turns to ways in which termination can become a constructive part of the therapy process.

CHALLENGES TO ASSUMPTIONS ABOUT TERMINATION AS CRISIS

In a discussion of termination in short-term psychotherapy, Quintana (1993) argues that too much has been made of the notion that termination will inevitably be experienced as a crisis by clients. Referring primarily to planned termination, i.e. termination that is mutually agreed upon and not imposed by therapist departure, Quintana cites literature to indicate that most therapists and clients handle termination well. Indeed, studies reviewed by Quintana show that clients whose therapy was successful describe termination in positive terms, focusing on the progress they have made and on the ending of therapy as a beginning of something new. For clients whose therapy was less successful, termination is less likely to be described in positive terms, with the focus placed instead on disappointment over the limited progress.

Based on his own research and review of the empirical literature, Quintana proposes that instead of focusing solely or primarily on the loss involved in termination, therapists should address termination as an opportunity for development and transformation. Of special importance is the process of helping clients internalize the therapeutic relationship, the gains that have been made, and a new image of themselves as the result of their growth in therapy. Quintana cites a particularly valuable statement by Edelson (1963):

> The problem of termination is not how to get therapy stopped, or when to stop it, but how to terminate so that what has been happening keeps going inside the patient. (p. 23)

In order to help "keep therapy going" inside the client, Quintana asserts that:

> . . . clients need to acknowledge the steps they have taken toward more mature functioning. Perhaps most important to clients is for therapists to acknowledge and validate their sense of accomplishment. (Quintana, 1993, p. 430)

Ideas similar to Quintana's have been voiced by Siebold (1992) in relation to forced terminations. Like Quintana, Siebold challenges the view that termination is necessarily experienced as a crisis.

> . . . instead of processes fraught with peril and little benefit, premature endings, although not optimal conditions, are opportunities for mastery, growth and maturation. The therapist is an active participant who facilitates expression of the full complement of feelings present during this experience, and who believes in the client's ability to survive the loss and to use the process productively. (p. 339)

Fundamental to the assertion that termination can present an opportunity for further growth is the phrase "if handled properly" by the therapist. What are some of the key ingredients to successful termination?

CLIENT SELECTION

In Chapter 2 of this book it was emphasized that internships are time limited and this fact must be considered by interns and supervisors throughout their work with clients. Penn (1990) also stressed this point, adding that:

Certain patients for whom a forced termination could be countertherapeutic, such as patients with a history of multiple losses, should be referred elsewhere whenever possible. It is also important to try to avoid a patient's being assigned and transferred to a series of therapists, each of whom will need to terminate. (p. 382)

This point is repeated here for two reasons. First, if it happens that the intern has been working with clients for whom termination might be unusually difficult due to past experiences, that possibility must be considered and addressed in the therapy process as termination nears. A second consideration in termination should be careful selection of another therapist to take the case when the intern leaves. As Penn suggested, efforts should be made to avoid referring clients to other therapists or interns with whom the client is likely to experience another forced termination. Transfers between therapists will be addressed further in a moment.

WORKING WITH SUPERVISORS TO PREPARE FOR TERMINATION

Before addressing termination in therapy with clients, interns should prepare themselves for the termination process. This self-preparation process includes several elements: self-reflection, discussions with instructors and supervisors, and study of termination issues and techniques.

Siebold advises that:

> Before announcing an impending departure, the therapist may want to explore his or her own feelings and fantasies about leaving, and the repercussions of such feelings on clients. (p. 330)

In my internship classes, we typically devote at least one or two class periods (or group discussions plus individual sessions) to discussing both general and personal termination issues with interns. This process often involves exercises such as those presented earlier in the chapter. We also use the group format of our classes to facilitate discussion about personal termination experiences of interns and about shared reactions to their work in therapy.

In addition to exploring termination in the academic context, interns should raise termination issues with their onsite supervisors. Two critical issues must be addressed between interns and their supervisors. First, interns should work closely with supervisors to understand their own reactions and possible approaches to termination with clients. Second, the intern and supervisor must also address the fact that the intern is simultaneously experiencing a termination with the supervisor.

Several authors have noted that the way supervisors address termination issues with their interns provides a model to help interns learn how to address termination with clients. Gavazzi and Anderson (1987) refer to the "parallel process" that occurs between supervisor and therapist, and therapist and client. They suggest that supervisors and therapists should engage in a cognitive and affective review of their work together. The cognitive element would address areas such as the therapist's strengths and weaknesses, progress made during training, future directions, etc. The affective review would entail talking about feelings toward one another, the supervisory experience, and termination itself. A similar review on both cognitive and affective levels is recommended as part of the termination work with clients.

One caveat should be mentioned in regard to the supervisor-intern termination process serving as a model for termination with clients. In their study of trainees' impressions of the termination process, Geller and Nash (1987) found that many of the trainees they surveyed were disappointed with how their supervisors handled the termination process with them. Some supervisors were described as offering virtually no help with termination, while others focused solely on the patients' feelings about termination and neglected the reactions of the trainees. Commenting on these results and on their findings regarding differing termination styles among trainees, Geller and Nash postulate that:

> . . . supervisors may collude with residents by avoiding discussions about their feelings around termination. If, for example, both supervisor and resident are given to the more distancing style they may in a variety of ways reinforce each other's need to dilute the intense feelings aroused by the anticipated end of their relationship. (p. 23)

This suggests that although the ideal supervisory relationship will address termination issues well, it may also happen that supervisors neither help interns deal with client terminations nor effectively address termination of their own relationship with the intern. If supervisors do not introduce the subject of termination, interns may need to raise it themselves. If a supervisor seems uncomfortable dealing with the topic, interns may wish to discuss termination with other experienced professionals or with their peers. It may also be possible for interns to observe how other practitioners manage termination. McRoy et al. (1986) suggest that this observation could occur either directly or via video or audio tapes of skillful termination sessions.

Exercise

In the next chapter, more will be said about the issue of termination with supervisors. However, because termination with supervisors is so closely tied to how one terminates with clients, additional reflection on the topic is warranted here. I have found that the following questions help interns become more aware of some of the cognitive and affective issues evoked by termination with their supervisors.

1. As you anticipate termination with your supervisor, what kinds of positive experiences during your placement will be easy for you to discuss? What positive experiences may be more difficult or awkward for you to talk about?
2. Having considered positive experiences, what negative experiences or unfulfilled expectations are you aware of? What are your thoughts and feelings as you consider raising these with your supervisor?
3. Does considering the questions above enhance your appreciation of what your own clients might be experiencing as they address their own positive and negative feelings about their work and relationship with you?

When and How to Notify Clients

In order to allow sufficient time to work through termination, it is essential to notify clients well in advance of the actual termination date. Opinions vary about how much advance time is necessary. Some writers suggest that six weeks is a minimum (Penn, 1990), while others prefer substantially more time (Siebold, 1992). As noted earlier, if interns know from the beginning of therapy that they will be leaving at a specified date, they should probably notify clients of that fact from the outset of treatment.

Penn (1990) advises that therapists and interns need to be careful not to let good intentions about advanced notification become lost because of their own anxiety. If one is not comfortable about termination it can be easy to "run out of time" in a session, "forget" to raise the topic, or generate a host of good clinical reasons for delaying the discussion. In part to reduce this possibility, and to allow time in a session for a client's initial responses to the information, Penn suggests raising the topic at the start of a session.

I agree with the idea that time must be allowed in the session for patients to respond to the news of termination, but I prefer to first get a sense of how the client is doing that day and what issues seem to be present. To begin a session by announcing that one is leaving, before knowing what is happening with the client, could obscure critical information that may impact how the client will react. As such, my practice is to begin sessions in a usual fashion, checking out what has happened since our last session and what issues the client is interested in addressing during the present session. After listening to these, I then set my "mental clock" to be sure to raise the issue of termination by at least mid-session. Sometimes this means interrupting the client, and it often means shifting the topic, but I do this in order to avoid the aforementioned temptation to avoid or delay telling clients.

One of the reasons interns are reluctant to tell clients they are leaving is the intern is not sure what to say or how to deal with the client's reaction. One intern told me he mentally practiced what to say, much as he had when he broke up with a girlfriend. Another said that she thought about handling terminations in the same way she handled leaving her family at the conclusion of holiday visits. "I just get on the plane and go," she said. "No long good-byes, no tears, I don't like to get emotional, or at least I don't like to show it." These examples reveal both the awkwardness of the subject and how therapy termination tends to evoke previous termination experiences for therapists as well as clients.

I do not have a fixed recommendation for what to say to introduce termination, but I suggest that you think carefully about what your choices may reflect about yourself and may imply for your clients. For example, one intern announced termination to all of his clients by saying "I have some bad news to discuss with you today." This statement assumes both that the intern knows what the client's reactions will be and that the news will necessarily be received as "bad." Introducing the subject this way is likely to make it much more difficult to then review the positive gains the client has made or to explore the potential for further growth during the termination process.

My preference is, first, to be sure to address what has happened in the immediate session to that point. Then, proceed in a more neutral, open-ended fashion, to introduce the news about termination and offer a chance to discuss it. For example, an intern might say: "From what you've said so far today it sounds like. . . . That is something we may need to talk some more about, but today I need to raise another issue and I want to be sure we have time to talk about it. On (date) I will be finishing this internship, so we need to begin to discuss what that means and what you will want to do from that point. We should also talk about what you feel about the fact that we'll be finishing our work together."

At that point I usually leave some silence, sometimes a rather lengthy silence, to allow the client to think about what has been said. Even though I may have some idea about how a client will react, I do not presume the client's immediate reaction nor do I impose a plan of my own design. This practice allows clients to respond in whatever way they need and it encourages clients to be in control of their future. I will, of course, discuss clients' responses and plans with them as they respond, but I think it important to let the response and plans be the clients' own, not something I impose upon them.

ISSUES TO ADDRESS IN TERMINATION

Assuming the preparatory steps described above have been taken and sufficient time is allowed, termination should address several key topics. These include: progress the client has made, future directions for the client either in or out of therapy, and reactions to the termination process itself. Within these areas it is important to address cognitive, affective, and behavioral components of the client's reactions and plans.

Quintana (1993) suggests that:

Termination is a particularly critical opportunity for clients and therapists to update or transform their relationship to incorporate clients' growth. For this transformation to occur, clients need to acknowledge the steps they have taken toward more mature functioning. Perhaps most important is for therapists to acknowledge and validate their sense of accomplishment. (p. 430)

Quintana goes on to suggest that techniques for termination should help clients "internalize" positive images of themselves. Such images, developed from therapy and successful termination, could help clients cope with future crises.

Similar recommendations are offered by Penn (1990), who recommends that therapists, ". . . focus with patients on the therapeutic tools that they have grown to use over time and therefore take away with them" (p. 383). Penn suggests that therapists can facilitate this process by citing specific examples in which patients made connections, observed and questioned their own behaviors, or did other work in therapy for themselves. Therapists and clients may also review specific instances in which the client thought, felt, or acted differently than would have been the case prior to therapy. Such concrete examples help strengthen the client's sense that changes have, in fact, occurred and will likely continue after therapy ends.

Recognizing gains is clearly important, but it can be equally necessary to acknowledge any frustrations that may exist over ongoing problems or unrealized goals. This realistic appraisal helps clients and therapists recognize the reality that no treatment can "solve" all of a person's problems and no relationship is without its difficulties.

Acknowledging difficulties becomes especially important if clients will be transferred to other therapists. Gavazzi and Anderson (1987) observe that the outgoing therapist may not want to admit any shortcomings in therapy or identify unmet goals. Similarly, the client may not want to raise these issues, in part so that they will not appear disloyal to the therapist. At the same time, however, if therapy up to the present is not reviewed openly and honestly, subsequent treatment may be undermined before it begins. Gavazzi and Anderson state the matter directly:

Quite simply, it is the outgoing therapist's job as translator to address the shortcomings of the past therapeutic effort in order to establish just what has been accomplished and what has not. (p. 152)

The one caveat I would place on this is that therapists must be careful not to "blind-side" clients by suddenly confronting them at the end of treatment with a list of shortcomings. One can imagine the deleterious effect it could have if a client has been encouraged to review his or her accomplishments and progress only to then be confronted by the therapist identifying all the things that have not been accomplished or the areas in which personal improvement is still wanting. Thus, although it can be important and valuable to acknowledge frustrations or shortcomings in therapy, this must be done with discretion and sensitivity.

In addition to evaluating the gains and challenges of therapy, termination work should also address the reactions of therapist and client to ending their relationship. Earlier in this chapter we explored some of the feelings and thoughts therapists and clients might experience as therapy ends. The closing sessions of treatment are a time to discuss and work through those reactions. Penn (1990) points out that patients may be reluctant to discuss their feelings about termination. To help them do so, she recommends asking "what they are feeling" rather than "if they have any feelings." The first question assumes there will be some feelings without presuming what those feelings are. This, as Penn notes, makes it less risky for the clients to begin to talk about how they are feeling about termination.

While encouraging therapists to provide opportunities for patients to verbalize their reactions, Penn also reminds us that patients may express their emotions indirectly. Apparent changes in attitude toward the therapist, missed or late appointments, sudden appeals for more help, or sudden denials of the need for further assistance, may all be manifestations of underlying reactions to ending the therapy relationship. Penn urges therapists to be alert for such disguised responses and to help patients recognize and understand them.

TECHNIQUES FOR TERMINATION

Beyond the usual methods of therapy, several authors have proposed specific techniques to bring out and help deal with issues relating to termination. Gutheil (1993) relates therapy termination to other sorts of endings or transitions and notes that rituals are often used to demarcate and aid in such transitions. Common elements of rituals that Gutheil sees as relevant to termination include:

1. The sense of specialness;
2. The connection to both past and future;
3. The ability to hold both sides of the contradiction;
4. The capacity to deal with emotions; and
5. The communication component. (p. 167)

Having identified these functions of rituals, Gutheil proceeds to describe three termination procedures and how they serve each function. The procedures she identifies are evaluation, goal attainment scaling, and the "eco-map." Space does not allow a thorough review of each technique here, but several of Gutheil's key points are worth mentioning.

Gutheil offers the insight that although evaluation is often viewed as a research or program assessment tool for measuring therapy effectiveness, well-constructed evaluations can also serve to promote useful discussion between therapists and clients. Topics that evaluations raise include where treatment has gone, what has worked and what has not, how each person feels about termination, and what lies ahead. Gutheil notes that the objective nature of a structured evaluation,

> . . . can be used as a bridge to the subjective discussion of the loss and the gains. If there are fewer gains than the client hoped for, the objective discussion can give permission to move into the expression of anger or frustration as termination approaches. (p. 171)

To help this "bridging" come about, several questions are proposed for inclusion in the evaluation process. These include:

> What did it feel like to ask for help?
> What did you like best about our work together?
> What did you like least about our work together?
> What will you miss about our work together?
> What do you look forward to when we stop working together? (p. 171)

These questions clearly promote discussion of many of the key elements of termination that have been addressed in this chapter. They also fit well within the previously mentioned characteristics of rituals as described by Gutheil and with the earlier discussion of client reactions to termination.

Accompanying her endorsement of evaluation and other "termination rituals," Gutheil also cautions that the use of rituals should facilitate, not "bind" the expression of emotion. If therapist or client become "stuck in the procedure" of the ritual, they may lose sight of its purpose. Gutheil stresses that termination rituals, like all rituals, should be used as means to ends, not ends in themselves. Citing Fox (1992), Gutheil emphasizes that it is important to address both the accomplishment of therapeutic tasks and the fact that the therapy relationship is ending.

> Clients may have achieved their goals yet not want to end the relationship. If attention is focused exclusively on goal achievement and the accompanying gains, the pain of the impending separation may be overlooked. (p. 173)

EXERCISE

Think of relationships that have ended in your own life and any "rituals" that might have been part of that process. What functions did such rituals serve for you and the others in the relationship? What similar or different functions would need to be served by rituals to conclude therapy, and what types of activities might best serve those functions?

TRANSFERRING CLIENTS TO OTHER THERAPISTS

Unless the work of therapy is considered to be completed, therapists who must end their work with clients typically make arrangements with other therapists to take the case. Just as problems can arise when therapists terminate their own work with clients, the process of transitioning from one therapist to another also presents a number of challenges that must be managed therapeutically. Wapner et al. (1986) provide an informative review of literature regarding transfer. They note that the issue of transferring clients tends to receive insufficient attention in training but often presents a problem for clients. They also suggest that clients who are transferred between therapists tend to terminate prematurely with the second therapist.

Gavazzi and Anderson (1987) listed a number of common pitfalls that can impede effective case transfers. Several of these have already been alluded to. For example, if departing therapists do not deal effectively with their own issues about termination, they may undermine the possibility of the client building a therapeutic relationship with the new therapist. As Gavazzi and Anderson described this process in family therapy, the departing therapist may attempt to:

> . . . set him/herself up as an absent but integral member of the clients' system. Such a maneuver potentially guarantees the clients' unswerving loyalty to their previous therapist and may possibly block further work toward change with the new therapist. (p. 148)

A second obstacle to effective transition is the tendency for the current therapist to allow too little time for transfer work with the incoming therapist. Just as therapists often allow too little time to work through their own termination with clients, they may allot insufficient time to work with the incoming therapist. I have seen many instances in which outgoing interns attempted to transfer their entire case load to another person during a one-hour meeting. Such transactions typically involve exchanging case files, offering a few descriptive phrases about each client and their therapy, then moving on to describe the next client in comparably limited terms. Gavazzi and Anderson advise against this practice, noting that unless sufficient time is provided for personal interaction between incoming and departing therapists, subtle aspects of the therapy process are likely to be lost in the rush.

Another common obstacle to transitions is the failure of the outgoing therapist to ask or discuss with the client how the client feels about switching to a new therapist. Therapists may simply assume their clients are still in need of treatment without checking with the clients to see how they feel about the matter. Again, this practice may reflect therapists' attempts to assuage their own guilt about leaving. Whatever the therapist's motives, the results are not likely to be positive. At the very least, the client who is transferred without discussion or consent will not feel respected, and this feeling could undo much of the therapy work that has been accomplished up to that point. Further, if a client reluctantly accedes to seeing another therapist, it is unlikely that interaction will be successful.

TOWARD EFFECTIVE TRANSFERS

Based on cluster analyses of survey results, Robison et al. (1986) identified four different types of reassignment practice that typify the process in college and university counseling centers. Briefly, their results showed that practices differ in terms of how clients are involved and the types of practices therapists follow in preparing clients for transfer. Some centers provide almost no preparation and give the client no say in selecting subsequent therapists. Others offer extensive preparation and involve the client working jointly with their present therapist to select and transition to a new therapist. Robinson et al. draw no firm conclusions about which practice is best, but they recommend further research to determine how different strategies affect client outcome.

Gavazzi and Anderson (1987) suggest that one of the keys to successful transfers is the ability of the current therapists to fill the role of "translator" as they help build connections and exchange information with the incoming therapist. Four key phases are identified within the transfer process. These are:

> 1) preparing clients for termination and transfer; 2) orienting clients and incoming therapist with one another; 3) bringing clients and incoming therapist together; and 4) facilitating the continuation of the therapeutic process. (p. 145)

The first task in relation to transferring patients is to determine which patients are in need of, and would likely benefit from, continued therapy. As noted earlier, it is a mistake to assume that all patients will desire transfer to other therapists. It can also be a mistake for the therapist to unilaterally determine that a client does not need or want further treatment. If transfer is a viable option at a given placement, one recommendation is for interns or therapists to raise the possibility of transfer to all clients as part of the termination process. The option can then be discussed jointly between therapist and client.

In regard to discussing transfers with clients, Gavazzi and Anderson point out that clients' reactions to working with another therapist are not necessarily indicative of desires to make further changes. It is possible that clients still feel a need for further work but the prospect of starting over with a new therapist is not appealing. It may also happen that if termination with a current therapist is not handled well, clients will be reluctant to risk a relationship with someone new. This latter point highlights the fact that transferring clients to other therapists in no way eliminates the need for the present therapist to deal effectively with termination issues. Indeed, if anything, the prospect of transferring only makes the termination more important because it will have a direct bearing on how well the subsequent therapy proceeds.

If clients are willing to work with another therapist, or if they are willing to consider the possibility but are unsure, the outgoing therapist's next task is to help orient the clients to the new therapist and vice versa. Clients, as well as incoming therapists, will have a number of questions and the outgoing therapists should help address these. As discussed earlier, this part of the process must involve more than a mere exchange of content information, case notes, etc. Gavazzi and Anderson suggest that the departing therapist should anticipate and explore client concerns, address these with the clients, and communicate them to the incoming therapist.

The third phase of the transfer process involves the initial meeting between the incoming therapist and clients. Some therapists prefer that the outgoing therapist participate in these initial sessions. Others prefer to allow the new therapist and clients to meet separately. Whichever course is chosen, the outgoing therapist must in this phase begin to relinquish the role of therapist in order to allow a new relationship to build.

Also important to this phase is the process of exploring comparisons between therapists as individuals and their therapy styles. Clients will inevitably look for similarities as well as differences between the therapists and it may be helpful for both therapists to discuss these differences openly and noncritically. I find it helpful in this phase for therapists to remember, and gently to remind clients, that the "real work" of therapy will continue to reside with the client. Different therapists will have different ways of aiding this work, but clients can and should continue with the work that has already been initiated even though the therapists have changed. When I am in the role of incoming therapist, I find it helpful to encourage clients to let me know if something I am doing clashes in some way with their expectations or needs. By sincerely offering this opportunity I hope to reassure clients that my aim is to assist their progress, not to compete in some way with their former therapist. This also takes some pressure off of me, because I do not have to worry that I am going to do something at odds with what has been happening in therapy. Should I in fact do so, clients have the chance to let me know so we can discuss the issue together.

As termination issues are worked through and the client builds a relationship with the new therapist, it eventually becomes time for the present therapist to say good-bye. This should probably be done with just the outgoing therapist and the client present. An important task of this meeting is to "solidify the fact that the outgoing therapist and client will not see each other again" (Gavazzi & Anderson, 1987, p. 153).

Interns often find it difficult to accept and state that the ending of therapy is indeed the ending of the relationship. Because they may feel guilty about terminating and are concerned about what will happen after they leave, interns sometimes try to "reassure" clients by promising to visit, write, or

in some other way maintain contact. Such promises may be made with the intent of helping the clients feel better, but generally the real function is to help interns cope with their own feelings. I recommend that interns avoid such practices.

There are two important problems with offering to stay in contact with clients after termination. First, if continued contact in fact occurs, it can inhibit the relationship of clients with their new therapist. Second, in spite of their best intentions at the time of termination, the reality is that in almost every case the intern will not be able to maintain the kind of contact they may have promised. After an internship or rotation ends, interns move on to other things and cannot find the time to keep in touch with former clients. The result is that the intern feels guilty at not keeping up his or her end of the promise and clients feel let down.

Even though it may be difficult, interns would do better to deal with endings as precisely that: endings. If this is hard, working with peers or supervisors may be helpful, but avoid the temptation to deny the reality of termination by making promises that will not be fulfilled.

Before concluding the discussion of transferring cases, it should be added that, although the focus has been primarily on situations in which clients will be continuing in therapy, this does not mean the issue of transfer should be ignored for clients who do not elect to work with another therapist at the time. Many clients will, in fact, later return for additional therapy. In anticipation of this possibility, it can be very useful to at least introduce them to another therapist and briefly discuss their case with that person. That way, both will be more prepared should the client choose to seek therapy some time in the future.

REFERENCES

Edelson, M. (1963). *The termination of intensive psychotherapy.* Springfield, IL: Charles C. Thomas.

Fair, S. M., & Bressler J. M. (1992). Therapist-initiated termination of psychotherapy. *The Clinical Supervisor, 10*(1), 171–189.

Fox, R. (1992). *Elements of the helping process: A guide for clinicians.* Binghamton, NY: Haworth.

Gavazzi, S. M., & Anderson, S. A. (1987). The role of "translator" in the case transfer process. *The American Journal of Family Therapy, 15,* 145–157.

Geller J. D., & Nash, V. (1987). *Termination as experienced by therapists-in-training as viewed by psychiatric residents.* Unpublished manuscript. Yale University, Department of Psychology, New Haven, CT.

Gutheil, I. A. (1993). Rituals and termination procedures. *Smith College Studies in Social Work, 63*(2), 163–176.

McRoy, R. G., Freeman, E. M., & Logan, S. (1986). Strategies for teaching students about termination. *The Clinical Supervisor, 4*(4), 45–56.

Penn. L. S. (1990). When the therapist must leave: Forced termination of psychodynamic therapy. *Professional Psychology: Research and Practice, 21,* 379–384.

Quintana, S. M. (1993). Toward an expanded and updated conceptualization of termination: Implications for short-term, individual psychotherapy. *Professional Psychology: Research and Practice, 24,* 426–432.

Robison, F. F., Hutchinson, R. L., Barrick, A. L., & Uhl, A. N. (1986).

Reassigning clients: Practices used by counseling centers. *Journal of Counseling Psychology, 33,* 465–468.

Siebold, C. (1992). Forced termination: Reconsidering theory and technique. *Smith College Studies in Social Work, 63,* 323–341.

Wapner, J. H., Klein J. G., Friedlander, M. L., & Andrasik, F. J. (1986). Transferring psychotherapy clients: State of the art. *Professional Psychology: Research and Practice, 6,* 492–496.

FINISHING THE INTERNSHIP

The previous chapter focused primarily on the process of termination with clients. This chapter addresses other important elements of finishing the internship. These include such things as concluding the supervisory relationship, bidding farewell to staff members, expressing your appreciation, and requesting letters of recommendation.

Internship opportunities are not easy to come by and the willingness of an agency or individual to accept interns depends on each intern doing quality work and leaving a positive impression. Because future interns depend on the good will of a placement site and staff for their opportunities, it is extremely important that interns attend carefully to how they conclude their placement.

CONCLUDING THE SUPERVISORY RELATIONSHIP

Several things must be accomplished as part of concluding the supervisory relationship. Without reiterating material from the previous chapter, there are a few remaining ideas to introduce in the context of termination with supervisors.

ENSURING THERAPEUTIC TERMINATION WITH CLIENTS

Because there are so many things to attend to in the termination process, it can be very helpful to follow some form of structured format in order to ensure that termination planning is adequate and critical issues are addressed. An instrument that may be very helpful in this regard was developed and tested by Fair and Bressler (1992). The 55-item "Termination Scale" is designed for use by supervisors and trainees before, during, or after the termination process. This instrument includes two subscales, "Termination Planning" and "Emotional Response to Termination." Items within the Termination Scale are answered on a 6-point Likert-type format with responses ranging from strongly disagree to strongly agree. Sample items from the Termination Planning Subscale include:

> I understand what this client wants to accomplish before our last session.
> My supervisor and I have discussed the pros and cons of transferring this client to another therapist when we terminate.
> I have reviewed the other times in this client's life when he or she has ended relationships. (pp. 186–187)

Items from the Emotional Response to Termination Subscale include:

> I feel more burdened with this client than I have previously.

I feel guilty about terminating with this client.
I have more feelings of love for this client than I used to
I more often feel an anxious urgency to cure and help
this client (p. 187–188)

In relation to the topics discussed in the preceding chapter, it should be evident that this instrument addresses many of the key areas and issues of termination. Fair and Bressler suggest that their Termination Scale can serve several functions. Among these are: helping to objectify termination in spite of painful elements, bringing out countertransference feelings, identifying areas for therapist improvement, and providing a structure to conceptualize termination. Use of the scale is also deemed to help supervisors encourage trainees to deal with a process that supervisors know can be challenging emotionally.

EXERCISE

Whether one uses Fair and Bressler's instrument or another, it is helpful to follow some format to be sure one covers all the bases and to review one's own responses to termination. Taking into account what has been said about termination in this and the previous chapter, generate a "checklist" for yourself in which you identify key logistical details about termination. For example, your list might include details regarding notification of clients, arrangements for transfer, etc. Then, generate a second checklist that you can use to help monitor your own emotional reactions to termination and how you are coping with those reactions. When you have completed your own scale, you might want to compare it with Fair and Bressler's to see what they have included that you may have overlooked and vice versa. It would also be helpful to review your ideas with peers, instructors, and supervisors for their feedback.

REVIEWING THE INTERN'S PROGRESS AND AREAS FOR FURTHER GROWTH

An important part of the termination process is to review the progress the client has made in treatment. A comparable process is equally important to the work of concluding supervision. In this process, interns and supervisors should allocate sufficient time to discuss both the development the intern has shown during the placement and any areas in which further growth is needed.

The most common format for reviewing the intern's progress is typically through some type of evaluation procedure. Appendix D presents a form that can be used for evaluations of interns by site supervisors. Although faculty instructors will often ask that such forms be sent directly to them as part of the grading process, the intern and supervisor should first review the evaluation jointly to directly exchange and discuss their ideas and impressions.

Perhaps the most difficult part of the evaluation process is being able to give and accept critical feedback constructively. It is natural for interns to hope to hear nothing but praise from supervisors. It is equally understandable that supervisors would want to give all their interns glowing reviews. Praise is, of course, important, and one hopes that all supervisors will think carefully about and acknowledge the achievements and efforts of even their most challenging interns. At the same time, however, constructive criticism is essential if interns are to develop beyond their existing levels. While praise helps give one the strength and hope to carry on, constructive criticism helps show the directions to be traveled for further progress. Thus, interns are advised to seek and welcome critical feedback as a means of helping identify what they need to work on for the future.

One way to help interns receive criticism constructively is to have them write an evaluation of themselves identifying the things they did well during the placement and areas in which they recognize a need for improvement. Interns can then imagine that their supervisors are not as positive about the intern's strengths and raise a number of additional issues that need work. The purpose of this is to anticipate the affective reaction that accompanies negative feedback in order to better enable the intern to process the feedback cognitively if it comes. This process of self-evaluation also helps set a precedent of personal reflection that should be part of the intern's regular practice throughout his or her career.

EXERCISE

An exercise was just described in which interns are invited to identify their own strengths and weaknesses before meeting with their supervisor to discuss their evaluations. If you do this exercise yourself, be particularly aware of your affective reaction as you imagine as vividly as possible some of the critical things your supervisor might say. Notice any feelings of defensiveness, hurt, or other responses that could interfere with your ability to receive the comments constructively. If you detect such responses, practice relaxing and listening attentively without feeling a need to respond or defend. As part of this imagery exercise, you might also imagine yourself receiving critical feedback yet still thanking the supervisor for giving you his or her impressions. This may not be easy, and it does not necessarily mean you must agree with all the feedback, but it will help you be more open to at least hearing what your supervisor has to say.

FEEDBACK TO SUPERVISORS

As a supervisor, I believe feedback should be mutual. I encourage interns to tell me what they thought I did well as a supervisor and ways in which I could have done better or can improve in the future. This process helps me become a better supervisor and it gives the interns an opportunity to practice giving honest feedback. Giving mutual feedback also helps to bring better closure to the relationship. If the communication is only one directional, interns may be left with a feeling of unfinished business. Talking about their impressions of supervision helps reduce the feeling that something is left unsaid or incomplete.

If you have an opportunity to give your impressions to your supervisor, try to keep in mind the principles we have discussed about giving and receiving constructive feedback. Supervisors are human just like anyone else, and they are always glad to receive positive reviews. At the same time, well-intentioned and sensitively communicated criticism can also be welcomed.

Because there is an inherent imbalance in the power structure of the relationship between supervisors and interns, interns may be well advised to think carefully about how they deliver any negative comments to supervisors. If a supervisor invites you to offer your impressions, it is probably a good idea to begin by clarifying what the supervisor is really requesting. You might tactfully inquire about the specific kinds of information the supervisor is interested in. The response to this question can help you determine how best to phrase your comments. Whatever the response, it is a good idea to present your impressions in a way that the supervisor is most likely to take well.

ENDING THE SUPERVISORY RELATIONSHIP

Even as they attend to all the tasks that have been described above and in the previous chapter, interns and supervisors are also involved in the process of concluding their personal relationship with one another. Depending on the level and nature of the relationship, this may be a very simple matter or it could be quite emotional. Whichever is the case, relationship issues should be addressed as part of concluding the supervisory relationship.

Unfortunately, in many cases, neither the supervisor nor the intern raises this issue. The reason is probably that it is not easy to do. Discussing termination issues with clients, ensuring that case notes are in order, and even the process of evaluating the intern's clinical performance are all easier than dealing with how the intern and supervisor feel about one another and about the conclusion of their relationship. Nevertheless, to the extent that the supervisory termination is a model for therapy termination, and if it is accepted that dealing with relationship issues is a necessary part of terminating therapy, those same issues should also be addressed in termination.

The breadth of feelings expressed at termination ranges from bland to profound. I have supervised interns with whom lasting relationships were developed and with whom I still maintain contact. On the other hand, in some cases it seems I have scarcely known interns and they have known little about me. Talking about these issues at termination helps bring a resolution to the supervision relationship. This resolution makes it easier for both intern and supervisor to move on.

As you think about your relationship with your supervisor and about discussing that relationship during termination, you might want to keep in mind a fundamental difference between your experience and that of your supervisor. It sometimes happens that interns hope to form exceptionally close relationships with supervisors but the intern is disappointed to discover that the supervisor maintains distance or relates primarily in an objective or didactic, as opposed to a friendly or personal, way. There may be many reasons for this. One of the most common is the fact that although the supervisory experience may be unique for the intern, in many instances the supervisor and staff will have worked with numerous interns before and will anticipate more in the future. Thus, an experience that stands out as unique and perhaps profound for the intern may, for the supervisor, be somewhat routine. This does not mean the relationship is unimportant, but it does mean that supervisors may not invest the relationship with the same emotional energy or sense of specialness as interns.

I point this out for two reasons. Because students who are at internship placements often express frustration at not getting closer to their supervisors, it can be helpful for them to understand the dynamics just described. This also helps interns appreciate how clients might have different feelings about termination than do interns or therapists. Once again, understanding the supervisory process helps one understand much about the therapy process.

LETTERS OF RECOMMENDATION

Interns who plan to go on to further studies or employment may want to request letters of recommendation from their supervisors. Because such letters can be exceptionally important, interns should think carefully about requesting them and should follow certain basic courtesies to make the supervisor's task as easy as possible.

REQUESTING LETTERS

The most important thing interns must do if they plan to request a letter is be sure they did the best job/work possible at the internship. If your work was not of the highest level, you might want to think twice about asking for a recommendation. Just as positive letters can be the key to open doors, negative letters may well lock them shut.

Even though you believe your work would likely merit a positive letter, you should not take this for granted. Whenever you are thinking about asking someone for a recommendation on your behalf, and this applies to all settings, before requesting an actual letter it is a good idea to ask the person directly if she or he can write you a supportive letter. You may want to talk about your specific goals with your supervisor and ask how he or she would feel about writing a letter of recommendation. In this process it is very important to be specific about your goals before requesting the letter. The reason is that your supervisor might feel very comfortable about recommending you for a certain type of employment or educational program, but less comfortable supporting other aspirations.

When you do ask for a letter, be attentive to the supervisor's first reaction. If it is immediately enthusiastic and supportive you will probably receive a positive letter. If the supervisor thinks a long time, asks if you have thought of seeking letters from others, or otherwise seems reluctant, it is possible he or she has some hesitation about writing a very supportive letter. If you detect such hesitancy, it is acceptable, indeed probably advisable, to ask about your impression in a tactful but forthright way.

Asking if instructors or supervisors have any doubts or concerns about recommending you might put them on the spot and this can be uncomfortable. On the other hand, if you raise the question it might be easier for them to express any reservations. Most supervisors are reluctant to be as blunt as they perhaps should be when they have reservations about a student. As such, they may speak in vaguely positive terms that would result in a rather lukewarm letter. It is better for you to know this in advance so you can make an informed decision and perhaps select an alternative reference.

Apart from the matter of trying to solicit positive letters, it can be extremely beneficial for you to hear any concerns your supervisor might have. You might want to take that into consideration in your deliberations about what jobs or positions to apply for. If you respect your supervisors and believe they are caring and honest with you, it is worth listening carefully to their feedback and advice. If a supervisor encourages you to pursue a chosen career or plan of study, that can be a heartening boost to your goals. On the other hand, if a supervisor expresses reservations or suggests alternatives, you may wish to reevaluate your aims.

GUIDELINES FOR SOLICITING LETTERS

If supervisors or instructors indicate that they are willing to write a letter on your behalf, you can make their job much easier and increase the chances of a good letter by following a few simple steps. Whenever students request a letter from me, I give them the following set of guidelines that help ensure the students do all they can to prepare forms, envelopes, etc., and give me the information I need to write a strong letter of support.

PROCEDURES FOR THOSE SEEKING LETTERS OF RECOMMENDATION

This following describes my procedures for completing letters of recommendation requested by students.

1. Advance Notice. As a general rule, I require a minimum of two to three weeks advance notice between the time a letter is requested and the time the letter must be postmarked. Please plan ahead to allow at least this amount of time and preferably more. As it often happens that many students request letters at the same time, I may not always be able to get a letter out quickly. Therefore, it is advisable wherever possible to give me at least a month notification.

2. Preparation of Forms. Many programs request that specific forms be completed by reference sources. If you will be asking me to complete forms please make my job easier by completing portions of the form that request the following information: my name, my address at the University, the amount of time we have known each other and the nature of our relationship, my rank, which is _____ in the Department of _____ at _____ College/University. Complete this portion of *every* recommendation form prior to giving them to me. I suggest you type the information as it will be clearer for others to read. Also, be sure to sign your own name on forms where you are asked. This is mandatory. I will not send forms unsigned by students.

3. Preparation of Envelopes. For each program for which you will request a letter, please provide a pre-addressed and stamped envelope. Be sure you have enough postage for the envelope, the forms, and several pages of my letter. Submit the envelope and the aforementioned forms, paper clipped together such that it is easy for me to locate the form and the corresponding envelope for each program.

4. Clear Instructions. If you have any special requests or instructions regarding letters or the completion of forms for different programs, clearly indicate those in a cover letter that you give me when you request letters of recommendation.

5. To Help Me Write the Best Letter Possible in Your Behalf. Please provide me with a brief summary of your academic achievements, internships or field experience, research, service, and other personal accomplishments. In this information please clearly indicate the nature of our contact. In which classes or activities have we worked together, what did you do in the class or activity that was noteworthy, what other achievements stand out? Also, if there are any special points I should note, e.g., GPA in Psych better than overall GPA, etc., please let me know. Finally, if you have written a personal statement for the schools, it might help me to see a copy.

6. Follow-up. To ensure that requested letters are actually sent in a timely fashion, please take it upon yourself to contact me several days before the request is actually due to be sure I have completed and mailed the letters. My schedule is often very busy and I would hate to become so tied up in other things that I fail to send a letter that was requested. You can help me avoid this by following up in a timely fashion.

7. Notification of Results. Although it is not necessary, I would very much appreciate if students for whom I write a letter would let me know the results of their application process. As faculty we are very interested in how our students fare and it is a much appreciated courtesy when students for whom we have written letters write to us and let us know how their applications went.

Thank you for your attention to the details above. If you have any questions, please feel free to ask me.

CONCLUDING RELATIONSHIPS WITH STAFF

Although interns will interact most closely with their immediate supervisors, they will also come into varying degrees of contact with other staff members. As you prepare to conclude your internship, do not forget to let other staff members know you will be leaving. In most instances this may simply involve letting people know a few weeks in advance, perhaps by making a brief announcement at a staff meeting, or by posting some form of notice in a lounge. If closer relationships developed, more personal farewells are in order.

If you have been working with a client who is also being treated by another staff member other than your supervisor, you should schedule some time to meet with that person to discuss the case and your work to date. In this process you must be careful not to violate confidentiality and to consider how information you share might influence the client's future treatment. In most instances the other staff member will appreciate and make beneficial use of whatever information you provide. There may be occasions, however, when a client might feel betrayed if certain information were divulged to other staff members. If you are unsure about what information to share, or how a specific staff member might use that information, consult with your supervisor to discuss the matter beforehand.

LETTERS OF THANKS

Most people who work with interns do so because they care about interns and the profession and want to contribute. Usually, they receive no or minimal compensation for their added responsibilities. Because of this, it is vital that as part of concluding your placement you express your gratitude and appreciation. Unfortunately, writing to say thank you is a custom that is seldom taught and sometimes seems lost. Even though one has said good-bye in person, taking just a few minutes later on to write a letter of thanks is a simple gesture that will be much appreciated.

As a supervisor and instructor I can personally attest to how it can really make my day to receive a card expressing genuine appreciation for my work. It is not something I necessarily expect, but when I receive a card from a student or intern, the hours of work, time taken from other tasks, stress, etc., all feel worthwhile.

I encourage our interns to write several thank you notes after their internship. Obviously, the first should go to the immediate supervisors. These notes need not be lengthy, but at least a few lines acknowledging the supervisor's efforts, time, and what the intern learned as a result would certainly be welcomed. If other individuals in addition to the supervisor were particularly helpful to the intern, special notes of thanks to them would also be in order.

Interns sometimes ask if they should write a thank you even though a supervisor was not "the best." Except in rare instances of extreme conflict, virtually all supervisors should be thanked. Even if supervisors were busier than they had hoped, or other factors somehow diminished the experience, the supervisor still made it possible for the intern to have a real-world learning opportunity. That is valuable and merits an expression of appreciation.

In addition to the note sent to one's immediate supervisor, it is also a good idea to drop a note of thanks to the overall agency director. Although an intern may have had no personal contact with the director, the director is ultimately responsible for what happens in the program and it is through his or her good graces that interns are allowed to train. Recognizing this and acknowledging the work of your immediate supervisor will please both the director and supervisor.

Next, I suggest writing a "group" thank you addressed to all the staff the intern worked with at the placement. These notes typically consist of one or two lines and are addressed "To everyone at. . . ." This kind of note is often posted on a staff bulletin board for all to see. Again, it is a small gesture but it helps everyone you worked with feel appreciated and acknowledged.

The other person to whom you may wish to send a note is your faculty instructor. Whether or not the instructor had extensive contact with you during the internship, faculty instructors do a great deal of work "behind the scenes" helping to arrange for placements, keeping in touch with site supervisors, resolving conflicts, etc. Faculty are like anyone else and would certainly welcome your thanks.

Finally, I also want to suggest that if someone was especially helpful to you it would be nice to keep them in mind down the road as you progress in your training or work. Just as thank-you notes right after an internship are much appreciated, people value learning what happens to their interns over the long run. It is gratifying to receive a letter saying that an intern has gone on in some way and that the efforts of supervisors, instructors, and others contributed to that. Because it is easy to get occupied with other things and let matters like this slip away, you may want to find a strategy to remind yourself in the future to get in touch with those who helped you in the past. Interns who keep personal schedule books might write a note in a yearly planner. Others might put a memo several months away on a calendar. Other creative possibilities are to leave notes in places you might discover later, such as dictionaries or other reference works. Whether or not and how you leave such notes is, of course, up to you, but some kind of follow up correspondence is a nice gesture. This is especially in order if you have asked someone for a letter of recommendation. They will want to know how things turned out for you and it can be fun for you to fill them in.

REFERENCES

Fair, S. M., & Bressler, J. M. (1992). Therapist-initiated termination of psychotherapy. *The Clinical Supervisor, 10,* 171–189.

CHAPTER 14

FRUSTRATIONS, LESSONS, DISCOVERIES, AND JOY

At the conclusion of their internship placement, many interns feel a strong sense of accomplishment and satisfaction. They have enjoyed the opportunity to work with clients, have encountered professionals whom they respect and admire, and they are pleased with their own work and what they have learned. This is the ideal. On the other hand, many interns also experience a sense of frustration and disillusionment as they end their internship.

Whatever your experience, this chapter is offered as a way to help put the internship into perspective. The comments that follow are based on impressions gathered from students, interns, supervisors, instructors, and during my own experience from the past twenty years. I begin by describing certain experiences and lessons that can dim one's enthusiasm for the profession. Then, I conclude by offering some more positive thoughts that may help you keep perspective and keep your spirits up through the hard times that inevitably come with any profession.

LEARNING FROM WHATEVER HAPPENS

Whatever happens at your internship, remember that it is just one experience. Do not make judgments about all settings, staff, clients, or yourself based on a very limited sample. Even in the worst settings, with the most difficult clients, and most pathological staff members, there are valuable lessons to be learned. You may actually hate a certain setting and want to get out as soon as possible, but that does not mean you should give up or that the experience was a waste of time.

To help you get a handle on what might frustrate or trouble you about your internship, I offer the following list of "lessons" that eventually occur to us all, but are never pleasant. The point of the list is not to add to whatever woes you may already have discovered on your own. Rather, it is to validate some of what you may have encountered already or may experience in the future.

EXERCISE

Before reading my ideas, write your own impressions of the negative and positive lessons you have learned during your internship experience. Try to identify some of the things you have learned about people, systems, the function and outcome of treatment, and yourself as a person and as a helping professional.

LESSONS WE WISH WERE NOT TRUE

THE PEOPLE IN THE PROFESSION

1. Not everyone in the helping professions is equally able to help others. There are some people who are grossly incompetent. For some clients, tasks, or situations, we must include ourselves in the incompetent category.
2. Very few people who are in fact incompetent are willing to acknowledge that fact. Instead, most are terribly defensive about their skills and their work and many believe themselves to be outstanding and gifted professionals.
3. Not everyone in the helping professions is really there to help others. Regardless of what they may profess outwardly, some are in the field primarily to satisfy their own needs. In some instances, this means they will act in ways that may be detrimental to clients, their agency, and to you if they stand to benefit as a result.
4. For some people, honesty, openness, caring, and learning are not as important as power, status, appearance, and control. When working with these people, many of the things you assume are the right thing to do may have exactly the opposite effect you intended.
5. The people described in 3 and 4 above will probably not be interested in changing themselves. Either they do not think of themselves as just described, or they accept that description but do not find anything wrong with their view of the world. They may also think everyone else is just like them or worse.
6. Not everyone will like or respect you, no matter who you are or what you do.

THE SYSTEMS IN WHICH WE WORK

1. Ultimately, any system is only as good as the people who operate and use it. No system can succeed if it is run by incompetent or negatively motivated people.
2. Frequently, the people described in 3, 4, and 5 of the preceding section are in charge of systems.
3. Even well-intentioned programs run by healthy, caring people sometimes do not work efficiently or well. Sometimes the very best efforts of the very best people are thwarted by bad systems or incompetent people running them.

4. Mental illness and a host of other social ills are given very little attention and real support in our society. There is a lot of talk and substantial sums of money are spent, but much of this is symbolic. In relation to where other monies and energy are allocated, what does go to these needs is a drop in the bucket.
5. Many of the problems we deal with as human service workers are rooted in the larger social and economic conditions of our society. Unless the root causes are addressed, systems implemented to deal with the effects are likely to have only limited success.
6. Prevention would work better than most treatments, but money for prevention is very hard to come by and most people do not want to take personal responsibility for prevention.
7. Coordination between different service systems can be nightmarishly complicated, inconsistent, and inefficient.
8. Sometimes rules and policies seem stupid but are based on sound reasons. Sometimes they are just stupid.
9. Much of your professional life, far too much, will be spent in meetings in which little gets accomplished.

THE CLIENTS WITH WHOM WE WORK

1. Not all clients are motivated to get "better."
2. Not all clients are decent and likable people.
3. Some clients are self-serving predators. They will steal from other people, will lie to you, and would probably hurt or even kill you if they thought it would help them.
4. Some clients do not look, dress, act, talk, or even smell very nice.
5. Some clients are well motivated but simply lack the mental or emotional capacity to accomplish what they need to do to help themselves.
6. There will be many clients who are indeed decent, deserving, and well-motivated people who, for a variety of reasons, you will be unable to help no matter how hard you try.
7. Some clients encounter such incredibly bad luck that it is hard to imagine how they survive. It is also hard to believe that life is in any way "fair." Simply put, it isn't. Part of what we are about is trying to make the unfairness livable.

THE NATURE OF THE PROBLEMS

1. The kinds of people and problems we deal with are often overwhelmingly complex. They include psychological, social, economic, physical, and genetic factors. This is one of the reasons treatment is so challenging.
2. You will have clients who are in desperate straits because of the social system in which they live. Unemployment, lack of insurance, abusive families, sexism,

racism, dangerous neighborhoods, and more all add to whatever other factors the client may present and few if any of these factors can be dealt with directly by you.

3. In spite of what we might wish to believe, everyone may be created equal in rights, but not everyone is created equal in abilities or temperament. Genetics plays a far bigger role than we realize in shaping who we are, and in causing or contributing to certain illnesses. Some clients are apparently predisposed to become alcoholic, schizophrenic, bipolar, etc. Others will simply be less able mentally to prosper in this world or to comprehend certain therapy approaches. Still others will be quite well endowed intellectually, but their emotional responsiveness will be minimal.

4. In the past twenty years, our understanding of biochemistry and behavior has increased immensely but it still pales in comparison to what there is left to discover and what we need to know to help our clients. Many of the illnesses clients present have biological bases or will result in biochemical changes, yet our ability to understand and correct the condition is meager at best. On the other hand, many of the illnesses that are often treated biochemically have their roots in situational factors that, if changed, would largely "cure" the individual problems.

5. Chance, pure dumb luck, can make everything else irrelevant. A perfectly healthy individual is in a car accident and his or her life is changed forever. A woman is raped on her way home from work. A client who is unstable but coping loses his job and girlfriend on the same day and it pushes him over the edge. You can try to reduce some of these things by changing systems and people, but a degree of luck will always be present and can impact us all in profound and sometimes terrible ways.

6. Many of the problems you deal with will be part of repeating cycles that are difficult to interrupt. A father who beats his children was, himself, beaten as a child. Children of alcoholic parents become alcoholic themselves. A child who lives in poverty and whose parent is in jail winds up committing crimes her- or himself.

7. Some of the problems we deal with are givens of existence. As such, we must not only help clients deal with those problems, we must deal with the same problems ourselves. Death, relationships, meaninglessness, responsibility, freedom, and uncertainty are part of being alive for client and clinician alike. We, too, are vulnerable.

THE LIMITS TO OUR KNOWLEDGE AND TOOLS

1. In the face of the lessons mentioned thus far, you will often feel you have no idea what the real problem is or how to treat it.

2. There will be times when you have a clear theoretical explanation about the nature of the real problem and its treatment and you are sure you are right. Some of these times, you will be dead wrong.

3. In the face of the lessons mentioned thus far you will often feel you know exactly what the real problem is but it is part of the socioeconomic structure or other system that you are powerless to influence or to change soon enough for a particular client.

4. Blaming the system rarely helps if that is all you do.

5. Change takes time. In fact, it often takes lots of time. You may never see the long-term effects, good or bad, of what you do for individuals or for the society.

6. Often, no one, not the client, their family, their friends, you, or anyone else really knows what is going on with a client. Yet, somehow, you are expected to proceed anyway and do the best you can.

7. Many in the public, including perhaps your friends, family, and other professionals, will doubt the validity or value of what you do. This may be due to lack of knowledge, but it may also be due to very good reasons. This can make it hard to believe in what you do yourself.

LESSONS ABOUT OURSELVES

1. You will not always live up to your own ideals as a professional or as a person.

2. You will not always be as competent as you would like.

3. There will be times when you do not work as hard as you believe you should. There will be times when you work too hard.

4. You will find yourself doing many of the negative things you believe clients should not do.

5. You will find yourself not doing the positive things you tell your clients to do.

6. There will be times when your own conduct could lead others to wonder about your motives and intentions.

7. There will be many times when you wonder if it is all worth it or if you should be doing something else.

LESSONS ABOUT THE LESSONS

The lessons above could easily lead one to abandon the field entirely or to stay with it but become cynical, jaded, and part of the problems rather than the solutions. Do not let this happen to you.

The lessons above are only part of the picture. You need to know that part because it is real and you will have to learn to deal with it. The good news is that you can learn to deal effectively with even the most difficult of these realities. Further, in spite of the negative aspects of clinical work, there are many positive rewards and, in balance, these tend to outweigh the negatives. It is an honor and a privilege to get to do the kind of work we do. Even in the most down times it is worth remembering that and finding the joy.

DISCOVERIES AND JOY

PEOPLE IN THE PROFESSION

1. There are many fine people in the profession. They are drawn to human services out of genuine concern and caring for others and they have dedicated their lives and talents toward that end. In many cases, these people could make far more money doing something else, but they have chosen instead to pursue occupations that serve others.
2. People differ in skills and wisdom. By working closely with those more skilled than yourself, and by continually being open to learning, your own skills can rapidly advance. By working patiently with others and sharing you own knowledge, you can help others learn and grow. We can all pass on what has been given to us.
3. Perhaps more than any other profession, the human services offer an expectation and opportunity for personal exploration and growth. This is not just about knowledge and technical skills, it is about who we are as people.
4. If you have certain natural abilities, do your best, work hard, listen, and learn, you will probably get along with most folks and will make some wonderful friends along the way. You may also do some excellent work for your clients and their lives will be better as a result.

THE SYSTEMS IN WHICH WE WORK

1. No system is perfect, but most can be improved by dedicated and competent effort.
2. Some systems really do help people. They may not be perfect, but without them the lives of many would be much worse.
3. It is possible to gradually change the root causes of problems. That process may involve personal change and political action alongside clinical work. The history of civilization is a history of painfully slow advances in how we care for and treat one another, but advances are indeed made and each of us can contribute to them.
4. Change in systems begins with changes in ourselves.

THE CLIENTS WITH WHOM WE WORK

1. The task of personal understanding and growth is difficult and frightening. Although some clients will be unmotivated to change, many will show great courage in the face of incredible obstacles.
2. Some of your clients will be extremely grateful for the help you provide as they struggle to improve their lives.
3. It is a privilege and responsibility to work with people who entrust a portion of their lives to our care. We must respect that responsibility and do our best to honor it.
4. Some of our clients will have lived lives and learned lessons that we have never dreamed of. We may learn more from working clients than the clients benefit from their work with us.

THE NATURE OF THE PROBLEMS

1. The problems we deal with are extremely complex, but little by little we make strides in understanding them. This is how all knowledge progresses. We may not know everything we would like, but we do know some things and that can be very helpful. Our task is not to know everything already, but to apply what we have learned and keep moving forward.
2. Social change is slow, but change does happen thanks to the dedication and sacrifice of a few individuals working for the good of many. You can be part of that change process. To paraphrase Joe Hill, "Don't whine; organize!!"
3. Differences in abilities and traits may be genetically influenced, but people are not ruled entirely by genes. Even those with severe limitations in many areas have certain abilities that bring them joy. Nurturing those abilities and strengthening others can make some extraordinarily challenging lives more pleasant. That can be a very rewarding goal.
4. Life is uncertain and bad things do happen to good people. For some that is cause for despair, for others it is the reason we must make the most of every moment. The choice is ours. Watch out for simplistic answers.

THE LIMITS TO OUR KNOWLEDGE AND TOOLS

1. Although our tools are limited, overall, the research evidence shows that the treatment we offer can and does make significant positive differences in people's lives.
2. Differences in theories can be confusing and frustrating. Given the complexity of human existence, we should not expect it to be otherwise. Each theory adds to our understanding and can help us in our work. The trick is to use theories as tools and fit them to our clients rather than fitting clients to our theories.
3. No matter how frustrated you might become with the limits to knowledge or to your techniques, you are not alone. Every job or activity eventually has its limits. The challenge is to learn to deal with them constructively. That, indeed, is the challenge of life itself.

LESSONS ABOUT OURSELVES

1. You do not have to be absolutely perfect in order to help people. Some of your own most difficult struggles can help you find insights that will later serve your clinical work well.

2. You will make mistakes but for the most part clients are resilient and if you do your best and recognize your limits things will work out.

3. Each of us can make changes, but change takes time. As you work to improve yourself you will come to understand the task your clients face.

4. There will be times when you wonder if it is all worth it, but there will also be times when it is crystal clear that something you have done has made a difference. Moments like that are rare enough in any work. When they happen in clinical work they are especially valuable because people's lives are affected for the better.

5. You must find joy in your clinical work, but you must also find it elsewhere in your life. Because clinical work is so important, it will bring with it both highs and lows. Therefore, you must be dedicated as a clinician, but do not let that be the only thing that brings you satisfaction. Take care of yourself so you can care for others.

CLOSING COMMENTS

Throughout the book, from the opening chapter to this sentence, I have encouraged interns to be open to new learning and to seek consultation frequently. Now it is my opportunity to put that advice into practice one more time myself. A book of this sort is never really finished. As soon as I write the final words for this page, I will begin to gather information from journals, colleagues, and students for the next edition. This is where I have the chance to learn from you, the reader.

If you found this book helpful, if there are parts that were not useful, if I left things out that should have been included, if you have any suggestions for improvements, or if you care to share any personal anecdotes, I would welcome your input. You can write me at the address below and if you include your address I will try to get back in touch with you.

My goal in writing this book was to contribute to the quality of internship training and thereby enhance the quality of the helping professions. I hope that goal has been met and I welcome your contributions to making the next edition still more useful.

Thank you for reading this book, I hope it has been helpful. I wish you success in your future studies and work.

Brian N. Baird, Ph.D.
Department of Psychology
Pacific Lutheran University
Tacoma, WA 98447

A P P E N D I X   A

INTERNSHIP SELECTION CHECKLIST

This checklist is designed to help interns and supervisors select placements that will best meet the intern's educational and training needs.

PREVIOUS FIELD EXPERIENCE
List any previous field experience you have had.

ACADEMIC CLASSES OR SKILLS TRAINING
List any coursework or skills training that would be relevant to an internship. (E.g., Human Development, Abnormal Psychology, Theories of Counseling, Assessment, etc.)

TIME
Carefully considering the requirements for your program and the various other commitments in your life, how much time can you realistically allocate to this placement each week? Please be specific about days and times you will or will not be available.

TREATMENT SETTING
What treatment settings would best match your abilities and interests at this time?

Indicate any prior course work or experience relating to such settings.

CLIENTS SERVED

What types of clients, e.g., ages, presenting concerns, ethnic or cultural backgrounds, etc., are you most interested in working with at this point in your training?

Indicate any prior courses, training, or experience working with this group.

TREATMENT APPROACH

What theoretical orientation or treatment approach is most interesting to you at present?

Indicate any prior courses, training, or experience working with this approach.

LEARNING OPPORTUNITIES

What sorts of learning opportunities do you hope to have at your internship and what level of involvement and responsibility would you like? For example, you might want to learn about intake interviews by first observing, then doing part of them with supervision, then doing a complete interview, and then doing a complete interview with a written report. List any opportunities you think would be interesting here. Also note if you already have some experience in an area.

SUPERVISION STYLE AND PERSONALITY

What personal qualities of a supervisor do you think you would work with best?

What personal styles might challenge you but help you learn?

CAREER PLANS

What experiences will be most useful in helping your candidacy for a job or academic admission?

Safety and Risks

List any concerns you might have about the limits of your abilities or knowledge.

Identify any concerns or questions you have about your personal safety or risks relating to placements.

Peers

Are there any other interns with whom you would particularly like to be assigned? If so, please indicate who and briefly describe your reasons.

Are there any other interns with whom you would particularly NOT like to be assigned. If so, please indicate who and briefly describe your reasons.

Other Comments

Please identify or discuss any issues that you have not had an opportunity to address above.

PLACEMENT INFORMATION FORM

Instructions: This form is designed to provide information about agencies and programs interested in offering placements to interns. Copies of this form will be kept on file for students to review when seeking internships. Please answer all items and feel free to include any additional information that you think important. Thank you for your time and interest in working with us.

Placement Name: _____

Placement Address: _____

_____

_____

_____

Phone: _____-_____-_____

Contact Person: _____

Position Title: _____

Phone: _____-_____-_____ ext._____

Please provide a brief description of the services provided and the clients served by your program or institution:

_____

_____

_____

Please indicate the qualifications you would like interns to have.
Degree Level or Year in School:
Freshman Sophomore Junior Senior   BA/BS   MA/MS   Ph.D./PsyD./Ed.D.

Majors Acceptable: _____

Prior Experience: _____

_____

_____

Other Required Qualifications: _____

(continued)

Briefly describe the learning opportunities, responsibilities, and expectations for interns at your placement site:

_____

_____

_____

_____

Please indicate what days and times are available for interns to be at your placement. If you require that interns be present on certain days or times, please indicate those times:

_____

_____

_____

_____

Briefly describe the supervision opportunities available to interns:

Supervisor Name: _____

Supervisor Position: _____

Frequency of Available Supervision: _____

Supervisor's Theoretical Orientation: _____

Other information about supervision: _____

_____

Additional information about your program or the internship:

_____

_____

_____

A P P E N D I X   C

INTERNSHIP LEARNING AGREEMENT RECORD FORM

Date:_____

Intern Name: _____   Intern ID#_____

Intern Address:

Street   _____

City   _____

Zip   _____

Intern Home Phone: _____

Internship Site: _____

Internship Address:

Street   _____

City   _____

Zip   _____

Internship Phone: _____

Supervisor Name: _____

Supervisor Title: _____

Supervisor Phone: _____

Description of Internship Setting:

_____

_____

Intern's Schedule:

Day Hours

Sun _____ Mon _____ Tue _____ Wed _____ Thu _____ Fri _____ Sat _____

Internship Goals and Learning Activities:

In the space below please list your learning goals for the internship and the activities you and your supervisor agree upon to help you achieve those goals. Leave space under "evaluation" to record an evaluation at the end of the internship.

Learning Goals	Learning Activity	Evaluation
1.		
2.		
3.		
4.		
5.		

Intern Signature: _____   Date:_____

Supervisor Signature: _____   Date:_____

INTERN EVALUATION: SUPERVISOR FORM

Intern Name: _____

Date of Evaluation: ____/____/____

Supervisor: _____

Internship Site: _____

Instructions:

This form is designed to help supervisors provide feedback about the performance of interns. I know you are probably busy, but the form usually takes just five or ten minutes to complete and your answers and comments will be much appreciated. This form will become part of the intern's record for this course and may be considered in assigning grades for the internship. Please answer each item using the scale provided. Space is provided following each category group for specific comments. There is also space at the end of this form for general comments. If you feel it would be helpful to put anything into context from the outset, please feel free to do so below.

Initial Comments:

_____

_____

_____

_____

_____

_____

_____

_____

Answer Code for Evaluation Items

NA. Not Applicable or not enough information to form a judgment
1. Far Below Expectations—needs much improvement, a concern
2. Below Expectations—needs some improvement to meet standards
3. Acceptable—meets standards at average level for interns
4. Above Expectations—performs above average level for interns
5. Far Above Expectations—a definite strength, performs well beyond average levels for interns

I. Basic Work Requirements

_____ Arrives on time consistently

_____ Uses time effectively

_____ Informs supervisor and makes arrangements for absences

_____ Reliably completes requested or assigned tasks on time

_____ Completes required total number of hours or days on site

_____ Is responsive to norms about clothing, language, etc., on site

Comments: _____

_____

Suggested areas for further study: _____

_____

II. Ethical Awareness and Conduct

_____ Knowledge of general ethical guidelines

_____ Knowledge of ethical guidelines of internship placement

_____ Demonstrates awareness and sensitivity to ethical issues

_____ Personal behavior is consistent with ethical guidelines

_____ Consults with others about ethical issues if necessary

Comments: _____

_____

Suggested areas for further study: _____

_____

Answer Code for Questions

NA. Not Applicable or not enough information to form a judgment
  1. Far Below Expectations—needs much improvement, a concern
  2. Below Expectations—needs some improvement to meet standards
  3. Acceptable—meets standards at average level for interns
  4. Above Expectations—performs above average level for interns
  5. Far Above Expectations—a definite strength, performs well beyond average levels for interns

III. Knowledge and Learning

A. Knowledge of Client Population
_____ Knowledge level of client population at beginning of internship
_____ Knowledge level of client population at end of internship

B. Knowledge of Treatment Approaches
_____ Knowledge of treatment approach at beginning of internship
_____ Knowledge of treatment approach at end of internship

C. Knowledge of Treatment Setting
_____ Knowledge of treatment setting at beginning of internship
_____ Knowledge of treatment setting at end of internship

D. Learning
_____ Receptive to learning when new information is offered
_____ Actively seeks new information from staff or supervisor
_____ Ability to learn and understand new information
_____ Understanding of concepts, theories and information
_____ Ability to apply new information in clinical setting

Comments: _____

_____

Suggested areas for further study: _____

_____

IV. Response to Supervision

_____ Actively seeks supervision when necessary
_____ Receptive to feedback and suggestions from supervisor
_____ Understands information communicated in supervision
_____ Successfully implements suggestions from supervisor
_____ Aware of areas that need improvement
_____ Willingness to explore personal strengths and weaknesses

Comments: _____

_____

Suggested areas for further study: _____

_____

V. Interactions with Clients
_____ Appears comfortable interacting with clients
_____ Initiates interactions with clients
_____ Communicates effectively with clients
_____ Builds rapport and respect with clients
_____ Is sensitive and responsive to client's needs
_____ Is sensitive to cultural differences
_____ Is sensitive to issues of gender differences

Comments: _____

_____

Suggested areas for further study: _____

_____

VI. Interactions with Coworkers
_____ Appears comfortable interacting with other staff members
_____ Initiates interactions with staff
_____ Communicates effectively with staff
_____ Effectively conveys information and expresses own opinions
_____ Effectively receives information and opinions from others

Comments: _____

_____

Suggested areas for further study: _____

_____

VII. Work Products
_____ Reliably and accurately keeps records
_____ Written or verbal reports are accurate and factually correct
_____ Written or verbal reports are presented in professional manner
_____ Reports are clinically or administratively useful

Comments: _____

_____

Suggested areas for further study: _____

_____

Overall, what would you identify as this intern's strong points?

_____

_____

_____

_____

What would you identify as areas in which this intern should improve?

_____

_____

_____

_____

Would you recommend this intern for employment at his or her present level? Please explain:

_____

_____

_____

_____

Would you recommend this intern for continued graduate studies?
Please explain:

_____

_____

_____

_____

Supervisor's Signature:_____   Date:_____

Thank you for your time in supervising this intern and in completing this evaluation.

INTERN EVALUATION: INTERN FORM

Intern Name: _____

Date of Evaluation: ____/____/____

Supervisor: _____

Placement Site: _____

Instructions:
Your supervisor will be asked to complete an evaluation form designed to assess your performance during your internship. In order to help you assess your own performance, this form is provided. It is essentially identical to the one given to your supervisor. The form usually takes just five or ten minutes to complete. This form will become part of your record for this course and may be considered in assigning grades for the internship. Please answer each item using the scale provided. Space is provided following each category group for specific comments. There is also space at the end of this form for general comments. If you feel it would be helpful to put anything into context from the outset, please feel free to do so below.

Initial Comments: _____

_____

_____

_____

_____

_____

_____

_____

_____

Answer Code for Evaluation Items
NA. Not Applicable or not enough information to form a judgment
1. Far Below Expectations—needs much improvement, a concern
2. Below Expectations—needs some improvement to meet standards
3. Acceptable—meets standards at average level for interns
4. Above Expectations—performs above average level for interns
5. Far Above Expectations—a definite strength, performs well beyond average levels for interns

I. Basic Work Requirements
_____ Arrives on time consistently
_____ Uses time effectively
_____ Informs supervisor and makes arrangements for absences
_____ Reliably completes requested or assigned tasks on time
_____ Completes required total number of hours or days on site
_____ Is responsive to norms about clothing, language, etc., on site

Comments: _____

_____

Suggested areas for further study: _____

_____

II. Ethical Awareness and Conduct
_____ Knowledge of general ethical guidelines
_____ Knowledge of ethical guidelines of internship placement
_____ Demonstrates awareness and sensitivity to ethical issues
_____ Personal behavior is consistent with ethical guidelines
_____ Consults with others about ethical issues if necessary

Comments: _____

_____

Suggested areas for further study: _____

_____

Answer Code for Questions

NA. Not Applicable or not enough information to form a judgment
1. Far Below Expectations—needs much improvement, a concern
2. Below Expectations—needs some improvement to meet standards
3. Acceptable—meets standards at average level for interns
4. Above Expectations—performs above average level for interns
5. Far Above Expectations—a definite strength, performs well beyond average levels for interns

III. Knowledge and Learning

A. Knowledge of Client Population

_____ Knowledge level of client population at beginning of internship
_____ Knowledge level of client population at end of internship

B. Knowledge of Treatment Approaches

_____ Knowledge of treatment approach at beginning of internship
_____ Knowledge of treatment approach at end of internship

C. Knowledge of Treatment Setting

_____ Knowledge of treatment setting at beginning of internship
_____ Knowledge of treatment setting at end of internship

D. Learning

_____ Receptive to learning when new information is offered
_____ Actively seeks new information from staff or supervisor
_____ Ability to learn and understand new information
_____ Understanding of concepts, theories and information
_____ Ability to apply new information in clinical setting

Comments: _____

_____

Suggested areas for further study: _____

_____

IV. Response to Supervision

_____ Actively seeks supervision when necessary
_____ Receptive to feedback and suggestions from supervisor
_____ Understands information communicated in supervision
_____ Successfully implements suggestions from supervisor
_____ Aware of areas that need improvement
_____ Willingness to explore personal strengths and weaknesses

Comments: _____

_____

Suggested areas for further study: _____

_____

V. Interactions with Clients

_____ Appears comfortable interacting with clients
_____ Initiates interactions with clients
_____ Communicates effectively with clients
_____ Builds rapport and respect with clients
_____ Is sensitive and responsive to clients' needs
_____ Is sensitive to cultural differences
_____ Is sensitive to issues of gender differences

Comments: _____

_____

Suggested areas for further study: _____

_____

VI. Interactions with Coworkers

_____ Appears comfortable interacting with other staff members
_____ Initiates interactions with staff
_____ Communicates effectively with staff
_____ Effectively conveys information and expresses own opinions
_____ Effectively receives information and opinions from others

Comments: _____

_____

Suggested areas for further study: _____

_____

VII. Work Products

_____ Reliably and accurately keeps records
_____ Written or verbal reports are accurate and factually correct
_____ Written or verbal reports are presented in professional manner
_____ Reports are clinically or administratively useful

Comments: _____

_____

Suggested areas for further study: _____

_____

Overall, what would you identify as your strong points?

_____

_____

_____

_____

What would you identify as areas in which you should improve?

_____

_____

_____

_____

Do you believe you are prepared for employment at your present level? Please explain:

_____

_____

_____

_____

Do you believe you are ready for continued graduate studies?
Please explain:

_____

_____

_____

_____

Intern's Signature:_____   Date:_____

A P P E N D I X   F

EMERGENCY CONTACT INFORMATION

Intern
Name:_____   Location in Placement _____
Primary Work Phone: ____–____–_____ ext_____ Pager #
Secondary Work Phone: ____–____–_____ ext_____ Pager #
Primary Home Phone: ____–____–_____ ext_____ Pager #
Secondary Home Phone: ____–____–_____ ext_____ Pager #

Placement Supervisor
Name:_____   Location in Placement _____
Primary Work Phone: ____–____–_____ ext_____ Pager #
Secondary Work Phone: ____–____–_____ ext_____ Pager #
Primary Home Phone: ____–____–_____ ext_____ Pager #
Secondary Home Phone: ____–____–_____ ext_____ Pager #

Alternative Contact Person at Placement
Name:_____   Location in Placement _____
Primary Work Phone: ____–____–_____ ext_____ Pager #
Secondary Work Phone: ____–____–_____ ext_____ Pager #
Primary Home Phone: ____–____–_____ ext_____ Pager #
Secondary Home Phone: ____–____–_____ ext_____ Pager #

Faculty Supervisor
Name:_____   Office Location _____
Primary Work Phone: ____–____–_____ ext_____ Pager #
Secondary Work Phone: ____–____–_____ ext_____ Pager #
Primary Home Phone: ____–____–_____ ext_____ Pager #
Secondary Home Phone: ____–____–_____ ext_____ Pager #

Alternative Faculty Contact
Name:_____   Office Location _____
Primary Work Phone: ____–____–_____ ext_____ Pager #
Secondary Work Phone: ____–____–_____ ext_____ Pager #
Primary Home Phone: ____–____–_____ ext_____ Pager #
Secondary Home Phone: ____–____–_____ ext_____ Pager #

Crisis Line Number: ____–_____–_____

Other Resources
Name:_____ Number: ____–_____–_____
Name:_____ Number: ____–_____–_____

A P P E N D I X   G

ETHICAL GUIDELINES

All those taking part in internship opportunities are expected to adhere to certain guidelines for ethical, responsible conduct. This is necessary for the benefit and protection of the interns themselves, as well as for the clients, placement agencies, instructor, supervisor, and the university. Certain basic guidelines are described below but these are not exhaustive. Interns are also expected to learn and adhere to the broader ethical guidelines dictated by their relevant profession (e.g., APA, NASW, ACA, etc.), as well as the guidelines specific to their placement agency. If, at any time, interns have questions about ethics or responsible conduct, they should contact their instructor or the placement supervisor. At a minimum, interns agree to adhere to the following principles:

1. *Confidentiality.* The identity of clients, or information that would reveal the identity of clients, cannot be revealed without the specific permission of the client. The only exceptions to this are cases in which the client may be dangerous to themselves or others and in cases of child abuse. In such situations, there may be legal requirements that responsible agencies be informed. There are also certain legal proceedings in which case notes and other records can be ordered to be released by the courts. Interns must familiarize themselves with, and adhere to, confidentiality procedures of their placements and the laws of the state. Case material discussed in class must be prepared in such a way that confidentiality is maintained.

2. *Recognition of Qualifications and Limitations.* Interns must recognize the limitations to their training and abilities and must not exceed these in work with clients. It is incumbent upon interns that they recognize when clinical situations are beyond their knowledge or ability. When such situations arise, interns will seek assistance from their supervisors and instructor.

3. *Identification as Interns.* Interns will explicitly identify themselves as interns to their clients, in reports, and in other professional activities. They will not misrepresent their training, qualifications, or status. Interns who will be at a placement for a limited time will inform clients of that limitation at the outset of therapy and will consider it in their work with clients.

4. *Record Keeping.* Interns will accurately and reliably maintain written and other records as required by their placement agency.

5. *Dual Relationships.* Interns will refrain from clinical work with persons with whom the intern is already involved in other types of relationships. Such "dual relationships" may inhibit the effectiveness of the intern's clinical work and may jeopardize both the client and the trainee. For example, it would not be ethical for a trainee to take as a client someone who was a fellow student in class. Similarly, coworkers, friends, and others should not be seen as clients.

6. *Prohibition Regarding Sexual Conduct or Harassment.* Under no circumstances shall interns become involved in sexual or romantic relationships of any sort with clients of their placement agency. Interns will also refrain from sexual harassment and will respect the sensitivity of others regarding sexual matters.

7. *Self-Awareness and Monitoring.* Interns will monitor their own emotional and physical status and should be aware of any conditions that might adversely impact their ability to serve their clients or placement agencies. If such conditions arise, interns should inform their placement supervisor and instructor.

8. *Ethics Discussion with Supervisor.* Each intern must discuss the ethical standards of their placement with their supervisor before performing any clinical work or patient contact. Space is provided at the bottom of this form to indicate that such discussions have taken place and the intern has been informed of ethical expectations.

By signing below the intern agrees to adhere to the guidelines listed above as well as those of the professional discipline and the specific placement agency.

Intern Signature _____   Date _____

Site Supervisor _____   Date _____

Instructor _____   Date _____

TREATMENT AGREEMENT AND INFORMED CONSENT

This form is designed for use as an example and template to help you develop a form suited to your own situation. Feel free to use parts of it to draft your own form. Be aware, however, that no claim is made of the legal standing of this model. You must craft your own information with an awareness of the legal and ethical requirements of your position, profession, setting, and state. Discuss any document such as this with your instructor and supervisor before using it with clients.

LETTERHEAD FOR YOUR AGENCY

INTRODUCTION
As a way of introducing myself to clients I have prepared this brief description of my background, approach, and other information that is important for you to know. Please read this carefully and feel free to ask me any questions about what you have read or any other elements of your treatment. I know this may seem rather formal and that it covers a lot of information, but I believe it is very important for clients to have as much information as possible so they can make informed decisions about their treatment. Again, if you have any questions or concerns at any time please feel free to discuss them with me.

My name is _____ and I am a/an (intern, practicum student, etc.) presently studying at (institutional name) and working toward my (degree). I have (previous academic qualifications and practical experience).

Throughout my work here I will be under the supervision of (supervisor name). His/her qualifications include (list qualifications). The nature of our supervision will include (describe activities and frequency). If you have any questions or concerns please feel free to contact (supervisor name and agency phone number).

My placement at this agency is scheduled to run from (start to stop dates). On (end date) I will (move on, continue, or other plans). At that time clients I am working with will be (transfer or termination plans).

FEES
Fees for services are (describe fees). All fees will be collected at the time services are provided. Billing procedures will be (describe billing procedures).

In addition to fees for time when I am meeting with you directly, it is also my practice to charge for time required for preparing assessment reports, telephone conversations lasting longer than ___ minutes, consultations, or meetings you have authorized as part of your treatment. I will be pleased to provide you with details of any such costs should they be necessary.

If it happens that you are involved in some way in a lawsuit that requires my participation, you will be responsible for fees associated with my professional time. Because of the demands of preparing for and participating in legal proceedings, my fees for this are _____.

Please be aware that in receiving my services you, not your insurance company, are responsible for full payment of fees. If you want your insurance company to pay for my services, please read your policy carefully to be certain what your coverage provides. If you have any questions, call your insurance provider to be sure. I will be pleased to help in whatever way I can with this process. If conditions of your insurance policy limit the number of sessions your provider will pay for (indicate your policy for managing this situation).

Please also be aware that your insurance company may request diagnostic information, a copy of your treatment plan, and case records in order to provide compensation. This information will then become part of their files. Insurance companies are generally quite responsible about keeping this matter confidential, but that is something I cannot control or be responsible for. If you wish, I will provide you with copies of any material or correspondence I send to your insurer.

CONFIDENTIALITY AND LIMITATIONS TO CONFIDENTIALITY

I place a high value on the confidentiality of information clients share with me and I will make every effort to ensure that information about your case will be kept confidential. You should, however, be aware that legal and ethical requirements specify certain conditions in which it may be necessary for me to discuss information about your treatment with other professionals. If you have any questions about these limitations, please ask me about them before we begin treatment or at any time during our treatment. Such situations include (check your state laws before completing this):

1. If I believe there is a danger that you may harm yourself or others or that you are incapable of caring for yourself.
2. If I become aware of your involvement in abuse of children, elderly, or disabled persons.
3. If I am ordered by a court to release your records. This sometimes happens when clients are plaintiffs in lawsuits and psychological records are subpoenaed as part of that process.
4. If your insurance company requests records in order to verify the services received and determine compensation.
5. (In the case of minors, list any limitations and requirements requiring parental notification, etc.)
6. As part of the supervision process I may discuss your case and share records and other materials (note if tapes will be used) with my supervisor (supervisor's name).
7. (Depending on policy and law) I may also discuss information about your case with other personnel within the agency.

TREATMENT PHILOSOPHY AND FREQUENCY

Briefly, my approach to treatment is best described as (approach used). In essence, this means (lay person's terms description of approach).

The length of a typical session is (length). The number and frequency of sessions depends on the client and the nature of their concerns. Typically, I see clients for (average number of sessions), but this can vary from as few as (   ) to as many as (   ). By the (number of sessions) we will discuss how treatment is going and how we expect it to proceed.

CLIENT RESPONSIBILITIES

In order for our work together to be successful, it is essential that clients attend sessions, make a sincere effort to work on the issues we are addressing, and follow through with elements of treatment such as things to do between sessions, readings, etc.

If for some reason you cannot attend a scheduled session, please call well in advance and at least 24 hours before your appointment. My schedule tends to be rather full and if clients do not cancel appointments with sufficient time that means others who could receive services are unable to.

Repeated failures to attend sessions or to provide adequate rescheduling notice may lead to termination of our work together.

Contacting Me

Because of the nature of my work, there will be many times when I am with clients and am not immediately available by telephone. My normal office hours are _____ on _____. If I do not answer the phone, please leave a message and a number so I can return your call. If there is an emergency and I cannot be reached, please contact your physician, the emergency room at your local hospital, or the mental health center crisis line at _____.

Additional Issues

I appreciate the time you have taken to read this. As I have said before, if you have any questions or concerns now or at any point during your treatment, please feel free to let me know. Please sign below to indicate that you have read this and have had a chance to ask any questions. When we meet, I will give you a copy of this to keep and refer to if you like.

I am looking forward to our work together.

Sincerely,

(Your name)

I have read this document, discussed it with (intern's or professional's name), understand the information contained, and agree to participate in treatment under the conditions described.

Client's Name_____   Date_____

A P P E N D I X I

SUPERVISOR EVALUATION FORM

This form is designed to give interns the opportunity to provide feedback about the supervision they receive during their internship. This information will be useful in discussions with supervisors and will help your faculty instructor evaluate the learning opportunities at various internship sites.

Each item that follows asks you to indicate the frequency with which activities of supervision occurred, your satisfaction with the activities, or both frequency and satisfaction. Please rate frequency based on percentage from 0 to 100 with 0 meaning that something never happened, and 100 indicating that the activity happened each time there was an opportunity as described in the item. Please rate satisfaction on a rating scale from 0 to 100 with 0 indicating that you were completely dissatisfied and 100 signifying that you were completely satisfied. Frequency and satisfaction ratings need not be the same. For example, if you met for fewer than the agreed upon times for supervision, you might rate the frequency at 75 percent. Your satisfaction might be anywhere from 0 to 100 depending on what you felt about this issue. Please try to evaluate each item separately from other items. Space is provided at the end for general comments.

PRELIMINARY REMARKS
If you think it will be useful to preface your responses with any introductory comments, please feel free to do so here. Additional space is available at the end of this form for general evaluative comments.

_____

_____

_____

_____

_____

_____

_____

_____

_____

_____

_____

_____

_____

_____

_____

SCHEDULE AND AVAILABILITY

1. ____Frequency
   ____Satisfaction
   Overall during the internship, approximately how closely did the actual super vision contacts match the agreed upon plan?

2. ____Frequency
   ____Satisfaction
   Apart from scheduled meetings, how available was your supervisor if you requested additional contact?

INTRODUCTION TO SETTING

3. ____Yes ___No
   ____Satisfaction
   Did your supervisor give you a tour or arrange for a tour of the internship site?

4. ____Yes ___No
   ____Satisfaction
   Did your supervisor introduce you to other staff when you began the internship?

5. ____Yes ___No
   ____Satisfaction
   Did your supervisor discuss procedural matters, agency policy, etc., when you began the internship?

6. ____Yes ___No
   ____Satisfaction
   Did your supervisor discuss ethical and legal issues when you began the internship?

ACTIVITIES AT THE INTERNSHIP

Approximately what percentage of your time at the internship was spent in each of the following activities:

7. ____Frequency
   ____Satisfaction
   Observing the milieu of your setting or interacting informally with clients, but not directly observing or participating in treatment or other services

8. ____Frequency
   ____Satisfaction
   Interacting informally with staff members

9. ____Frequency
   ____Satisfaction
   Observing treatment, assessment, or other direct service with clients

10. ____Frequency
    ____Satisfaction
    Participating in or providing treatment, assessment, or other direct service with clients

11. ____Frequency
    ____Satisfaction
    Attending meetings other than supervision or informal conversation

12. ____Frequency
    ____Satisfaction
    Reading records, reports, etc.

13. ____Frequency
    ____Satisfaction
    Writing case notes, assessments, reports, correspondence, etc.

In the spaces below describe and evaluate any other activities you participated in during your internship.

14. ____Frequency
    ____Satisfaction

15. ____Frequency
    ____Satisfaction

16. ____Frequency
    ____Satisfaction

17. ____Frequency   Overall, were you able to participate in the activities you had hoped to in the
    ____Satisfaction   internship?

18. What additional activities would have been useful to you during the internship?

_____

_____

_____

ACTIVITIES OF SUPERVISION

Approximately what portion of supervision time was spent in the following activities.

19. ____Frequency   Using case notes or material to review your interactions with clients
    ____Satisfaction

20. ____Frequency   Observing the supervisor providing treatment, assessments, or other services
    ____Satisfaction   to clients

21. ____Frequency   Providing services yourself under the direct observation of your supervisor
    ____Satisfaction

22. ____Frequency   Discussing institutional issues
    ____Satisfaction

23. ____Frequency   Didactic instruction in specific topics or skills
    ____Satisfaction

24. ____Frequency   Reviewing assessments or other reports you have written
    ____Satisfaction

25. ____Frequency   Reviewing case notes or other records you have written
    ____Satisfaction

26. ____Frequency   Reviewing assessments or other reports written by your instructor or other pro-
    ____Satisfaction   fessionals

27. ____Frequency   Reviewing case notes or other records written by your instructor or other
    ____Satisfaction   professionals

28. ____Frequency   Discussing your personal impressions, reactions and adjustment to the intern-
    ____Satisfaction   ship

29. ____Frequency   Discussing your relationship with your supervisor
    ____Satisfaction

In the space below please describe and evaluate any other activities of supervision in which you participated.

30. ____Frequency
    ____Satisfaction

31. ____Frequency
    ____Satisfaction

32. What additional activities would have been useful to you in supervision?

_____

_____

INTERPERSONAL ISSUES AND FEEDBACK FROM YOUR SUPERVISOR

The items below refer to how you were given feedback by your supervisor and to the quality of your relationship to one another. Please comment on your supervisor's performance in each of the following areas.

33. ____Frequency   Recognizing areas in which your skills or knowledge are relatively strong.
    ____Satisfaction

34. ____Frequency   Recognizing areas in which your skills or knowledge need improvement.
    ____Satisfaction

35. ____Frequency   Recognizing and complimenting you for accomplishments or things you
    ____Satisfaction   have done well at your internship

36. ____Frequency   Letting you know when your performance has not been good in certain areas
    ____Satisfaction

37. ____Frequency   Providing emotional support
    ____Satisfaction

38. ____Frequency   Dealing with differences between you
    ____Satisfaction

39. ____Frequency
    ____Satisfaction

40. Based on your experience, briefly describe the ways in which you feel supervision was most helpful to you during your internship.

41. If there was anything about supervision that was not helpful, please explain.

42. In what ways do you think supervision could have been more beneficial to you?

INDEXES

SUBJECT INDEX